TO

THE MEMORY

OF THE

LATE WILLIAM L. STONE, ESQ.,

OF

NEW YORK CITY,

THIS WORK IS AFFECTIONATELY INSCRIBED, BY HIS SON,

THE AUTHOR.

THE

LIFE AND TIMES

OF

SIR WILLIAM JOHNSON, BART.,

BY

WILLIAM L. STONE.

VOL. I.

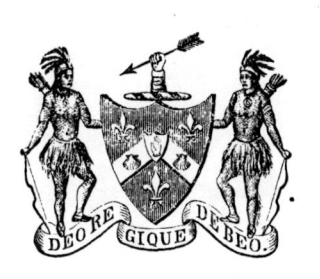

ALBANY:
J. MUNSELL, 78 STATE STREET
1865.

Entered according to Act of Congress in the year 1864,
By WILLIAM L. STONE,
In the Clerk's Office of the District Court of the United States for the Southern District of New York.

Printing Statement:

Due to the very old age and scarcity of this book, many of the pages may be hard to read due to the blurring of the original text, possible missing pages, missing text and other issues beyond our control.

Because this is such an important and rare work, we believe it is best to reproduce this book regardless of its original condition.

Thank you for your understanding.

PREFACE.

It may not be generally known that my father, the late William L. Stone, Esq., commenced a history of the LIFE AND TIMES OF SIR WILLIAM JOHNSON, BART. He had employed several years in collecting the materials for this work, and had written the first seven chapters of it, when death cut short his labors in 1844. Esteeming it a sacred duty, I have completed the work; and in so doing, have endeavored to carry out, as far as possible, his original design. The result is before the reader.

Perhaps the character of no man prominent in our colonial history has been less understood, and less fairly judged, than that of SIR WILLIAM JOHNSON, BART. His death occurred just on the eve of the Revolutionary war; and the troublous times which followed, and the immediate removal of his private papers, by his son, Sir John Johnson, into Canada, prevented any trustworthy estimate either of the man or of his services. As a natural consequence, the innumerable wild and improbable traditions afloat concerning him, have been eagerly seized and believed as veritable history. It was therefore evident, that until access could be had to his papers and private correspondence, it would be impossible to prepare a faithful and accurate biography of him. After years of search, my father procured from the Johnson family in England, and from various other sources, a large portion of Sir William's manuscripts, which, with the collection of the Johnson MSS. presented to the New York State Library by General John Tayler Cooper, amounts to more than seven thousand letters and documents. Although many letters are evidently lost, yet enough remain to answer the purpose of the present work; while the original records of Indian treaties and conferences, of which nearly all are in existence, afford a sure test of the accuracy of their relation.

Of this large collection, I have read and carefully compared each letter and document; and throughout the work have made abundant reference to authorities, in order that whoever desires may avail himself of the same sources of information.

To Hon. Jared Sparks of Cambridge, Hon. George Bancroft of New York, Francis Parkman, Esq., of Boston, Professor Robinson P. Dunn of Brown University, and Edward F. De Lancey, Esq., of New York, I am indebted for counsel and material aid. My thanks are also due to Anthony Lamb, Esq., of Cambridge, Doctor O'Callaghan of Albany, Dr. R. L. Allen, Hon. Judge Hay, and Daniel Sheppard, Esq. of Saratoga Springs, for valuable suggestions. Nor must I forget to make special mention of the kindness of the Regents and Librarians of the New York State University and

Library, in affording me every facility for examining the books and original documents under their control. To Thomas Simons, Esq., of Albany, and Elnathan Judson, Esq., of New York, I am truly grateful for assistance in copying many pages of manuscript.

In conclusion I may add, that in the preparation of this work, I have made no statement, and drawn no inference, that I did not conscientiously believe was fully warranted by the original authorities to which I have had immediate access.

WILLIAM L. STONE.

Saratoga Springs, January 1st., 1865.

CONTENTS.

CHAPTER I.
1534—1741.

Plan of the present work, 9—Success of the French in winning the confidence of the Indians; one exception to this success, 10—Inconsiderable attention paid to the Five Nations by the first three English governors, 11—Enterprise of the Jesuit missionaries during the peace of 1667, 12—Efforts of Governor Dongan to thwart the influence of the French, 14—Convention of the Five Nations at Albany in 1684, 15—Success of Dongan's efforts, 16—Neglect of Indian affairs in the colony of New York during the Leislerian administration, 17—Count Frontenac vainly attempts to detach the Confederates from the English interest, 18—Defeat of De Calliers, Governor of Montreal, by Major Peter Schuyler, 19—Colonel Fletcher succeeds Ingoldsby as governor. Ingoldsby holds a council with the Five Nations at Albany, in 1692, 20—Governor Fletcher takes Major Schuyler into his councils, 20—Count Frontenac captures two of the Mohawk castles, 21—Schuyler takes the field in pursuit. The purpose of the Oneidas to make peace with the French frustrated by Governor Fletcher, who calls a council of the Confederacy in July, 1693, 22—Count Frontenac makes another effort to subjugate the Five Nations, 23—The Earl of Bellamont succeeds Governor Fletcher, 24—Colonel Schuyler visits England in 1710 with five Iroquois chiefs, 26—Senecas prevented from turning their arms against the English by the peace of Utrecht in 1713, 27—The Confederates mediate hostilities against the Catawbas and Cherokees. Numerical strength of the Tuscaroras, 28—They are taken into the Iroquois Confederacy, which is henceforth known as the Six Nations, 29—General Hunter goes back to England, leaving Schuyler at the head of the colonial administration. The latter holds a treaty with the Six Nations, 29—Failure to expel the Jesuit emissary, Joncaire, from the Senecas, 30—William Burnet takes the reins of government in 1720. Endeavors to break up the Indian trade between Albany and Montreal, 30—Passage of an act for that purpose, 31—Trading post established at Oswego in 1722. Beneficial effects of Burnet's policy, 31 —The establishment of an English post at Oswego, a source of great displeasure to the French. Mr. Burnet meets the Confederates at Albany in 1727, 32—Mr. Montgomery succeeds Mr. Burnet in the government, 33—Revival of the trade between Albany and Montreal, 34—Death of Montgomery. Rip Van Dam succeeds him for a short period, 34—Stormy administration of Governor Cosby, 35—The Six Nations again resume hostilities against the southern Indians. The latter are defeated with the loss of twelve hundred braves, 35—George Clarke, after a brief struggle with Rip Van Dam, is commissioned lieutenant governor, 36—Recommends to the assembly various important measures, 37—The election between Adolphe Philipse and Gerrit Van Horn contested. Eloquence of Mr. Smith on the occasion, 39—Increased political excitement during the years 1738—1739. Reasons for it, 41—Demand for a permanent supply bill. Dissolution of the assembly. Temper of the new one, 43—The governor yields to the assembly, 44—Mr. Clarke complains bitterly of the continued encroachments on the crown by the people, 45—The assembly decline making an appropriation for rebuilding the chapel among the Mohawks, 47—War declared against Spain, 47—Grand council of the Confederacy held at Albany by the lieutenant governor in 1741. Satisfactory result, 51—The famous negro plot. Incidents connected with it, 52.

CHAPTER II.
1742—1744.

Prominence of SIR WILLIAM JOHNSON in the colonial annals of the United States. His life and character hitherto but imperfectly understood, 56—Family and descent. His uncle Sir Peter Warren, 57—Marriage of Sir Peter Warren. Birth of Sir William Johnson, 59—Arrival in America, 69—Takes charge of his uncle's estate in the Mohawk valley, and keeps a country store. Means of both uncle and nephew, at this time, small, 60—Receives advice from his uncle, 61—His style of living. Description of his person. His success in winning the confidence and affection of the Mohawks, 64—Proposes to erect a saw mill. His education, 65—Difficulty in fixing the exact date of his marriage. Character of his wife, Catharine Weisenberg, 66—the Six Nations in 1742, send a large delegation to Philadelphia. Its object, 66—Proceedings of the council, 68—Tact of Lieutenant Governor Thomas, 69—Interesting historical incident during the sitting of the council, 71—Complaint made by the Indians against the governor and people of Maryland. Misunderstood on the part of Virginia, 73—A party of Indians invade the county of Augusta, and kill several Virginians. Correspondence between Lieutenant Governor Gooch and Lieutenant Governor Clarke in relation to it, 73—Jacobus Bleecker sent to Onondaga by the Indian commissioners, 74—Another embassy sent to Onondaga. Result of these missions, 76—Arrival of Admiral George Clinton as the successor of Lieutenant Governor Clarke, 77—Opening speech of the new governor probably moulded by Chief Justice De Lancey. Tone of the speech, 79—Sketch of Chief Justice De Lancey, 59—De Lancey, in behalf of the assembly, draws up an humble address, 80—The governor signs all the bills presented to him, 81—Removal of Mr. Johnson from the south to the north side of the Mohawk. Opens a correspondence on his own account with the opulent house of Sir William Baker & Co., London. Grows in the public estimation, 81—Lays the foundation of his future prosperity on the basis of honorable dealing, 82—The government of New York authorized to issue letters of marque against Spain, 82—Activity of Captain Warren at sea. Captures a privateer and is promoted, 86—Clinton communicates to the assembly advices of the intended invasion of England by "a Popish Pretender," 87—Holds a conference with the Six Nations at Albany, 88. —Expresses apprehensions for the post at Oswego, 89—Lays before his council a communication from the commandant at Oswego, in relation to the designs of the French against that post, 90—Grand Indian council at Lancaster in 1744. Its proceedings in detail, 91—109.

CHAPTER III.
1744—1745.

Repose of the colonies under the administration of Sir Robert Walpole, broken by the declaration of war against France. Attempts of the French upon Acadia and Placentia, 110—Declaration of hostilities announced to the general assembly by Clinton. Strong measures urged for the protection of the colony and city of New York, 111. The building of a strong fort in the vicinity of Crown Point recommended, 112—Cowardly retreat of the English traders from Oswego. The house pledge

CONTENTS.   XI

the ways and means for putting the colony in a posture of defence, 113—
The Caughnawagas take up the hatchet against the English, 114—Special
allowances voted for the defence of Albany and Schenectady, 115—The
French again active in their endeavors to win the Six Nations from the
English, 116—Mr. Bleecker is despatched into the Seneca country.
Returns and reports favorably. Another report from a French deserter,
117—Arrest and discharge of David Leisberger and Christian Frederick
Post. Governor Shirley proposes the capture of Louisburg, 118—
Description of the harbor and defences of Louisburg, 119.—Shirley communicates his plan to the ministry, 120—Circular letters sent to the
several colonial governors, 122—Lukewarm reception of the scheme by
New York. Its cause, 122—Conduct of the assembly, and its dissolution
by the governor, 122—128—Preparations of Shirley for the capture of
Cape Breton, 129—The command of the land forces given to Colonel
William Pepperell, 130—Circumstances which favored the undertaking,
132—Unfitness of Shirley to direct the conduct of the expedition, 133—
Commodore Warren assumes command of the naval forces, 136—Progress
of the seige, 138—Success of Warren in cruizing off the harbor, 142—
Surrender of the city, 146—The Mermaid despatched to England with
the tidings. Effect of the conquest in Europe and America, 148—Honorable rewards to the master spirits of the expedition, 149—Unwillingness
of the parent government to reimburse the colonies for their expenses,
150—Efforts to detract from the just fame of the Provincials defeated,
151—Discussion respecting the relative merits of Pepperell and Warren,
156.

CHAPTER IV.
1745—1746.

David Jones of Queens county, elected speaker of the new assembly, 157—
Clinton urges upon the assembly the importance of reinforcing the
forces of Pepperell and Warren. Both branches of the assembly respond
cordially. Indian relations of the colony again critical, 158—Dissatisfaction among the Six Nations. Examination of John Henry Lydius,
159—Animosity between the Mohawks and the people of Albany.
Conrad Weiser sent on a friendly tour among the Six Nations, 160—
Reception of Weiser. Accusations against the Albanians by the Confederates, 161—The commissioners of Indian affairs announce the
approach of scalping parties of Canadian Indians. Barbarities of these
Indians on the frontier of New Hampshire, 162—Attention of the assembly called to these outrages. A general council with the Indians recommended, 163—Proceedings of the council. Speech of Hendrik, 164—
Suspicions of the Massachusetts commissioners, 170—Clinton communicates the result of the council to the assembly in a special message, 172
—Burning by the French and Indians of the settlement at Saratoga, 173
—Destruction of the village of Hoosick, 174—Governor Clinton reproves
the assembly for its indifference, 175—Communication from Colonel
Philip Schuyler laid before the privy council. Dissatisfaction at the
removal of the local militia from the city, 176—Prospect of a gloomy
winter. Exciting rumors, 177—Clinton asks for an appropriation to
build a stone fort at the great carrying place between Hudson River and
Lake Champlain, 178—Doubtful position assumed by the Confederacy, 179.
The importance of an alliance with New England for mutual protection
appreciated. Commissioners appointed for that purpose, 180—The question of parliamentary law and prerogative before the council and assembly, 181—The assembly driven from the city by the small pox, 182—Discussion of the revenue bill by the council and assembly, 183—The victory
with the representatives of the people, 185—Resolution adopted directing
the erection of six strong block-houses. Appropriations for other important objects, 185—Clinton again asks for reinforcements for Pepperell

and Warren, and is refused. Reluctance of the assembly to coöperate with the New England colonies not easily explained, 186.

CHAPTER V.
1746.

Commencement of the brilliant public career of SIR WILLIAM JOHNSON. He erects a valuable flouring mill. Builds an elegant stone mansion, and calls it Mount Johnson. Becomes known to Governor Clinton, probably through the influence of Chief Justice De Lancey, 187—His commercial affairs widely extended. Is engaged in shipping furs to London. Is commissioned a justice of the peace for Albany county. Begins to participate largely in the political concerns of the colony, as shown by the return of Mr. Holland to the assembly from Schenectady, 188—The exact date of his wife's decease not known. Birth of a son— John Johnson, and of two daughters—Mary and Nancy. Is rapidly gaining an ascendency over the Iroquois Confederacy. Manuscript letter from James Wilson to Johnson, 189—Comprehensive views of Shirley, 190—Communicates them to the government of New York, 191—The duke of Newcastle's letter laid before the council, 192—Joyful reception of these communications by the legislature and people, 193—Inaction of the parent government, 196—Expedition against Quebec abandoned, 198—Activity of the French, 199—Alarm of the North American seaports on the approach of D'Anville's fleet, 200—Quarrel of Chief Justice De Lancey with Governor Clinton. Causes which led to it, 201—Governer Clinton arrives in Albany to meet the Six Nations. Finds very few Indians in attendance, 202—Rumors of a French expedition against Schenectady communicated to Clinton by Johnson, 204—Growing disaffection of the Six Nations, 205—The Jesuits succeed in gaining over some of the chiefs, 206—Mr. Clinton avails himself, in the Indian department, of the services of Mr. Johnson. Qualifications of the latter for this branch of the public service, 207—Mr. Johnson exerts himself successfully in winning back the friendship of the Confederates. Prevails upon them to attend the council, 208—Is adopted by the Mohawks, and invested with the rank of a war chief, 209—Receives from the Mohawks an Indian name. Enters Albany at the head of a party of Mohawks, dressed and painted as a warrior, 210—Dr. Colden opens the council with a speech, 211—Reply of the Indians, 213—An alliance defensive and offensive formed with the Iroquois Confederacy. 216— Astonishing ignorance of Mr. Clinton in relation to affairs in New England, 217—Efforts of the Canadian governor to neutralize Mr. Clinton's proceedings, 218—The Caughnawagas, instigated by the French, vainly attempt to dissuade the Six Nations from their recent alliance, 219— Impossibility of the Iroquois Confederacy, from their geographical position, remaining neutral, 219.

CHAPTER VI.
1746.

The Canadian Indians desolate the New England frontier, 221—Number Four. Upper Ashuelot and Bernardstown attacked, 222—Command of the posts west of Hoosick mountain confided to Captain Ephraim Williams, 224—Vaudreuil invests Fort Massachusetts, 225—Bravery of the garrison, 226—Its capture, 227—Remarkable conduct of the Indians, 228— Active operations against Crown Point abandoned, 229—Mr. Johnson directed to organize war parties of Indians to harrass the French settlements, 230.—The preparations of the French for the reconquest of Cape Breton prove abortive, 232—Disasters to D'Anville's fleet, 233—Suicide of D'Estouraelle, 234—Governor Clinton returns to New York. Dissatisfaction with the Indian commissioners. The management of the Indian department devolves chiefly upon Mr. Johnson,

CONTENTS. XIII

235—Trouble between Governor Clinton and his assembly, 236—Henry Holland, by order of Colonel Roberts, breaks open the public store houses in Albany, 238—The assembly urged to their opposition of the governor by De Lancey, 240—Holland declared guilty of a high misdemeanor, 241 —Review of Holland's conduct, 242—The Schuylers take offence at the growing influence of Johnson, 243—Johnson becomes contractor for supplying the Oswego garrison. First step taken toward the establishment of Kings, now Columbia college, 245—Mr. De Lancey makes another demonstration against his rival, Dr. Colden, 246—Johnson pays a visit to Governor Clinton in the autumn. Receives from the governor the rank of colonel. Is recommended by Clinton, through the duke of Newcastle, to his majesty's favor, 247—The operations of the New Englanders in Nova Scotia end disastrously. Inactivity of the enemy during the winter, 248.

CHAPTER VII.
1747.

Shirley conceives the project of a descent upon Crown Point, 249—New York deems the plan impracticable, 250—Active correspondence between Clinton and Johnson in relation to the Indian service, 251—Exertions of Colonel Johnson, 254—Letter from Colonel Johnson to Governor Clinton, 255—Enumeration of scalps taken from the enemy, 257—Attack on Charlestown, N. H., 258—Raising of the seige, 260—Rebuilding of Fort Massachusetts, 261—Clinton again involved in controversies with his legislature, 262—Letter from Clinton to Johnson regarding the disloyalty of some Albanians, 266—Mutiny of the levies at Saratoga, 267—Report of the committee, charged with the preparation of an address to the governor, 273—The attention of the assembly called to the disaffection among the northern levies. Reply of the house, 274—Movements of Sir Peter Warren. Appointed second in command under M. Anson, 275 —Is promoted to the rank of rear admiral of the white, 277—Meets with great success in his cruizes, and is returned to parliament, 278.

CHAPTER VIII.
1747.

Military affairs in the north in a deplorable condition. Desertion of the troops. Murders by the enemy, 279—Captain Chew defeated near Lake Champlain by M. Lacose, and taken prisoner. Schuyler marches to repel the invaders, 280—The Six Nations complain to Schuyler. Clinton concerts measures with Schuyler for relieving Oswego. Governor Shirley meditates an attack upon Crown Point, 281—Clinton lays Shirley's plan before the assembly, 282—Is received coldly, 283—Activity of the enemy. Saratoga surrendered. Johnson writes to Clinton, 284—He demands a guard to escort the stores to Oswego, 286—The assembly refuse to allow them, 287—Letter from Clinton to Johnson, 288—High estimation in which Johnson was held by Clinton. Cause of Johnson's jealousy toward Lydius, 291—Johnson returns from an expedition against Crown Point. The fort at Saratoga in danger of being evacuated through want of provisions, 292—More trouble between Clinton and the assembly, 293—Colonel Roberts directed to send three companies to Saratoga, 294—Colonel Johnson visits New York to consult with the governor respecting the condition of the colony. His advice, 295—Clinton and Shirley still cling to the expedition against Crown Point. The former again appeals to his legislature and dwells upon the views of Johnson, 296—The assembly respond coldly, 299—The assembly in secret sitting attack Colonel Johnson. Reasons for this attack, 301—Clinton charges the house with falsehood, and adverts to the services of Johnson in terms of high praise, 305—The hopes of the colonies fall to the ground. The duke of Newcastle orders Clinton and Shirley to desist from the intended expedition, 310—Trouble with James Parker, printer to the assembly, 311—Clinton proposes to detail large bodies of the militia for the defence of the frontiers, 312—The assembly charge the governor with inconsistency, 314—Clinton again involved in controversies with the assembly on the question of prerogative, 315—He dissolves the assembly much to its surprise, 318—Review of the controversy, 320—Difficulty between Commodore Knowles and the citizens of Boston on the subject of press gangs. Shirley's house mobbed, 222—Order restored, 225—Governor Clinton presses the command of the northern frontier upon Colonel Johnson. The latter is entrusted with the duty of effecting a complete reorganization of the militia. All confidence reposed in him, 326.

CHAPTER IX.
1748.

Prominence of Johnson in the affairs of the colony—Accepts the command of the troops for the defence of the frontiers. Devotes himself to the management of the Indian department. Becomes favorably known to the colonial and British government. Employs as his housekeeper, Molly Brant, 327.—Beneficial effects of this Indian alliance, 328.—New assembly chosen. The governor's opening speech conciliatory. Arent Stevens succeeds Mr. Bleeker, deceased, as government interpreter to the Indians, 329.—The dissolution of the old assembly produces a better state of feeling in the new one. The answer of the council to the governor's speech moved by De Lancey, 330—Resolutions passed for repairing the fortifications along the frontiers. Robert Charles appointed agent for the colony, to reside in London with a salary of £200 per annum, 331—The action of the assembly attributed to a desire to supplant Clinton in the gubernatorial chair by Sir Peter Warren. Warren not a party to this intrigue, 332—Discontent of the Six Nations. Alarming intelligence from Colonel Johnson and Lieutenant Lindesay of Oswego, 332—Colonel Johnson directed by Clinton to make a tour in the Indian country, 333—Objects to be attained by this tour, 334—Johnson summons a council of the Confederacy at Onondaga. Arrives at the Onondaga castle, and meets with a flattering reception, 335—Proceedings of Johnson at the council, 336—Communicates to the Indians, the intention of Clinton to meet them at Albany, 339—He recommends to the governor strong legislative enactments to prevent the sale of rum to the Indians, 341—A grand council of the Six Nations at Albany, long in contemplation by Clinton and Shirley, 341—Clinton's efforts to second Shirley's plan for an expedition against Crown Point fruitless, 342—Complains to the lords of trade of the continued encroachments of the assembly upon the crown. Lays before the assembly Colonel Johnson's report of the council at Onondaga, 343—Urges an immediate exchange of prisoners. The assembly recommends the sending of a flag of truce to Canada, 344—Colonel Beekman prefers a charge against the governor, 344—Important tidings received from Europe, 345—Letter from Clinton to Johnson, announcing that preliminaries of peace had been signed at Aix la Chapelle, 346—Clinton, accompanied by Dr. Colden, arrives in Albany to attend the grand council. Unprecedented number of Indians present, 348—Proceedings of the council not important, 349—Massacre at Schenectady. No accurate account of it in existence, 350—General result of the council satisfactory, 353—Heart rending tragedy in the town of Hoosick, 354—The borders of Massachusetts and New Hampshire again suffer from the enemy, 361—Narrow escape of Captain Melvin and his party, 362—The enemy generally successful in these border skirmishes, 363—Captain Eph. Williams narrowly escapes capture, 364—Serious trouble among the troops stationed at Albany and along the frontiers. The commissioners refuse to execute the orders of the governor, 365—

CONTENTS. XV

Complains of this in a letter to Colonel Johnson, determines to reassert the prerogative in the strongest terms, by bringing the supply-bill to a direct issue, 366—The assembly refuse to grant it, 368—Various successes of the English fleet in the West Indies, 369—Definite treaty of peace signed at Aix la Chapelle. End of the old French war, 370—The Confederates demand the release of their braves in Canada. Negotiations between Clinton and La Galissonière in relation to the exchange, 371—Embassy of M. Francis Marie. Suspicions of Johnson, 372—Mutual dissatisfaction of all parties, 373.

CHAPTER X.
1749–1750.

Johnson is entrusted with the transfer of the prisoners. Success of his negotiations, 374—Apprehensions of the Mohawks artfully increased by La Galissonière. Johnson writes Clinton upon the subject. Reply of the governor, 375—Johnson summons both of the Mohawk castles to a conference. Happy results, 376—Trouble between the Indians and a few Albany traders. Proclamation of the governor in regard to it, 377—General exchange of prisoners effected, 377—Remarkable energy of Colonel Johnson, 378—He thwarts all the plans of Galissonière and his priests, 379—Encroachments of the French in Nova Scotia, 379—Colonel Johnson is appointed by the crown to a seat in his majesty's council for the province of New York, 380—This appointment, though unsought, by no means a surprise, 381—Wranglings between the governor and his assembly continue. The post at Oswego in danger of being given up. The assembly dissolved and writs issued for a new one, 382—The assembly allow Colonel Johnson part of the debt due him for provisioning the Oswego garrison, 383—Contemptible conduct of the assembly toward Johnson. Falsely charges him with peculation, 384—Resignation of Johnson as superintendent of Indian affairs. The step not entirely unexpected by Clinton, 385.

CHAPTER XI.
1750–1751.

The peace of Aix la Chapelle received by the colonies with strong feelings of dissatisfaction, 386—Proves to be a peace only in name. Boundaries between the English and French possessions left undetermined, 387—The French occupy the valley of the Ohio. La Presentation founded by Rev. Abbè Piquet, 388—Sagacity of Piequet. La Presentation destroyed by Gage in 1757, 389—Jean Cœur, a French emissary, stirs up the Six Nations against the Catawbas. Johnson advises Clinton of the fact. 390—Clinton acting upon the suggestions of Johnson, summons the Confederacy to meet the Catawbas in Albany. Determines to have the ends of the council take a wider scope, and asks the different colonial governors to send delegates, 391—Johnson informs the Mohawks of the governor's intentions. The invitation of Thomas Lee of Virginia declined by the Six Nations, 392—Commissioners present at the council, 393—The Six Nations are grieved at the resignation of Colonel Johnson. They despatch a fleet runner for him, 394—Johnson arrives in Albany to attend the council. Is requested by Clinton to continue in the charge of the Indian department, but peremptorialy declines, 395—Is willing to render every assistance in an individual capacity, 396—Johnson takes the oaths of office as a councillor. Clinton opens the council, 396—Reply of the Confederates. Address of Mr. Bull, commissioner from South Carolinia, 397—Speech of the Catawba king to the Six Nations, 398—Treaty between the Six Nations and the Catawbas concluded, 400—Clinton lays before his council letters from Colonel Johnson and Captain Stoddard of a startling nature. Designs of the French upon Oswego, 402—Col Johnson sent down to the house by the council to demand certain vouchers. They are refused, 403—Churlish treatment of the governor by the house, 404—Master stroke of policy on the part of Mr Clinton, 405—The French plan farther encroachments upon the territory of New York. Meditate the establishment of a missionary and military post at Oswego. The design frustrated by Johnson. The council grant him Onondaga lake with the land around it for two miles in width. Otherwise than this his debt from the colony never paid, 406.

CHAPTER XII.
1752–1753.

Dawning of a new era in American literature, 407—Johnson indulges in literary pursuits, and sends to London for books, 408—Takes special interest in the intellectual culture of the Mohawk children. Becomes a prominent patron of the mission school at Stockbridge, 409—Places Joseph Brant under the charge of Dr. Eleazer Wheelock at Lebanon Ct., 410—Closing years of Sir Peter Warren. His death announced to Johnson in a letter from his brother Warren Johnson, 411—William Smith appointed to the seat at the council board, left vacant by Sir Peter Warren's decease, 412—Principal features of the new assembly, 413—Clinton consults Colonel Johnson in the appointment of a new board of Indian commissioners, 414—Fears of Chief Justice De Lancey, 415—He ceases his opposition to the governor, 416—Difficulty in collecting the Oswego duties John De Peyster and Peter Schuyler Jr. charged with peculation. Johnson requested to sift the matter, 416—Makes his report, 417—Hostile Indians still hover along the northern frontier, A party of St. Francis Indians surprise and capture John Stark, afterward the hero of Bennington, 418—Clinton's opening message to the assembly, 418—French again active, 419—Johnson apprised of the movements of the enemy. Alarm of the Six Nations. 420—Indian affairs sadly neglected since the resignation of Johnson. King Hendrik visits Clinton in New York. Complains bitterly of the frauds to which the Indians were subjected in the sale of their lands, 421—Reply of the governor. Disgust of Hendrik, 422—The general assembly request Clinton to send Johnson to Onondaga to pacify the Six Nations, 424—Johnson summons the Mohawks to Mount Johnson, 425—Sets out on his mission, 426—Conference at Onondaga attended with happy results, 427—Arrival of Sir Danvers Osborne as the successor of Governor Clinton, 428—Strange conduct of the new governor. He commits suicide. Suspicions of foul play clearly without foundation. 429—Mr. De Lancey takes the reins of government, 430—His opening message to the assembly, 431—Change in the administration productive of one good result, 433—Death of Governor Clinton. His character, 434.

CHAPTER XIII.
1753–1754.

Period reached when the active public life of Colonel Johnson begins, 436—Claims of England and France to the Ohio valley, 436—Formation of the Ohio company, 437—Christopher Gist sent to explore the country. Commissioners treat at Logstown with the Mingoes and Shawanese, 438—The French call to their aid the spiritual arm, 439—La Jonquère seizes the English traders. George Washington sent by Governor Dinwiddie to remonstrate with the French commander, 440—His reception by St. Pièrre, 441—Mr. De Lancey informs the assembly of the encroachments of the French, 441—Niggardly spirit of the assembly, 442—The lieutenant governor answers the quibbles of the assembly and prorogues that body, 444—Virginia raises a regiment of six hundred men, 445—Washington with his troops reaches Will's creek, 446—The fort at the Monongahela captured by Contrecœur, who names it Du Quesne, 447—Washington is put on his guard by the half king. 447—Defeats De Jumonville,

CONTENTS.   XVII

Builds a fort at the Great Meadows which he called Fort Necessity, 448—
Surrenders Fort Necessity to De Villiers. The French left in undisputed
possession of the basin of the Ohio, 449.

CHAPTER XIV.
1754.

Congress of commissioners assemble at Albany. Its object, 450—Colonies
represented. Backwardness of the Six Nations in arriving. Jealousy
of the Indian commissioners toward Johnson, 451—True cause of the
reluctance of the Indians to attend the council. Lieutenant Governor
De Lancey called to the chair, 452—Opening speech of De Lancey to the
Indians, 453—King Hendrik replies, 454—The venerable Mohawk brave
utters a scathing phillipic, 456—Speech of his brother Abraham.
Desires that Colonel Johnson may be reinstated. Biting irony of his
speech, 456—Johnson prepares an answer, which is delivered by the
lieutenant governor, 457—Johnson, at the request of the commissioners,
submits a paper on the management of the Six Nations, 458—Measures
urged by him, 459—Origin of the Wyoming lands, 460—The Connecticut delegates purchase the lands of the Six Nations. Extent of the
land thus purchased, 464—Plan of a general federal union taken into
consideration, 465—Plan not adopted. Why it was not, 466—Savage
hordes let loose upon the whole frontier. The storm bursts with all its
fury, 467—Dutch Hoosic burned by Schaghticoke Indians. Vigorous
measures of Shirley, 468—Captain Ephraim Williams given a command
with the rank of major. De Lancey vies with Shirley in efficient preparations for defence, 469—The French meditate a descent upon the
lower settlements. Johnson places the militia in a condition for efficient
service. Difficulties between the militia and regulars at Schenectady,
470—De Lancey announces to the general assembly the defeat of Washington at the Great Meadows, 471—Want of harmony in the assembly,
472—Origin of the famous college controversy, 472—The church party
writhe under the lash of William Livingstone, 474—Charter of the college granted by Lieutenant Governor De Lancey. He and Johnson
become warm friends, 475—Rev. Mr. Barclay resigns his post among
the Mohawks for the rectorate of Trinity Church, 476—A fort on the
Hudson river above Albany ordered to be built, 477—End of the college
controversy, 478.

CHAPTER XV.
1755.

Vascillating course of the Newcastle ministry. Edward Braddock sent to
America with two regiments, 479—Dieskau and Vaudreuil arrive at
Quebec. Surrender of two French men-of-war. General assembly again
convened, 480—Johnson arrives in New York to take his seat at the
council board. Delivers to the lieutenant governor a letter from the
Mohawks, 481—Shirley again agitates the question of a descent on
Crown Point. Thomas Pownal sent as commissioner to New York.
Meets with a cold reception, 482—Braddock calls a conference at Alexandria. Four separate expeditions against the French planned, 483—
Johnson receives the command of one of them, with the rank of major
general. Form of his commission. Receives also the appointment of
Indian affairs, 484—Summons the Confederacy to a grand council at
Mount Johnson. Informs the Indians of the arrival of General Braddock, 485—The Confederacy, through Hendrik, express great satisfaction at his being "again raised up," 486—Johnson, by a stirring speech,
persuades them to take up arms in favor of the English, 488—Shirley
hastens to Boston to prepare for the expedition under his command,
489—The assembly of New York, urged by De Lancey, enter with alacrity into the work of raising troops for Major General Johnson, 490—

Conquest of Acadia, 491—Character of the Acadians, 492—Brutality of General Monckton, 493—Cruel fate of the Acadians, 494—Expedition of Braddock, 494—His defeat, 496—The half king at the solicitation of Johnson, offers his services to Braddock, and is refused, 497—The French prevail on several Indian tribes to take up the hatchet. Susquehannas and Catawbas remain faithful, 498—Shirley's expedition against Niagara, 498—It proves abortive, 499—All eyes turned to the expedition under Major General Johnson, 500.

CHAPTER XVI.
1755.

The forces destined against Crown Point assemble at Albany. General Lyman is sent forward with the greater part of the troops. Johnsonl delayed by the leaky condition of the bateaux, 501—Difficulty between himself and Shirley. Shirley's conduct, 502—He is piqued at the seeming neglect shown to his position, 504—Johnson heals the dissensions sown among the Indians by Lydius. Arrives at the great carrying place, accompanied by Hendrik and Brant, 505—The New England troops burn to retrieve the disgrace of Braddock's defeat. General Lyman builds Fort Edward, 506—Johnson reaches Lake St. Sacrament, and names it Lake George. Is joined by Lyman, 507—His dissappointment at finding so few of the Six Nations at the lake. Hendrik attributes it to Shirley, 508—Johnson's plan of operations, 510—Movements of Dieskau. A courier sent out by Johnson killed by the enemy, 511—A council of war called. Hendrik's advice, 512—Dieskau arranges an ambuscade. Deaths of Hendrik and Williams, 513—The French fail to take advantage of their first success. The attack on Johnson's camp begun by the French regulars, 514—Dieskau attempts to turn Johnson's right. He fails. Desperate fighting by the Provincials, 515—Utter route of the French. Dieskau, seriously wounded, is taken prisoner. Last words of Gardeur St. Pierre, 516—General Johnson receives a severe wound and is forced to retire to his tent. Captain Maginnis defeats the remnants of the French army at Rocky Brook, 517—Losses of the English and French. Singular historical fact, not generally known, 517—Johnson sends circular letters to the colonial governors. His treatment of Shirley vindicated. The Indians return home, 518—Building of Fort William Henry. Want of alacrity shown by the New England troops, 519—Efforts of Johnson to allay all jealousy, 520—Favorable opinion of Johnson by a New England officer. Scouting parties, under Rogers, annoy the enemy in the vicinity of Crown Point. Johnson disbands his army and returns to Mount Johnson, 521—He is severely censured. Review of his conduct, 521—Manuscript letters now first brought to light, afford a complete vindication of his conduct, 523—He is created a Baronet of Great Britain, and receives the thanks of parliament. Is greeted with an illumination and a triumphal procession by the citizens of New York, 525—Summing up of the results of the battle of Lake George, 526.

CHAPTER XVII.
1755-1756.

Sir Charles Hardy arrives in New York as the successor of Sir Danvers Osborne. His first message to the assembly, 530—Good feeling between the new governor and his legislature, 531—Hardy appoints a day of thanksgiving, and sets out for Albany to hasten the departure of the levies 532—Accomplishes little by the visit. Announces to the assembly Johnson's victory over Dieskau. Demands the settlement of a permanent revenue on a solid foundation. The assembly allude especially to the advantage gained by Johnson, 533—Governor Hardy's demand for a permanent support met with quiet indifference, 534—The St. Francis

Indians resume their incursions in the New Hampshire border, 535—Shirley, now commander-in-chief of the forces in America, arrives in New York and summons a grand congress of colonial governors, 536—Lays before it his plan for the next year's campaign, which meets with the general approval of the congress, 537—The assembly of New York look coldly upon the proposed expedition against Ticonderoga, and Shirley, in disgust, returns to Boston, 538—Tart correspondence between Johnson and Shirley, 538—The latter yields the point, 539—Johnson is appointed by the crown, "SOLE SUPERINTENDENT OF THE AFFAIRS OF THE SIX NATIONS AND OTHER NORTHERN INDIANS,"540.

APPENDIX.

I. Letter from Colonel William L. Stone to the chiefs and warriors of the Senecas, acknowledging his adoption as a chief of that nation, 541.

II. "A memorandum for trifles sent to London for through Captain Knox," by Sir William Johnson, 546.

III. Sketch of Colonel Ephraim Williams, 547.

IV. Sketch of King Hendrick, 549.

V. Sketch of Fort William Henry (engraving) 553.

VI. Manuscript letter; Sir William Baker to Sir William Johnson, 554.

THE LIFE AND TIMES

OF

SIR WILLIAM JOHNSON, BART.

CHAPTER I.

1534—1741.

THE annalist is the narrator of events in exact order of time: the biographer is a relator, not of the history of nations, but of the actions of particular persons: the office of the historian is to digest and record facts and events in a narrative style, but of yet greater security and dignity. Such, at least, should be the office of the writer who aspires to the more elevated walks of history. It is not intended that the present work shall be confined within the limits of either of the preceding definitions; but rather that it shall to an humble extent, combine the characteristics of all. Were it strictly biographical, it would be in order to introduce the principal personage concerning whom it is written, upon the stage of action in his own proper person, at the outset. But, as the life of Sir William Johnson was, for a long series of years, identified with the Indian history of the colony of New York, it seems to be necessary, in order to a proper understanding of the relations subsisting between the English and the Six Nations, at the time when he was appointed to the head of the Indian Department,—and in order, also, that the difficulties he was required to surmount may be adequately appreciated,—to give a summary review of the intricate and curiously interblended history of the Iroquois Confederacy, as connected with the English and French colonies, from the time of the Dutch conquest, and the cession of the colony to the Duke of York, down to the year in which Johnson, in his youth, established his residence in the valley of the Mohawk.

It is not to be denied that the French, from the day of their arrival in the St. Lawrence to the fall of their power in America, were generally more successful in winning the confidence and affections of the Indians with whom they came into immediate contact, than any other European people, not even excepting the Dutch. Their traders threaded the forests, and navigated the lakes and rivers, from the Gulf of the St. Lawrence to the Delta of the Mississippi,— planting posts among them at pleasure, adopting their habits, and intermarrying with their women. Their missionaries went forth unarmed and alone, everywhere exhibiting the most beautiful examples of patience, meekness, and self-denial; and, with rare exceptions, gaining the confidence of even the most savage hordes whom they encountered. Still there was one exception to this general success; and the time was long after their establishment in Canada, before they succeeded in making any favorable impressions upon the Iroquois. This delay was probably owing to the circumstance that when the French first ascended the St. Lawrence, they found the Confederates, upon whom they bestowed that name,[1] at war with the Hurons and Adirondacks, or Algonguins,— with which latter nations their first amicable relations were established, and as the allies of whom, under Champlain,

---

[1] "Iroquois," I need scarcely remark, was not an Indian, but a French name. The Five Nations called themselves "*Aquanu Schioni,*" or "*The United People.*" Iroquois is a generic term, bestowed by the French on that type of languages of which the Five Nations — the Tuscaroras, and, originally, the Wyandots, spoke dialects. The term, however, was early restricted to the two former; and the latter, for distinction's sake, and owing to striking events in their history, were called Hurons.

they engaged in the contest. The consequence of that alliance was a bitter hostility on the part of the Iroquois toward the French, which continued until after the conquest of New York from the Dutch, in 1664.¹ During that long period even the artful Jesuits failed to make any considerable impression upon them,— especially upon the Mohawks, at whose hands three of their number suffered martyrdom with the spirit of a primitive apostle.² More than once, likewise, before and after that date, the Iroquois swept over the French settlements with the torch and tomahawk, tracking their paths in blood, and carrying consternation even to the gates of Quebec. But the French and Adirondacks having successfully invaded the country of the Mohawks with a strong force, in the spring of 1666, a peace was concluded in the following year, through the influence, in chief, of the English colonial government, acting in obedience to instructions from the Duke of York,— afterward King James II.,— to whom the colony had been granted by his brother, the second Charles, of profligate memory.

The first three English governors of the colony, or rather lieutenants of the Duke of York, viz: Colonels Nicholls, Lovelace, and Major, afterward Sir Edmund Andross, bestowed but inconsiderable attention upon the Five Nations,³ not seeming to appreciate either the impor-

---

¹ Dr. Colden's *Memoir on the Fur Trade*.

² Father Joques, Brebœuf, and Lallemand. Vide Bancroft's *United States*, vol. iii, pp. 135–142.

³ Nicholls, the first English governor, was the commander of the expedition to whom Governor Stuyvesant capitulated, August twenty-seventh, 1664. Francis Lovelace, a colonel, succeeded Nicholls in 1667. He was a man of moderation, under whom the people lived very happily until the re-surrender of the colony to the Dutch, which ended his administration in 1673. But on the peace between the English and the states general, in February, 1674, the colony reverted back to England; and Major Andross (afterward Sir Edmund), was appointed to the government; the province being resigned

tance of their trade, or of their friendship.[1] Still, the mortal hatred they had borne the French, inclined them rather to prefer the friendship of the English. But the Duke of York, in his affection for the Church of Rome, shutting his eyes to what unquestionably should have been the true policy of the English toward the Indians, had conceived the idea of handing the Confederates over to the Holy See, as converts to its forms, if not to its faith. Hence the efforts to mediate the peace between the Iroquois and the French, of 1667; which were followed by invitations to the Jesuit missionaries, from the English, to settle among the Confederates, and by persuasions to the latter to receive them. The Mohawks were either too wise, or too bitter in spirit toward the French, to listen to the proposal. But not so with the other nations of the alliance; and the Oneidas, Onondagas, Cayugas and Senecas opened their arms to the insidious strangers in holy garb, causing infinite mischief in after years, as will appear in the sequel.

This peace of 1667 continued several years, during which time both the English and French prosecuted their trade with the Indians to a great and profitable extent. The French, especially, evinced a degree of energy, and a spirit of enterprise, almost unexampled in the history of colonization — planting their trading posts, under the lead of the adventurous La Salle, at all the commanding points of the great lakes, and across the country of the Illinois to the Mississippi; and stealing the hearts of the Indians through the arts of the crafty ministers of the order of Jesus, whom they sprinkled among the principal nations

---

to him in October following. Andross continued in the government of New York until 1682. In 1686 he was appointed by King James to the government of New England, where he displayed a tyrannical disposition. In 1688 New York was annexed to the jurisdiction of New England.

[1] Smith's *History of New York.*

over the whole country of the exploration. By these bold advances deep into the interior, and the insidious wiles which everywhere characterized their movements, the French acquired a decided advantage over the English colonists in the fur trade, which it was evidently their design exclusively to engross; while the direct tendency of the Duke of York's policy, originating in blindness and bigotry, was to produce exactly the same result.

The error was soon perceived by Colonel Dongan, who arrived in the colony as the successor of Major Andross, in 1683. Though his religious faith was in harmony with that of his royal master, he nevertheless possessed an enlarged understanding, with a disposition, as a civil governor, to look more closely after the interests of the crown than those of the crosier. He had not been long at the head of the colony, before he perceived the mistakes of his predecessors in the conduct of its Indian relations. In fighting men, the Five Nations at that time numbered ten times more than they did half a century afterward;[1] and the governor saw at once their importance as a wall of separation between the English Colonies and the French. He saw, also, the importance of their trade, which the Jesuit priests were largely influential in diverting to Canada. He saw that M. de Courcelles had erected a fort at Cadaraqui, within the territory of the Iroquois, on the north side of Lake Ontario,[2] and that La Salle had built a bark of ten tons upon that lake, and another of fifty upon Lake Erie; planting, also, a stockade at Niagara. He saw that the French were intercepting the trade of the English upon the lakes, and that the priests had succeeded in

---

[1] Memoir of Dr. Colden, concerning the fur trade, presented to Gov. Burnett, in 1724.

[2] The site of Kingston, Canada West.

seducing numbers of the Mohawks and river Indians[1] away from their own country, and planting their colonies upon the banks of the St. Lawrence, in the neighborhood of Montreal, through whose agency an illicit trade had been established with the city of Albany, by reason of which Montreal, instead of Albany, was becoming the principal *depot* of the Indian trade.[2] He saw, in a word, that the subtle followers of Ignatius Loyola were rapidly alienating the affections of the Confederates from the English and transferring them to the French,[3] and that unless the policy respecting them was changed, the influence of the English would, at no distant day, be at an end with them. Nor had the priests confined their efforts simply to moral suasion; but as though aiming to separate the Confederates from the English at a blow, and by a gulf so wide and deep as to be impassable, they had instigated them to commit positive hostilities upon the frontier settlements of Maryland and Virginia.

Having made himself thouroughly acquainted with these matters, Colonel Dongan lost no time in seeking to countervail the influence of the French, and to bring back the Indians to a cordial understanding with his own people. His instructions from home were to encourage the Jesuit missionaries. These he not only disregarded, but he ordered the missionaries away, and forbade the Five Nations to entertain them.[4] It is true this order was never enforced to the letter, — the priests, — some of

---

[1] The Mahickanders, or Stockbridge Indians. This tribe was composed of Mohegans, Narragansetts, the Farmington Indians, and refugees from what were called the Seven Nations of Connecticut Indians, who, fleeing before the march of civilization in New England, united with the Schaghtikoke Indians, and afterward settled together, as one people, at Stockbridge, and subsequently were generally known as the "River Indians."

[2] Dr. Colden's memorial.

[3] Idem.

[4] Smith's *History of New York*.

them at least,—maintaining a foothold at several points of the Confederacy,—dubious, at times, certainly,—but yet maintaining it for three-quarters of a century afterward. Still, the measures of conciliation adopted by Colonel Dongan, made a strong and favorable impression upon the Indians.

Availing himself of the difficulty between the Confederates and Virginia, consequent upon the outrages just adverted to as having been instigated by the priests, Colonel Dongan was instrumental in procuring a convention of the Five Nations, at Albany, in 1684, to meet Lord Howard of Effingham, Governor of Virginia, at which he (Dongan), was likewise present. This meeting, or council, was attended by the happiest results. The difficulties with Virginia were adjusted and a covenant made with Lord Howard for preventing further depredations.[1] But what was of yet greater importance, Colonel Dongan succeeded in completely gaining the affections of the Indians, who conceived for him the warmest esteem. They even asked that the arms of the Duke of York might be put upon their castles;—a request which it need not be said was most readily complied with, since should it afterwards become necessary, the governor might find it convenient to construe it into an act of at least partial submission to English authority, although it has been asserted that the Indians themselves looked upon the ducal insignia as a sort of charm, that might protect them against the French.[2]

There was likewise another fortunate concurrence of events just at that time which revived all the ancient animosity between the Iroquois and the French. While the conferences between Lord Howard and the Indians were yet in progress, a message was received from M. De la

---

[1] Smith's *History of New York*.

[2] Colden's *History of the Five Nations*.

CHAP. I.
1684.

Barre, the Governor of Canada, complaining of the conduct of the Senecas in prosecuting hostilities against the Miamies and other western nations in alliance with the French, and thus interrupting their trade. Colonel Dongan communicated the message to the Iroquois chiefs, who retorted by charging the French with supplying their enemies with all their munitions of war. "Onontio[1] calls us children," said they, "and at the same time sends powder to our enemies to kill us!" This collision resulted in open war between the Iroquois and the French,—the latter sending to France for powerful reinforcements, with the design of an entire subjugation of the former in the ensuing year. Meantime the French Catholics continued to procure letters from the Duke of York to his lieutenant, commanding him to lay no obstacles in the way of the invaders. But these commands were again disregarded. Dongan apprised the Iroquois of the designs of the French, not only to march against them with a strong army, but simultaneously to bring down upon them the western Indians in their interest. The English governor also promised to assist them if necessary.

1685.

Thus by the wisdom, and the strong sense of justice, of Colonel Dongan, was the chain of friendship between the English and the Five Nations, brightened, and the most amicable relations re-established. Yet for the course he had taken, he fell under the displeasure of his bigoted master on his accession to the throne, in 1685.[2]

It is not, of course, within the purpose of this retrospect, to trace the progress of the long and cruel wars that succeeded the negotiations between Colonel Dongan and

---

[1] The name by which the Iroquois were wont to speak of the French governors of Canada.

[2] Colonel Dongan continued in the government of the colony from 1683 to 1688. He was highly respected as governor, being upright, discreet and of accomplished manners. He gave the colony its first legislative assembly, and after his return home became Earl of Limerick

the Confederates. Briefly it may be said, in respect to the expedition of M. de la Barre, that it failed by reason of sickness in his army at Cadaraqui, before crossing the lake. He was succeeded in the government of Canada by the Marquis Denonville, who invaded the Seneca country in 1687 with a powerful force; gaining, however, such a victory over the Indians, in the Genesee Valley, as led to an inglorious retreat. This invasion was speedily recompensed by the Confederates, who descended upon the French settlements of the St. Lawrence like a tempest and struck a blow of terrible vengeance upon Montreal itself.

New York, was at this time, torn by the intestine commotions incident to the revolution which drove the Stuarts from the English throne, and ended the power of the Catholics in the colony. It was a consequence of these divisions, that the English could afford the Indians no assistance in their invasion of Canada, at that time, else that country would then doubtless have been wrested from the crown of France. But the achievements of the Indians were, nevertheless, most important for the colony of New York, the subjugation of which was at that precise conjuncture meditated by France, and a combined expedition by land and sea, was undertaken for that purpose,—Admiral Caffiniere commanding the ships which sailed from Rochefort for New York, and the Count de Frontenac, who had succeeded Denonville, being the general of the land forces. On his arrival at Quebec, however, the count beheld his province reduced to a field of devastation, and he was therefore constrained to abandon the enterprise.

During the civil feuds of the revolution, and those that followed under the contested Leislerian administration, the Indian affairs of New York were neglected. Meantime the New England colonies becoming involved in a war with the Eastern Indians, sent a deputation to Albany to invite the Five Nations to take up the hatchet in their cause; but the invitation was declined.

1687. The revolution which brought William and Mary upon the throne having been followed by war between England and France, the colonies were of course involved in the conflict; whereupon Count Frontenac revived the policy of attempting to detach the Confederates from the English interest. To this end, through the efforts of a Jesuit residing among the Oneidas, all the Confederates save the Mohawks were induced to meet the emissaries of the French in council at Onondaga. At the same time, with a view of making an unfavorable impression upon the Mohawks, as to the power of the English to defend their own settlements against the arms of the French king, a secret expedition was set on foot against Schenectady, which resulted in a frightful massacre of the slumbering inhabitants of that devoted town, on the night of the eighth 1690. of February, 1690. But the Five Nations were neither won to the interests of the French by the persuasions of the agents at Onondaga, nor by the terrors of the scene at Schenectady. The veteran chief, Sadekanaghtie, an Onondaga orator of great eminence acted the skillful diplomatist at the council, while the Mohawks deeply sympathized with their suffering neighbors of Schenectady, and harrassed the invaders to good purpose on their retreat,— sending their war parties again into Canada, even to the attack once more of the island of Montreal.

It required, however, as will often appear in the present work, the most unremitted attention of the government to maintain those close relations of amity with the Five Nations which were essential to the true interests and safety of the province. Their jealousies were far more easily awakened than allayed; and unless continually caressed and propitiated by frequent largesses, they became restless and frowning. Hence, notwithstanding the alacrity with which the Mohawks had sought to avenge the murders of Schenectady, in February, 1690, the neglect they experienced during the agitations attending and following the foul judicial murder of Leisler and his son-in-law, not only disaffected them toward the English, but they even went so far as to send an embassy of peace to Count Frontenac. Meantime, in order to defeat this purpose, Colonel Sloughter, who had superseded Leisler in the government,[1] succeeded in holding a council with the four nations of the Confederates, exclusive of the Mohawks, which was attended by happy results,— the designs of the Mohawks, moved, probably, by a sudden impulse, being frustrated, and they themselves renewing their covenant chain.

In order to maintain the advantages secured by these negotiations, and keep in action the hostile feelings of the Confederates against the French, Major Peter Schuyler, the white man of all others in whom the Five Nations reposed the greatest confidence, planned and executed his bold irruption through Lake Champlain into Canada during the same season,— defeating, with his Indians, De Callieres, governor of Montreal, and keeping the whole

---

[1] Colonel Sloughter was commissioned to the government of New York in January, 1689, but did not arrive until the nineteenth of March, 1691. The selection of Sloughter was not fortunate. According to Smith, he was utterly destitute of every qualification for government; licentious in his morals, avaricious, and base. Leisler, who had administered the government after a fashion, since the departure of Dongan, intoxicated with power, refused to surrender the government to Sloughter, and attempted to defend the fort in which he had taken refuge against him. Finding it expedient, however, very soon to abandon the fort, he was arrested, and, with his son-in-law Milburne, tried and executed for treason. Still, on the whole, the conduct of Leisler during the revolution had been considered patriotic, and his sentence was deemed very unjust and cruel. Indeed, his enemies could not prevail upon Sloughter to sign the warrant for his execution, until, for that purpose, they got him intoxicated. It was a murderous affair. Sloughter's administration was short and turbulent. He died July twenty-third, 1691.

CHAP. I.
1691.

Canadian country in constant alarm by frequent incursions of war-parties against the French settlements. Active hostilities were likewise prosecuted by the Confederates against the French traders, and their posts, upon Lake Ontario. The celebrated Onondaga chief, Black-Kettle, one of the bravest and most remarkable warriors of his race, was the leader in that quarter. Being taken in the same year, he was put to death by the most frightful torments.

On the death of Sloughter, Richard Ingoldsby, the captain of an independent company, was made president of the council, to the exclusion of Joseph Dudley, who, but for his absence in Boston, would have had the right to preside, and upon whom the government would have devolved. But although Dudley very soon returned to New York, he did not contest the authority of Ingoldsby, who administered the government until the arrival of Colonel Fletcher, with a commission as governor, in August, 1692. In the preceding month of June, Ingoldsby met the Five Nations in council at Albany, on which occasion they declared their enmity to the French in the strongest possible terms. Their expressions of friendship for the English were also renewed. "Brother Corlaer," said the sachem, "we are all the subjects of one great king and queen; we have one head, one heart, one interest, and are all engaged in the same war." They nevertheless condemned the English for their inactivity, "telling them that the destruction of Canada would not make one summer's work, against their united strength, if ingeniously exerted."[1]

1692.

In conducting the Indian affairs of the colony, Colonel Fletcher took Major Schuyler into his councils, and was guided by his opinions.[2] No man understood those affairs

[1] Smith's *History of New York*.

[2] Fletcher was by profession a soldier, a man of strong passions, and inconsiderable talents; very active, and equally avaricious. His adminis-

better than he; and his influence over the Indians was so great, that whatever Quider,[1] as they called him, either recommended or disapproved, had the force of a law. This power over them was supported, as it had been obtained, by repeated offices of kindness, and his single bravery and activity in the defence of his country." Through the influence of Quider, therefore, Colonel Fletcher was placed upon the best footing with the Indians, by whom was conferred upon him the name of Cayenguinago, or "The Great Swift Arrow," as a compliment for a remarkably rapid journey made by him from New York to Schenectady on a sudden emergency.[3]

Despairing, at length, of accomplishing a peace with the Five Nations, Count Frontenac determined to strike a blow upon the Mohawks in their own country,— which purpose was securely executed in the month of February, 1693. For once this vigilant race of warriors were taken by surprise, two of their castles being entered and captured without much resistance — the warriors of both having been mostly absent at Schenectady. On assailing the third, or upper castle, however, the invaders met with a different reception. The warriors within, to the number of forty, were engaged in a war-dance, preparatory to some military expedition upon which they were about

---

tration was so energetic and successful, the first year, that he received large supplies, and a vote of special thanks from the assembly. He was a bigot, however, to the Episcopal form of church government, and labored hard to encourage English churches and schools, and was shortly involved in a violent controversy with the assembly, who inclined rather to favor the Dutch churches. He was also unpopular because of his extravagant demands for money. He continued in the administration of the government until the year 1695, inclusive.

[1] Quider, the Iroquois pronunciation of Peter. Having no labials in their language, they could not say Peter

[2] Smith's *History of New York*.

[3] Colden's *Six Nations*.

entering; and though inferior in force, yet they yielded not without a struggle, nor until thirty of the assailants had been slain. About three hundred of the Mohawks were taken prisoners in this invason, in respect to which the people of Schenectady have been charged with bad conduct. They neither aided their neighbors, nor even apprised them of the approach of danger, although informed of the fact in due season themselves. But Quider, the fast friend of the Indians, took the field at the head of the militia of Albany, immediately on hearing of the invasion, and harassed the enemy sharply during their retreat. Indeed, but for the protection of a snow-storm, and the accidental resting of a cake of ice upon the river, forming a bridge for their escape, the invaders would have been cut off.

The loss of the Mohawks by this incursion, added to dissatisfaction arising from the many unfulfilled promises made to them by the English, disheartened them so much that, in the spring of 1693, the Oneidas sued the French for peace,— a purpose which was frustrated only by the promptness of Fletcher's movements. A timely supply of presents for the Indians, received from England, enabled him to convene a council of the whole Confederacy at Albany, in July, and by a liberal distribution of arms and ammunition, knives, hatchets, and clothing, they were pacified, and, to use their own figure of speech, made "to roll and wallow in joy, by reason of the great favor the king and queen had done them." Yet, a Jesuit priest, resident with the Oneidas, named Milet, soon afterward succeeded in persuading all the nations, excepting the Mohawks, to open their ears to the propositions of certain emissaries dispatched upon the insidious errand to Onondaga. But the demands of the French, particularly for permission to rebuild the fort at Cadaraqui, were greater than the Indians were willing to concede, and the war was renewed in 1694, during which year Count

Frontenac sent an expedition of three hundred men against such of the Five Nations as might be found in the region of the Niagara peninsula. Only a small number of Indians were met with, some of whom were killed, and others made prisoners. These latter were taken to Montreal and tortured to death by fire. The Five Nations likewise, renewed their incursions into Canada, and the fate of their brethren was avenged by a holocaust, in which ten of their Indian captives were burnt.

In the year 1696, the Count de Frontenac made a yet more formidable effort for the subjugation of the Five Nations. To this end, an army, consisting of two battalions of regular troops, four battalions of militia, together with the warriors of all the Indian tribes, under his influence, was assembled, with which the count ascended the St. Lawrence to Cadaraqui, and crossing thence to Oswego, made a descent upon the Onondagas. But it was a bootless expedition. The Indians, apprised that the French were bringing several small pieces of artillery against them, before which they knew they could not stand, set fire to their principal towns, and retired with their women and children, and their old men, to their wilderness labyrinths. One only of their nation remained to receive the invaders,— an old man, whose head was whitened with the snows of a hundred winters. He refused to leave his lodge, and was put to death by torture,— dying as bravely as he had lived, and laughing to scorn the efforts by his tormentors to wring a groan or a murmur of complaint from his bosom. It is difficult to conceive how the officers of a civilized and gallant people, like the French, could have permitted such a murder. One would have thought that in admiration of his fortitude, his patriotism, and his courage, a hundred swords would have leaped from their scabbards for the defence of a venerable brave like him. But it was not thus; and the death of the old sachem was the only exploit which crowned the last campaign of the Count de Frontenac against the indomitable Iroquois. Not a single Onondaga captive was made, and their conquest was a field of smouldering ashes. Subsequently, by treachery, thirty-five Oneidas were taken prisoners and carried into Canada; but on the retreat of the army, the Onondagas fell upon its rear and cut off several bateaux. Nor was this all, the warriors of the Five Nations renewed their incursions, even to the gates of Montreal, and by tomahawk and fire caused another famine in Canada. On the other hand, the scalping parties of the French and the Indians in their alliance, hung upon the skirts of the English colonies, infesting even the precincts of Albany.

The peace of Ryswick, in 1697, put an end to these barbarities. The Earl of Bellamont had by that time succeeded Colonel Fletcher in the government of New York[1] and some difficulties arose between his lordship and the French governor, in the negotiations that ensued for a mutual release of prisoners. In these negotiations the earl claimed the Iroquois as the subjects of, or dependents upon, the crown of Great Britain,— a claim in which Count Frontenac was by no means inclined to acquiesce. Pending these diplomatic proceedings, the count died, and the exchange of prisoners was effected by the Indians

---

[1] Richard, Earl of Bellamont, was appointed governor of New York, Massachusetts, and New Hampshire, in May, 1795, but did not arrive in New York until May, 1698. He was appointed by King William with a special view to the suppression of piracy in the American seas — New York, at that time, having been a commercial *depot* of the pirates, with whom Fletcher, and other officers in the colony, had a good understanding. Kidd was fitted out with a ship by Bellamont, Robert Livingstone and others, including several English noblemen. Turning pirate himself, Kidd was afterward arrested in Boston by the Earl, and sent home for trial. The Earl was a nobleman of polite manners, a great favorite of King William, and very popular among the people both of New York and Boston. He had been dissipated in his youth, but afterward became penitent and devout. He died in New York, in March, 1701.

themselves, without the earl's consent, leaving the disputed point unsettled. Still, the Five Nations declared their continued attachment to Corlaer, and refused a residence at Onondaga to the Jesuit missionary Bruyas, who had acted as an ambassador in the negotiation.

Nevertheless the French were far from relinquishing their designs of supplanting the English in the affections of the Iroquois; to which end so many Jesuit priests were introduced among them that in the year 1700 an act was passed by the provincial assembly for putting to death by hanging, every Popish priest coming voluntarily within the bounds of the colony.

In the spring of 1702, hostilities were again proclaimed by England against France and Spain. Happily, however, the Five Nations had just previously concluded a treaty of neutrality with the Canadian French, and the murderous border-forays incident to Indian hostilities, were not renewed.

But even the terrors of the halter were insufficient to deter the Jesuits from communicating with the Five Nations, nor were their artful dealings with them persisted in without partial effect. The indications were indeed such in the year 1708, as in the opinion of Lord Cornbury,[1]

---

[1] Edward Hyde, Lord Cornbury, was the son of the Earl of Clarendon. On the death of Earl Bellamont, the government devolved upon Mr. Nanfan, the lieutenant-governor, until the appointment of Lord Cornbury, in 1702. He was a very tyrannical, base, and profligate man, and was appointed to the government of New York by King William, as a reward for his desertion of King James, in whose army he was an officer. He was a savage bigot and an ungentlemanly tyrant. He imprisoned several clergymen who were dissenters, and robbed the Rev. M. Hubbard, of Jamaica, of his house and glebe. He was wont to dress himself in women's clothes, and thus patrol the fort. His avarice was insatiable, and his disposition that of a savage. Becoming at length an object of universal abhorrence and detestation, he was superseded by the queen (Anne), who, in the autumn of 1708, appointed Lord Lovelace in his place. He was then thrown into prison by his creditors, where he remained until the death of his father, when he became Earl of Clarendon. He died in 1723.

then at the head of the colony, to require such an appropriation as would enable him to meet them in council, and conciliate them with the needful presents. This timely measure was successful. The rusty spots upon the chain were again rubbed off; and in the succeeding year, through the indefatigable exertions of Colonel Schuyler,— Quider,— the Five Nations were engaged heartily in Colonel Nicholson's remarkable though entirely abortive expedition for the subjugation of Canada,— an expedition the organization of which cost the colonies, — that of New York in particular,— a vast amount of money, and the failure of which caused deep and wide-spread mortification.

Colonel Schuyler was greatly beloved by the Five Nations, and having excited their expectations to a high pitch of enthusiasm in regard to the projected conquest of Canada, he felt keenly the miserable failure of Nicholson's expedition. Still, distinctly perceiving the importance of effecting that conquest, and with a view, probably, of diverting the attention of the Indians from their disappointment, he determined upon a voyage to England to represent the actual state of the country, in person, to the parent government. His views were seconded by the colonial assembly, and he took with him the five Iroquois chiefs whose appearance in the British capital created so great a sensation, according to the chroniclers of those days.[1] This visit was made in 1710. Schuyler returned with his chiefs in the autumn of the same year,— the latter being highly gratified with their voyage, and their reception by the great queen, before whom they had strongly seconded the arguments of Quider for the speedy reduction of Canada, as the only effectual measure of peace and security to the northern English colonies.

In accordance with this advice, another expedition for

---

[1] Vide, one of the numbers of Addison's *Spectator*.

that object was undertaken in the next year — 1711; great preparations being made therefor, both by the parent government and the colonies. The French, aware of the design, were equally active in concerting measures of defence. The Indians in their immediate alliance were induced to take up the hatchet, and renewed attempts were made upon the fidelity of the Iroquois. No perceptible impression was made upon their virtue, however; but the expedition resulted in another sad miscarriage, alike upon the land and the wave,— whereat the Confederates were greatly disheartened, and at length, under their repeated disappointments, they again began to "open their ears" to the insidious counsels and persuasions of the French. Indeed, but for the peace of Utrecht, concluded in the spring of 1713, it was believed that the Senecas, and perhaps others of their Confederacy, would then have turned their arms upon the English. Yet one important point connected with the Indian relations of the English, was secured by this treaty, if no more. By its provisions the long contested question of English supremacy over the Five Nations and their territory, which in his negotiations with the Earl of Bellamont, Count Frontenac had refused to recognize, was conceded by the French. The Indians of this Confederacy had previously, under the administration of Colonel Fletcher, thrown themselves upon the English for protection,— as they likewise did again at a susbequent period, for the same object,— making a formal surrender of their country to the English; not as an unqualified cession, however, but to be held and protected by the crown for *their use*. In other words, the Indians seem to have supposed that they were investing the English with a sort of superior jurisdiction over their territory, reserving to themselves their own distinct sovereignty in every other respect.

Brigadier-General Hunter, who was appointed to the government of New York, as the successor of Lord Lovelace, was required to take no very active part in the Indian affairs of the colony.¹ The peace of Utrecht being followed by several years of repose, the colonies were relieved from the terrible inflictions of Indian hostilities,—a species of warfare the most frightful that can be imagined, as well from its certain as from its uncertain character,—uncertain, always, when, or where, the dreaded enemy might strike, and equally certain that his path would be illumined by fire, and made red with blood. Meantime the Confederates, being likewise relieved from hostilities with the French, and the Indians in their interest, again directed their arms against their ancient enemies in the south,—in the countries of the Carolinas and Georgia,— among the Catawbas and the Cherokees, even to the head waters of the Mobile. The most powerful nation in the midlands of Carolina, were the Tuscaroras, kindred, as their speech testified, either of the Wyandots, or the Five Nations, or both. In either case, their language, having no labials, bore so strong an affinity to that of the Five Nations, that they were claimed by the latter as relations; and with their own consent were transplanted to the north, within the bosom of the Iroquois Confederacy. It has been asserted by a high authority, that at a date so recent as the year 1708, the Tuscaroras possessed fifteen towns, and could count twelve hundred warriors as brave as the Mohawks.² This enumeration must have been erroneous, or else their numbers were rapidly diminished by pesti-

---

¹ John, Lord Lovelace, Baron of Hurley, appointed to supersede Lord Cornbury, entered upon the government of the colony on the 18th of December, 1708. He died on the 5th of May in the next year, of a disorder contracted in crossing the ferry at his first arrival in New York. His lady remained in New York many years after his death. On the death of his lordship, the government once more devolved upon Richard Ingoldsby, the lieutenant-governor of the colony, until the arrival of Governor Hunter, in the summer of 1710.

² Bancroft's *History of the United States*, vol. iii.

lence or war, or by some other calamity, since at the time of their transplantation, five years afterward, they were but a comparatively feeble clan. Yet they were counted as a nation; and the Iroquois Confederacy was thenceforward called THE SIX NATIONS.[1]

General Hunter continued at the head of the colonial administration until the summer of 1719, when he went back to England on leave of absence, as well on account of his health, as to look after his private affairs. He intimated that he might return to the government again, but did not.[2] The chief command on his departure, devolved on the Hon. Peter Schuyler, as the oldest member of the council, but only for a brief period. He however held a treaty with the Six Nations at Albany, which was considered satisfactory; yet it would have been more so, had his efforts to induce the Confederates to drive Joncaire,

---

[1] The history of the Tuscaroras, and the manner or cause of their removal to the north, and their incorporation with the Iroquois Confederacy, are involved in doubt. According to some accounts, they are said to have been first conquered by the Five Nations, and then adopted among them because of discovered relationship. Dr. Colden says they fled to the Five Nations, before the arms of the people of Carolina. Smith gives a still different account of their southern locality, thus: "The Tuscaroras possessed a tract of land near the sources of James river, in Virginia, whence the encroachments of the English induced them to remove, and settle near the southeast end of the Oneida lake."—SMITH.

[2] Hunter was a Scotchman, and when a boy, an apprentice to an apothecary. Leaving his master, he entered the army, and being a man of wit and beauty, gained promotion, and also the hand of Lady Hay. In 1707 he was appointed lieutenant-governor of Virginia, but being captured by the French on his voyage out, on his return to England he was appointed to the government of New York and New Jersey, then united in the same jurisdiction. Governor Hunter was the man who brought over the three thousand Palatines from Germany, who founded the German settlements in the interior of New York and Pennsylvania. He administered the government of the colony "well and wisely," as was said to him in an affectionate parting address by the general assembly, until the summer of 1719, when he returned to England on leave, to look after his private affairs.

the artful agent of the French, out of their country, been successful. This Jesuit emissary had resided among the Senecas from the beginning of Queen Anne's reign. He had been adopted by them, and was greatly beloved by the Onondagas. He was incessant in his intrigues in behalf of the French, facilitating the missionaries in their progress through the country, and contributing greatly to the vacillating course of the Indians toward the English. Schuyler was aware of all this; but notwithstanding his own great influence over the Six Nations, he could not prevail upon them to discard their favorite. In other respects the government of Schuyler was marked by moderation, wisdom, and integrity.[1]

1720. William Burnet, son of the celebrated prelate of that name who flourished in the reign of William and Mary, succeeded to the government of the colony, in the year 1720; and of all the colonial governors of New York, with the exception of Colonel Dongan, his Indian policy was marked by the most prudent forecast and the greatest wisdom. Immediately after the peace of Utrecht, a brisk trade in goods for the Indian market, was revived between Albany and Montreal,— the Caughnawaga clan of the Mohawks residing near Montreal serving as carriers. The chiefs of the Six Nations foresaw the evil and inevitable consequences to result from allowing that trade to pass round in that direction, inasmuch as the Indians would of course be drawn exclusively to Montreal for their supplies, to be received immediately at the hands of the French, — and they cautioned the English authorities against it. Mr. Hunter had indeed called the attention of the general assembly to the subject at an antecedent period; but no action was had thereon until after Mr. Burnet had assumed the direction of the colonial administration. The policy of the latter was at once to cut off an intercourse, so unwise and so dangerous, with Montreal, and bring the

---

[1] Smith's *History of New York*.

entire Indian trade within the limits and control of New York. To this end an act was passed at his suggestion, subjecting the traders with Montreal to a forfeiture of their goods, and a penalty of one hundred pounds for each infraction of the law. It likewise entered into the policy of Mr. Burnet to win the confidence of the Caughnawagas, and reunite them with their kindred in their native valley. But the ties by which the Roman priesthood had bound them to the interests of the French, were too strong, and the efforts of the governor were unsuccessful.

In furtherance of the design to grasp the Indian trade, not only of the Six Nations, but likewise that of the remoter nations of the upper lakes, a trading post was established at Oswego in 1722. A trusty agent was also appointed to reside at the great council-fire of the Onondagas,— the central nation of the Confederates. A congress of several of the colonies was held at Albany, to meet the Six Nations, during the same year, which, among other distinguished men, was attended by Governor Spottswood, of Virginia, Sir William Keith, of Pennsylvania, and by Governor Burnet. At this council the chiefs stipulated that in their future southern war-expeditions they would not cross the Potomac, and in their marches against their southern enemies, their path was to lie westward of the great mountains — the Alleghanies meaning. Mr. Burnet again brightened the chain of friendship with them, on the part of New York, notwithstanding the adverse influences exerted by the Chevalier Joncaire, the Jesuit agent residing alternately among the Senecas and Onondagas.

The beneficial effects of Mr. Burnet's policy were soon apparent. In the course of a single year more than forty young men plunged boldly into the Indian country as traders, acquired their languages, and strengthened the precarious friendship existing between the English and the more distant nations; while tribes of the latter previously unknown to the colonists, even from beyond Michilimackinac, visited Albany for purposes of traffic.

1722. The establishment of an English post at Oswego was a cause of high displeasure to the French, who, in order to intercept the trade from the upper lakes that would naturally be drawn thither, and thus be diverted from Montreal, determined to repossess themselves of Niagara, rebuild the trading-house at that point, and repair their dilapidated fort. The consent of the Onondagas to this measure was obtained by the Baron de Longueil, who visited their country for that purpose, through the influence of Joncaire and his Jesuit associates. But the other members of the Confederacy, disapproving of the movement, declared the permission given to be void, and dispatched messengers to Niagara to arrest the procedure. With a just appreciation of the importance of such an encroachment upon their territory, the Confederates met Mr. Burnet in council upon the subject, at Albany, in 1727. "We come to you howling," said the chiefs; "and this is the reason why we howl, that the governor of Canada encroaches on our land and builds thereon." Governor Burnet made them a speech on the occasion, beautifully expressed in their own figurative language, which gave them great satisfaction.[1] The chiefs, declaring themselves unable to resist this invasion of the French, entreated the English for succor, and formally surrendered their country to the great king, "to be protected by him for their use," as heretofore stated. But Governor Burnet being at that period involved in political difficulties with an assembly, too short-sighted, or too factious, to appreciate the importance of preserving so able a head to the colonial government, was enabled to do nothing more for the protection of the Indians than to erect a small military defence at Oswego; and even this work of necessity he was obliged to perform at his own private expense. Meantime

---
[1] Smith's *History of New York.*

the French completed and secured their works at Niagara without molestation.

In the course of the same year, having been thwarted in his enlarged and patriotic views by several successive assemblies, Mr. Burnet, the ablest and wisest of the colonial administrators, retired from the government of New York, and accepted that of Massachusetts and New Hampshire.[1] Mr. Montgomery succeeded him in New York, in 1728. He was an indolent man, and had not character enough to inspire opposition. The French, enraged at the erection of a fort at Oswego, were now menacing that post. The new governor thereupon met the Six Nations in council at Albany, to renew the covenant chain, and engage them in the defence of that important station. Large presents were distributed among them, and they declared their willingness to join the reinforcements detached from the independent companies for that service. Being apprised of these preparations, the French desisted from their threatened invasion.[2]

Much of the opposition to the administration of Governor Burnet, had been fomented and kept alive by the Albanians who, by the shrewdness of his Indian policy, and

---

[1] Governor Burnet was not only a man of letters, but of wit — a believer in the Christian religion, yet not a serious professor. A variety of amusing anecdotes has been related of him. When on his way from New York to assume the government at Boston, one of the committee who went from that town to meet him on the borders of Rhode Island, was the facetious Colonel Tailer. Burnet complained of the long graces that were said before meals by clergymen on the road, and asked when they would shorten. Tailer answered: 'The graces will increase in length till you come to Boston; after that they will shorten till you come to your government of New Hampshire, where your excellency will find no grace at all."

[2] Colonel John Montgomery succeeded Mr. Burnet in the government of the colonies of New York and New Jersey, in the month of April, 1728. He was a Scotchman, and bred a soldier. But quitting the profession of arms, he went into parliament,— serving also, for a time, as groom of the bed-chamber to his majesty George II, before his accession to the throne. He was a man of moderate abilities and slender literary attainments. He was too good-natured a man to excite enmities; and his administration, cut short by death in 1731, was one of tranquil inaction.

the vigorous measures by which he had enforced it, had been interrupted in their illicit trade in Indian goods with Montreal,— and also by the importers of those goods residing in the city of New York. Sustained, however, by his council-board, and by the very able memoir of Doctor Colden upon that subject, Mr. Burnet, as the reader has already been apprised, had succeeded in giving a new and more advantageous character to the inland trade, while the Indian relations of the colony had been placed upon a better footing, in so far at least as the opportunities of the French to tamper with them had been measurably cut off. But in December of the succeeding year, owing to some intrigues that were never clearly understood, all these advantages were suddenly relinquished by an act of the crown repealing the measures of Mr. Burnet; reviving, in effect, the execrable trade of the Albanians, and thus at once re-opening the door of intrigue between the French and the Six Nations, which had been so wisely closed.

On the decease of Colonel Montgomery, the duties of the colonial executive were for a brief period exercised by Mr. Rip Van Dam, as president of the council.[1] His administration was signalized by the memorable infraction of the treaty of Utrecht, by the French, who then invaded the clearly defined territory of New York, and built the fortress of St. Frederick, at Crown Point, a work which gave them the command of Lake Champlain,— the highway between the English and French colonies. The pusillanimity evinced by the government of New York on the occasion of that flagrant encroachment upon its domains, excites the amazement of the retrospective reviewer. Massachusetts, alarmed at this advance of the rivals, if not natural enemies, of the English upon the settlements of the latter, first called the attention of the au-

---

[1] Mr. Van Dam was an eminent merchant in the city of New York, " of a fair estate," says Smith, the historian, " though distinguished more for the integrity of his heart, than his capacity to hold the reins of government."

thorities of New York to the subject; but the information was received with the most provoking indifference. There was a regular military force in the colony abundantly sufficient, by a prompt movement, to repel the aggression; yet not even a remonstrance was uttered against it.

During the stormy administration of Colonel Cosby, from 1732 to 1736 inclusive, no attention whatever appears to have been directed to Indian affairs. The incessant quarrels of this weak and avaricious man with the people and their representatives, left him apparently no time to bestow upon the external relations of the colony; and the Six Nations, in the absence of other employment, again resumed hostilities against their enemies at the South. One of their expeditions, directed against the Chickasaws, was fearfully disastrous. They fell into an ambuscade, and fought until all but two of a strong body of warriors were slain. One only of those two returned to rehearse the tale. He struck off deep into the forest, and supporting himself by game on the way, succeeded in traversing the whole distance back to his own country without meeting a single human being during the journey.[1] Another expedition, yet stronger, was sent against the Catawbas and Cherokees. They met upon the banks of the Cumberland river, now in Kentucky, at a place called "the bloody lands." Ascertaining that their enemies were advancing to meet them, the Six Nations in turn drew them into an ambuscade, and a terrible battle followed, in which the southrons, after a contest of two days, were defeated, with a loss of twelve hundred braves killed on the field.[2]

These retrospective glances have now been brought down to the year 1735 — the date of the arrival in America of

---

[1] Relation of General Schuyler to Chancellor Kent. Vide note in Kent's *Commentaries*, vol. iii.

[2] *Life of Mary Jemison*, the Seneca white woman. Hiockatoo, her husband, was in the battle. Still, the numbers said to have been killed may be an exaggeration.

the extraordinary youth whose life will form a prominent subject of these memoirs. And although that individual does not yet appear upon the theatre of public action, still, in order to the completeness of his "*life and times*," it will be necessary henceforward to set forth both the Indian and the civil history of the colony with more fullness of detail than in the preceding pages.

On the demise of Colonel Cosby,[1] Mr. George Clarke, long a member of the council, after a brief struggle with Mr. Van Dam for the precedency, succeeded to the direction of the government; and being shortly afterward commissioned as lieutenant-governor, he continued at the head of the colonial administration from the autumn of 1736 to that of 1743,— seven years. Mr. Clarke was remotely connected, by marriage, with the family of Lord Clarendon,— having been sent over as secretary of the colony in the reign of Queen Anne. Being, moreover, a man of strong common sense and of uncommon tact; and by reason of his long residence in the colony, and the several official stations he had held, well acquainted with its affairs; his administration,— certainly until toward its close,— was comparatively popular, and, all circumstances considered, eminently successful. In the brief struggle for power between himself and Mr. Van Dam, the latter had been sustained by the popular party, while the officers of the crown, and the partisans of Cosby, with few if any exceptions, adhered to Mr. Clarke.[2] This difficulty had been speedily ended by a royal confirmation of the somewhat

---

[1] Colonel William Cosby, appointed to the government of New York in 1732, had formerly been governor of Minorca, where he acquired no very enviable name by the scandalous and corrupt practices to which he was prompted by his avarice. His administration was turbulent and exceedingly unpopular, and deservedly so, for his conduct was atrocious. He died universally detested, on the tenth of March, 1736.

[2] Mr. Van Dam had been privately, and, as he and his partisans contended, illegally removed from the council-board by Cosby, in a fit of passion, almost upon his death-bed. Hence the struggle to which I have referred in the text.

doubtful authority assumed by Mr. Clarke. His own course, moreover, on taking the seals of office, was conciliatory. In his first speech to the general assembly he referred in temperate language to the unhappy divisions which had of late disturbed the colony, and which he thought it was then a favorable moment to heal. The English flour-market being overstocked by large supplies furnished from the other colonies, the attention of the assembly was directed to the expediency of encouraging domestic manufactures in various departments of industry. To the Indian affairs of the colony, Mr. Clarke invited the special attention of the assembly. The military works of Fort Hunter being in a dilapidated condition, and the object of affording protection to the Christian settlements through the Mohawk valley having been accomplished, the lieutenant-governor suggested the erection of a new fort at the carrying-place between the Mohawk river and Wood creek,[1] leading into Oneida lake, and thence through the Oswego river into Lake Ontario; and the transfer of the garrison from Fort Hunter to this new and commanding position. He likewise recommended the repairing of the block-house at Oswego, and the sending of smiths and other artificers into the Indian country, especially among the Senecas.[2]

These recommendations were repeated in the executive

---

[1] The site, afterward, of Fort Stanwix,— now the opulent town of Rome.

[2] In the course of this session of the general assembly, Chief Justice De Lancey, speaker of the legislative council, announced that his duties in the Supreme Court would render it impossible for him to act as speaker through the session. It was therefore ordered that the oldest counselor present should thenceforward act as speaker. Under this order, Doctor Cadwallader Colden first came to the chair.

On the twenty-sixth of October, the council resolved that they should hold their sittings in the common council chamber of the City-Hall. The House immediately returned a message that they were holding their sessions, and should continue to hold them in that chamber; and that it was conformable to the constitution that the council, in its legislative capacity, should sit as a distinct and separate body.

CHAP. speech to the assembly in the spring of 1737, and also
I.
again to a new assembly which had been called in the
1737. summer of the same year. The lieutenant-governor farther informed the new assembly that it had become necessary for him to meet the chiefs of the Six Nations in council at Albany in consequence of certain negotiations pending between the Senecas and the French, by virtue of which the latter were on the point of obtaining permission to erect a trading-post at Tierondequot, which would enable them to intercept the fur-trade of the upper lakes on its way to Oswego.[1]

For the purpose of defeating this sagacious movement of the French, and if possible yet further to circumvent them by obtaining the like permission for the English to establish a trading-post at the same point, the meeting with the Confederate chiefs took place in Albany, as suggested in the speech. The objects of the interview, however, were only obtained in part. The Senecas agreed not to allow the French agent, John Cœur, to build at Tierondequot; but neither would they permit the English to plant themselves there. Still they gladly acceded to the proposition of the lieutenant-governor to send a gun-smith to reside among them,— with whom were also dispatched an interpreter, and three other agents, to assist in circumventing the intrigues of the French. At the succeeding autumnal session of the assembly, these measures were sanctioned by that body, and provisions made for strengthening Oswego, and for the farther promotion of commerce with the Indians.[2]

---

[1] Irondequot, now well known as an inlet, or bay, a few miles east of the mouth of the Genesee river,— the place where Denonville landed in his memorable expedition against the Senecas, half a century before.

[2] Vide *Legislative Journals.* Also Smith's *History of New York.* At the session of the Assembly, October thirteenth, of this year, the council having sent a message to the house by the hand of a deputy clerk, a message was transmitted back, signifying that the house considered such a course disrespectful. Until that time, messages had been conveyed between the houses, with bills, resolutions, &c., by the hands of their members respect-

During the greater part of the year 1738 but little attention was paid to Indian affairs,— the principal historical incident of that year being the memorable contested election between Adolphe Philipse and Gerret Van Horne, in connection with which, owing to the extraordinary skill and eloquence of Mr. Smith, father of the historian, and of counsel for Van Horne, the Hebrew freeholders of the city of New York, from which place both parties claimed to have been returned to the assembly, were most unjustly disfranchised, on the ground of their religious creed, and their votes rejected.[1] The colony was greatly excited by this question, and the persuasive powers exerted by Mr. Smith, are represented to have been wonderful,— equalling, probably, if not surpassing, those of Andrew Hamilton, four years previously, in the great libel case of the Zengers,— and possibly not excelled even by Patrick Henry, a few years afterward, when he dethroned the reason of the court, and led captive the jury, in the great tobacco case in Virginia.[2]

Yet the movements of the Indians, and the designs of the French in Canada were not entirely overlooked. On the thirteenth of October, the general assembly being in session, the lieutenant-governor summoned the house before him, and announced the receipt of intelligence of a design by the French, to establish themselves at the carrying-place upon Wood creek, between the head, or south-

---

ively. The house considered the sending of a clerk an innovation upon their privileges; and Col. Phillipse, Mr. Verplank, and Mr. Johnson, were appointed a committee to wait upon the council and demand satisfaction. The council healed the matter by a conciliatory resolution, declaring that no disrespect had been intended.

[1] For an animated account of this celebrated case, drawn, however, by the partial hand of a son writing of his father, see Smith's *History*, vol. ii.

[2] See Wirt's *Life of Patrick Henry.*

ern end of Lake Champlain, and the Hudson river,[1] and calling for means to enable him to build a fort and plant a colony of settlers there for the defence of the northern frontier, to be composed of emigrants from North Britain.[2] The lieutenant-governor also announced, in the same speech, that a delegation of the Senecas had departed for Quebec, to treat, as it was understood, with M. Beauharnois, then the governor of Canada, with a view, after all, of allowing the French to plant themselves in the beautiful valley of the Tierondequot,— a measure which, said the speech, "would put an end to the Oswego trade." In conclusion the lieutenant-governor asked for an appropriation of money to enable him to frustrate their designs, and to make another effort for the purchase of the Tierondequot. The assembly having been suddenly dissolved a few days subsequent to the delivery of this speech, no steps were taken in reference to either of its recommendations, and they were each pressed urgently upon the new assembly summoned in the spring of the next year, 1739.

[1] The Wood creek here mentioned is altogether a different stream from that spoken of a few pages back, at the Mohawk carrying-place, which leads into the Oneida lake. These duplicated names are apt to create confusion. The present town of Whitehall stands upon *the* Wood creek spoken of here in the text, which pours into Lake Champlain.

[2] The North Britons here spoken of, whom Mr. Clarke proposed colonizing at the head of Lake Champlain, were a company of between four and five hundred adult Highlanders, with their children, who had been brought to the colony by Captain Laughlin Campbell, in the expectation of settling them upon a manor of thirty thousand acres of land, which he, Campbell, alledged had been promised him by the lieutenant-governor,— Campbell, who was a Highland chief, calculating to become, as it were, "lord of the manor." Smith roundly asserts that Clarke had stipulated to make the grant to Campbell; but the statement was contradicted by Dr. Colden, who was at the time in question a member of the executive council. Certain it is, however, that Campbell had the emigrants with him in New York; yet Colden says that many of them came out at their own expense, and that no more land had been promised to Campbell than he could bring into cultivation. Be this as it may, the disappointment of the emigrants was great, and they suffered much keen distress before they could take care of themselves.

The years 1738 and 1739, were marked by increasing political excitement, and the dividing line of parties, involving the great principles of civil liberty on the one side, and the prerogatives of the crown on the other, were more distinctly drawn, perhaps, than at any antecedent period. The administrations of the earlier English governors, Nicholls and Lovelace, were benevolent, and almost parental. Andross, it is true, was a tyrant; and during his administration parties were formed, as in England, upon the mixed questions of politics and religion, which dethroned the last and most bigoted of the Stuarts, and brought William and Mary upon the throne. Dongan, however, the last of the Stuart governers in New York, although a Roman Catholic, was nevertheless mild in the administration of the government, and a gentleman in his feelings and manners. It was upon his arrival in the autumn of 1683, that the freeholders of the colony were invested with the right of choosing representatives to meet the governor in general assembly.[1] For nearly twenty years subsequent to the revolution of 1689, the colony was torn by personal, rather than political factions, having their origin in the controversy which compassed the judicial murder of the unhappy Leisler and his son-in-law Milborne. These factions dying out in the lapse of years, other questions arose, the principal of which was that important one which always, sooner or later, springs up in every English colony,— involving, on the

---

[1] Two years previous to the arrival of Dongan, the aldermen of New York, and the justices of the peace of the court of assize, in consequence of the tyranny of Andross, had petitioned the duke that the people might be allowed to participate in the affairs of the government by the construction of a general assembly, in which they might be represented. Through the interposition of William Penn, who enjoyed the favor both of the king and the duke, the point was yielded, and Colonel Dongan was instructed to allow the people a voice in the government. Greatly to the joy of the inhabitants, therefore, who had become turbulent, if not disaffected, under the despotic rule of Andross, writs were issued to the sheriffs summoning the freeholders to choose representatives to meet the new governor in assembly on the seventeenth of October, 1683.

one hand, as I have already remarked, the rights of the people, and on the other the claims of the crown. Invariably, almost, if not quite, the struggle is originated upon some question of revenue,— either in the levying thereof, or in its disposition, or both. Thus in the origin of those political parties in New York, which continued with greater or less acrimony until the separation from the parent country, Sloughter and Fletcher had both endeavored to obtain grants of revenue to the crown for life, but had failed. Subsequently grants had been occasionally made to the officers of the crown for a term of years; but latterly, especially during the administration of Governor Cosby, the general assembly had grown more refractory upon the subject,— pertinaciously insisting that they would vote the salaries for the officers of the crown only with the annual supplies. This was a principle which the governors, as the representatives of the crown, felt bound to resist, as being an infringement of the royal prerogative. Henceforward, therefore, until the colony cast off its allegiance, the struggle in regard to the revenue, and its disposition, was almost perpetually before the people, in one form or another; and in some years, owing to the obstinacy of the representatives of the crown on one side, and the inflexibility of the representatives of the people on the other, supplies were not granted at all. Mr. Clarke, although he had the address to throw off, or to evade, the difficulty, for the space of two years, was nevertheless doomed soon to encounter it. Accordingly, in his speech to the assembly at the autumnal session of 1738, he complained that another year had elapsed without any provision being made for the support of his majesty's government in the province,— the neglect having occured by reason of "a practice not warranted by the usage of any former general assemblies." He therefore insisted strongly upon the adoption of measures for the payment of salaries; for the payment of the public creditors; and for the general security of the public credit by the creation of a sinking fund for the redemption of the bills of the colony.

The assembly was refractory. Instead of complying with the demands of the lieutenant-governor, the house resolved unanimously that they would grant no supplies upon that principle; and in regard to a sinking fund for the redemption of the bills of credit afloat, they refused any other measure than a continuance of the existing excise. These spirited and peremptory resolutions gave high offence to the representative of the crown; and on the day following their adoption, the assembly was summoned to the fort, and dissolved by a speech, declaring the said resolutions "to be such presumptuous, daring, and unprecedented steps that he could not look upon them but with astonishment, nor could he with honor suffer their authors to sit any longer."

The temper of the new assembly, summoned in the spring of the succeeding year, 1739, was no more in unison with the desires of the lieutenant-governor, than that of the former. The demand for a permanent supply bill was urged at several successive sessions, only to be met with obstinate refusals. The second session, held in the autumn, was interrupted in October, by a prorogation of several days, for the express purpose of affording the members leisure "to reflect seriously" upon the line of duty required of them by the exigencies of the country; for, not only was the assembly resolutely persisting in the determination to make only annual grants of supplies, but they were preparing to trench yet farther upon the royal prerogative, by insisting upon specific applications of the revenue, to be inserted in the bill itself. Meantime, on the thirteenth of October, the lieutenant-governor brought the subject of his differences with the assembly formally before his privy council. In regard to the new popular movement of this assembly, insisting upon a particular application of the revenues to be granted in the body of the act for the support of the government, the lieutenant-governor said they had been moved to that determination by the example of New Jersey, where an act of that nature had lately been passed. He was unwilling to allow any encroachment upon the rights of the crown. Yet, in consideration of the defenceless situation of the colony, he felt uneasy at such a turn of affairs; and not being disposed to revive old animosities, or to create new ones by another summary dissolution, he asked the advice of the council. The subject was referred to a committee, of which the Hon. Daniel Horsmanden, an old member of the council, was chairman. This gentleman was one of the most sturdy supporters of the royal prerogative; but, in consequence of the existing posture of affairs, and the necessity of a speedy provision for the public safety, the committee reported unanimously against a dissolution. They believed, also, that the assembly, and the people whom they represented, had the disputed point so much at heart that it would be impossible to do business with them unless it was conceded; and, besides, it was argued, should a dissolution take place, there was no reason for supposing that the next assembly would be less tenacious in asserting the offensive principle. Since, moreover, the governor of New Jersey had yielded the point, the committee advised to the same course in New York.[1] The point *was* conceded; and the effect, for the moment, was to produce a better state of feeling in the assembly. Supplies were granted, but only for the year; and various

---

[1] See the old minutes of the executive or privy council, in manuscript, in the secretary of state's office in Albany. To avoid confusion hereafter, it may be well to state in this connection, that the council acted in a two-fold capacity: first, as advisary; second, as legislative. "In the first," says Smith, in his chapter, entitled Political State, they are a privy council to the governor." When thus acting they are often called the executive or his majesty's council. Hence, privy council and executive council are synonimous. During the session of the legislature, however, *the same council* sat (without the presence of the governor) as a legislative council; and in such capacity exercised the same functions as the senate of the present day — so far as regards the passing of laws. The journals of this last or legislative council have recently been published by the state of New York under the supervision of Dr. E. B. O'Callaghan.

appropriations were made for placing the colony in a posture of defence. The Mohawks, among other things, required either that the dilapidated defences of Dyiondaroga (Fort Hunter) should be repaired or rebuilt, and that a garrison should be continued there, under a threat of leaving their own country and removing into Canada; and they were considered of too much importance as a line of defence against the French, to allow their demand in this respect to be disregarded.

But it is seldom that the wheels of revolution roll backward, and the concession which allowed the general assembly to prescribe the application or disposition of the supplies they voted, ever before claimed as the legal and known prerogative of the crown, appeased the popular party only for a very short time. Indeed, nothing is more certain, whether in monarchies or republics, than that the governed are never satisfied with concessions, while each successful demand only increases the popular clamor for more. Thus was it in the experience of Mr. Clarke. It is true, indeed, that the year 1740 passed without any direct collision upon the question of prerogative; although at the second short session of that year, the speech alleged the entire exhaustion of the revenue, and again demanded an ample appropriation for a term of years. But the controversy was re-opened at the spring session of the following year,—1741,—on which occasion the lieutenant-governor delivered a speech, long, beyond precedent, and enumerating the grievances of the crown by reason of the continued encroachments of the general assembly. The speech began by an elaborate review of the origin and progress of the difficulties that had existed between the representatives of the crown and the assembly, in respect to the granting of supplies,—evincing—such, indeed, is the inference,—a want of gratitude on the part of the latter, in view of the blessings which the colony had enjoyed under the paternal care of the government since the revolution of 1688. But it was not in connection with the supplies, only, that the assembly had invaded the rights of the crown. It was the undoubted prerogative of the crown to appoint the treasurer. Yet, the assembly had demanded the election of that officer. Not satisfied with that concession, they had next claimed the right of choosing the auditor-general. Failing in that demand, they had sought to accomplish their object by withholding the salary from that officer. These encroachments, he said, had been gradually increasing from year to year, until apprehensions had been seriously awakened in England "that the plantations are not without thoughts of throwing off their dependence on the crown." He, therefore, admonished the assembly to do away such an impression "by giving to his majesty such a revenue, and in such a manner, as will enable him to pay his own officers and servants," as had been done from the revolution, down to the year 1709 — during which period the colony was far less able to bear such a burden than now.[1]

Thus early and deeply were those principles striking root in America, which John Hampden had asserted, and poured out his blood to defend, in the great ship-money contest with Charles I., — which brought that unhappy monarch to the block, — and which, — fulfilling the apprehensions of Mr. Clarke, — thirty-five years afterward, separated the colonies from the British crown; — although in the answer of the house to the "insinuation of a suspicion" of a desire for independence, with real or affected gravity, they "vouched that not a single person in the colony had any such thoughts; adding — "for under what government can we be better protected, or our liberties or properties so well secured?"[2]

The Indian relations of the colony were not forgotten

---

[1] Vide *Journals of the Colonial Assembly*, vol. i, Hugh Gaine's edition. This (1741), was the year in which the chapel, barracks, secretary's office, &c., of Fort George (the Battery), were burnt, and the speech referred to in the text, asked an appropriation for their rebuilding — but without success.

[2] Smith, vol. ii.

at any time by Mr. Clarke. The Mohawks having requested an appropriation for the rebuilding of their chapel, the attention of the assembly was invited to the subject, and the occasion was improved to bestow a well-deserved compliment to the English missionary among that people — the Rev. Mr. Barclay, who, it was said, "had opened a glorious prospect of spreading the Christian faith and worship throughout the Six Nations."[1] The assembly declined making the grant — alleging that if the Christian converts in that nation were increasing, the funds required for a new chapel should be raised by private contributions.

But there were other considerations connected with the Indian policy, which it would not answer to neglect. War had been declared by the parent government against Spain; and lively apprehensions were entertained of an approaching rupture with France. In anticipation of such an event, fortifications were required for the security of the harbor of New York, and also for the defence of the frontiers — particularly of Oswego, — to the importance of strengthening which the lieutenant-governor repeatedly called the attention of the assembly. In the event of a war with France, he was greatly apprehensive that this post would be taken, in which case there was reason to fear from the temper of late manifested by the Six Nations, that they would all fall away to the enemy. In this emergency, appropriations were asked to enable the lieutenant-governor to convoke a grand council of the Confederates at Albany, which was accordingly held in the

---

[1] The missionary thus mentioned in the text, was the Rev. Henry Barclay, afterward a doctor of divinity, and rector of Trinity Church in the city of New York. He was a native of Albany, and a graduate of Yale College of the year 1734. He received orders in England; and after several years' service in the Mohawk country, as a missionary, was called to New York. The translation of the litugy into the Mohawk language, was made under his direction, and that of Rev. W. Andrews and the Rev. J. Ogilvie. Mr. Ogilvie succeeded him both in the mission, and also, on his decease, in Trinity Church. Mr. Barclay died in 1765.

month of August. The lieutenant-governor's opening speech to the assemblage of sachems and warriors was both happily conceived and expressed — creditable alike to his head and his heart. After an apology for not having met them at an earlier day, in consequence of the prevalence of the small-pox in New York, the infection of which he was apprehensive might be conveyed among their people, he admonished them against the dangers arising from the propensity of their young warriors to join the Indians in the interest of the French, in their hostile expeditions against the more distant tribes of their own kindred. The enticing of their young men in those expeditions, he argued, was an artful device of the French to divide and weaken them. "When united," said he, "you are like a strong rope, made of many strings and threads twisted together, but when separated, weak and easily broken. Thus they attempt to divide and weaken you, by leading your rash young men upon their distant wars. They hope so to weaken you by degrees, as by and by to be able to conquer you. If they were lovers of liberty themselves, they ought not to try to enslave other nations."

It was doubtless owing in a great measure to this species of intercourse between the Iroquois and the Indians on the Canadian side of the line, that the former were so frequently disposed to join the French — a disposition requiring so many largesses, and so much tact and activity to counteract. The lieutenant-governor likewise drew a contrast between the tyrannical and overbearing conduct of the French toward the Indians, as compared with the liberal and humane treatment which the red-men had always received at the hands of the English. Whether that contrast was in all respects a just one, it were bootless now to inquire.

In the course of the speech, the lieutenant-governor attempted to impart to the sachems and warriors some wholesome lessons of filial piety, and to infuse into their hearts some juster and loftier notions of true courage than were prevalent among that rude people. He endeavored to impress it upon their minds that wars upon women and children were the opposite of brave, and that the scalps of such when brought in from the war-path, were the trophies of cowards. He also exhorted them to abandon the cruelties practiced by their people in war — reminding them that the cruelties they inflicted upon others, were sure in the end to be visited upon themselves in return; and in again admonishing them against their associations with the French, he reminded them of the fact, that in some of their distant expeditions in company with the Indians in that interest, they had been compelled to strike the heads of their own remote allies, and sometimes it had been proved that they had struck down their own people — probably unawares.

In connection with this intimacy with the French, Mr. Clarke complained that some of the Onondaga chiefs had even been to converse with the governor of Canada, after the council they were then holding had been summoned. Still, he thanked them for the disposition they had shown to keep the path open to the trading-post at Oswego, and complimented them for their wisdom in keeping the French from Tierondequot. In conclusion he informed them that he had it in charge from the great king their father, to negotiate a general peace among all the Indians, so that they, with all the red-men south and west to the great Mississippi, should form a mighty chain, strong and bright. This work, he said, he was determined to do.

The sachems were shrewd in their replies. In regard to Oswego, they wished "their brother Corlaer,[1] would

---

[1] The name or title by which the Six Nations always designated the English governors of New York. The original Colaer was a German trader greatly beloved by the Six Nations. He was drowned in Lake Champlain while on one of his trading trips.

make powder and lead cheaper there, and pay the Indians better for helping to build their houses." Of the Tierondequot matter they replied: "You said that we had acted very wisely in not suffering the French to settle at Tierondequot, and that if they only had liberty to build a fishing-hut there, they would soon build a fort. *We perceive that both you and the French intend to settle that place, but we are fully resolved that neither you nor they shall do it.* There is a jealousy between you and the governor of Canada. If either should settle there it would breed mischief. Such near neighbors can never agree. We think that the trading-houses at Oswego and Niagara are near enough to each other." Touching the simile of the rope, they said it was their desire to make it strong by preserving friendship with as many nations as they could. "As our great father the great king has commanded us that we should be as one flesh and blood with the Indians to the southward and westward as far as the Mississippi, so we accept of them as brethren, that we may be united as one heart and one flesh, according to the king's commandment. But we desire that some of the sachems of those southern Indians do come here, which will strengthen and confirm this treaty. We will give them two years time to come in, and in the mean time keep at home all our fighting men."

In his rejoinder, the lieutenant-governor told them he could perceive no necessity for any meeting between them and the chiefs of the south and west. He was already clothed with power to conclude for them a general peace. He farther informed them that he had some presents from the governor of Virginia, but was instructed not to deliver the articles unless they first received all the Indians under his majesty's protection into the covenant chain.

The result of the conference, after the chiefs were made to understand that Corlaer was empowered fully to treat in behalf of the southern Indians, was, that they agreed to receive them all into the covenant chain,— adding: "and we shall ever look upon them as our own brethren, and as our own flesh, as if they had been born and bred amongst us. And as we have never yet been guilty of violating treaties, so you may depend that we will keep this inviolable to the end of the world."[1]

The council broke up amicably, and the Indians, well laden with presents, returned to their homes, professing a friendship for Corlaer which was to endure so long as the Great Spirit should cause the grass to grow and the water to run. But however firm the grasp by which they purposed to hold on to their end of the covenant chain, their good resolutions were liable to be shaken by every trifling circumstance that awakened their unslumbering jealousy, while the hold upon the affections of the Onondagas, Cayugas, and Senecas, which the Jesuits retained till the last, in all times of peril, rendered their constancy an object of doubtful solicitude in the minds of the English. Still, the pacification effected by Mr. Clarke contributed largely to the repose of the Six Nations for the two ensuing years,— 1741 and 1742.[2] The lieutenant-governor, it

---

[1] Unpublished minutes of the executive council, secretary of state's office, in Albany.

[2] In the manuscript journals of the privy council which have never been published, and which are only to be found in the office of the secretary of state in Albany, it is stated, under the date of May thirty-first, 1742, that the lieutenant-governor announced to the council-board that he had summoned the Six Nations to meet him in Albany, on the seventh of June; but that he had not been able to obtain the necessary funds from the treasurer to purchase presents for the Indians. The treasurer alledged that he had not the money nor could he obtain it. He had, however, some other funds, to the amount of £600, which he offered to furnish toward the necessary supply. But the lieutenant-governor said he could not go unless an amount sufficient to answer the object could be procured. Whereupon Mr. Livingston offered to make the necessary advance. It is not however certain that the council was held, since I have not been able to find any account of it either in the council minutes or elsewhere.

is true, adverted to the defenceless condition of the Indian frontiers occasionally in his speeches to the general assembly, especially to the important post of Oswego. But the popularity of Mr. Clarke was rapidly on the wane. Chief Justice De Lancy, the master spirit of the council, having rather abandoned him, and attached himself to the popular party, managed to preserve a considerate coolness on the part of that body toward their executive head, while the house heeded but little his recommendations.

The only subject of local excitement, however, during the year 1741, was the celebrated plot supposed to have been discovered on the part of the negroes, to murder the inhabitants of New York, and ravage and burn the city,—an affair which reflects little credit either upon the discernment, or the humanity, of that generation.

The burning of the public buildings, comprising the governor's residence, the secretary's office, the chapel and barracks, in March, 1741,— an occurrence which has already been anticipated in a note to a preceding page, was first announced to the general assembly by the lieutenant-governor as the result of an accident,— a plumber, who had been engaged upon some repairs, having left fire in a gutter between the house and chapel. But several other fires occurring shortly afterward, in different parts of the city,— some of them, perhaps, under circumstances that could not readily be explained, suspicions were awakened that the whole were acts of incendiaries. Not a chimney caught fire,—and they were not at that day very well swept,—but the incident was attributed to design. Such was the case in respect to the chimney of Captain Warren's house, situated near the ruins of the public buildings, by the taking fire of which the roof was partially destroyed, and other instances might be enumerated. Suspicion, to borrow the language of Shakespeare, "hath a ready tongue," and is "all stuck full of eyes," which are not easily put to sleep. Incidents and circumstances, ordinary and extraordinary, were seized upon and brought together by comparison, until it became obvious to all that there was actually a conspiracy for compassing such a stupendous act of arson as the burning of the entire town and murder of the people. Nor was it long before the plot was fastened upon the negro slaves — then forming no inconsiderable portion of the population. A negro, with violent gesticulation, had been heard to utter some terms of unintelligible jargon, in which the words "fire, fire, scorch, scorch," were heard articulated, or supposed to be heard. The crew of a Spanish ship, brought into the port as a prize, were sold into slavery. They were suspected of disaffection, as well they might be, and yet be innocent; seized, and thrown into prison. Coals were found disposed, as was supposed, for burning a haystack; a negro had been seen jumping over a fence, and flying from a house that had taken fire, in another place; and in a word a vast variety of incidents, trifling and unimportant, were collated, and talked over, until universal consternation seized upon the inhabitants, from the highest to the lowest. As Hume remarks of the Popish plot in the reign of Charles II, "each breath of rumor made the people start with anxiety; their enemies, they thought, were in their bosoms. They were awakened from their slumbers by the cry of *Plot*, and like men affrighted, and in the dark, took every figure for a spectre. The terror of each man became a source of terror to another. And, an universal panic being diffused, reason, and argument, and common sense, and common humanity, lost all influence over them."[1] A Titus Oates was found in the person of a poor weak servant-girl in a sailor's boarding-house, named Mary Burton, who, after much importunity

---

[1] Quoted by Dunlap, who has given a good collection of facts respecting this remarkable plot, though not rendered into a well-digested narrative. See chapt. xxi, of his *History*.

confessed that she had heard certain negroes, in the preceding February, conferring in private, for the purpose of setting the town on fire. She at first confined the conspirators to blacks; but afterward several white persons were included, among whom were her landlord, whose name was Hughson, his wife, another maid-servant, and a Roman Catholic named Ury. Some other information was obtained from other informers, and numerous arrests were made; and the several strong apartments in the City Hall, called "the jails," were crowded with prisoners, amounting in numbers to twenty-six whites and above one hundred and sixty slaves.[1] Numerous executions took place, upon the most frivolous and unsatisfactory testimony; but jurors and magistrates were alike panic-stricken and wild with terror. Among the sufferers were Hughson, his wife, and the maid-servant, as also the Romanist Ury, who was capitally accused, not only as a conspirator, but for officiating as a priest, upon an old law of the colony, heretofore mentioned as having been passed at the instance of Governor Bellamont, to drive the French missionaries from among the Indians. "The whole summer was spent in the prosecutions; every new trial led to further accusations: a coincidence of slight circumstances was magnified by the general terror into violent presumptions; tales collected without doors, mingling with the proofs given at the bar, poisoned the minds of the jurors; and this sanguinary spirit of the day suffered no check until Mary, the capital informer, bewildered by frequent examinations and suggestions, began to touch characters which malice itself dared not suspect." Then, as in the case of the Popish plot, and the prosecutions for witchcraft in Salem, the magistrates and jurors began to pause. But not until many had been sent to their final account by the spirit of fanaticism which had bereft men of their reason,

---

[1] Smith's *History of New York*, vol. ii, pp. 70, 75.

as innocent of the charges laid against them as the convicting courts and jurors themselves. Thirteen negroes were burnt at the stake, eighteen were hanged, and seventy transported.[1]

---

[1] Smith. Daniel Horsmanden, the third justice of the supreme court, published the history of this strange affair in a ponderous quarto. He was concerned in the administration of the judicial proceedings, however, and wrote his history before the delusion had passed away. Chief Justice De Lancey presided at least at some of the trials; and he, too, though an able and clear-minded man, was carried away by the delusion.

CHAPTER II.

1742—1744.

FEW names in the colonial history of the United States, have descended to the present day with greater renown, than that of SIR WILLIAM JOHNSON, BART. Yet, notwithstanding its frequent occurrence in the annals of his times, and its intimate association with the public affairs of the country during the period of nearly forty years immediately preceding the American revolution, it may well be questioned whether the life and character of any other public man, equally distinguished, have been so inadequately appreciated, or so imperfectly understood. Coming to America at the instance of a relative, when, if not a mere youth of fifteen, he was certainly a very young man, he threw himself boldly into the wilderness, and with but little assistance, became the architect of his own fortune and fame. From the subordinate station of an agent in charge of the landed property of his relative, he became successively a farmer, a dealer in peltries, a merchant, a government contractor, a general in the armies of his adopted country, and a baronet of the British realm,—possessed of an estate of great value, and transcending in extent the broadest domains of the nobles of his parent-land. The hero alike of veritable history and of romance, his actual career being withal more romantic by far than any of the tales which the writers of fiction have succeeded in inventing for him, his character,—from the wild border-life which he led, and from his associations, both in civilized life and as connected with the Indians, and the wonderful influence he acquired over the latter,— has been invested, both in books and by tradition, with qualities strange and undefinable,—such indeed as are believed to have appertained to no other man of his own, or of any other age.[1]

WILLIAM JOHNSON,—afterward SIR WILLIAM JOHNSON, BART., was the eldest son of Christopher Johnson, Esquire, of Warrentown, county of Down, Ireland,— of a family ancient in its descent, and honorable in its alliances. His mother was Anne Warren, sister of the brothers Oliver and Peter,— afterward Sir Peter Warren, K. B.— whose names are identified with the naval glory of England. The Warrens were of an old and honorable family, possessing an estate in the county of Down from the first arrival of the English in Ireland. Oliver Warren, the eldest son of his father, was a captain in the royal navy, and served with reputation during the reigns of Queen Anne and George the First.[2] Peter, the youngest son, having been trained to the nautical profession under the immediate eye of his brother, was appointed in the summer of 1727, to the command of the Grafton, one of the four ships of the line sent out under Sir George Walton, to join Sir Charles Wager, then in the Mediterranean command. Captain Warren did not long continue in the Grafton, having been soon after his arrival at Gibraltar, transferred to the Solebay frigate, for the purpose of carrying to the West Indies the orders of the king of Spain

---

[1] See the admirable satire by Charles Johnson, entitled *Chrysal, or the Adventures of a Guinea;* vol. iii, book ii, chapters 1, 2, and 3. *The Dutchman's Fireside*, by Paulding; and also *The Gipsey*, by G. P. R. James; to say nothing of minor tales and romances. Neither of the writers of the first mentioned three works appears to have understood the true character of Sir William Johnson. The satire in *Chrysal* is a gross exaggeration of the errors in the baronet's life. Paulding's exaggerations are equally great in another respect; while the delineation attempted by James is an utter failure.

[2] MSS. of Sir William Johnson.

for executing the preliminaries of peace agreed upon between that monarch and Great Britain. He sailed upon this service in May, 1728; and having executed the commission with which he was charged, in pursuance to his instructions, he sailed from the West Indies to South Carolina,— returning to England in the following year. Immediately on his arrival he was appointed to the Leopard, of fifty guns, one of the fleet which during the years 1729 and 1730, rendezvoused at Spithead, under the command of Sir Charles Wager. Captain Warren commanded the Leopard until after 1735, in which year he accompanied Sir J. Norris to Lisbon.

This account of the earlier service of Sir Peter Warren, after his promotion to the command of a ship, has been drawn from Charnock's *Biographia Navalis*, and is conceived to be at least not irrelevant, from the relations which subsisted between him and the immediate subject of these memoirs. During the period under consideration, and long afterward, the domicil of Captain Warren was in the city and colony of New York[1] He married the

---

[1] The dwelling-house No. 1, Broadway, formerly the residence of Nathaniel Prime, and now (1864), the Washington Hotel, was built by Captain Warren. Neither pains nor expense were spared to make it one of the finest mansions in this country. The plans were all sent out from Lisbon, the exterior and interior being similar in every respect to that of the British ambassador residing at the Portuguese capital. The house was fifty-six feet on Broadway, and when erected, the rear of the lot was bounded by the North river. Greenwich street was not then opened or built — the North river washed the shore. One room of this edifice deserves particular notice, being the banqueting room, twenty-six by forty, and was used on all great occasions. After the British forces captured New York, in the war of the American revolution, being the most prominent house, it was the head-quarters of the distinguished British commanders. Sir William Howe, Sir Henry Clinton, and Sir Guy Carlton, afterward Lord Dorchester, all in succession occupied this house, and it is a memorable fact that the celebrated Major Andre, then adjutant-general of the British forces, and aid to Sir Henry Clinton, resided in this house, being in the family of Sir Henry, and departed from its portals never to return,

sister of James De Lancey, long the chief justice of the colony, and for several years lieutenant-governor.[1] I have not been able to ascertain the time when Captain Warren came to America to reside. Equally difficult, among conflicting authorities, is the task of fixing upon the date of his nephew's arrival in this country. No farther mention is made of Captain Warren in the naval history of England from the time of his sailing to Lisbon, in 1735, until after the rupture with Spain, when, in the year 1741, he was in command of the Squirrel, a twenty-gun ship, on the American station.

It seems hardly probable, from the age of Warren, and from the active service in which he was engaged, that he could have settled in America at an earlier period than the year 1735. He was born in 1704, and was consequently but twenty-three years of age when appointed to the command of the Grafton.

William Johnson, his nephew, was born in the year 1715. According to Doctor Dwight, as written in his travels, and according to the biographical dictionaries also, Mr. Johnson was called to America by his uncle, Sir Peter Warren, in the year 1735, to superintend a large estate which the latter, shortly after his marriage, had purchased in the Mohawk valley. I have besides an old manuscript, furnished by the Sammons family of

---

when he went up the North river, and arranged his treasonable project with the traitor Arnold at West Point.

[1] The name of James De Lancey will be of frequent recurrence in the progress of this work. He was the son of Stephen De Lancey, a French Huguenot gentleman from Caen, in Normandy, who fled from persecution in France. Settling in New York in 1686, he married a daughter of Mr. Van Courtlandt, and was thus connected with one of the most opulent families in the province. He was also an active member of the house of assembly during the administration of Governor Hunter. His son James was sent to Cambridge University (England), for his education; and bred to the profession of the law. On being elevated to the bench, such was his talents and application, he became a very profound lawyer.

Johnstown, which states that the young adventurer came to America *with* Captain Warren at the age of fifteen. Neither of these dates, however, is correct, as Johnson himself distinctly states in a letter written to the lords of trade under date of October thirteenth, 1764, that he came to America in the year 1738. Johnson was then twenty-three years of age; and his arrival must have been shortly after the weak and turbulent administration of Governor Cosby. Although in the letter to the lords of trade just cited, the writer does not state the season of the year in which he came to America, yet it was probably in the spring, since in the fall of 1738, he was already settled in the Mohawk country and had begun the cultivation of his land. The document of the earliest date which I have found among the Johnson manuscripts, is a letter from Captain Warren to his nephew, whom he familiarly addresses as "*Dear Billy.*" It was dated at Boston, November twentieth, 1738, at which place the captain probably passed several months, since he suggested a shipment of wheat, corn, and other farming produce, to be made by his nephew from Albany to his order in Boston, early in the following spring.

The estate purchased by Captain Warren in the Mohawk country, heretofore alluded to, consisted of a tract of land lying on the south side of the river, near the junction of the Mohawk and Schoharie kill, called Warrensbush. From the letter just cited, it appears that young Johnson was engaged in the double capacity of forming a settlement upon the lands of his uncle, and bringing lands into cultivation for himself — keeping, also, though upon a small scale, a country store, in which his uncle was a partner. But the means of neither of the parties could have been great at that time; such at least is the inference from the letter, which is long, and abounds in many details and directions, in what was evidently at that time a comparatively limited business. The captain writes: "I have received yours of the twenty-sixth and thirtieth of October, and am glad to hear that you are in health, and go on briskly with your settlements." Respecting the means for prosecuting the enterprise, the letter says: "I am sorry you have been obliged to draw for more on New York than I directed; but as it is, I presume, for goods that will bring part of the amount in again, I am not displeased with it; yet I will not go beyond two hundred pounds per annum in making the settlement, and that to be complete in three years from your first beginning, which will make the whole six hundred pounds. I desire in your next you will let me know how much you have had from New York in money and goods." Sailor that he was, the captain understood the policy of cutting his patent into small farms. "The smaller the farms," he remarks, "the more the land that will be sold, and the better the improvements will be." The captain had also some taste for horticulture: "I hope you will plant a large orchard in the spring. It won't hinder your Indian corn, nor grass, as you will plant your trees at a great distance." He had likewise taste and forecast on the subject of clearing lands: "As you have great help now, you will girdle many acres;[1] in doing which I would be regular, and do it in square fields, leaving hedge-rows at each side, which will keep the land warm, be very beautiful, and subject you to no more expense than doing it in a slovenly, irregular manner." This prudential suggestion

---

[1] "Girdling trees," is a preliminary process often adopted in the clearing of wild land, which facilitates the labor by relieving the ax-man of a part of his labor. The operation consists in making a deep circular cut around the trunks of the trees of any magnitude, which draws off the sap, and causes the tree to die in the course of a couple of years. The trunks and limbs of the trees, becoming dry, are then readily subject to the action of fire, and the foresters are thereby often relieved of much heavy labor; while by the absence of the foliage, the earth has already been partially warmed by the sun, and is in respect of decaying roots rendered much easier of cultivation.

in favor of leaving hedge-rows of trees and shrubs for ornament, proves that Captain Warren had not yet imbibed that vandal taste so characteristic of the early Anglo-American proprietors, inducing them to think that the finest country, and most beautiful, from which the timber and every verdant object has been most carefully removed. The following passage from the letter, shows that the patron and his nephew were in a kind of partnership, in the mercantile line. After enumerating various articles of goods, of small amounts, which the captain had ordered from England and Ireland, the letter proceeds: "You see you will have a pretty good cargo. The whole proceeds of it must be remitted as soon as possible, to be laid out again, till you with your increase will have a very large store of goods of all kinds proper for the country. Pray let me know what rum, and all things sell for there, such as axes, and other wrought iron. These I would send from hence; if I found the profit great, I would soon have a thousand pounds worth of goods there." The following sentence indicates that the nephew had already commenced the fur-trade, which he afterward prosecuted to a great extent, and doubtless to great profit: "As for what skins you can procure, I will send them to London, and the produce of them shall be sent you in proper goods." Captain Warren, as already stated, was brother-in-law to James De Lancey, afterward chief justice of the province and subsequently lieutenant-governor. But the date of his marriage I have not been able to ascertain. It must, however, have been some years before that of the letter under consideration; for in this the captain remarks: "My wife and two daughters are very well." The letter concludes thus, "I will send for books for you to keep your accounts, which you must do very regularly. I have no more to add at this time but my service to all friends and to wish you well. Captain Nelson, who, I hear, is going to Fort Hunter,[1] has been so kind as to promise to spare you some muskets for your house. If he be there, my service to him. Keep well with all mankind. Act with honor and honesty. Don't be notional, as some of our countrymen are often foolishly; and don't say anything of the badness of the patroon's horses, for it may be taken amiss. He is a near relation of my wife, and may have it in his power very much to serve you.[2] Get the best kind of fruit-trees for the orchard, if they cost something more, and a good nursery would not be amiss. My love to Mick. Live like brothers, and I will be an affectionate uncle to you both.

P. WARREN."

Who was "Mick," I do not know, but his name occurs twice. The letter itself forms a singular medley, in which matters of every description are set down without arrangement, just as they came into the mind of the writer. I have made the greater use of it not only because it is the only manuscript I have been able to obtain from a man who afterward became illustrious in the service of his country, but also because that while it sheds a few glimpses of light upon a portion of his own private life, it affords authentic information as to the comparatively humble beginnings of one, whose career in after-life filled so wide a space in the public eye, and whose name is of such frequent and honorable record in the history of his adopted country.

Other testimony to the same point might be adduced, were it necessary. I have a manuscript, giving some ac-

---

[1] Fort Hunter was at the mouth of the Schoharie kill,— the site of the lower castle of the Mohawks. The Indian name of the place was Dyiondarogon.

[2] Mr. De Lancey through the Van Courtlandt family was connected with that of the patroon of Albany. Hence the relationship referred to in the text.

count of Sir William's life, furnished by the late Thomas Sammons, who in his boyhood knew the baronet. It speaks of his humble beginning at Warrensbush, but dates his settlement there in 1734, at the age of nineteen; which, for reasons already stated, must have been at least four years too early. According to this authority, young Johnson was wont to ride to mill, on horse-back, with very indifferent equipments, to Caughnawaga, on the opposite or north side of the river, distant from Warrensbush fifteen miles. He showed himself a man of enterprise from the first, clearing a large farm for himself, erecting a storehouse, and immediately opening a trade with the white inhabitants and also with the Indians. His style of living was plain, and his industry great. His figure was robust, and his deportment manly and commanding. Yet he made himself very friendly and familiar among the people, with whom he mingled in their rustic sports, and speedily became popular. Of this fact he was not unconscious himself. In a letter to his uncle, dated May tenth, 1739, he says: "As to my keeping in with all people, you may assure yourself of it, dear uncle, for I dare say I have the good will of all people whatsoever, and am much respected,— very much on your account,— and on account of my own behaviour, which I trust in God shall always continue."

Young Johnson likewise succeeded, beyond all other men, in winning the confidence and affection of the Mohawk Indians, whose most considerable town, Dyiondarogon, was but a few miles distant. His trade with them had already become considerable, and the spirit of enterprise which was rapidly to raise him to fortune, was manifested in the letter to his uncle just cited, wherein he thus early spoke of opening a trading-house at Oghkwaga,[1]— a

---

[1] It is a perplexing matter to fix the orthography of Indian names, either of men, or places, or things. For example, this place is now usually

settlement of the Six Nations on the Susquehanna river, some two hundred miles south of the Mohawk. The advantages of a trading expedition to Oghkwaga he thought better than were offered at Oswego, where there were already a parcel of mere sharpers in the trade. It appears farther by this letter, that Mr. Johnson had given offence to his uncle by the purchase of a lot of land, on the opposite side of the river, to which his patron was apprehensive he might remove. From the description, or rather the tenor of the nephew's letter in reply, the purchase was of the lot upon which he subsequently settled, known to this day as Mount Johnson, and where the old massive stone mansion erected by him yet stands. But Mr. Johnson protested to his uncle that he had no design of removing to his new purchase, having made it, he said, for the purpose of securing a valuable water-power, on which he proposed to erect a saw-mill, that would be certain to yield a profit of full forty pounds per annum.

In regard to the early education of Mr. Johnson, I have succeeded in obtaining no satisfactory information. It is presumed that he did not receive the advantages of a university course of instruction; while the presumption is equally strong that he had enjoyed the benefit of some classical school where other languages than the English were taught. I have found among his private correspondence, letters addressed to him both in French and Latin, which were filed away with endorsements in his own hand-

---

written Oquago. The Rev. Mr. Hawley, however, a missionary to the Indians, and a cotemporary of Sir William Johnson, in his journal to this place, spells it Onohoghgwáge. I have adopted, in the *Life of Brant*, from his own manuscript, the orthography given above in the text. The place and river now known as Unadilla, are spelt by Mr Hawley, Teyondélhough. By Brant it was contracted to Tunadilla. The large creek flowing into the Susquehanna some ten or fifteen miles south of Cooperstown, called Otego, was written by Mr. Hawley, Wautĕghe; which is the better Indian.

writing, always in the language in which the letters themselves were respectively written. And it will subsequently appear from the invoices of books ordered for his private library from his correspondents in London, in the days of his prosperity, that his selections indicated not only a mind of considerable cultivation, but also of a scientific turn. There is yet greater difficulty in fixing the date of his marriage, or giving any satisfactory account of the family with which he became thus connected. It is believed that he married young, probably about 1740,— certainly in the earlier years of his residence in the Mohawk country,— and the object of his choice is supposed to have been a young German woman by the name of Catherine Wisenberg, a plain country girl of no social position, but gifted with good sound sense, and a mild and gentle disposition.

Having thus introduced to the reader the principal biographical subject of these memoirs, with some of his family connections, it is necessary for the preservation, as far as may be, of chronological order, to resume again the thread of Indian history, at the point of its termination in the preceding chapter.

In the summer of 1742, the Six Nations, by a large delegation of counselors, chiefs, and warriors, numbering in all upward of seventy persons, visited Philadelphia to hold a treaty with their brother ONAS, governor of Pennsylvania.[1] It appears that by an antecedent treaty, the Six Nations, claiming the country of the Delawares by right of conquest, had released to ONAS their claim to all the lands on both sides of the Susquehanna, from the Endless mountains, or Kittochtinny hills, to the southern boundary of Pennsylvania. At the time of making that relinquish

---

[1] ONAS, in the Iroquois language, signifies a PEN, and was the title by which William Penn was addressed by the Indians, and the governors who succeeded him.

ment, they had received payment in goods, for the territory ceded on the east side of the river; but preferred waiting for the balance due for the lands on the other side until a more convenient season. It was for the purpose of closing that negotiation, therefore, that the council of 1742 was convened. The deputation was headed by the celebrated Onondaga counselor, Canassateego,— one of the ablest orators and wisest sachems of his race,— and by the Cayuga chief Shicolamy, or Shikellimus, father of the famous Logan, who was afterward immortalized by Mr. Jefferson, in his *Notes on Virginia*. Shicolamy was at that period residing with a clan of his people at Shamokin. It was the policy of the Iroquois Confederacy, in accidental conformity with that of the Romans, to plant military colonies in the countries they conquered, and that at Shamokin was one of them. Deputations were also present from the Shawanese, then residing at Wajomick, or Wyoming; from the Nantikokes, who had removed from the eastern shore of Maryland to the southern extremity of the Wyoming valley; from the Delawares; and from the Canestogoes,— a clan of the Oneidas, planted in Central Pennsylvania. The interpreter was Conrad Weiser, a faithful man, enjoying the fullest confidence of the Indians, and long in the service of Pennsylvania in her intercourse with the Six Nations.[1]

The governor, or rather the lieutenant-governor of Pennsylvania, under the proprietaries at that time, was Mr. George Thomas, a man of talent and resolution, who managed the Indian affairs of the colony for several years with excellent tact and address. The Indians were received by Mr. Thomas and his council at the house of the then venerable James Logan, the learned and philosophic friend and cotemporary of William Penn. Mr. Logan had

---

[1] Weiser was of German blood, a native of Schoharie, in the colony of New York.

preceded Mr. Thomas in the colonial administration, as president of the council. He had long been a man of distinction in the colony, and enjoyed the unbounded respect and confidence of the Indians. This reception took place on the second of July, and the council was continued from day to day until the twelfth.

The proceedings of the first day were rather informal,—being confined to an exchange of salutations, and to certain explanations which the sachems desired to make. In the first place, they disclaimed a certain sale of land which some of their "foolish young men," when out upon a hunting expedition, had made, or pretended to make, to a few individuals, for a very small number of strouds,—the sale conflicting with a previous contract of the Confederacy with their brother Onas. The sachems had wrested the strouds from the young men, and now produced them that they might be returned to those who had made the invalid purchase. Another explanation which they desired to make, or rather which had been required of them by Mr. Thomas, related to the murder of two or three white people some time before, by a returning war-party of Twightwees, or Miamies, which murders had been accidentally detected by the Shawanese, through whose town they were passing, when scrutinizing the scalps they had taken. The Twightwees, said Mr. Thomas, had sent a message that "their hearts were full of grief" when they heard that "the road had been made bloody" by some of their young men, "with the blood of white people;" and the Shawanese had sent a message "that they would sweep the road clean and wipe all the blood away;" desiring that their white brethren "would be satisfied with this, and not weep too much for a misfortune that might not happen again as long as the sun and moon shone." The governor expressed a wish that the Six Nations might take up the matter, ascertain the facts of the case, and obtain satisfaction for the outrage. The chiefs promised to consider the subject on their return home, and send an answer.

The times being critical, and another French war supposed to be unavoidable, it was deemed advisable by Governor Thomas and his counselors, to endeavor to sound the Indians, and ascertain if possible what would be their probable temper and disposition in such an event. A grand entertainment was therefore provided for them, with the design of extracting their sentiments in the flow of the wine-cup,— upon the well known principle, "*in vino veritas.*" It happened that although the deputation was numerous, there were no representatives from the Mohawks, and but three from the Senecas,— the most powerful nation by far, of the Confederates. Mr. Thomas approached the object at which he was aiming warily, by inquiring why so few Senecas were present, since they were equally interested with the others in the business that had called them together. The answer of Canassateego was prompt and painfully satisfactory. "The Senecas," he said, "were in great distress on account of a famine that had raged in their country, which had reduced them to such want that a father had been obliged to kill two of his children to preserve his own and the rest of his family's lives." Their situation, therefore, was such that they could not attend the council, but the necessary instructions had been given in regard to their share of the goods. The lieutenant-governor next, with seeming carelessness, inquired whether any of the Seneca chiefs were in Canada, and whether the governor of Canada was making any warlike preparations. Both questions were answered in the affirmative; whereupon Mr. Thomas playfully remarked: "Well, if the French should go to war with us, I suppose you would join them?" Canassateego was evidently not put off his guard by the apparent indifference of the querist, and therefore did not reply until after a brief consultation with his people. He then said, frankly, that the French governor was paying great court to the Indians, and had informed them that he was uncovering the hatchet and sharpening it; but at the same time he had told them that if he was obliged to lift it up against the English, he hoped they would not espouse the cause of either side, but remain neutral. The orator, however, assured his brother Onas, that in the event of a war, they should be faithful and true to their old allies, and lift the hatchet in their cause, adding: "The governor of Canada talks a great deal, but ten of his words do not go so far as one of yours; we do not look toward them; we look toward you, and you may depend on our assistance." Yet it will be seen hereafter that when the crisis came, great reluctance was manifested by the Confederates to engage in the contest.

At the next subsequent meeting in council, after having delivered the goods which the Indians had come to receive, Mr. Thomas opened the subject of the probable rupture with France, with more directness. It was his desire, he said, in the event of a war, that the road between the English and the Indians, should be kept clear and open. More fuel should then be added to the fire between them, that it might burn brighter and clearer, and give a stronger light, and more lasting warmth. "We must hear with our ears for you, and you must hear with your ears for us,"—terms all significant, and well understood by these metaphor-loving sons of the forest. Nor were they employed without effect. Having taken a day for consideration, Canassateego replied to the speech of the lieutenant-governor at length, and in regard to the threatening storm, to the entire satisfaction of the English, and with the seemingly cordial assent of his dusky associates.

In discussing the business matters which they had assembled specially to consider, the Onondaga orator, though prepared fully to confirm the prior contract for the sale of the lands on the western side of the Susquehanna,—but how far west does not appear, the terms in the records of the council being quite indefinite,— had nevertheless complaints to make, as has ever been the case on such occasions, of the encroachments of the white people upon their lands. "The pale-faces think we do not know the value of our lands," said the veteran counselor; but we are sensible that the land is everlasting, and the few goods that we receive for it are soon worn out and gone. The specific complaint adduced by Canassateego, was, that the white people were settling all along the banks of the Juniata river,— one of the large western tributaries to the Susquehanna,— "to the great damage of our cousins, the Delawares." This encroachment had been the ground of a complaint before; and Mr. Thomas now replied that magistrates were then sent expressly to remove the trespassers. "Those persons who were sent did not do their duty," interposed Canassateego. "So far from removing the people, they made surveys for themselves, and they are in league with the trespassers!" A common occurrence, I believe, in the great catalogue of Indian wrongs.

But the most interesting historical incident during the sittings of this council, affording proof at once of a disputed fact, and an illustration of Indian character, occurred toward its close. Mr. Thomas had complained at one of their meetings that a clan of the Delawares, residing at the forks of the Delaware river, had not only refused to yield the occupancy of a tract of land which had been sold to William Penn fifty-five years before, but had presumed to make sales of some portions of the same lands,— notwithstanding that their fathers had made the treaty with Penn, and received the value of the sale; and notwithstanding also that they themselves had subsequently ratified the treaty anew. It was in reply to this statement of Mr. Thomas, that Canassateego uttered a speech of bitter and biting reproof of the Delawares, in which he reminded them in terms of severity of their subjugated condition.

"You," said he, "you take it upon yourselves to sell land!" "You don't know what ground you stand upon!" "You ought to be taken by the hair of your head and shaken till you recover your senses, and become sober!" "We conquered you. We made women of you. You know you are women, and can no more sell land than women!" This speech, which was full of indignant irony and invective, was closed by a peremptory order for the Delawares to remove forthwith from the disputed territory, either to Shamokin, or Wyoming, as they might prefer. The following was the closing injunction of the mandate: "After our just reproof and absolute order to depart from the land, you are now to take notice of what we have further to say to you. This string of wampum serves to forbid you, your children and grand-children, to the latest posterity forever, from meddling with land affairs; neither you, nor any who shall descend from you, are ever hereafter to presume to sell any land. For which purpose you are to preserve this string, in memory of what your uncles have this day given you in charge. We have some other business to transact with our brethren, and therefore depart the council, and consider what has been said to you."

The obedience of the Delawares to the order was as prompt as the mandate itself was summary,— some of them going to Shamokin, but the greater number settling at Wyoming, on the eastern side of the Susquehanna,— a large clan of the Shawanese residing at that time on the western side opposite. This transaction sufficiently proves the state of abject subjection to which the Delawares had been reduced, and in which at that time they were held by the Iroquois, notwithstanding the efforts of the benevolent Heckewelder to sustain a loftier position for his favorites among the aborigines.

In the course of the proceedings at this treaty, while complaining of the trespasses of the white men upon the lands along the Juniata, Canassateego uttered a further complaint "that some parts of their country had been taken up by persons whose place of residence is south of this province (Pennsylvania), and from whom we have never received any consideration." It was their desire that Mr. Thomas should "inform 'the person' whose people were thus seated on those lands, that that country belongs to us, in right of conquest, we having bought it with our blood, and taken it from our enemies in fair war;" and, in their behalf, require compensation for it. It was understood by Mr. Thomas and his board of counselors, that this complaint was directed against the governor and people of Maryland; and a letter was addressed to the former upon the subject. But from the vague and indefinite terms in which the Indian counselor had spoken,— referring to the aggressors only as "persons living south of Pennsylvania,"— the government and people of Virginia by some means became impressed with the idea that the illusion was pointed at them.

An unlucky occurrence in December following strengthened this impression. It appeared from a communication addressed to Lieutenant-Governor Clarke, by Mr. Gooch, lieutenant-governor of Virginia, that in the month of December, a body of Indians had made an incursion into the frontier county of Augusta in that colony, and committed some very serious outrages,— killing several people, and carrying away numbers of cattle and horses. The invaders were pursued by a small body of Virginia militia, commanded by Captains M'Dowell and Buchanan, and overtaken on the eighteenth of December, when a smart engagement ensued,— the Indians having commenced the fight by shooting down a messenger of peace who was approaching them with a flag. The action lasted about forty-five minutes, during which eleven of the Virginians were killed, among whom was Captain M'Dowell. The Indians fled, leaving eight or ten of their warriors dead upon the field. Such was the magnitude of the affair, and such its result, as stated to Lieutenant-Governor Clarke by Mr. Gooch. The Virginians alleged that there were several white men with the Indians, believed to be French. Mr. Gooch stated that the affair had occurred at an unfortunate moment, since at that very time he was preparing to send a friendly deputation to meet the Six Nations; and being uncertain whether these hostile Indians might not belong to that Confederacy, he was in doubt what course to pursue. Under these circumstances he requested the assistance of the authorities of New York, in enabling him to ascertain whether the aggressors belonged to the Six Nations. He also desired Mr. Clarke to ask the chiefs of the Six Nations where the land in Virginia was, to which they had referred in the Philadelphia council as belonging to them.

1743. The communication from Mr. Gooch was forwarded to the Indian commissioners at Albany, on the fifth of April, with instructions to adopt the necessary measures for ascertaining the facts.[1] Should it prove true that the outrages had really been committed by the Six Nations, in consequence of any dispute with Virginia about their lands, the Indians were to be rebuked for the adoption of such a barbarous course. They ought rather to have sought an adjustment by treaty, as they had done with Pennsylvania and Maryland. Had they adopted such a course, the governor of New York would cheerfully have aided them in the negotiation. The commissioners had previously heard of the Virginia affair, from the Mohawks, who stated that the Indians were feeling very uneasy upon the subject. On the receipt of the dispatches, therefore, Mr. Jacobus

---

[1] The board of Indian commissioners at that time consisted of the following persons, viz: Captain Rutherford, Cornelius Cuyler, Myndert Schuyler, Hendrick Ten Eyck, Peter Winne, Rutger Bleecker, Nicholas Bleecker, John De Peyster, Ryer Garretson, Dirck Ten Broeck and John Lansingh.

Bleecker, a competent interpreter, was sent to Onondaga, where a council had already been convened to receive a deputation from Philadelphia. The errand of these messengers, however, was merely to invite the chiefs to make another visit to Pennsylvania. But the invitation was declined by the chiefs expressly upon the ground of what had happened at the south. They sent word that "they could not come this year, but would do so the next."

The contents of Mr. Gooch's letter having been communicated to the chiefs and sachems, they gave quite a different version to the story. They denied that they were preferring any claims against Virginia for lands. Their warriors, they said, had been first fired upon by the Virginians, and four of their number killed. In return for which they had killed eight of the Virginians, and severely wounded two more. There were no white men in the party, which consisted of thirty warriors, twenty-six of whom had returned. They thanked the commissioners for the efforts they were making to have the difficulty adjusted, as they hoped it would be. Still, apprehending the possibility of a war as the consequence of the affray, they had sent messages to the Ottawas, and their friends at the west, to remain at home, and be prepared to aid them in the event of hostilities.

Mr. Clarke's council, to whom the papers connected with these transactions were communicated, on the seventeenth of April, were by no means satisfied with the explanations of the Indians, nor with the proceedings of the commissioners, against whom they more than insinuated a lack of energy. They wrote back that the interpreter should have been instructed to demand why the war party went to Virginia? Why they had killed some of the people, and carried away horses and cattle before the battle? Why they had killed the man who was approaching them with a signal of friendship? The council thought the Indians were dealing with subtilty in this matter, and insisted that they ought to be told explicitly that they were breaking the covenant chain whenever they killed any of his majesty's subjects, no matter in which of the colonies. Yet if the Indians disclaimed all knowledge of the murders, and their abhorrence of the act, and would restrain their young men from such unwarrantable expeditions hereafter, the council hoped that the governor of Virginia would come to such a temper as would enable them to heal the breach. In regard to the land-claim to which Mr. Gooch had referred, the council thought the inference was warranted from the undeterminate phraseology of Canassateego's speech at Philadelphia, although some had supposed that Maryland, not Virginia, was intended. However, it was necessary that the commissioners should inform the Six Nations that such outrageous acts against any of his majesty's colonial settlements, must be put an end to. The Indians themselves had complained to Mr. Bleecker, the interpreter, of the intrigues of the French; and it was evident to the mind of the council, that in order to put a termination to those outrages, the emissaries of the French must be prevented from coming among them.

The consequence of this letter to the commissioners, was another embassy in May to the Six Nations, in council at Onondaga, with a more peremptory message. In reply to which the Indians again explicitly disclaimed any claim to land in Virginia. In regard to the unhappy occurrence in Virginia, they denied with solemnity that any people had been killed before their braves were fired upon thrice by the soldiers of M'Dowell and Buchanan. Their young men were going on a fighting expedition to the south when the affair happened,— but not to fight against the Virginians. They had only taken a few cattle on their way, and they thought the Virginians had treated them too severely by following and firing upon them for so small an offence. They regretted the occurrence; but it was out of the power of the chiefs to prevent their young warriors from occasionally going off upon such expeditions. In transmitting this reply, the commissioners wrote to the council that the Indians were really anxious for a reconciliation. They thought great good would ensue, were Mr. Gooch to come and meet them himself; and it would be yet better if some of the chiefs of those remote southern Indians, against whom the Six Nations had been so long at war, could be persuaded to come also and meet them in council. A general peace might then be effected, whereas it was now almost impossible for the chiefs to restrain the formation of war parties among the scattered Indians residing at a distance from their castles, notwithstanding the stipulations of peace negotiated by Mr. Clarke at the council of 1740.

A pacific letter, giving the results of these conferences with the Indians was written to Mr. Gooch by Mr. Clarke; and at the earnest solicitation of the latter, the matter seems to have been pressed no farther.

The administration of Lieutenant-Governor Clarke was ended in the autumn of 1743, by the arrival of Admiral George Clinton, uncle of the earl of Lincoln, and a younger son of the late earl, who had been appointed to the government of New York through the interest of his friends, to afford him an opportunity of mending his fortunes. Mr. Clarke, who in the commencement of his administration had succeeded in conciliating the leaders of both political parties, had contrived before the close of his career to lose the confidence of both,— so that his retirement from the government was regarded with universal satisfaction.[1] Especially had he incurred the resent-

---

[1] George Clarke, Esq., who, in various official stations was for almost half a century connected with the colonial government f New York, was an Englishman by birth. "His uncle, Mr. Blaithwait, procured the secretaryship of the colony for him early in the reign of Queen Anne. He had

ment of the chief justice, De Lancey; who, strangely enough, though usually a staunch supporter of the prerogatives of the crown, had now become to some extent a favorite of the general assembly. The new governor had spent the most of his life in the navy; and, according to the earliest English historian of New York, "preferring ease and good cheer to the restless activity of ambition, there wanted nothing to engage the interest of his powerful patrons in his favor, more than to humor a simple-hearted man, who had no ill nature, nor sought anything more than a genteel frugality and common civility, while he was mending those fortunes, until his friends at court

---

genius, but no other than a common writing-school education; nor did he add to his stock by reading, for he was more intent upon improving his fortune than his mind. He was sensible, artful, active, cautious; had a perfect command of his temper, and was in his address specious and civil. Nor was any man better acquainted with the colony and its affairs." He successively held the offices of secretary, clerk of the council, counselor, and lieutenant-governor; and from his official position he had every opportunity of enriching himself by obtaining grants and patents of land — which, from his knowledge of the colony he was enabled to choose in the most advantageous locations. He was a courtier, and was careful never to differ with the governors of the colony; although during Cosby's stormy career, he usually kept himself quiet at his country villa upon the edge of Hempstead plains. "His lady was a Hyde, a woman of fine accomplishments, and a distant relation of that branch of the Clarendon family. She died in New York. Mr. Clarke returned to England in 1745, with acquisitions estimated at one hundred thousand pounds. He purchased an estate in Cheshire, where he died about the year 1761. George Clarke, his grandson, and the heir to his estates, after a residence in America of about thirty-five years, died at Otsego, about the year 1835. His eldest son, George Hyde Clarke, with his young wife, was lost in the ship Albion, wrecked on the coast of Ireland, in the summer of 1820, on his passage from New York to England. His second son then returned to England, and entered into possession of the fortune of his father's estates situated in that country. By the vast increase in price of his American lands, Mr. Clarke's estates in this country became of princely value before his death. They are inherited by his youngest son, George Clarke, Esq., who now (1843), resides in the noble mansion erected by his father a few years before his decease, upon the margin of Otsego lake.

could recall him to some indolent and more lucrative station."[1]

Mr. Clinton arrived in New York on the twenty-second of September, and was received with demonstrations of universal satisfaction by the people. Finding that the general assembly stood adjourned to meet in a few days, and ascertaining that the people would be pleased with an opportunity of holding a new election, the assembly was dissolved on the twenty-seventh and writs for the return of another assembly issued the same day.[2] The elections were conducted without political acrimony, and all the old members, with but seven exceptions, were returned. The session opened on the eighth of November. Meantime the governor had fallen into the hands of De Lancey, who doubtless had the moulding of his excellency's speech. Its tone was conciliatory, although the sore subject of a permanent revenue was opened afresh. But this was done in gentle terms, the governor asking for a grant " in as ample a manner, and for a time as long, as had been given under any of his predecessors." The assembly was informed that owing to the critical state of affairs in Europe, and the doubtful attitude in which Great Britain and France stood toward each other, a large supply of military stores for the defence of the colony had been received from the parent government; and the governor hoped the assembly would show their thankfulness by making an adequate provision for the purchase of others. The usual recommendations in regard to the Indian intercourse of the colony were renewed, and an appropriation was asked for rebuilding the barracks, and public offices, together with the house of the governor, which had been destroyed by fire. The latter recommendation was insisted on

---

[1] Smith's *History of New York*, vol. ii, page 85.

[2] Idem.

as being necessary for the comfort of the governor's family.

"An humble address" was voted by the council in reply, drawn up by De Lancey. The appointment of the new governor was received "as an additional evidence of his majesty's affection for his people, and his zeal for the liberty of mankind, lately most evidently demonstrated in his exposing his sacred person to the greatest dangers in defence of the liberty of Europe."[1] In all other respects the answer was an echo of the speech. The address of the house was more than an echo,— it was couched in language of excessive flattery to the new governor, and of fawning adulation toward the sovereign, who was designated "the darling of his own people, and the glorious preserver of the liberties of Europe." There was, however, a disposition on all sides to be pleased. The assembly responded to the demanded appropriations,— voting the governor fifteen hundred pounds for his salary, one hundred pounds for house rent, four hundred pounds for fuel and candles, one hundred and fifty pounds to enable him to visit the Indians, and eight hundred pounds for the purchase of presents to be distributed amongst them. Other appropriations were made upon a scale of corres-

---

[1] The battle of Dettingen, in Germany, in which the British troops and their allies obtained a brilliant victory over a powerful division of the army of the Mareschal de Noailles, commanded by the Duke de Grammont. The English troops, commanded by the Earl of Stair, were joined by the Duke of Cumberland, to make his first campaign, and by his majesty (George II), on the ninth of June. The English with their allies, were moving, on the twenty-sixth of June, toward Hanau, to obtain supplies, and to join the Hanovarians and Hessians, when they were met in a difficult position by the French, thirty thousand strong. The king behaved very gallantly in the engagement, exposing his person to a severe fire of cannon as well as musketry. He rode between the first and second lines with his sword drawn, and encouraged the troops to fight for the honor of England. The French were defeated with the loss of five thousand men. They might have **been destroyed had the advantage been promptly followed up.**

ponding liberality; and the governor was so well pleased with the good temper of the assembly, that he signed every bill presented for his approbation, without a murmur of disapprobation, not even excepting the supply-bill, which, notwithstanding his demand to the contrary, in the opening speech, was limited to the year.

But notwithstanding these reciprocal manifestations of good feeling; and notwithstanding also the amiable traits of the governor's natural disposition, it will be seen in the progress of events that the bluff characteristics of the sailor were not always to be concealed; and his administration, in process of time, became as tempestuous as the element upon which he was certainly more at home than upon the land.

Until after the arrival of Governor Clinton Mr. Johnson seems to have taken no part in the public affairs of the colony. His name appears in none of the public records of that day; and such of his private papers as have escaped the ravages of time and revolution, exhibit him only in the character of a country merchant, enlarging his business from year to year, increasing rapidly in wealth, and assiduously cultivating the friendship and language of the Indians. Before the year 1743, he had removed from the south to the north side of the river, and settled at the place heretofore described as Mount Johnson. He had also in the last mentioned year become connected with the fur-trade at the important trading post of Oswego. Nor was it long before he opened a correspondence on his own account with the opulent house of Sir William Baker & Co., in London. As his fortunes improved rapidly, he grew with equal pace in the public estimation, not only among the people of his own region, but likewise in Albany and New York. His correspondence during this period was considerable, indicating an extensive business in all the multifarious departments of a country trading establishment, independently of the fur-trade, in which he

CHAP. II.
1743.

was now engaged, and his commerce with the Indians. In his business transactions "he by no means lost sight of his own interests, but on the contrary raised himself to wealth in an open and active manner, not disdaining any honorable means of benefiting himself; but at the same time the bad policy, as well as meanness of sacrificing respectability to snatching present advantages, were so obvious to him, that he laid the foundation of his future prosperity on the broad and deep basis of honorable dealing, accompanied by the most vigilant attention to the objects he had in view; acting so as without the least departure from integrity on the one hand, or inattention to his affairs on the other, to conduct himself in such a manner as gave an air of magnanimity to his character, that made him the object of universal confidence."[1]

Meantime the relations between Great Britain and Spain had undergone a change demanding the services of Mr. Johnson's uncle and patron, Captain Warren, upon his own element. After a long series of aggressions upon the commerce of England in the West India seas, committed by the Spaniards, attended often by the utmost insolence, cruelty, and rapine,[2] the former power, appealing in vain to the court of Madrid for indemnification, granted letters of marque and reprisal against the Spaniards in the year 1739. It was on the seventeenth of August of that year, that Mr. Clarke, the lieutenant-governor, laid before his council his majesty's warrant, authorizing the government of New York to issue letters of marque and reprisal against the commerce of Spain. Measures to

---

[1] *Memoirs of an American Lady*, by Mrs. Grant.

[2] Smollett's continuation of Hume. Bancroft, I am aware, gives another aspect to the case, vide *History of the United States*, vol. iii, pp. 435 and onward. He contends that England was the aggressor, and the cause of war was with Spain. So seems to have thought Walpole, but so thought not Pulteney, Pitt, afterward Earl of Chatham, and their followers in and out of parliament. Nor has the brilliancy of Bancroft's style and argument won me to his side of the question.

that end were immediately adopted by the council, including the specification of the bonds to be taken, and the forms of commissions to be granted.[1]

This measure was soon followed by an open rupture. The British squadron in the Mediterranean having taken two richly laden Spanish merchantmen from Caraccas, his Catholic majesty ordered all the English ships in his harbors to be seized and detained. A declaration of war could no longer be avoided by Sir Robert Walpole, although that able and crafty minister had labored long and earnestly to avoid such an issue.[2] The declaration by the king of England, was proclaimed in October, 1739, and Admiral Vernon was forthwith dispatched in the command of a fleet against the Spanish West India possessions; but it was not until the thirtieth of June in the following year that the fact that such a declaration had been issued, was officially communicated to the general assembly by Lieutenant-Governor Clarke. He then called upon the assembly to encourage, by bounty, enlistments of volunteers to join his majesty's troops engaged in the West India expedition; and a bill was shortly afterward passed making provision for the victualing and transportation of five hundred volunteers in that service.[3] From

---

[1] MS. records of the executive council of New York. It appears by these records, however, that the privateering business had been carried on briskly from the port of New York for the two or three preceding years.

[2] Smollett. It was upon this subject of their Spanish relations, that Sir Robert Walpole was compelled to encounter the fierce opposition which marked and embittered his closing career. Before the issuing of the letters of marque, a convention had been concluded between England and Spain (though never regarded by the latter), which was the subject of the severest condemnation by the opposition, and was denounced with the strongest invective by Sir William Wyndham and Mr. Pulteney, in the commons; to whom Walpole, losing his temper, replied in a manner that induced the famous secession of the minority from the house, in 1738. Those debates have been greatly extolled for their eloquence and power. In the following year, however, the seceding members resumed their seats, with Mr. Pulteney at their head.

[3] *Journals of the Provincial Assembly.*

the West Indies, Vernon directed his course to Porto Bello, which became an easy conquest. The fortress of Chagre was also taken and demolished by Vernon, and Europe was made to resound with his praises for these exploits. Lord Cathcart, to whom the command of the land forces of the expedition was entrusted, having died at Dominica, a victim to the climate, the command devolved upon "the inexperienced and irresolute Wentworth."[1] Expectation was high in regard to anticipated triumphs; and in May, 1741, more levies were required from the northern colonies, and the assembly of New York was required by Mr. Clarke to make farther appropriations for this service. It was hoped, said the speech, that "the glorious beginning would excite the assembly to speedy and generous resolutions." But this "glorious beginning" was shortly followed by the miserable ending of the expedition against Carthagena, where, weakened by sickness in its most frightful forms, and discouraged by the ill-judged movements of their commanders, the British troops were repulsed in an attempt to storm the citadel, or castle commanding the town. In escaping thence, Vernon and Wentworth attempted to retrieve their sad reverses at Carthagena by a descent upon Cuba. A landing was effected in a bay, on the south-eastern part of that island, in July, 1741, and the troops ascending a river, encamped about twenty miles from the bay. This event was announced by Mr. Clarke, in a speech to the assembly, in September. General Wentworth, it was said, had obtained a secure footing on the island, and recruits and supplies were called for to secure the conquest.[2] But they were not needed. After remaining inactive in their position till the month of November, enfeebled by the cli-

---

[1] Bancroft.

[2] See *Journals of the Provincial Assembly*. In this speech the lieutenant-governor recommended the enactment of laws regulating the manufacture and sale of flour and bread — denouncing the bolters and bakers for their frauds, &c.

mate, and their numbers wasted by sickness, the troops were re-embarked, and sailed to Jamaica.[1] The whole expedition was a deplorable failure. The levies, from the colonies nearly all perished from the pestilence, and the entire loss of lives was estimated at twenty thousand. England had made no acquisitions, and had inflicted on the Spanish West Indies far less evil than she herself had suffered."[2]

Simultaneously with these operations in the West Indies, the invasion of Florida from the colonies, had been determined on, the command being entrusted to General Oglethorpe,— the benevolent founder of Georgia,— who was ordered to raise levies of provincials for that purpose from South Carolina and his own infant plantations. This expedition, though successfully commenced by the capture of Fort Diego, distant twenty-five miles from St. Augustine, owing to a combination of untoward circumstances, ended in disaster — the general having been compelled to raise the siege of the last mentioned fortress, under circumstances that caused great and mutual dissatisfaction between the troops and their commander.[3]

These hostilities, as I have already remarked, required the services of Captain Warren at sea, to which he seems to have been ordered very soon after writing the letter to his nephew cited in the early part of the present chapter; inasmuch as he was engaged in the squadron of Commodore Price, co-operating with General Oglethorpe against St. Augustine. The vessel commanded by Captain Warren at this time is not mentioned; but he was certainly there at the time in question, for when it was found that the town could not be effectively cannonaded from the batteries erected by Oglethorpe on an island in the river opposite, because of the distance, a plan was proposed for a night attack upon the Spanish galleys which prevented the

---

[1] Smollett.

[2] Bancroft.

[3] Marshall's *Colonial History*.

CHAP. II.
1743.

passage of the river for a direct assault, and Captain Warren volunteered to conduct the enterprise. "But, on sounding the bar, the water was found too shallow to admit the passage of one of the large ships to the attack, and the project was necessarily abandoned."[1] Probably, however, Captain Warren was then in command of the Squirrel, a twenty-gun ship, in which he was certainly cruising upon the American station eighteen months afterward. In 1742 he commanded the Launceton, of forty guns, in which he captured the Peregrina privateer, mounting fourteen carriage, and four swivel guns, in company with Captain Edward Aylmer, of the Port Mahon. Warren was subsequently promoted to the Superbe, of sixty guns, in which he was ordered to the West Indies, where he was left by Admiral Sir Chaloner Ogle in command as commodore of a small squadron on the Antigua station.[2] The activity of his after-life probably left him but little time to reside on shore in New York, before his return to and settlement in England. But of this hereafter.

France was at that time an ally of Spain, in the wars of the continent; and had well nigh been drawn into the contest with England in 1741. The queen of Spain having formed a plan for erecting a kingdom for her second son, Don Philip, from some of the Italian dominions, an army of fifteen thousand men was embarked for that object at Barcelona, for Orbitello, which was convoyed thither by the united squadrons of France and Spain — passing the straits of Gibraltar in the night, while Admiral Haddock, with a fleet of twelve sail of the line was lying in the bay. The British admiral sailing from Gibraltar, fell in with them in a few days, and discovered both squadrons drawn up in order of battle, having been joined by the French squadron from Toulon. When bearing down to

---

[1] Marshall's *Colonial History*.

[2] Charnock.

give the Spaniards battle, the French admiral sent a flag to the English, informing him that inasmuch as the French and Spanish fleets were engaged in a joint expedition, he should be obliged to act in concert with his master's allies. The combined fleets amounted to double the number of the English ships; and the interposition of the French admiral prevented an engagement.[1] Still the time was not far distant when France became involved in the contest with England, by reason of espousing the cause of the Chevalier de St. George, usually called "the pretender." And an expedition in behalf of this prince, with a view of placing him upon the throne of his ancestors, the Stuarts, under a belief that he would be received in Scotland with acclamation, was set on foot by France during the present year.

Advices of the intended invasion of his majesty's dominions, in behalf of "a Popish pretender," were communicated to the general assembly of New York by Governor Clinton, in April, 1744. In connection with this anticipated act of hostility, which would of course extend to the contiguous colonies of the two countries, efficient measures were urged for placing the country in a posture of defence. The temper of the colony, in regard to this movement of France, may be inferred from the immediate action of the assembly. In the council, Chief Justice De Lancey, in moving an address of thanks for the speech, offered also a resolution expressive of the abhorrence of that body of the designs of France in favor of the pretender, and declaring that the civil and religious rights of his majesty's subjects depended on the Protestant succession. The house was invited to join in the address, which request, though a very unusual procedure, was readily acquiesced in, and the address was prepared by a joint committee of the two houses.[1] From all this it was evi-

[1] Smollett.

[2] *Journals of the Colonial Assembly.*

88   LIFE OF SIR WILLIAM JOHNSON, BART.

CHAP. II.
1744.

dent that a war was very near at hand, and that the frontiers of the colony might again, very soon, be subjected to the ravages of a foe than whose tender mercies nothing could be more cruel.

An appropriation had been made in the preceding December, to enable Governor Clinton to meet the Six Nations in general council. But no such conference had yet taken place. Happening to be in Albany, however, in June of the present year, and a considerable party of the chiefs and sachems happening to be there also at the same time, an interview took place at which the formalities almost of a general council were interchanged. The governor commenced his speech by informing them that he had it in command from the great king their father, to tell them of his desire that the covenant chain between them should be kept bright and strong. He then informed them how his majesty had sent an army into Germany the preceding year, which had been treacherously attacked by the French, contrary to the faith of treaties. But by the courage of the English they were beaten, and obliged to fly across the Rhine.[1] Not only so, but the governor told them that at a subsequent day, the French fleet had joined itself to the fleet of his majesty's enemies, the Spaniards, and having attacked the British fleet, the French had again been beaten.[2] After this, the French king had de-

---

[1] Referring to the battle of Dettingen, of which a brief account has been given in a preceding note.

[2] Referring to the irregular and unfortunate engagement between the English and the combined French and Spanish fleets, off Toulon, on the eleventh and twelfth of February, 1744. The English commander was Admiral Matthews, under whom was Vice Admiral Lestock. The French commander was M. de Court; the Spanish Don Navarro. The combined fleets had been blockaded in Toulon. But on attempting to get to sea, they were attacked by Matthews, who himself, behaved with great intrepidity; but failed in his tactics. Between Matthews and Lestock, a bitter antagonistical feeling existed; and perceiving the erroneous manœuvers of his commander, Lestock furnished a precedent for Captain Elliott, in the American service, on Lake Erie, seventy years afterward, by manœuvering on both days, so as to keep entirely out of the action. For this con-

clared war against their great father, who in turn had declared war against him.[1] For the present, the governor would not urge them upon the war-path. He wished them to remain at home,— to be on their guard against the arts of the French,— and to communicate whatever information they could obtain to the Indian commissioners at Albany. In recompense for their fidelity, they were promised protection by the English; but they were also told by the governor that he should expect them to assist in the prosecution of the war whenever called upon for that purpose. The governor farther spoke of the importance, to them, of maintaining the post of Oswego, where they could always purchase goods cheaper than they could of the French. The French had their eye upon this post, to defend which six pieces of ordnance had recently been forwarded thither; and should it be attacked, the governor expected the Six Nations to assist in its defence. In conclusion, the governor reminded them of the promise formerly made by the Cayugas and Senecas, that they would concentrate their people and unite their castles. If this measure had not been executed, he hoped they would attend to it as soon as possible; since, in this time of war, a union of their nations would greatly add to their strength and reputation. They had likewise promised that no Frenchmen should be suffered to live among them; which promise the governor hoped they had kept.

This speech was delivered on the eighteenth of June. Two days afterward the chiefs replied; but not in a manner altogether satisfactory to the governor upon the main subject of his speech — the war with France. True, they reciprocated his excellency's professions of friendship with

---

duct, Lestock was brought to a court marshal, but instead of being punished, as he deserved, Matthews, who had really fought with gallant daring, was dismissed the service for allowing the fleets to escape him! Such is the caprice of fortune.

[1] The French declaration of the war of 1744, was dated on the twentieth day of March. On the thirty-first day of March, the English declaration published amidst the acclamations of the people.

as much apparent cordiality as ever. It was their determination to strengthen the covenant chain, and keep it strong and bright as long as the sun endures. Indeed, "we will preserve it so strong and keep it so bright, that it shall not be in the power of the devil himself, with any of his wiles and arts, to break or rust it." Yet they were not remarkably anxious to prove their friendship by going upon the war-path. They said they understood all that had been said in regard to the conduct of the French and the war. But, as to engaging in it, that seemed to be another affair. They were indeed a warlike people, and they had never yet been engaged in a war in which they had not sooner or later prevailed. But they did not now like to begin the war with Canada. It would be time enough when the enemy himself had taken up the hatchet. When the enemy should have attacked any of the subjects of the great king, their father, they would be ready to join in defending themselves against them. In reference to the post of Oswego, they were glad it was to be preserved; but, as to its immediate advantages to them, in their trade, these were not so great as when first established; they sold goods cheaper to the Indians then, than they do now. They liked the officer in command there, and wished goods might become as cheap as before. Yet, should it be attacked, they would aid in its defence. In regard to the proposed concentration of their two western nations, the Cayugas and Senecas, they were too busy to do it now. Nor would they send from among them any of the French that might be residing with their people. "We have just told you we are for peace, and must await the attacks of the enemy. Should we take hold of any French that came among us, we should be the first aggressors."[1]

The apprehensions expressed by the governor, respecting Oswego, were by no means groundless. On the twenty-fourth of June he laid before the council letters

---

[1] The proceedings of this incidental council may be found at large in the *Council Minutes*.

from the commandant of Oswego, advising that Monsieur Micol Hayden had ascended Lake Ontario past that post, with a small force (probably of observation); and some Indian scouts had returned from Cadaracqui, with intelligence that the French were collecting a force of eight hundred men for the purpose of attacking Oswego, and were only waiting for the arrival of their fleet in the St. Lawrence to complete their arrangements and make the descent.[1]

But the largest and most important Indian council of the year 1744, and upon which the principal sachems and chiefs of the Six Nations were in attendance nearly at the same time that Mr. Clinton was holding his conference with others of their chiefs at Albany, took place at Lancaster, in the colony of Pennsylvania, commencing on the twenty-second day of June, and ending on the fourth of July. This council was convened at the solicitation of Lieutenant-Governor Thomas, of that colony, who had assumed the office of mediator between the Six Nations and the colonies of Maryland and Virginia, in regard to the ownerships of certain districts of country within the extending borders of those colonies, claimed by the Six Nations. It will be remembered that complaints of trespasses upon those lands, especially by the people of Maryland, were uttered by the Six Nations in Philadelphia two years before, and also that the governor of Maryland was written to upon the subject by the council of Pennsylvania at that time,— the Indians having intimated a threat that, if their complaints were not attended to, they were able to do justice to themselves. Mr. Thomas had also acted as a mediator between the Virginians and the Six Nations, touching the skirmish between a party of Iroquois warriors and a small body of Virginia militia-men, under Captains M'Dowell and Buchanan, which occurred in the back part of the colony, in December, 1742, the particulars of which have already been related. By means of this interposi-

---

[1] *Council Minutes.*

tion, the difficulty had been adjusted;—both parties agreeing to lay down their arms and bury the transaction in oblivion; Virginia cementing the reconciliation by a present of goods to the amount of one hundred pounds. Yet the land-controversy remained for adjustment; although it was not apparent at the council of 1742, that the claim of the Indians extended to any lands upon which the pale faces had trespassed in Virginia. They were indeed reported by the Indian commissioners at Albany, in their dispatches to Lieutenant-Governor Clarke, to have disavowed making any such claim. But that was a wide misunderstanding between the parties, since the claim was advanced upon Virginia as well as Maryland; and this council was invited by Mr. Thomas, for the purpose, if possible, of effecting such an adjustment of the controversy between the parties respectively, as should be satisfactory to them all.

No doubt the anxiety of Mr. Thomas to bring about a reconciliation, was quickened by the impending conflict with France. He saw the importance of the Six Nations as a barrier between the English and French colonies. If friends, to quote nearly his own language, they were capable of defending the English settlements; if enemies, of making cruel ravages upon them; if neutral, they could deny the French a passage through their country to strike the English settlements, and moreover give timely information of their designs. The advantages of cultivating a good understanding with them were therefore obvious, while equally evident were the disadvantages of a rupture. Hence the exertions of Mr. Thomas to gather the present council, to which Virginia had commissioned as delegates the Honorable Thomas Lee, and Colonel William Beverley, and Maryland the Honorable Edmund Jennings, Philip Thomas, Esquire, and Colonels Robert King and Thomas Calvil. Mr. Witham Marshe was appointed secretary to the commission, and the Rev. Mr. Craddock chaplain.[1]

---

[1] Witham Marshe — afterward Sir William Johnson's secretary — has left a very particular and edifying journal of his journey to and from this

The number of Indian deputies present — chiefs and sachems, — is not stated; but they came like a caravan, accompanied by warriors who were not chiefs, and by women and children and old men, to the number of more than two hundred and fifty persons. Several of their women and children were mounted on horseback, "a thing very unusual with them;" and their warriors were armed with muskets, bows and arrows, and tomahawks.[1] On entering the village of Lancaster, "a great multitude of people followed them. They marched in very good order, with Canassateego, one of the Onondaga chiefs at their head; who, when he came near to the quarters of the commissioners, sung, in the Indian language, a song, inviting to a renewal of all treaties heretofore made, and to the negotiation of a new one."[2]

The Oneidas, Onondagas, Cayugas, Senecas and Tuscaroras were each represented. The Mohawks were not. Canassateego and Tachanoontia, Onondagas, and Gachradodow, a Cayuga, were the speakers, and Conrad Weiser, whose Indian name was Tarachawagon, as usual, the interpreter.

The chiefs with their retinue, formed an encampment in the precincts of the town, which, from the descriptions of honest Witham Marshe, must have presented a rare example of the picturesque in human life. While the sages were in council, the women occupied themselves with their usual domestic concerns, and the children frolicked about at their option — the boys making strong their arms by stringing the bow, and improving their skill by speeding the arrow, or hurling their little hatchets — acquiring the art, in anticipation of going upon the war-path, of planting the hatchet in the trunk of a tree within the

---

council, and of its proceedings from day to day, to which I shall have occasion more than once to refer. This curious itinerary may be found in vol. vii, *Mass. His. Coll*.

[1] Marshe's Journal.
[2] Idem.

diameter of a hair of the mark. In the evenings, when the graver affairs of the day were ended, and the fires were lighted, the young men indulged in their favorite sports and games, wild and grotesque, before the groups of pale faces that gathered around their encampment; now illustrating the pow-wow dance, and now seizing a spear in one hand and a hatchet in the other, making the woods ring with the shrill war whoop, as around the blazing fire they performed the threatening war-dance. Among the friends to the mission was the celebrated Catherine Montour,— a princess of the Senecas residing at the head of Seneca lake in the midst of a clan whom she ruled. Mrs. Montour was a half-breed, her father according to tradition and her own story, having been governor of Canada, and her mother a Huron. Until about ten years of age, she had been carefully reared and educated, and her manners, even then, in her old age, were affable, and comparatively polite. During the war between the Six Nations and the French and Hurons, she was captured and carried into the country of the Senecas, by whom she was adopted. On arriving at years of maturity she was married to a famous war-captain, who was in great esteem for the glory he achieved for his people in their wars against the Catawbas, by whom she had several children. About fifteen years before the date of this council, her chief was slain by the Catawbas. She had two daughters, both married to war-captains, who were then upon the war-path at the south. She had also a son, John, a man of great prowess, then absent against the Catawbas. He was a brave partisan warrior at a later period, and a great favorite of Sir William Johnson — being often in his service. Although so young when made a prisoner, she had nevertheless preserved her language; and being in youth and middle age very handsome, and of good address, she had been greatly caressed by the gentlewomen of Philadelphia during her occasional visits to that city with her people on business. Indeed she was always held in great esteem by the white people, invited to their houses, and entertained with marked civility.[1]

The business of the council was opened by Mr. Thomas, in a speech addressed chiefly to the commissioners of Maryland and Virginia, who at its close were formally introduced to the dusky ambassadors "as brethren who had come to enlarge the fire which had almost gone out, and to brighten the chain which had contracted some rust." To the chiefs he said: "receive these your brethren with open arms, and unite yourselves to them in the covenant chain as one body and one soul." The speech was closed with exhortations to the Indians of fidelity toward the English, and by the oft-repeated cautions against the arts and designs of the French. Canassateego replied that the Indians had always considered Assaragoa,[2] and the governor of Maryland as their friends; but inasmuch as they had met to adjust disputes about land, he preferred having that business settled first, after which they could proceed "to confirm the friendship subsisting between them."

The Maryland commissioners opened their case first. They were surprised when they heard of the claim of the Six Nations two years ago, to any of their lands, and were displeased at the threat with which they had accompanied their complaint,—as though they had designed to terrify the people of Maryland into a compliance with their demands. The people of Maryland had been in possession of the lands in question more than a hundred years, without having heard of this claim. Ninety years ago the Susquehanna Indians had by treaty relinquished those lands. Sixty years ago the Six Nations had acknowledged, at Albany, that they had given up their lands and submitted themselves to the king of England. In a word, they believed the Six Nations had no rightful claim whatever to the territory in dispute. "They had now laid

---

[1] Witham Marshe's Journal.

[2] The name which the Indians had conferred upon the governor of Virginia, and by which they always addressed him or his representatives.

their bosoms bare;" and yet they were willing, in order to remove every cause of contention, to make the Six Nations a valuable present of goods, which they had brought along "in a chest, with the key in their pocket."

Canassateego replied.[1] It was true that the Indians, in making their complaint against the trespasses upon their lands by the people of Maryland, had used language "that looked like a design to terrify you." He admitted that they had done so. They had complained in regard to trespasses upon their lands about seven years ago. But no notice was taken of their complaint. "Two years ago, therefore, they resolved to use such language as would make the greatest impression on your minds, and we find it has had its effect. You will soon have understood our expressions in their true sense. We had no evil design,— no desire to terrify you, but to put you on doing the justice you have so long delayed." Having thus explained the intention of their menace, and added the strongest assurances of their good disposition toward the commissioners, the chief proceeded to discuss the nature of their claim, and its history,— commencing in true Indian style, with the first planting of the European colonies in America. "When you mentioned the affair of the land yesterday, you went back to old times. You told us you had been in possession of the province of Maryland above one hundred years; but what is one hundred years, in comparison of the length of time since our claim began? since we came out of this ground? Long before one hundred years our ancestors came out of this very ground, and their children have remained here ever since. You came out of the ground in a country that lies beyond the

---

[1] For some account of this Indian counselor, and an interesting anecdote concerning him, see Proud's Pennsylvania, and also the author's history of Wyoming. Witham Marshe says of him: "He was a tall, well made man; had a very full chest, and brawny limbs. He had a manly countenance, mixed with a good natured smile. He was about sixty years of age; very active, strong, and had a surprising liveliness in his speech, which I observed betwixt him, Mr. Weiser, and some of the sachems."

seas. There you may have a just claim, but here you must allow us to be your elder brethren. It is true that above one hundred years ago the Dutch came here in a ship, and brought us goods — such as awls, hatchets, knives, guns, and other things. And when they had taught us how to use them, and saw what sort of people they were, we liked them so well that we tied their ship to the bushes on the shore. Afterward, liking them still better the longer they staid with us, and thinking the bushes too slender, we removed the rope and tied it to the trees; and as the trees were likely to be blown down by the high winds, or to decay of themselves, we, from the affection we bore them, again removed the rope, and tied it to a strong and big rock.[1] Not content with this, for its further security, we removed the rope to the *Big Mountain*, and there we tied it very fast, and rolled wampum about it;[2] and, to make it still more secure, we stood upon the wampum and sat down upon it. To prevent any hurt coming to it, we did our best endeavors that it might remain uninjured forever." During all this time, he maintained, the Dutch never disputed their title to the land, but purchased by league and covenant, as they needed. Then came the English, who, the Indians were told, became one people with the Dutch. The English

---

[1] Here the interpreter said they meant the Oneida country. They were called the People of the Rock, from a large and peculiar stone in their country, which, according to their tradition was moving westward, and the nation moved with that stone, or rock. Indeed the name, Oneida, signifies an *upright stone*. By some of the Oneidas, this *Oneida stone* was regarded as a proper emblem, or representation of the divinity whom they worshiped. "This stone," says the late Rev. Jeddediah Morse, D. D., in one of his missionary tours, "we saw. It is of a rude, unwrought shape, rather inclined to cylindrical, and of more than a hundred pounds weight. It bears no resemblance to any of the stones found in that country. From whence it was brought, no one can tell. The tradition is that it follows the nation in their removals. When set up in the crotch of a tree, the people were supposed invincible."

[2] This was an allusion to the Onondaga country — the People of the Big Mountain.

governor came to Albany, and approving mightily of the friendship between the Dutch and Indians, wished likewise to form a league with the Six Nations. "Looking into what had passed between us, he found that the rope which tied the ship to the great mountain, was only fastened with wampum, which was liable to break and rot. He therefore told us he would give us a silver chain, which would be much stronger, and would last forever. This we accepted, and fastened the ship with it, and it has lasted ever since." Glancing rapidly over the history of their intercourse with the English, and arguing that on the whole that intercourse had been of no advantage to them, the arrival of William Penn was thus referred to: "Our brother Onas, a great while ago, came to Albany, to buy the Susquehanna lands of us; but our brother the governor of New York, who, as we supposed, had not a good understanding with our brother Onas, advised us not to sell him any land, for he would make an ill use of it; and, pretending to be our good friend, he advised us, in order to prevent Onas, or any other person's imposing upon us, and that we might always have our land when we should want it, to put it into his hands; and told us he would keep it for our use, and never open his hands, but keep them close shut, and not part with any of it, but at our own request. Accordingly we trusted him, and charged him to keep the land safe for our use. But some time after, he went to England, and carried our land with him, and there sold it to our brother Onas for a large sum of money; and when afterward, we were minded to sell our brother Onas some of our lands, he told us that we had sold them to the governor of New York, already, and that he had bought them of him in England! But when he came to understand how the governor of New York had deceived us, he very generously paid us for the Susquehanna lands over again."

Notwithstanding the dishonesty thus practiced upon them by New York, however, the orator admitted that in their wars with the French, they had received such assistance from New York as had enabled them "to keep up their heads against their attacks." In regard to the immediate question as to the lands now in controversy, the orator said they had examined the titles adduced by the commissioners, to the Susquehanna lands, and admitted their validity. The Conestoga or Susquehanna Indians had sold them to the governor of Maryland before their subjugation by the Six Nations, and therefore they had a right to sell them. But those were not the lands in dispute. The Six Nations demanded satisfaction for no part of those lands, but their claim was from the Cohongorontas lands.[1] Those, they were sure, had not been in the possession of the people of Maryland one hundred years, no, nor even ten years; and the Six Nations had demanded satisfaction so soon as they were apprised that the people of Maryland had settled down upon them. They had never been sold; but understanding that the commissioners were provided with goods to pay for them, they were willing to treat for their sale. Canassateego added, that inasmuch as the then governors of Virginia, Maryland and Pennsylvania had divided the lands among them, the Indians could not tell how much had been taken by each, nor were they concerned on that account, provided they were paid by the parties upon the principles of honor and justice.[2]

Next in order the discussion was resumed by Mr. Lee, of the Virginia commission, who acknowledged that seven years before, Onas had written to Assaragoa in behalf of the Six Nations, requesting compensation for certain lands claimed by them, upon which they alleged some of the Virginians had taken their seats; but as they had heard that the Six Nations had given up their lands to the great king long ago, and as Virginia had been in possession one hundred and sixty years, Assara-

---

[1] Cohongorontas, the name by which the Potomac was called by the Six Nations.

[2] Dr. Colden's account of the treaty.

goa thought there must be some mistake in the matter. He had therefore requested the governor of New York, nearly two years ago, to make some inquiry upon the subject. That governor sent a message to the great council-fire at Onondaga more than a year ago, to which the chiefs answered, "that if they had had any demands or pretensions upon the governor of Virginia, they would have made it known to the governor of New York." It was clear, therefore, that the Six Nations had no claim upon Virginia for the Cohongorontas lands, nor for any other. Yet, continued the commissioners, " tell us what nations of Indians you conquered lands from in Virginia, how many since, and what possessions you have had; and if it appears that there are any lands on the borders of Virginia to which you have a right, we are willing to make you satisfaction.

This speech was pronounced by Canassateego to be very good and agreeable; and after the usual time for consideration with the Indians had elapsed, Tachanoontia replied.[1] He said they claimed the lands on the Susquehanna and on the Cohongorontas, and back of the great mountains by the right of conquest — "a right too dearly purchased, and which cost too much blood, to be given up without any reason at all, as you say we did at Albany." He denied, explicitly, the answer said to have been returned to Governor Clarke's message from Albany the year before. No such answer had been given either by the chiefs, or by anybody else. If they held the fact to be otherwise, he demanded the letter. He next proceeded

---

[1] Tachanoontia was an Onondaga sachem and warrior. "He was a tall, thin man; old, and not so well featured as Canassateego, but about the same age. He is one of the greatest warriors that ever the Six Nations produced, and has been a great war-captain for many years past. This chief was also called The Black Prince, because, as I was informed, he was either the son of an Indian woman by a negro, or of an Indian chief by a negress; but by which of the two I could not be well assured. The governor of Canada will not treat with any of the Six Nation, unless Tachanoontia is personally present, he having a great sway in all the Indian councils."—*Witham Marshe.*

to enumerate five several nations of Indians in Virginia whom the Six Nations had conquered, " and who feel the effects of our conquests, being now a part of our nations and their lands at our disposal. However, the chief was not disposed to prolong the discussion concerning the lands, as, understanding that commissioners were provided with goods, he thought that question could be easily adjusted.

Before closing his speech, however, Tachanoontia referred, for the purpose apparently of making an explanation, to the skirmish that had taken place in the back part of Virginia, in December, 1742, between a party of the Six Nations' warriors and a detachment of Virginia militia, under Captains M'Dowell and Buchanan, the particulars of which have been already stated. This affair, he asserted, had been occasioned solely by the aggressions of Virginia. Twenty years ago, at the treaty held by Governor Spotteswood in Albany, the Six Nations had agreed to remove their road to the middle of the ridge of the great mountains. But the Virginians, contrary to the stipulations of that treaty, had settled on that road; and this was the cause of the affray. The Six Nations then removed their road again to the foot of the mountains; " but it was not long before your people came like a flock of birds, and sat down on both sides of it." They could not remove their road any farther back, and this matter, said the chief, must be settled before we can make any grant of land. " The Virginia people must be obliged to remove farther easterly, or, if they stay, our warriors must share what they plant."

The proceedings were interlocutory, the Maryland commissioners interposing at this stage of them, and after a speech denying, peremptorily, the claim of the Six Nations, yet, for the purpose of harmony,— that they might all be of one heart,— offering to pay for a title to the lands in dispute the sum of three hundred pounds in goods.

The Virginia commissioners thereupon renewed the

discussion,— insisting that "the king held the entire territory of Virginia by right of conquest, to the westward as far as the great sea." Even if the Six Nations had conquered any Indians beyond the great mountains, they yet had never possessed any lands there. When the English came those lands were deserted. But aside from this fact, the Indians were reminded once more of their relinquishment of their lands to the great king fifty-eight years before, in a treaty with the governor of New York, at Albany. Lord Howard, the governor of Virginia, being also there. They had then not only given up their lands to the king for his protection, but declared themselves his subjects.[1] In respect to the affair between Captain M'Dowell and a party of their warriors, the commissioners maintained that the Indians had not kept their agreement with Governor Spotteswood, not to pass or repass within certain boundaries without written passports, either from the governor of New York or of Virginia. "What right can you have to lands that you have no right to walk upon, but upon certain conditions? Nor would there have been any collision, had the Six Nations kept the peace with the southern Indians, which had been confirmed at Albany with Governor Clarke. It was owing to the war they were continuing against the Catawbas, that the skirmish had taken place. Yet, after all, they, the commissioners, were willing to adjust the difficulty upon the basis of Governor Spotteswood's treaty, and furthermore to pay any reasonable demand which the Six Nations sup-

---

[1] This was in the year 1687. The following passage from the speech of the Six Nations on that occasion, was cited by the Virginia commissioners: "Brethren, you tell us the king of England is a very great king, and why should you not join with us in any just cause, where the French join with our enemies in a very unjust cause? O brethren, we see the reason of this; for the French would fain kill us all, and when that is done, they would carry all the beaver trade to Canada, and the great king of England would lose the land likewise; and therefore, O great sachem, beyond the great lakes, awake, and suffer not those poor Indians, that have given themselves and their lands under your protection, to be destroyed by the French without a cause."

posed themselves to have for the territory they claimed, although, as they had been informed, the southern Indians were claiming the same lands.

It is quite probable that in all these discussions, there was duplicity on both sides. The Indians saw that their own importance was magnified by the condition of the country; while the commissioners, for the same cause, were prepared to accede, to a considerable extent, even to groundless claims, rather than give such umbrage to the Indians as might by any possibility drive them over to the French.

The Virginians were answered by a Cayuga chief named Gachradodow — a name which appears in this negotiation only, so far as I am acquainted with Indian history. Addressing "Brother Assaragoa"—"The world," said he, at the first, was made on the other side of the great water, very different from what it was on this side, as may be known from the different colors of our skin and our flesh; and that which you call justice, may not be so among us. The great king might send you over to conquer the Indians, but it looks to us that God did not approve of it. If He had, He would not have placed the great sea between us where it is. Though great things are remembered among us, yet we don't remember that we were ever conquered by the great king, or that we have been employed by that king to conquer others. If it was so, it is beyond our memories. We do remember we were employed by Maryland to conquer the Conestogas, and the second time we were at war with them, he carried them all off." Gachradodow next proceeded to explain their conduct respecting the Catawbas. They had, it was true, at Albany, when their brother Assaragoa sent them some belts of wampum from the Cherokees and Catawbas, agreed to a peace with those nations, on the condition that they should send some of their great men "to confirm it face to face." The Cherokees came, and after the peace was confirmed, the Six Nations escorted them back to their own country in safety. But the Catawbas refused to come, and sent a taunting message. "They sent word that we were but women; that they were men,— double men,— and that they would be always at war with us. They have been treacherous, and know it; so that the war must be continued till one of us is destroyed. Be not troubled at what we do to the Catawbas." The orator proceeded to touch upon other points in the speech of the Virginia commissioners,— but intimated that if the goods they had brought were sufficient in quantity and value, their difficulties might be adjusted. "You told us that you had a chest of goods, and the key in your pocket. But we have never seen the chest, or the goods. It may be small, and the goods few. We want to see them, and come to some conclusion. We have been sleeping here these ten days, and have done nothing to the purpose."

The public discussions of the land questions, of which I have barely attempted to sketch the leading features, ceased at this point. It had been all along evident that the Indians were willing to grant whatever Maryland and Virginia desired; while, as has been seen, both of those colonies, while in terms denying the Indians any rights in the premises, were from policy disposed to buy them off at reasonable sums. The commissioners having prepared maps of the districts, the Indian title to which they were now finally to extinguish, and the Indians having assented thereto, the goods to be given in consideration were brought for the examination of the purchasers. By a previous stipulation with Mr. Thomas, Virginia was to pay one hundred pounds value in goods, to heal the border skirmish in which Captain M'Dowell fell. To this amount was now added two hundred pounds in goods, and one hundred in gold. The commissioners of Maryland, also, as an equivalent for the disputed land already in their possession, proposed a payment of goods to the amount of two hundred pounds, and a like addition of one hundred pounds in gold. The negotiation was thus closed, and the deeds executed. The lands in Maryland were "confirmed to Lord Baltimore with definite limits. The deed to Virginia extended the claim of that colony indefinitely to the west and northwest." ¹ But in executing this last conveyance, the Indians stipulated that their case should be commended to the consideration of the great king, should their brother Assaragoa push his settlements yet farther back beyond the line of their "great road"— the right to which road was again confirmed. But vain were all these stipulations to save the red man from his doom!

These matters having thus been adjusted to the satisfaction of the parties, it was determined by the Maryland commissioners to give the chiefs by special invitation, a grand entertainment,— at which, of course all the distinguished gentlemen in attendance upon the council were guests. Twenty-four Indian dignitaries attended the feast, which was served with uncommon preparation and ceremony, in the court-house, Governor Thomas presiding. Five tables were spread, the sachems being seated by themselves, with Canassateego at their head. "The chiefs seemed prodigiously pleased with their feast, for they fed lustily and drank heartily," says honest Witham Marshe. After dinner, being warmed into a glow of good feeling, the Indians, through the interpreter, informed Governor Thomas, that as Lord Baltimore, the proprietary and governor of Maryland was not known to the Indians by any particular name, they had agreed in council to take the first convenient opportunity when a large company should be present, to confer one upon him. Such a transaction being with them a matter of great form and ceremony, the deputies of the several nations had drawn lots for the honor of performing it, and the lot had fallen upon the Cayugas, who had designated their chief Gachradodow for that purpose. The name with which the lord baron of Baltimore was then honored was TOCARRY-HOGON, "denoting precedency, excellency, or living in the middle, or honorable place between Assaragoa and our brother Onas, by whom our treaties may be the better carried on." The ceremony

---
¹ Bancroft's United States.

was performed "with all the dignity of a warrior, the gesture of an orator, and in a very graceful posture."[1]

All the differences between the Indians and their brothers Tocarry-hogon and Assaragoa having thus been adjusted, and some explanations having been interchanged between Onas and the chiefs, respecting the murder by a party of Delawares, of an Indian trader, named John Armstrong, and two of his men, and also in regard to the alleged murder of several Indians on the Ohio, by white men; and the lieutenant-governor having congratulated the council upon the happy issue of their deliberations, the next business in hand was to sound the chiefs on the yet more important subject of the French war. Rehearsing, as Governor Clinton had done at Albany, the story of the battle of Dettingen, for the purpose of magnifying the personal prowess of the king, and the sea-fight of Toulon, and announcing the declarations of war that had followed those transactions, Mr. Thomas reminded them of their obligations by treaty to assist their brethren of Pennsylvania against the French, and especially to prevent them from passing through their country to make war upon the English.

A conciliatory speech was then delivered by the Virginia commissioners, in which they were urged by all means to make peace with the Catawbas, in order that they might be the better prepared to meet their common enemies, the French and Spaniards. They closed by inviting them to send some of their promising youths to

---

[1] Witham Marshe,— who adds — "This Gachradodow is a very celebrated warrior, and one of the Cayuga chiefs, about forty years of age, tall, straight-limbed, and a graceful person, but not so fat as Canassatcego. His action, when he spoke, was certainly the most graceful, as well as bold, that any person ever saw; without the buffoonery of the French, or the over-solemn deportment of the haughty Spaniards. When he made the complimentary speech on the occasion of giving the new name to Lord Baltimore, he was complimented by the governor (Thomas), who said, 'that he would have made a good figure in the forum of old Rome.' And Mr. Commissioner Jennings declared, 'that he had never seen so just an action in any of the most celebrated orators he had heard speak.' "—*Witham Marshe*

Virginia, to be instructed in the religion, language and customs of the white people.

The chiefs required a day for special reflection, before replying to these addresses. Meantime, said Canassateego, archly, "You tell us you beat the French. If so, you must have taken a great deal of rum from them, and can the better spare us some of that liquor to make us rejoice with you in the victory!"

On the next day Canassateego delivered a formal reply to each of their addresses in order. He admitted that their people were bound by the faith of treaties to take part in the French war. "We have all the particulars of these treaties in our hearts. They are fresh in our memory. We shall never forget that we have but one heart, one head, one eye, one ear, and one hand. We shall have all your country under our eye, and take all the care we can to prevent any enemy coming into it." As an evidence at once of their fidelity and precaution, he said they had sent a message to Younondio, informing him that "there was room enough at sea to fight, where he might do what he pleased; but he should not come through our country to fight the English." The Six Nations, he added, had great authority over sundry tribes of Indians in alliance with the French, especially over "the praying Indians, formerly part with ourselves, who stand in the very gates of the French; and to show our care, we have engaged these very Indians for you. They will not join the French against you." [1]

In reply, specially, to his "Brother Assaragoa," Canassateego said, referring to their war against the Catawbas, "they are spiteful and offensive." Yet, although "they have treated us contemptuously," the Six Nations were willing to make peace with them, if they would come to

---

[1] These "praying Indians," were the Caughnawagas, residing near Montreal.

the north and treat for it. In reply to the invitation to send some of their children to Virginia to be educated, he replied: "Brother Assaragoa, we must let you know that we love our children too well to send them so great a way. The Indians are not inclined to give their children education. We allow it to be good. We thank you for the invitation; but our customs being different from yours, you must excuse us."[1] When acknowledging the gifts they had received from the proprietaries, the veteran orator was evidently affected in the contemplation of their own poverty, and the gloomy anticipations as to the fate of his race which he was too sagacious a man not to foresee: "We have provided a small present for you; but, alas! we are poor, and shall ever remain so, as long as there are so many Indian traders amongst us. Their's and the white people's cattle eat up all the grass, and make deer scarce. However, we have provided a small present for you." Saying which he presented three bundles of skins, one for each of the colonies represented in council.

Toward the conclusion of the council, while the several parties to it were engaged drinking healths, and exchang-

---

[1] Doctor Franklin, in his miscellaneous works, has given a more extended report of Canassateego's reply to the invitation. In addition to this remark which I have quoted from Colden's official account of the treaty, Franklin reports Canassateego to have continued his speech thus: "We have had some experience in this sending of our children to your schools. Several of our young people were formerly brought up at the colleges of the northern provinces; they were instructed in all your sciences; but when they came back to us, they were bad runners; ignorant of every means of living in the woods; unable to bear either cold or hunger; knew neither how to build a cabin, take a deer, or kill an enemy; spoke our language imperfectly; were therefore neither fit for hunters, warriors, or counselors; they were totally good for nothing. We are however, not the less obliged by your kind offer though we decline accepting it, and to show our grateful sense of it, if the gentlemen of Virginia will send us a dozen of their sons, we will take care of their education, instruct them in all we know and make *men* of them." This addition to the sachem's real speech, was doubtless one of Franklin's pleasantries.

ing parting compliments, Canassateego playfully remarked to Mr. Thomas, that they had given them *French* glasses to drink their liquor in. "We desire you to give us some in English glasses." The governor saw the point at which the shrewd savage was arriving,— the English glasses being the largest,— and improved the occasion by the ready reply: "Yes. We are glad to hear you have such a dislike to what is French. They cheat you in your glasses as well as in everything else."

CHAPTER III.

1744—1745.

CHAP. III.
1744.

THE repose which the colonies had so long enjoyed under the administration of Sir Robert Walpole,— owing, probably, not more to the policy of that minister than to the pacific temper of the duke of Orleans,— the regent of France during the minority of Louis XV,[1]— was of course ended by the receipt of the declaration of war against France, as stated in the preceding chapter. Indeed the news of this declaration had not reached New England, before Duquesnel, the French governor of Cape Breton, resolving upon the destruction of the English fishery on the north-eastern coast of Nova Scotia, or Acadia, as it was called by the French, invaded the island Canseau, burnt the houses, and made prisoners both of the garrison and the inhabitants.[2] Attempts were likewise made by the French upon Placentia, in Newfoundland, and upon Annapolis in Nova Scotia, in both of which enterprises they were unsuccessful,— owing to a miscarriage of the plan in one instance, and to the timely arrival of several companies of militia and rangers from Massachusetts, in the other.[3]

The flames of war having thus been lighted in the north, it required no special gift of prophecy to perceive that they would soon blaze along the whole lines of the English and French colonies, from Cape Breton to the

---

[1] Marshall's Introduction.

[2] Belknap.

[3] Idem. See also Marshall.

trading posts of Detroit and Michilimackinac, or Mackinaw, according to the orthography of later times. What rendered the pending war yet more frightful to the inhabitants of both of these extended chains of rival colonies, was the fact that a broad belt of territory between them, was peopled exclusively by the Indians,— ever ready to snuff blood in the breeze,— and generally disposed to rush forth upon the war-path at every opportunity. In fact the Micmacs, the Abenakies and Etchmims, or the canoe-men of St. John's river, with perhaps the remains of other and lesser tribes of the eastern Indians, whose partialities inclined ever toward the French, had already taken part with them in their expedition against Annapolis. These Indians, twenty years before, had been declared by resolution of the Massachusetts government, to be traitors and robbers;[1] and a formal declaration of war was now proclaimed against them, by that colony, with a bounty for scalps and prisoners.[2]

The declaration of hostilities was announced to the general assembly of New York, by Governor Clinton, at an adjourned session opening on the eighteenth of July, as a measure that had become indispensable to the honor and dignity of the crown, not only because of the attack upon the Mediterranean fleet, but above all because of the movements of France in behalf of the pretender. Immediate and strong measures were urged for the security of the city of New York, and for the general defence of the colony, especially of the frontiers. Measures, it was intimated, had already been taken for strengthening the posts of Oswego and Saratoga. In speaking of his interview with the Indians at Albany, it was stated that commissioners from Massachusetts and Connecticut were also present, the object of whose visit was to aid in cultivating a more firm

---

[1] Bancroft.
[2] Belknap.

and extensive alliance with that people. Their mission was a source of gratification to all parties. They were moreover clothed with full powers to enter into a strict union with New York and the other English colonies, for the purpose of devising and executing proper measures for the prosecution of the war offensively and defensively. Power was asked to enable the governor to appoint like commissioners to confer with them. The fitting out of privateers for the protection of the coast was also recommended,— not forgetting the supplies and the adoption of all such measures as would enable his excellency to support the power and dignity of the government, and pursue every method for its safety.

The speech was followed, on the twenty-fourth of July, with a special message setting forth the measures that had been taken by the executive for the security both of the city and the frontiers; and making requisitions for all such farther measures as were judged essential to the public defence. For the protection of Albany and the scattered settlements north of it, the governor strongly urged the erection of a strong fort in the neighborhood of Crown Point. As such a work would be calculated as well to guard the frontiers of the New England colonies as those of New York, it was suggested that it should be constructed at the joint expense of all. Some farther measures of defence had been adopted at Oswego; and it was recommended with great propriety that a strong fort should be built at Tierondequot, or at some other suitable point in the Seneca country,— as well for the defence of that country against invasion, as by means of a strong garrison, to check the wavering propensities of the Senecas,— the strongest of the Confederates, and the most easily tampered with by the French. Yet another message of a similar character, was sent down to the assembly on the thirty-first of July, recommending the erection of various works of defence for the harbor of New York; announcing the organization of a corps of rangers from the militia of Albany, to include a number of Indians, whose business it should be to traverse the country north to Canada, as perpetual scouts. The sending of troops to be stationed at Albany, was also recommended.

The precipitate and cowardly retreat of the English traders from Oswego, immediately on hearing of the declaration of war, elicited still another executive communication on the twentieth of August. This desertion of the trading houses had created a very unfavorable impression upon the minds of the Indians, particularly the remote nations, who, on coming thither to trade, had found the place really deserted, and the goods mostly brought away. The assembly were therefore earnestly urged to adopt the necessary measures for maintaining that important post, as a commanding mart for trade with the Indians, upon a more ample and efficient basis than had existed before. Disadvantages, other than such as might arise from a loss of trade, were apprehended by the governor. The Indians, inspired with contempt for the courage of men frightened, as it were, by a shadow, with the fall of Oswego, would be very likely to desert the English interests for the French.

The spirit of the general assembly was good. Resolutions were promptly passed by the house, *nemine contradicente*, pledging the ways and means for putting the colony in a suitable posture of defence by sea and land. In consequence of the demonstration made in Scotland "in favor of a Popish pretender," a resolution was adopted requiring all persons in the colony to take the oaths prescribed by act of parliament for the security of the government and the Protestant religion. Bills making liberal appropriations,— liberal considering the means of the colony,— for the public exigencies were initiated and in progress, when on the fourth of September, another message was received from the governor, calculated yet more rapidly to accelerate their action. It covered a communication from the commissioners of Indian affairs of an alarming character. Information had been received by a secret messenger from Canada, that, contrary to the declarations of Canassateego, at Lancaster, as to the temper and designs of the Caughnawagas, they, with the other Canadian Indians, had taken up the hatchet against the English, and the fall of Oswego was considered inevitable, unless its feeble garrison could be reinforced.[1] Information respecting the designs of the French upon that post, had also been received by the Six Nations.

This communication was considered so important that at the instance of Doctor Colden and Mr. Murray, of the council, a conference was held between the two houses in order to insure prompt and efficient action for the public welfare. Chief Justice De Lancey opened the deliberations of the conference, and after an interchange of opinions it was determined to apply to the governor for the addition of fifty men to the garrison of Oswego, and also for orders to the militia of Albany to hold themselves in instant readiness to march to the defence of that post in the event of an invasion. A joint address in accordance with these recommendations was made to the governor, in which the assembly pledged itself " cheerfully to contribute everything in its power for the defence and safety

---

[1] The commissioners at that time, signing this communication, were Messrs. Myndert Schuyler, Abraham Cuyler, Cornelius Cuyler, Dirck Ten Broeck, Nicholas Bleecker, Johannis Lansing, and John Depeyster. Among other matters detailed in the letter, was an account of their proceedings under an order from the governor to send Captain Walter Butler, with his son as an interpreter, upon a confidential errand to Oswego. The governor had enjoined perfect secrecy as to this mission; but the commissioners state that the fact was known in Albany before they had opened his excellency's dispatches. An admirable commentary this, upon the manner in which secrets are usually kept, in all times, in peace as in war.

of the colony, and for repelling any attempt of the enemy."

Difficulties were experienced in regard to the ways and means, arising chiefly from the reluctance of the popular branch, no uncommon thing in representative governments, to meet the question of direct taxation. Yet the liberality of their appropriations attested the general patriotism of the members. Special allowances were voted for the defences of Albany and Schenectady, and the round sum of three thousand two hundred pounds was granted in addition for the defence of the colony at large. Provision was likewise made for the support of the prisoners who had been brought into New York, pursuant to a suggestion of the governor,— who was commended in an address for his clemency, and requested to relieve the colony from the presence of those prisoners, and others that might be brought in, with all convenient dispatch.

Thus far in the session, no action had taken place in the house in regard to the propositions from the New England colonies for effecting a general alliance among the Indians friendly to the English, and also for a closer bond of union between the colonies, in order to the more efficient conduct of the war. Upon these points Governor Shirley was particularly anxious; and on the eighteenth of September Mr. Clinton sent a message to the assembly, covering an urgent letter from Shirley, and expressing surprise that the assembly had done nothing hitherto to enable him to appoint commissioners to meet those in attendance from Massachusetts and Connecticut, and confer together in a matter that must redound so much to the benefit of the colony. Instead, however, of complying with this request, the house sent up to the governor an address, reminding his excellency of the liberality of their appropriations,— ample, as they conceived, for the public exigencies,— but expressing a strong reluctance to any action upon the subject of the proposed plan of union.

They thought they ought not to enter upon any scheme the details of which had not been imparted to them that they might have an opportunity of exercising their own judgments upon it. This address was communicated by the governor to his council on the twenty-first of September, and a protracted conference between the two branches ensued; including also, another point of difference, viz: a refusal by the house, of an appropriation to erect a fort at the carrying-place between the Hudson river and Crown Point. The managers on the part of the council, De Lancey and Murray, presented urgent reasons in favor of appointing commissioners to meet those from the other colonies, for the organization of a league, or an alliance, against the French; as, for instance, the advantages of united action,— the increase of strength,— the confidence with which it would inspire the friendly Indians,— the discouragements which such a union would throw in the way of the French. The importance, likewise, of erecting the proposed military work at the carrying-place, was ably urged.[1] But without success. No appropriation was made either for the Indian alliance, or for the commissioners, or for the erection of the fortress; and the assembly adjourned, not meeting again until March, 1745.

The autumn and winter were passed with uncertainty as to the temper and intentions of the Six Nations, and with considerable anxiety. At the close of September, dispatches were received from the Indian commissioners, expressing lively anxiety for the fate of Oswego. The efforts of the commissioners to persuade the chiefs of the Six Nations to keep a number of their warriors from each of their tribes at Oswego for its defence, had been ineffectual. The French were active in their appliances to steal the hearts of that fickle people from the English, and had at that time no fewer than twelve emissaries among the

---

[1] *Journals of the Legislative Council.*

Senecas. Upon the receipt of these alarming reports, Mr. Bleecker, the interpreter, was dispatched into the Seneca country, with a message that to allow those emissaries to remain among them was breaking their covenant chain. The interpreter, however, returned in December with more favorable news. He had found but two Frenchmen, smiths, among the Senecas, and there were English smiths among them without molestation. It was not known to the Senecas that the French Indians had actually taken up the hatchet; yet they were told that the French had entertained them at a war-feast, and joined with them in their dances,— carrying aloft the heads of the beasts they had slain, and declaring that thus would they dance with the heads of the English.[1] Other reports, received by the governor and council from time to time during the winter, by correspondence and otherwise, tended to keep the eye of suspicion from slumber, and occasionally to quicken the public pulse. A deserter from the French post at Niagara, arrived in New York and was examined before the council on the twelfth of February, who gave a particular description of the strength and armament of that fortress. He had traversed Canada, from Quebec, stopping at Three Rivers, and Cadaracqui, before his desertion. There were one hundred men at Niagara, with four pieces of cannon. Cadaracqui was a stone fortress, the walls twelve feet high, with four bastions, and garrisoned by two hundred men. Lieutenant Butler, at Oswego, wrote that a scout returned from Canada, reported the organization of a force of fifteen hundred men, with a body of Indians, destined against that post in the spring. The French, moreover, were expecting large supplies from France.[2]

From the fickle disposition of the Indians, great caution

---

[1] Council Minutes.

[2] Idem.

was observed in regard to their intercourse with white people, whose nation, character, and designs, were known and understood. The laws of the colony forbade the residence of white men among the Indians, unless by express permission. Under these laws, and the watchful policy observed, two men, David Seisberger, and Christian Frederick Post, having been found residing at the Canajoharie castle,[1] without a license, were arrested in mid-winter and dragged to New York. On their examination before the council, however, they were found to be two worthy Germans, members of the Moravian congregation at the forks of the Delaware, who had been sent thither to learn the Mohawk language for missionary purposes. They were discharged as a matter of course.[2] Post had an Indian wife and family; and it will be seen farther on that he afterward performed valuable services among the Indians on the Ohio.

But, notwithstanding the alarms to which such a frontier as that of New York and New England, in such a contest, was liable, the winter passed away without active hostilities between the French and the English,— the pale faces, or the red. Yet this inactivity of matter did not extend to mind; and it was during this season of comparative repose, that William Shirley, governor of Massachusetts, suggested the plan for striking a blow at the power of France in America, which was as bold in its conception, as in its execution it was brilliant.

---

[1] Canajoharie, or, according to the orthography of the Rev. Samuel Kirkland, who passed his life as a missionary among the Six Nations, *Ca-na-jo-ha-roo*, the name of a small river flowing into the Mohawk, near the mouth of which stood one of the Mohawk castles. The meaning of the word, literally, is, "*The-pot-that-washes-itself*," applied to a large and beautiful basin, worn in the rock which forms the bed of the stream two miles back from the Mohawk, by the whirling action of the water falling from one of the cascades abounding upon this stream. This basin is perhaps twenty feet in diameter; but the water has been diverted to a mill-wheel.

[2] Council Minutes.

The harbor of Louisburg, on the south-eastern side of the island of Cape Breton, was considered the key to the American possessions of the French. By the treaty of Utrecht, Newfoundland and Novia Scotia, including the island of Canseau, had fallen to the crown of Great Britain, while by the same instrument Cape Breton, situated between them in the entrance to the Gulf of St. Lawrence, had been ceded to the French. Affording convenient harbors for the reception and security of ships of every burden — either for men of war, or ships engaged in commerce between the parent country and her Canadian possessions, or those of the West Indies, — this island had become of vast importance to France, as a security to her own navigation and fisheries, and also as affording in time of war, great facilities for interrupting the fisheries and navigation of England and her colonies.[1] It was therefore determined to build a fortified town upon this island, for the site of which the most commodious bay upon the south-eastern side was chosen. It had formerly been called "English harbor," but the name was changed to Louisburg. Twenty-five years of labor, and thirty millions of livres, had been expended upon the fortifications, which were now deemed almost impregnable. Indeed it was called the Dunkirk of America.[2] "Upon a neck of land on the south side of the harbor was built the town, two miles and a quarter in circumference; fortified in every accessible part with a rampart of stone, from thirty to thirty-six feet high, and a ditch eight feet wide. A space about two hundred yards was left without a rampart, on the side next to the sea, inclosed by a simple dyke and a line of pickets. There were six bastions and three batteries, containing embrasures for one hundred and forty-eight cannon, of which sixty-five only were mounted, and

---

[1] Belknap.

[2] Marshall's Colonial History.

sixteen mortars. On an island at the entrance of the harbor, was planted a battery of thirty cannon, being twenty-eight pounders; and at the bottom of the harbor, directly opposite to the entrance, was the grand or royal battery of twenty-eight cannon,— forty-two pounders,— and two eighteen pounders. On a high cliff opposite to the island battery, stood a light-house; and within the harbor, at the north-east part, was a magazine of naval stores. The town was regularly laid out in squares, with broad streets, built up with houses, mostly of wood, but some of stone. On the west side, near the rampart, was a spacious citadel, and a large parade; on one side of which were the governor's apartments. Under the ramparts were casemates to receive the women and children during a siege. The entrance to the town, on the land side, was over a drawbridge, near to which was a circular battery, mounting sixteen twenty-four pounders; and from its position, its reduction was an object as desirable to the English as that of Carthage was to the Romans."[1]

From the prisoners taken at Canseau by the French, and sent into Boston the preceding year, and from other sources, Governor Shirley had obtained such information respecting the situation and condition of these formidable works, as induced him to form the project of a sudden invasion, with a view of carrying them either by surprise or by storm. Shirley had indeed conceived this bold and adventurous enterprise in the autumn of 1744, and written to the British ministry upon the subject,— dispatching his letter by the hand of an intelligent officer, who had been captured at Canseau, and whose knowledge of the localities and strength of Louisburg, he doubted not would be available to the government. The enterprise was approved by the ministry, and orders were transmitted to Commodore Warren, then commanding a squadron in the West

---

[1] Belknap.

Indies, in January, to proceed northward in the spring and co-operate with the movements of Shirley. Of these instructions the latter was apprised; but impatient of delay he proceeded in his preparations for the expedition in anticipation both of the decision of the government, and the movements of Warren. These preparations were in truth accelerated by the ardent temperament of Colonel William Vaughan, of New Hampshire, a son of the lieutenant-governor of that state, and a man of a high and daring spirit, who, from the fishermen in his employ, had become well acquainted with the harbor and defences of the place it was intended to storm. Being in confidential correspondence with Governor Wentworth upon the subject, Shirley's project was communicated to Vaughan, who embraced it with all the ardor which so noble an exploit would be likely to inspire a man of his bravery and enthusiasm. Nothing, with him, was impracticable which he had a mind to accomplish; and so strong were his convictions of the practicability of the conquest, that he would fain have undertaken it in mid-winter, believing that the walls might be scaled by the aid of the drifts of snow.[1]

Thus far the project had been kept a profound secret by Shirley himself, and the very few trust-worthy men to whom it had been confided. But early in January it became necessary for the governor to communicate his design to the general court, at whose hands he must ask for the means of its execution. Secrecy was yet desirable, to which end an oath of confidence was administered to the members before the plan was laid before them. Startled at the magnitude of the project, as well as at its boldness, the proposition was at first rejected; but subse-

---

[1] It has been suggested, says Belknap, that the plan of this enterprise was first suggested by Vaughan. Several other persons have claimed the like credit. I have discovered no good reason, however, for depriving Shirley of the honor of its conception.

quently, advantage being taken of the absence of several members, the question was reconsidered, and the undertaking was sanctioned by a majority of a single voice. Yet, nothing daunted, the governor proceeded to arrange his measures with characteristic energy. Circular letters were addressed to the governors of all the colonies south to Pennsylvania inclusive, invoking their assistance in the enterprise, and asking for the imposition of an embargo upon their ports. Armed with one of these missives, Vaughan, who had been awaiting the authorization of the expedition in Boston, rode back express to New Hampshire, the legislature of which was then in session. Wentworth, the governor, was already enlisted in the scheme; and the legislature, catching fire from the enthusiasm of Vaughan, entered heartily into the project, and made the necessary grants for the quota of men and supplies expected from that colony. Equal readiness to forward the enterprise was now manifested by the general court of Massachusetts; and Shirley assumed the responsibility, in the face of his instructions from the crown, of sanctioning an extraordinary emission of bills of credit to meet the heavy expenditures to be incurred,— advising Wentworth to the same course.[1] Until the issuing of the circulars, moreover, the secret had been well kept; nor, probably, would the disclosure then have been made,— at least not so soon,— had it not been for the unguarded fervor of one of the praying members of the general court, who, at the family altar, while earnestly invoking the favor of Heaven upon the enterprise, forgot that he was also speaking to human auditors.

The colonies of Connecticut and Rhode Island entered into the design in the finest spirit. New York would have done likewise, had the wishes of Governor Clinton been

---

[1] In Massachusetts fifty thousand pounds of bills were emitted for this exigency, and in New Hampshire thirteen thousand.

seconded by the general assembly. That body met by adjournment on the twelfth of March, and the session was opened by a speech of a length and earnestness proportioned to the importance of the crisis. It commenced by announcing to the assembly the projected enterprise of Massachusetts and her sister colonies of New England against Louisburg, in retaliation, as it was alleged, for the attacks of the French during the preceding year upon Annapolis-Royal. Governor Shirley had written him a pressing appeal for co-operation in this enterprise; and concurring entirely in his views as to its importance, the governor informed the assembly that without awaiting their meeting, he had already acted in relation thereto, to the extent of his power and means. He had sent ten pieces of ordnance to Boston, with their necessary warlike implements; and he called upon the assembly to respond to the invitation of Mr. Shirley, by contributing its full proportion to the expedition, the success of which would be of infinite advantage to the province. Aside from this great undertaking, farther measures for the defence of the colony of New York itself were strenuously urged. There was an absolute necessity for the erection of two additional forts in the Indian country, not only for the protection of the frontiers, but to give the Indians confidence, and afford them places of refuge in hours of disaster. Already, for want of these, they were evidently becoming cool and indifferent toward the English. He renewed the recommendation for an appropriation that would enable him to appoint commissioners to meet those of the other colonies which were disposed to form a bond of union for the common defence. The advantages to flow from such a league, were forcibly set forth, to which was added an expression of regret at the course the assembly had adopted in relation to the proposition at the preceding session. It was indeed the expressed desire of his majesty, that in all important exigencies, the colonies should unite their councils, and their forces, for the common security. The speech, which was the longest thus far to be found in the colonial journals, closed with an exhortation to unanimity and dispatch.

The council promptly responded to the speech by an address, moved by Chief Justice De Lancey. It was an echo throughout, but especially in regard to the Louisburg expedition. High praise was awarded to Massachusetts for the energy she was exerting in this matter, and the council closed by pledging the co-operation of New York.[1] But this pledge was not sustained by the house. There were several points of the speech which that body received unkindly — among which were the rebukes which the governor had administered to it for neglecting his former recommendations,— particularly in regard to the proposed commissioners of union, and the appointment of a solicitor for the colony to attend to their interests in the parent country. Consciousness of their neglect of the public interests in those respects then, neither improved the temper of the members, nor prompted them to a performance of the obligations of patriotism now. Toward the governor they were not only guilty of the discourtesy of returning him no address in answer to his speech, but they manifested no disposition to comply with either of his present recommendations. A special message, on the fourteenth of April, announcing the arrival of a large French force in Martinique, the destination of which it was apprehended might be against New York, did indeed arouse the assembly for a moment to the importance of providing some farther defences for the harbor, and a conference with the council upon the subject was asked and granted. Still, although a show of liberality was exhibited in the appropriations proposed for this branch of the public service, the house sought to interfere

[1] Journals of the Legislative Council.

with what was claimed as a prerogative of the executive, by specifications as to the manner in which the money should be expended, and designations of the points to be fortified — an interference, certainly, with the appropriate duties of the commander-in-chief.

There was yet another cause of irritation on the part of the house, so early as the year 1709, the general assembly had found it necessary, in providing ways and means for the public service, — especially in the prosecution of the several wars in which the colony had been involved by the parent government, — to issue a paper currency called bills of credit. The operation had been repeated from time to time, in emergent cases, — sometimes with the approbation of the crown, and sometimes not, — until these paper issues had become a part of the policy of the colony. Others of the colonies, laboring under the same necessities, had resorted to the same measures of finance; but to which the crown, jealous of its prerogative in all matters of currency, had uniformly been opposed. For many years, therefore, antecedent to this period, the royal governors had arrived in the colony clothed with instructions against allowing farther emissions of bills of credit; — instructions, however, which the stern law of necessity had seldom allowed them to enforce. Still the crown, keenly alive to every step of independent action on the part of the colonies, was persisting in its war against a colonial currency even of paper; and a bill was now before parliament upon the subject, which gave great alarm to the people. Professedly, its design was merely for preventing these bills of credit from being made a legal tender; but it was discovered that the bill was to have a far more extensive operation, — "obliging and enjoining the legislatures of every colony to pay strict obedience to all such orders and instructions as might from time to time be transmitted to them, or any of them, by his majesty or his successors, or by or under his or their authority."

Such an act, it was justly held, "would establish an absolute power in the crown, in all the British plantations, that would be inconsistent with the liberties and privileges inherent in an *English* man, while he is in a *British* dominion."[1]

Vexed with themselves, and with the governor, for reasons already mentioned, and still more for their own remissness in not having made seasonable provision for a resident agent in London to watch over the interests of the colony, and who might perhaps successfully oppose this bill,—the house evinced a disposition, without any sufficient reason, as it seems to me, to thwart the governor upon every point. In addition to the discourtesies heretofore mentioned, in regard to the erection of fortifications, "it ordered the city members to inquire for and consult some engineer; intimated a design to lessen the garrison at Oswego; declined the project of a guard-ship; rejected the renewed recommendation for appointing joint commissioners to treat with the Indians for mutual defence; voted but three thousand pounds toward the Louisburg expedition; and declined the provision of presents for the Indians."[2]

It was very evident that no good could result from the action of an assembly between which, and the governor such an unpleasant state of feeling existed. The session had been extended already to more than two months, and nothing had been done for the public defence. Even the bill making the paltry appropriation of three thousand pounds toward the New England expedition, had not passed the council. Indeed only four bills, and those of no great importance, were awaiting the approval of the

---

[1] See report of a committee of the house of assembly, colonial journals, March 15, 1745.

[2] Smith's *History of New York*, vol. ii, pp. 90, 91.

governor.[1] In this situation of affairs, the governor, in no very pleasant humor, on the fourteenth of May required the assembly to meet him in the council chamber, in order to its dissolution. In his speech on the occasion, the governor said he was prompted to that measure by many reasons. From an inspection of their journals he observed they were bringing their proceedings to a close, without having heeded most of the recommendations he had made to them in his former speeches and messages, although the greater part of those recommendations had been confined exclusively to the public service. It was, indeed, true that he had expected but little from them after the disrespect they had manifested toward him by omitting to present an answer to his speech. But, notwithstanding this mark of disrespect, such had been his anxiety for the welfare of the province that he had paid no attention to it,—having made to them from time to time all necessary communications, and given them all the information relating to the state of the colony, within his power. Nothing that could enlighten them had been withholden. He spoke of difficulties threatening commotions among the Indians. He had signified to the assembly the necessity of frequent interviews with these people, and of making them presents, in order to retain their confidence, allay their disquietudes, and renew their treaties. No respect had been paid to his recommendations upon this subject,— nor for the erection of the forts wanted in the interior,— nor even for the payment of scouts, and the adoption of such other prudential measures as were necessary for the security of the frontier settlers. He spoke of the con-

---

[1] One of these four bills was for the encouragement of privateering. Another was a bill, originating in the house, which was passed by the council, on the tenth of May, to prevent the slaves in the city of Albany from running away to Canada. By this act the crime was declared a capital offence, and the council so amended the bill that the offender was to be put to death "without benefit of clergy."

tempt with which they had treated the petition of the people north of Albany, who were alarmed at the conduct of the Indians; and of the indecency of their conduct toward him in connection with that petition. Yet, so far as his own individual feelings were concerned, he said he could almost overlook all their ill treatment of himself, could he entertain the least hope of awakening them to a proper sense of their duty toward his majesty, and the people they represented; but they had treated his majesty's orders, conveyed in a letter from the duke of Newcastle, with equal indifference,— having even misrepresented its contents, particularly in regard to certain orders to Commodore Warren, and the service in which he was engaged. They had neglected to make provision for the maintenance and transportation home, of the French prisoners then in the city of New York. Nor had they even made an appropriation for the money he had advanced, by the advice of his majesty's council, for the defence of Oswego on the breaking out of the war. They had, moreover, undertaken to exercise the power of designating the points in the harbor to be fortified, and the number of guns to be mounted at particular ports, and even directed the issues of gun-powder and other articles of war, without consulting the commander-in-chief,— thus in effect assuming the entire administration of the government, and arresting his majesty's authority from the hands of the governor. "Thus from an invincible untowardness on the one hand, or an immediate thirst for power on the other, they had become a dead-weight on the other branches of the government." They had "protracted the assembly to a most unreasonable length, without doing anything effective for the honor of his majesty or the service, credit, or security of the province or the people." He was therefore constrained to put an end to the session; and the assembly was dissolved.[1]

---

[1] See *Journals of the Colonial Assembly.*

Meantime the preparations of Governor Shirley, for the invasion of Cape Breton, had been pushed forward with a degree of vigor characteristic of the sons of the Pilgrims when roused to action, and bent upon some achievement requiring energy and courage like their own. Indeed the expedition had embarked, and was

"In brave pursuit of chivalrous emprise,"

weeks before the dissolution of Governor Clinton's refractory assembly, which, with a parsimony not usual to New York, had refused to contribute a single pound sterling toward the undertaking.[1]

The design of Shirley was to dispatch an army of at least four thousand men well appointed, and if possible to take Louisburg by surprise — calculating, — correctly as the event proved, — that the floes of ice prevailing in the waters of Cape Breton in the early weeks of spring, and the dense fogs, would prevent any communication by means of which the enemy could be apprised of the intended invasion. The people caught the enthusiasm of their leaders; and although not a recruit was mustered from beyond the confines of New England, yet the full complement was promptly supplied. Massachusetts raised three thousand two hundred and fifty men; Connecticut five hundred and sixteen; and New Hampshire three hundred and four,[2]—

---

[1] "The government of New York," says Dunlop's imperfect and ill-digested history of the state, "was wise enough to join in this plan of conquest, and sent field-pieces and other military equipments to Governor Shirley." Again, on the same page, Dunlop says: "New York contributed in money to this expedition, but had none of the honor of reducing Cape Breton." Neither of these statements conveys the exact truth. The cannon, as has been stated in the text, were sent by the *governor* of the colony, on his own responsibility — not by the *government*. Nor was any money contributed until after the great object of the expedition had been gained. Even then, the appropriation was beggarly.

[2] Belknap claims that, including the crew of an armed vessel furnished by New Hampshire, there were four hundred and fifty men commanded by Colonel Moore; and one hundred and fifty men more raised in that colony, and aggregated to a regiment of Massachusetts.

in all, four thousand and seventy. Three hundred men were likewise raised in Rhode Island; but they did not reach the point of destination until the great object of the enterprise had been accomplished. These forces consisted, not of disciplined soldiers, but in the main of husbandmen and mechanics — unused to service, save as militiamen occasionally engaged in the border forays with the Indians,— or to the stern code of discipline under the law martial. Yet they went forth with a resolution, and performed their duties with a steadiness, that would have done credit to the veterans of the duke of Marlborough, or Turenne. The Connecticut division was commanded by Roger Wolcott, lieutenant-governor of that colony, bearing the commission of major-general. The command of the New Hampshire levies was entrusted to Colonel Samuel Moore. Vaughan, the bold adventurer from that colony, refused to accept any regular command; but being appointed a member of the council of war, held himself in readiness for any special service or situation which might offer. The command in chief of the expedition was devolved upon Colonel William Pepperell, a merchant of Kitberg, in what was then called the province of Maine, though subject to the colonial government of Massachusetts, who was thereupon raised to the rank of lieutenant-general. His second in command, from Massachusetts, was Brigadier-General Waldo. The selection of a commander for an army of undisciplined volunteers, going upon a fatiguing and hazardous service, required the exercise of profound judgment, and a shrewd knowledge of character — qualities which were happily illustrated in the choice of William Pepperell. His profession had not been that of arms; but he had probably had some experience in the border service, not unfrequently in those days. He was, however, a man widely known, and exceedingly popular,— of engaging manners, and a vigorous frame. His mind was of the firmest texture; his courage doubted by none; and his reputation unblemished. These qualities, united with the most admirable coolness in seasons of danger, amply supplied in the public mind the lack of any very extensive military experience.[1]

Each of the colonies engaged in the enterprise, supplied all the vessels for transports, provision ships, and cruisers, in their power; and all things being in readiness, the Boston forces embarked from Nantasket,[2] on the twenty-fourth of March. Judging from the long and minute instructions from Shirley to Pepperell, and also from a private letter from the former to Governor Wentworth, of New Hampshire, which has been preserved by Belknap, the governor of Massachusetts, though the author of the project, must have been wholly unskilled in both the arts of navigation and war. It had been his intention that the several divisions of the expedition should meet at a common rendezvous, and the entire fleet sail in company. According to the letter to Wentworth, it was his design, without making the least allowance in their sailing of different vessels, or for variations of wind, or for any other of the hundred casualties that might occur, that the

---

[1] The following curious passage occurs in Belknap's interesting account of this memorable expedition: "Before Pepperell accepted the command, he asked the opinion of the famous George Whitefield, who was then itinerating and preaching in New England. Whitefield told him that he did not think the scheme very promising; that the eyes of all the world would be upon him; that if he should not succeed, the widows and orphans of the slain would reproach him; and if it should succeed, many would regard him with envy, and endeavor to eclipse his glory; that he ought, therefore, to go with "a single eye," and then he would find his strength proportioned to his necessities. Henry Sherburne, the commissary of New Hampshire, another of Whitefield's friend, pressed him to favor the expedition, and give a motto for the flag; to which, after some hesitation, Whitefield censented. The motto was, "*Nil desperandum Christo duce.*" This gave the expedition the air of a crusade, and many of the missionary's followers enlisted. One of them, a chaplain, carried on his shoulder a hatchet, with which he intended to destroy the images in the French churches."

[2] Nantasket road — the entrance into the harbor of Boston

entire fleet, consisting of more than a hundred vessels of different tonnage,— guard-ships, transports, and every species of craft employed,— should arrive at Chapeaurouge bay at precisely the same hour, just after night-fall, to the end that the landing of the whole army might be effected under cover of darkness the same night, and all the fortresses of Louisburg be carried by surprise before morning![1] All this was, of course, impossible. Indeed the New Hampshire division was so impatient of delay, that it could not brook the idea of coming out of its course to Boston to join the common fleet, but took its departure in advance of the principal squadron. The idea of a simultaneous departure and arrival of the whole expedition having been abandoned by Shirley on finding that its execution must be impracticable, the island of Canseau was designated as the rendezvous, at which place the New Hampshire division arrived on the thirty-first of March — four days before Pepperell came up with the Massachusetts fleet. The veteran Wolcott, who was then sixty-six years old, and who, thirty-four years before, had served in a campaign against Canada, arrived with the Connecticut squadron on the twenty-fifth of April. The Rhode Island levies, owing to various mischances, were so unfortunate as not to reach the scene of action until the business upon which they went had been accomplished.

A number of circumstances, not depending upon human foresight, have been noted by Belknap, Douglass, and other authors, as greatly favoring this undertaking. The winter was remarkable for its mildness, so that the harbors and rivers of New England were open in February, and the people were enabled to perform every description of labor abroad without inconvenience. The earth had

---

[1] "The inventive genius of New England had been aroused, one proposed a model of a flying bridge to scale the walls,— even before a bridge could be made; another was ready with a caution against mines; a third, who was a minister, presented to the merchant general, ignorant of war, a plan for encamping the army, opening trenches, and placing batteries."— *Bancroft.*

yielded her increase by handfuls the preceding season, so that provisions were abundant. The Indians, in the interest of the French, remained so quietly in their lodges, that they obtained no information of the projected enterprise in season to allow them to communicate the design. On the other hand, the garrison of Louisburg was discontented and mutinous; they were in want of provisions and stores; their shores were so environed with ice that no supplies could arrive early from France, and those which came afterward were intercepted and taken by the English and colonial cruisers.[1] In short, if any one circumstance had taken a wrong turn on the side of the invaders, and if any one circumstance had not taken a wrong turn on the side of the French, the expedition must have miscarried."[2]

I have already said, incidentally, judging from his instructions to Pepperell, that Shirely must have been entirely unskilled in the arts both of war and of seamanship. Those instructions were drawn up at great length, and with a degree of minuteness, in regard to matters of possible occurrence even of trifling moment, resembling, in legal phrase, a bill of particulars. Every movement, to be made both upon land and water, was directed in the body of the instructions with as much precision as though it were not possible either for the winds or the waves to interpose contingencies in the way of the closet calculations of the writer. On reading them over, it would seem as though not the slightest particle of discretion was to be allowed to the commanding general. These general instructions were reiterated in a supplementary order on the eve of Pepperell's departure, even to the adjustment of hooks and lines to enable the cruisers to supply the camp with fresh fish. Directions thus minute and peremptory, might have been found exceedingly inconvenient in the varying circumstances of a protracted siege,

---
[1] Belknap.
[2] Douglass.

by land and water, but for a seasonable postscript appended to the last-mentioned order, in these words: "Upon the whole, notwithstanding the instructions you have received from me, I must leave you to act upon unforeseen emergencies according to your best discretion." It was indeed fortunate that this most important clause of the many folios of directions was given, since the expedition was detained at Canseau three whole weeks, waiting for the dissolution or removal of the ice which environed the islands, and, by coasting the bay of Chapeaurouge, or Gabarus, as it was called by the English, during all that period protected Cape Breton from invasion.[1] Indeed the absurdity of Shirley's original idea of keeping the squadron compactly together during the voyage, and of a simultaneous landing, regardless of ice, or storm, or fogs, or surf, was signally illustrated by the event; for what with tempestuous weather, and unequal sailing, the first point of destination, Canseau, was attained in the most desultory manner. Only twenty of the main squadron arrived with Pepperell; and more than a week elapsed before the vessels all came up.[2] But this time was not lost by the commanding general, whose vigilance in obtaining information was sleepless, and whose activity in imparting discipline to his troops was untiring. A strong squadron of armed colonial vessels, under Captain Edward Tyng, commander of the Massachusetts frigate, was kept cruising off Louisburg, to cut off such of the enemy's vessels as might attempt either to enter or depart, and the prizes taken by them afforded valuable additions to the provisions of the army.[3]

---

[1] Even the Rev. Dr. Belknap, whose trade was not of war, criticises these instructions, drawn, as he says, by a lawyer, to be executed by a merchant, at the head of a body of husbandmen and mechanics.

[2] Letter from General Pepperell to Governor Shirley.

[3] Letter of Pepperell to Shirley. Governor Shirley having directed Tyng to procure the largest ship in his power, he had purchased this ship when on the stocks, and nearly ready for launching. It was a ship of about four hundred tons, and was soon afterward launched at Boston. Tyng commanded her and was appointed commander of the fleet.—*Note in Holmes.*

Although, as I have already said, the design of this expedition had been communicated to the ministers of the crown, in the expectation of receiving assistance thence, yet it had been conducted thus far altogether upon the resources of the colonies themselves; confident, to a considerable extent, in their own strength, yet anticipating such assistance. In the hope, moreover, of securing the co-operation of Commodore Warren, then in the West India seas, even before he could receive direct instructions from home, an express boat had been dispatched to him, communicating the project on foot, and requesting the aid at least of a detachment from his squadron. But on a consultation with his officers he was dissuaded from engaging in the enterprise; and the boat, conveying the news of this determination, returned to Boston two days before the departure of the forces.[1] The intelligence, however, though unexpected, operated only as a partial discouragement,— strong confidence being entertained that Pepperell would be supported from England with ships and reinforcements of troops.[2]

The promotion of Captain Warren to the Superbe, of sixty guns, and his being left on the Antigua station by Sir Chaloner Ogle, as commodore of a small squadron, are circumstances in the career of this truly brave and illustrious man, that have already been noted. His success in making captures in the West India seas had been great; and perhaps his officers were reluctant to relinquish a genial winter climate, yielding such golden returns of prize-money, in exchange for the icebergs and bleak regions of the north. He had captured two French prizes on his way to Barbadoes a few months before;[3] and while occupying a station off Martinique, his extraordinary activity was rewarded by more than twenty valuable prizes, one of which was estimated at two hundred and fifty thousand

---

[1] Marshall.

[2] Letter from Shirley to Pepperell.

[3] MS. letter, Edward Holland to Johnson.

pounds sterling.[1] But notwithstanding his refusal of aid to the expedition on the application of Governor Shirley, his orders from the admiralty, upon the subject, brought him upon the New England coast with the Launceton and Eltham, of forty guns each, in addition to his own ship, and in addition, also, to the Mermaid of the same force, by which he was joined shortly after his arrival.[2] Without entering the harbor of Nantasket, the commodore placed himself in communication with Shirley, and having ascertained that the expedition had previously sailed, he proceeded directly to Canseau, where he arrived on the twenty-third of April; and after a conference with Pepperell, assumed the command of the naval forces by express orders from the admiralty. Previous to his arrival, the colonial squadron, under Captain Tyng, had taken several prizes,—vessels laden chiefly with provisions,— which were received in good time by General Pepperell. The New Hampshire armed sloop had been remarkably successful,— she having captured a ship from Martinique, and with her, recaptured one of the transports which had fallen into the hands of the French on the day before Warren's arrival.

The two commanders having concerted their plans, Warren sailed to cruise off the harbor of Louisburg, where he was soon afterward joined by the Canterbury and Sunderland, of sixty guns each, and the Chester of fifty, all from England, which enabled him to institute a vigorous blockade. Meantime, the ice no longer effectually impeding the navigation, the general, after having sent out a detachment which destroyed the village of St. Peters, and scattered the inhabitants, embarked with his forces on the twenty-ninth of April, for the point of the grand attack. Shirley, even in his final instructions, had not altogether abandoned his original idea of a landing by night, and an assault by surprise; so that Pepperell was

---

[1] Charnock.

[2] Idem.

still enjoined "to sail with the whole fleet from Canseau so as to arrive in Chapeaurouge bay at nine o'clock in the evening. The troops were to land in four divisions, and proceed to the assault before morning. In the event of a failure of surprisal, particular directions were given how to land, march, encamp, attack, and defend; to hold councils and keep records; and to send intelligence, and by what particular vessels;[1] and a hundred other minute instructions were given, to be nullified daily by a hundred unforeseen contingencies. Obedience to the letter was out of the question. Instead of making the point designated in the evening, the falling of the wind brought them off the mouth of the bay only at eight o'clock the next morning —[2] "the intended surprisal being thus happily frustrated," as Belknap *naively* observes. But notwithstanding the long delay at Canseau, the blockade of the cape by the ice and the fleet had been so effectual, that no knowledge of the approach of an enemy had been received in Louisburg, and the appearance of the fleet of a hundred transports in the bay, was the first intimation they had of his proximity.[3] It was a moment of intense interest to the army when they came actually in sight of Louisburg. "Its walls, raised on a neck of land on the south side of the harbor, forty feet thick at the base, and from twenty to thirty feet high, all swept from the bastions, surrounded by a ditch eighty feet wide, furnished with one hundred and one cannon, seventy-six swivels, and six mortars; its garrison composed of more than sixteen hundred men; and the harbor defended by an island battery of thirty twenty-two-pounders, and by the royal battery on the shore, having thirty large cannon, a moat, and bastions, all so perfect that it was thought two hundred men could have defended it against five

---

[1] Belknap. See, also, the instructions at large, in the first volume Massachusetts Transactions.

[2] Letter of Pepperell to Shirley.

[3] Belknap.

CHAP. III.
1745.

thousand.[1] Yet, as though forgetful of these advantages of strength and position, nothing could exceed the consternation into which the inhabitants and garrison were thrown by this very unexpected visit. The governor made a feeble attempt to prevent the landing by sending out a detachment of one hundred and fifty men for that purpose; but they were attacked with spirit and compelled to retire with the loss of several killed and a number who were made prisoners,— among whom were some persons of distinction. These enemies having been thus summarily disposed of, the debarkation was effected without the loss of a man. In their flight the French burnt several houses situated between the grand battery and the town. Several vessels were also sunk in the harbor, but for what particular design is not known.

The enthusiasm with which the expedition had been undertaken by the citizen-soldiers, was unabated, and preparations were made for investing the city without delay. The point of debarkation was about a league from the town. The first column that advanced was led through the woods in sight of the town, by Colonel Vaughan, the daring spirit who had been so earnest from the first in urging forward the enterprise, and by whom the enemy showing himself upon the ramparts, was saluted with three cheers. On the night following, the second of May, Vaughan marched at the head of a detachment, composed chiefly of New Hampshire troops, to the northeast part of the harbor, where he burned the enemy's ware-houses, containing their naval stores, and staved in a large quantity of wine and brandy. The smoke of this conflagration, driven by the wind into the grand battery, so terrified the French that they precipitately abandoned it, spiking their guns, and retiring into the city. The next morning while reconnoitering the works with a small party of only thirteen men, observing that no smoke issued from the chimneys of the battery, Vaughan prevailed upon an Indian to enter

---

[1] Bancroft.

through an embrasure and open the gate. Immediate possession was taken of the fortress, and one of the brave fellows of the band climbed the flag-staff, carrying aloft a red coat in his teeth, which he hoisted in triumph as a banner. The French immediately sent out one hundred men to retake the battery; but Vaughan held them at bay until a regiment arrived to his relief and the conquest was secured. The guns that had been spiked were mostly forty-two-pounders.[1] The trunnions had not been knocked off; and by active drilling, under the direction of Major Pomroy, of Northampton,—a gun-smith when at home,[2]—about twenty of them were soon rendered fit for service. The greater number of these guns were intended for the defence of the harbor; but four of them were brought to bear upon the town with great effect,—almost every shot being made to tell, and some of the balls falling upon the roof of the citadel.[3] The general was at a loss to conjecture why the enemy abandoned so fine a battery, but concluded that it must have been occasioned by a deficiency of men. The French turned some of their guns against this battery, not without making some considerable impression upon its walls. Twice, also, in the course of ten days, they rallied out for its recovery, but in both instances were repulsed with loss. The loss of the Americans in this affair was very slight.

The siege was pressed with vigor, but its prosecution was attended with almost incredible labor and difficulty. For fourteen successive nights the troops were employed in dragging their cannon from the landing place to the camp through a morass, so miry that neither cattle nor horses could be used for that purpose. The men sunk to their knees in the slough, and the cannon could only be drawn even upon sledges constructed for that purpose by Colonel Misseroè, who, fortunately was a carpenter before

---

[1] Letters of Pepperell to Shirley.
[2] Bancroft.
[3] Pepperell to Shirley.

he took to the profession of arms. What added essentially to the severity of this labor, was the circumstance that it could only be performed in the night, or when curtained by the heavy fogs resting upon the island; since the distance was not only within view of the town, but within reaching distance of their cannon.[1] The approaches of the besiegers were not made with strategic regularity. Indeed the ears of a martinet would doubtless have been shocked at the barbarisms of the provincials in using, or attempting to use the technicalities of military science — or rather at the jesting and mockery which they made of them.[2] Still, the approaches were made, generally under cover of night; and in ten days after the debarkation, they were within four hundred yards of the town, with cannon planted upon several commanding heights, while a fascine battery had been erected on the west side of

---

[1] The men who performed this severe service were much disappointed and chagrined when they found that it was not more distinctly acknowledged in the accounts which were sent to England, and afterward published. The siege was signalized by many meritorious exploits which were not mentioned by General Pepperell in his dispatches, as, for instance, Vaughan's expedition on the night after the landing, and his seizure of the great battery, with only thirteen men, on the next morning.

[2] Bancroft. There was doubtless much less of military seniority among the besiegers during this campaign, than would have been the fact in an army of regular soldiers; and much less of strict military discipline than their commanding officers could have desired. "It has been said," remarks Mr. Belknap, " that this siege was carried on in a random, tumultuary manner, resembling a Cambridge commencement. The remark is in a great measure true. Though the business of the council of war was conducted with all the formality of a legislative assembly; though orders were issued by the general, and returns made by the officers of the several posts; yet the want of discipline was too visible in the camp. Those who were on the spot have frequently, in my hearing, laughed at the recital of their own irregularities, and expressed their admiration when they reflected on the almost miraculous preservation of the army from destruction. They indeed presented a formidable front to the enemy; but the rear was a scene of confusion and frolic. While some were on duty in the trenches, others were racing, wrestling, pitching quoits, firing at marks, or at birds, or running after shot from the enemy's guns, for which they received a bounty, and the shot was sent back to the city."

the city upon which eight twenty-two-pounders were mounted.

On the seventh of May, after a conference between the naval and military commanders, it was agreed to summon Duchambeau, the French governor, to surrender. This summons having been refused, it was then determined to prosecute the siege in a yet more vigorous manner, and to attack the island battery, in boats, the first favorable opportunity.[1] It was a formidable undertaking. This "island battery" stood upon a small rock, almost inaccessible, about two hundred yards long by twenty in breadth, with a circular battery of forty-two pounders commanding the entrance of the harbor, and a guard house and barracks behind.[2] On the eighteenth of May, the besiegers had thrown up a battery within two hundred yards of the western gate, whereon were mounted two forty-two, and two eighteen pounders, which annoyed the town considerably; but several of the siege pieces of ordnance were defective, and by bursting, or otherwise, were soon rendered useless.[3] Indeed there was great defectiveness in the equipments of the rank and file; but the siege was, nevertheless, persisted in with the most indomitable perseverance. Between the eighteenth and twenty-eighth of the month five unsuccessful attempts were made by Pepperell to carry that battery, in the last of which he lost nearly two hundred men, killed, and many more drowned, before they could land, besides several boats which were shot to pieces. Although repulsed, the attack was bravely conducted. The troops who succeeded in landing made a noble stand, and an officer named Brookes nearly succeeded in striking the flag of the fortress. It was already half cloven when a French-Swiss, a dragoon, clove his skull with his cutlass.[4] The expediency of making yet another

---

[1] Letter from General Pepperell to Governor Shirley.
[2] Letter of "an old English merchant" to the earl of Sandwich.
[3] Pepperell's letters.
[4] Letter from "an old English merchant" to the earl of Sandwich.

attempt upon this fortress was discussed in council, but such was its strength, and the commanding advantage of its position, and so difficult was the landing rendered by the surf, that the project was abandoned as impracticable.[1]

During these operations upon land, Commodore Warren had been cruising off the harbor with splendid success. So closely was the entrance guarded that with the exception of a single sloop laden chiefly with zinc, everything that attempted to get in was captured; the consequence was that both town and garrison were soon reduced to great distress for provisions. A large ship, the Vigilante, commanded by the Marquis de la Maison Forte, from Brest, deeply laden with military and other supplies, having on board reinforcements to the number of five hundred and sixty men, and bringing also two or three years' pay for the troops[2] was known by Duchambeau to be on her passage, and great dependance was placed upon this arrival for relief. But this, the governor's last hope, was cut off by Warren,— the ship having been decoyed by one of the frigates into the centre of his squadron and captured on the ninteenth of May— "almost without resistance."[3]

---

[1] Letter of Pepperell to Commodore Warren, in which he states the exact loss in killed, in the last abortive attack upon the island, at one hundred and eighty-nine.

[2] Letter from Madame Warren to her brother, Chief Justice De Lancey, written after the capture of the Vigilante.

[3] So says Charnock, in the *Biographia Navalis*. But Bancroft says the Vigilante "was decoyed by Douglass, of the Mermaid, and taken after an engagement of several hours." I have seen another authority in which Douglass is named as the captain of this ship. Yet there is doubt upon the subject. Holmes, in a note, cites from Alden, the biographer of Captain Tyng, a statement that the Vigilante was taken by this officer, commanding, as we have seen, the Massachusetts provincial frigate. Other books and several private letters among the Johnson manuscripts attribute the capture to Warren. As the commander of the squadron, it is settled in general history, that the credit in chief should be awarded to him. Alden's authority for awarding the particular credit to Tyng I do not know.

Although the island fortress had not yet been taken, still a battery erected upon a high cliff at the light-house, greatly annoyed it. Nevertheless, in the eye of Warren, the opera.ions of the siege advanced so slowly, that, impatient of delay, even after the capture of the Vigilante, having taken the opinion of a council of his officers, he wrote to Pepperell, proposing that a decisive blow should be struck by a combined attack by land and sea. The fogs were a great annoyance to the commodore, being often so dense, that it was impossible for him to communicate with his consorts for two or three days at a time. On more than one occasion, interviews between the land and naval commanders had been prevented by the same cause. Furthermore the commodore had been more than three months at sea, and was wearied of the service of cruising upon such a limited station. But the plans submitted by the commodore for the proposed assault, were not agreeable to Pepperell and his board of officers, and a correspondence was maintained upon the subject for several days,—Warren occasionally showing a degree of earnestness, bordering perhaps, upon asperity. Yet he protested that his only desire was for the success of the expedition, and the honor and interests of the crown; and he distinctly disclaimed the disposition to give the least offence.[1]

At length, however, the batteries of Pepperell continuing to make considerable progress against the walls of the town, on the first of June it was determined between the two commanders that a combined assault should be made as soon as the necessary arrangements could be completed. For this purpose a large body of the land forces were to be embarked on board the fleet, which was to force the harbor and land them in front of the town, covered by the guns of the ships. A bombardment of the town was to ensue, while Pepperell was to make a simultaneous attack through the breaches at the west gate. Before this could

---

[1] Correspondence between Warren and Pepperell.

be done, however, there was a formidable obstacle to be surmounted — the "island battery," heretofore mentioned, and upon which several ill-starred attacks had already been made. It was deemed too hazardous an undertaking thus to enter the harbor before that battery should be silenced; it being generally doubted whether, having entered the harbor, in the event of a repulse from the town, the fleet would be able to get to sea again. Such was the opinion of the officers of Warren, at a council holden on the seventh of June; and plans were then considered for another attack upon the island, to be made by the ships,— former experience having proven that boats were entirely inadequate to such a severe and perilous service. An attempt of this kind the commodore was yet better enabled to make after the tenth of June, on which day his squadron was farther strengthened by the arrival of the Princess Mary, the Hector, and the Lark.[1]

Happily, however, a further effusion of blood was rendered unnecessary by a successful *ruse de guerre*, suggested by Warren, and executed jointly by Pepperell and himself. The French garrison, mutinous when the siege commenced, reduced in numbers during its progress, and to great distress by the blockade, was supposed to be not in the best possible humor for continuing the defence; and as advices had been received that a large fleet with provisions and reinforcements for the succor of the fortress, might shortly be expected on the coast, it was considered wise to hasten matters to a decision. It was moreover believed that Duchambon was yet ignorant of the fate of the Vigilante, and also of the capture of a large rice ship and several other vessels laden with supplies; and it was suggested by Warren that should a flag be sent into the town with this information, by the hand of a discreet officer able to act his part well, the French commander might be induced to capitulate from sheer discouragement or despondency. Another part of the scheme was to play

---

[1] Correspondence of Pepperell and Warren.

upon his fears. To this end it was proposed that the Marquis de la Maison Forte should be taken through the several ships of the squadron, that he might see how kindly the French prisoners were treated by the English. The Marquis was next to be informed that the English had been advised of the fact that several of their people who had fallen into the hands of the French and Indians, had been treated with horrible barbarity; and he was to be requested to ask for as good treatment of the English prisoners in the town, as they, (the French,) were receiving on board the fleet. The expedient was successful, and the captive commander of the Vigilante readily consented to address the desired letter to Duchambon, announcing the loss of his ship, and speaking of the other matters that had been concerted. In regard to the treatment experienced by himself and fellow captives, since their misfortune, the captive marquis said they were dealt with not as enemies, but as "very good friends;" and in conclusion, he cautioned the governor against allowing the cruelties complained of to be practiced upon the English prisoners in his power. Captain Macdonald, the officer to whom the flag was confided, discharged his duty well; and the threat which he bore of retaliation for the cruelties complained of, unless they should be ended, had its effect. The bearing of the captain, was that of a soldier sure of victory in a few days, and apparently indifferent whether the besieged continued their defence or not. Pepperell in his message by the flag, made no demand of a surrender; while on the other hand, the whole affair was conducted as though the commander of the besiegers, certain of a speedy conquest, scarcely thought it necessary again to speak of a capitulation. Meantime the flag-officer, Macdonald, affecting entire ignorance of the French language though understanding it well, heard all that passed between the French officers themselves, who, speaking without suspicion or reserve, unconsciously confirmed the suspicions of Pepperell and

Warren, that the besieged were in truth ignorant of the loss of the Vigilante, until that hour.

The news of this loss sank deep into the hearts of the French. They saw, moreover, that preparations were on foot for an assault, which, from the scattered positions of the beseigers, and the inequalities of the ground around the town, they could form no intelligent estimate of their numbers — such prisoners as had fallen into their hands having with singular uniformity reported the invading forces much more numerous than they actually were. Under all these adverse events and circumstances, and discouraged, moreover, by the menacing appearances without, Duchambon determined to surrender, and on the sixteenth of June articles of capitulation were signed. The terms of this capitulation were honorable to the vanquished, who were allowed to march out with drums beating and colors flying — their arms and colors then to be delivered into the custody of Pepperell and Warren, until the return of the prisoners to their own country, when they were to be returned to them.

At four o'clock in the afternoon of the same day Colonel Bradstreet, with a detachment of troops took possession of the town and its defences, the strength and magnitude of which, and the resources yet remaining to the French, had they persisted in the defence, astonished the victors, who saw at once that policy had stepped in very opportunely to aid their own bravery in the reduction of works so formidable, yet the siege had been powerfully directed, as the reader must have seen by the preceding details, to which many facts and circumstances might be added.[1]

---

[1] On entering the town Pepperell wrote to Shieley — "Such ruins were never seen before, which however, is not to be wondered at, as we gave the town about nine thousand cannon balls and six hundred bombs before they surrendered, which sorely distressed them, particularly the day before they sent out their flag of truce, when we kept up such a constant fire on the town from our batteries, that the enemy could not show their heads, nor stir from their covered ways. Our battery near the light-house played on

The time of the capitulation was exceedingly opportune for the besiegers in various respects yet unmentioned. Two days after it took place, information was received by General Pepperell that a body of two thousand five hundred Indians were hovering within a few miles of his camp. The capitulation of the fortress was doubtless a signal for their instant dispersion among their own deep forests. The weather, moreover, which had been remarkably favorable to the objects of the besiegers, for that climate, now suddenly changed, and a cold and driving storm of rain set in, which continued ten days, and which, but for the shelter afforded the enemy in the town, would have thinned its ranks to a frightful degree by sickness — the disorders usual among those not accustomed to camp duty, or to sleeping upon the earth, having already made their appearance among the soldiers.

Reinforcements from Boston, for which Pepperell had been urgently writing to Governor Shirley, arrived soon after the capitulation,— as also did the Rhode Island levies, after a protracted voyage,— together with supplies of provisions. These and other stores, were augmented by further captures from the enemy,—several rich prizes having been decoyed into the harbor after the fall of the town, by the artifice of keeping the French flag flying upon the ramparts. Among these were two Indiamen, and one South-sea ship, estimated, in all, at six hundred thousand pounds.[1] A dispute arose between the land forces and the

---

the island battery with our cannon and large mortars so that they were ready to run into the sea for shelter, as some of them actually did."

Still in the same dispatch notwithstanding these severe operations, Pepperell says: we have not lost above one hundred men by the enemy in this vast enterprise, including the disaster at the Island battery." This is in contradiction of his dispatch giving an account of that island disaster, in which he stated the loss by the enemy at one hundred and eighty-nine, exclusive of those who were drowned in attempting to land from the boats.

[1] On the eighteenth of July, a large schooner from Quebec, laden with flour and other provisions was brought into Louisburg by one of the colonial cruisers. On the twenty-second, the Charmante, a French East India ship of about five or six hundred tons, twenty-eight guns and ninety-nine men, surrendered

naval, as to the distribution of the prize money arising from these captures, the former under the circumstances of the case, claiming an equal proportion with the latter. But the booty went to the seamen,— to the strong and general dissatisfaction by the soldiers.

The Mermaid, Captain Montague, was dispatched to England with the tidings, bearing official advices from both commanders, enclosing the articles of capitulation. These dispatches were received by the ministry on the twentieth of July, and gazetted, but in substance only, on the twenty-third. It has been justly said, that the news of this important victory filled America with joy, and Europe with astonishment. The colonists, for the first time, began to feel the might that slumbered in their own strong arms, while the parent country gave no unequivocal evidence of jealousy at the development of so much energy and power. The letter of Pepperell, giving an account of the operations under his own command, was not allowed to transpire; but the publication of the general facts caused great rejoicing among the people. A court of evidence was immediately convened, and an address of congratulation for the success of his Majesty's arms was voted, though in rather subdued and formal terms. But as the news of the capitulation spread through the colonies, the feelings of the people broke forth in the most lively rejoicings. Boston was illuminated even to the most obscure bye-lane and alley; and the night was signalized by fire-works, bon-fires and all the external tokens

---

to the Princess Mary and Canterbury, without opposition. The Charmante had been descried in the offing, and the ships which took her, were sent out from here. This was as valuable a prize as had been taken during the war. On the first of August, the Chester and Mermaid brought in the Heron, a French East Indiaman, from Bengal,—"pretty rich,"—as Sir Peter wrote to the admiralty. On the second of August, the Sunderland and Chester brought in a French ship called the Notre Dame de la Deliverance, of thirty-two guns and about sixty men, from Lima,—having on board, in gold and silver, upward of three hundred thousand pounds sterling, with a cargo of cocoa, Peruvian wool, and Jesuit's bark.—*Dispatches of Sir Peter Warren to the Admiralty.*

of joy. A day of solemn thanksgiving to Almighty God, was likewise set apart by the civil authorities, which was observed throughout the colony. Nor was a thanksgiving festival ever more religiously kept in Massachusetts.[1]

But notwithstanding the studied design, so rarely manifested in England, to attribute the success of the enterprise, and the glory of the achievement, mainly to Warren, there was no reluctance evinced in bestowing deserved honors upon the provincials. Pepperell was created a baronet, and commissioned a colonel in his majesty's forces, with permission to raise a regiment in the colonies, to be placed upon the regular establishment, in the pay of the crown. Govenor Shirley was also appointed to a colonelcy, and confirmed in his government of Massachusetts, as also was Benning Wentworth, in that of New Hampshire. Commodore Warren was likewise promoted to the rank of rear admiral of the blue.[2]

---

[1] Letters to Pepperell from the Rev. Dr. Chauncey. After the surrender of the fortress, a grand entertainment was given on shore by Gen. Pepperell, as well to celebrate the event, as to honor Commodore Warren and the various officers of the navy who had coöperated in the capture. There was a circumstance attending this dinner, connected with the Rev. Mr. Moody, Pepperell's worthy chaplain, which has been preserved as being at once grave and amusing. Mr. Moody was somewhat remarkable for his prolixity in saying grace, before meat, and his friends were particularly anxious on this occasion that he should not fatigue their guests, and perhaps disquiet them by the length of this preliminary exercise. Yet his temper was so irritable that none of them ventured the hint, "be short." The chaplain, however, catching the spirit of the occasion, very agreeably disappointed those who knew him by preparing the service in the following words: "Good Lord, we have so much to thank thee for, that *time* would be infinitely too short to do it in. We must therefore leave it for the work of *Eternity*. Bless our board and fellowship on this joyful occasion, for the sake of Christ our Lord. Amen."

[2] Pepperell was gazetted as a baronet on the tenth of August,—less than a month after the news of the capitulation. Commodore Warren was gazetted as a rear-admiral of the blue on the same day. It it stated by Belknap, that Warren was also created a baronet as a reward for the same achievement, and the statement is repeated by Dunlop, and perhaps by other American writers. But the fact is not so. Warren was never a baronet. It is true that the knighthood of the Bath was conferred upon him; but

150 LIFE OF SIR WILLIAM JOHNSON, BART.

CHAP. III.
1745.

Yet notwithstanding these honorable rewards to the master spirits of the expedition, there was unquestionably a most discreditable reluctance on the part of the parent government to reimburse the colonies for the heavy expenses, which, without counting the cost to themselves, they had so nobly and so generously incurred; and by reason of which, conquest was achieved, so important, according to the testimony of their own historians, "as to prove an equivalent, at the peace of Aix-la-Chapelle, for all the success of the French upon the continent of Europe." The claim was prosecuted several years before parliament could be brought to sanction an appropriation to cover it. The grant was however obtained in the year 1749, amounting to the sum of one hundred and eighty-three thousand six hundred and forty-nine pounds sterling. It was received at Boston the same year, and equitably divided among the colonies which had incurred the expenditure.[1]

---

this was not done until in the year 1747; the order being then conferred as a reward for his conduct under Vice Admiral Anson, in the great naval engagement with the French fleet off Cape Finisterre, which was fought May third, of that year. Warren commanded on that occasion the Devonshire of sixty-six guns, and (with the Yarmouth) was first in the engagement. In July of the same year, Warren was gazetted admiral of the white, as also, on the same day, Mr. Clinton, then governor of the colony of New York, Sir Peter Warren and the unfortunate admiral Byng appear to have been fellow officers, considered at that time of high and equal merit. On the same day that Warren was promoted to the rank of rear admiral of the blue, Byng was promoted to the same rank, and Warren and Byng were on the same day farther promoted to the white. Yet how widely different the end of their career! Ten years afterward, poor Byng, as brave, doubtless, as Warren, but in a single instance unfortunate, was sacrificed by ministers a victim to popular clamor, and to screen their own imbecility. The judicial murder of Byng is one of the foulest blots upon England's escutcheon!

[1] The exact sum was £183,649 25s. 7½d. The agent who prosecuted the claim, encountering difficulties at every step, was William Bollan, whose account of the negotiation is presented in the first volume of the Mass. His. Coll. The money was told in specie. On its arrival in Boston it was immediately conveyed to the treasury-house. It consisted, according to a note in Holmes, of two hundred and fifteen chests (three thousand pieces of eight, on an average, in each chest) of milled peices of eight, and one hundred casks of coined copper. There were seventeen cart and truck loads of the silver, and about ten truck loads of copper.

Jealousy of the rapidly increasing strength of the colonies, as I have already intimated, was beyond all doubt the moving cause of the unworthy attempts made in England, to appropriate all the glory of the conquest to Commodore Warren. Mr. Bollan, the agent for prosecuting the claims of Massachusetts, found on his arrival in London, that in the first address of congratulation to his majesty on the event which he saw, it was spoken of as "a naval success"—not the least mention being made of the land forces employed on the occasion. But although these attempts to present it in the light of "a naval acquisition," were not without their influence, the colonists were not friendless, and the claims of the provincial troops were ably asserted. All credit was denied to the ministry in regard to the achievement, by some of the most influential journals. "Our ministers," said one of these, "have no more merit in it than causing the park and tower guns to fire."[1] Again says the same standard periodical, on the appointment of Charles Knowles as governor of Cape Breton, and commander of the fleet on that station: "it is hoped that General Pepperell, the gallant commander of those brave forces who took it, will be provided for in some other way."

In the spring of 1775,—thirty years afterward,—these attempts to detract from the just fame of the provincials, were revived by the earl of Sandwich, then first lord of the admiralty, in a speech before the house of lords. His lordship professed to speak upon no less authority than that of Admiral Warren, who, as the minister asserted, had pronounced the Americans engaged in the siege of Louisburg, as the greatest cowards and poltroons whom he had ever seen. His lordship also made Warren to say, that the fighting at Louisburg had been done by the marines of the ship's crews, landed by the commodore for that purpose; while at the same time he was compelled to

---

[1] The *Gentleman's Magazine*—the best historical record antecedent to Dodsley's Annual Register, the publication of which was begun in 1758.

praise the Americans for their endeavors to keep them from running away. It should be remembered, however that this speech was delivered at the breaking out of the, war of the American revolution, when it was the policy of the parent country to decry the character of the colonies. The minister, moreover spoke at random of conversations merely held with one, who had been dead more than thirty years. He was however, immediately and sharply answered through the London press, by a man who had been engaged in the seige,—who had known Sir Peter Warren, and conversed with him upon the subject.[1] This writer proved that Sir Peter could never have made any such statements to his lordship, nor to any one else—in the first place, from the perfect harmony that existed between the land and the sea officers; secondly, because of the very impossibility that the story could be true,—since the commodore had no power to command upon land, and could not have interfered with the authority of General Pepperell;—and for the yet more conclusive reason, that THE COMMODORE NEVER LANDED A PARTY, EITHER OF MARINES OR SEAMEN, DURING THE SEIGE.

How far Admiral Warren himself participated in these efforts at detraction, or whether in reality he engaged in them at all, is now a point of difficult determination. It is affirmed by one highly respectable American authority,[2] that "Warren deposed on oath, in the high court of admirality, seventeen months after the event, that with the assistance of his majesty's ships, &c., he, this deponent did subdue the whole island of Cape Breton." This declaration unexplained, presents indeed a most arrogant claim; but it ill accords with the declarations of the com-

---

[1] Letter to the earl of Sandwich by "an old English merchant."—*Mass. Hist. Coll.*, Vol. I.

[2] *Walsh's Appeal* from the Judgments of Great Britain, respecting the United States of America, in which the author cites the Registry of the High Court of Admiralty of England, Sept. twenty-ninth, 1747. I have not seen this authority to judge of the extent of the circumstances under which the deposition was made.

modore's letters written during the seige. In one of these addresses to Governor Clinton in New York, and dated off Louisburg, May twelve, 1745, the commodore says:

"Sir, I take the liberty to acquaint you that the New England troops have taken possession of one of the enemy's most considerable batteries at Louisburg, which gives them the command of the harbor; and they have now carried their approaches so near by land, that the city is blockaded, and its communication by land and sea entirely cut off, *and that before the arrival of any ship to their relief from any part of the world, except one small one laden with wine and brandy.*"[1]

Indignation at British arrogance upon the subject of this expedition, however, and a pretty general conviction that Warren was less magnanimous than he should have been, have on the other hand conspired to induce certain American historians to derogate from the substantial merits of this distinguished naval commander, in regard to that great achievement, whose conduct, within his own proper sphere of action, and beyond which he evinced no desire to go, was without fear, and without reproach. Owing to the fogs, the ice, and the storms, the difficulties of maintaining a rigid blockade were exceedingly difficult and hazardous. Yet never was a blockade more effectively maintained, and never did a naval commander evince a stronger desire to encounter yet greater hazards for the honor of the service, and of his royal master. It is indeed possible, that feelings of jealousy may have been growing like hidden fires in the bosoms of both commanders, even in the hour of triumph. And if such were the fact, there were doubtless, ill-disposed people at hand to fan the sparks into a flame. Yet there is nothing in the conduct or correspondence of the two commanders, during the seige, going to warrant any such conclusion. On the contrary, there was at all times, a generous coöperation between them. Once, in-

---

[1] This letter is preserved in the journals of the general assembly of New York.

deed,—but not until the day after the capitulation,—there was an imputation of jealousy thrown out ; but it is no more than justice to admit that it came from Warren himself, who thought he had reason for the impeachment against Pepperell. "I am sorry," said he, "to find by your letter a kind of jealousy which I thought you would never conceive of me." The residue of this letter is earnest, but relates to some unspecified complaint of Duchambon, who seemed to apprehend a disposition on the part of Pepperell not to observe with sufficient exactness, the terms of the capitulation. But the real or affected cause of the French governor's complaint is not given, nor does the letter seem to have been preserved in which Warren thought he discovered the shadow of the green-eyed monster.

There were, however, sharp jealousies entertained in another quarter. The people of Boston were alive to the honor of their merchant-general ; and having heard that the keys of Louisburg had been delivered, not to him, but to the commodore, were not a little incensed thereat.[1] Still greater was their displeasure on hearing that Warren had assumed the government of the conquered province—it being feared "that New England, from a sea-officer, would not have its full share of the glory of the conquest."[2] Hence it was requested by the legislature of Massachusetts that Governor Shirley should repair in person to Louisburg, which port it had been determined to repair and retain, to look after the interests and the glory of those who had effected the conquest. Yet the highest praise was at the same time, and on all hands awarded to Warren. Dr. Chauncey himself, in the letter to his friend Pepperell, immediately prior to the one just cited, says:—"I have no personal acquaintance with the brave Mr. Warren, but I

---

[1] If I understand Hutchinson correctly, this statement was inaccurate. "It was made a question," says their candid historian, "whether the keys of the town should be delivered to the commodore or to the general, and whether the sea or land forces should first enter. The officers of the army *they* say prevailed."

[2] Letter from the Rev. Doctor Chauncey to Sir William Pepperell.

sincerely love and honor him. Had his majesty given us the choice of a sea-commander on this occasion, we should have selected that gentleman from all the rest, and desired that he might be sent." But other jealousies also existed, as in the case of Colonel Bradstreet, and even of Shirley himself, against whom Pepperell was admonished before he sailed upon the expedition, "as a snake in the grass." These things only prove that human frailty exists among the best of men in every age. A careful study of the history of this memorable expedition will show any candid enquirer for the truth that Warren behaved throughout like a brave and skillful officer, and a patriotic and honorable man. Admitting, nevertheless, for the sake of argument, that in the course of events immediately after the first flush of victory had passed away, unpleasant feelings had arisen between the two distinguished commanders, they must have been very short-lived, since the two heroes afterward lived in bonds of friendship that were dissolved only by death. Sir Peter Warren passed the summer at Louisburg, during which time many valuable captures were made by his ships,[1] and Sir William Pepperell remained there a whole year after the conquest. He afterward visited England at the express invitation of Warren, by whom he was received with honor, and treated with marked distinction. He was received with great kindness by the royal family, and the city of London presented him with a silver table. In regard to the joint conquest, there certainly was little room for jealousy, for there was glory enough for all.

It was believed, that the capture of Louisburg, prevented the conquest of Nova Scotia by the French. Duvivier, who had embarked for France in 1744 to solicit an armament for the invasion of that province, sailed with seven ships of war and a large body of troops, in July, 1745.

---

[1] A Ms. letter from John Catherwood, then an officer in the household of Governor Clinton, to "Mr. William Johnson, dated Sept. 5th, 1845, says: "This commodore has had great success in captures at Louisburg. His share, at least, will be above £20,000."

CHAP. III.
1745.

His orders were to touch at Louisburg, and proceed thence in the execution of his plan. Hearing at sea of the fall of that place, and of the strength of the British squadron stationed there, he relinquished the enterprise against Nova Scotia, and returned to Europe.

The daring and enthusiastic Vaughan, however, appears to have been forgotten in the hour of triumph. He repaired to London shortly afterward to prefer his claims to the crown, but was seized with the small-pox in that capital, of which disease he died.

CHAPTER IV.
1745—1746.

Recurring again to the progress of affairs in New York, Mr. Clinton, the governor, it will be remembered, had dissolved the second assembly of his administration, on the fourteenth of May, in high displeasure, because, as he alleged in part, of the personal disrespect with which he had been treated by that body; but chiefly because of its inattention to the defenses of the colony, and its neglect of his recommendations of a coöperation with the New England colonies in the expedition against Cape Breton. Orders for such coöperation having been received from his majesty's ministers, the governor held that obedience was an imperative duty. But the people seem not to have sympathized with the feelings of the governor; and the uncomplying members, with few exceptions, and with singular unanimity, were returned to the new assembly, which met on the twenty-fifth of June, and elected Mr. David Jones, of Queens county, a gentleman distinguished for his rigid views of economy in public affairs, as their speaker. The news of the fall of Louisburg had not reached New York at the time of the meeting. Much of the governor's speech, therefore, after pressing again upon the attention of the assembly the importance of placing the colony in such a posture of defence, as the crisis demanded, was devoted to the Louisburg expedition. The governor had indeed himself only heard of the earlier operations of the siege, the capture of the first great battery upon land, and of the Vigilante by sea, and the latest dispatches thence consisted of urgent appeals from Governor Shirley and Commodore Warren, for troops, seamen, and provisions. These solicitations were in turn urged upon the assembly with all

CHAP. IV.
1745.

the force at the command of the executive mind. But although few changes had taken place in the representative body of the general assembly, yet the dissolution had wrought a wonderful improvement in its temper. The answer of the council, drawn by Chief Justice DeLancey, was an echo to the speech, and that of the house, reported by Mr. Henry Cruger, was equally cordial. The members declared their full persuasion that the governor had the service of the crown and the welfare of the colony sincerely at heart, and they were equally explicit in avowing their own readiness to consider with the greatest attention, the several particulars recommended for their action. Nor was their conduct inconsistent with their professions. A bill was passed with the utmost promptitude, appropriating five thousand pounds toward the Louisburg expedition; another for the necessary fortifications both upon the wild inland frontier and the defence of the seaboard; and yet another for completing the governor's house. These acts having been passed with great harmony, the assembly adjourned from the sixth of July to the thirteenth of August,— during which interval of time the glorious news of the fall of Louisburg was received,—an achievement the most important by far of the war, and "which proved an equivalent at the treaty of Aix-la-Chapelle, for all the successes of the French upon the continent of Europe."

The Indian relations of the colony were yet again becoming critical. Notwithstanding the efforts of the preceding year, both at Albany and in the grand council at Lancaster, to keep this jealous and fickle people true to their covenants with the English; and notwithstanding their repeated pledges of fidelity, the Six Nations were again wavering; and the misgivings of the govenor as to their designs, were communicated by a message to the house, on the twentieth of August, in which an appropriation was asked to enable his excellency to meet them in council, and if possible, ascertain the grounds of their discontents.

The governor also announced that some of the Canadian Indians had broken the treaty of neutrality existing between them and the Six Nations, by committing hostilities against some of the frontier settlements of New England, where several of the inhabitants had been barbarously murdered. In the apprehension that those Indians might be meditating an infliction of the like cruelties upon the frontiers of New York, it was necessary that due measures of precaution should be adopted.

There had been indications of dissatisfaction among the Six Nations for several months prior to this message. Indeed the governor had referred to their "disquietudes" and "commotions" in his speech dissolving the assembly in May; and it was well ascertained that during the preceding winter, emissaries from the French had been among them, while they in turn had sent several messengers with belts into Canada. Information to this effect was elicited on the examination of John Henry Lydius, of Albany, before the executive council in New York, on the sixth of April. Lydius was a man of extensive acquaintance with the Indians, having resided much among them,—in Canada several years,—and again at Lake George. He stated that he had recently seen a French Indian, from whom he had received information touching the designs of the enemy against Oswego, and also in regard to the feelings of the Six Nations. The Mohawks were very uneasy, and had sent several chiefs to confer with the Indians in Canada. The cause of this uneasiness was a suspicion awakened in their bosoms by evil disposed persons, that the English were preparing at no distant day entirely to destroy them. This apprehension, notwithstanding its absurdity, was seriously entertained by many of the people, and even by some of the chiefs; though the orators Abraham, and Brant, gave no credence to the tale.[1]

---

[1] Manuscript journals of the executive council, secretary of state's office, Albany. The Brant here spoken of, was probably the father or the reputed father of Joseph Brant of the revolution.

CHAP. IV.
1745.

It was unfortunately but too true, at the time under consideration, that no good feelings existed between the Mohawks and the people of Albany. At least the Mohawks looked upon the latter with great bitterness,—having been overreached in some land purchases, in which the Albanians were concerned. So they alleged; and by availing themselves of these prejudices, some evil-minded persons had to some extent persuaded the Mohawks that the Albanians were plotting the destruction of their nation, in order to possess themselves of their domain. Rumors were accordingly circulated among them from time to time to the end that measures for killing them were in actual preparation. They were thus kept in a state of feverish excitement and suspicion for several weeks. At length a runner arrived in the Mohawk country, in the night, with information that the Albanians were then actually upon the march against them, to the number of several hundreds, armed with muskets, and treading to the sound of arms and trumpets. The poor Indians of the lower castle, Dyiondarogon, fled in wild affright to their upper towns. All was confusion,— the women seizing their infants, and the children who were able to run, flying in the utmost consternation, and uttering the dead cry—"QUE!" QUE!" QUE!"[1]

The dissatisfaction having become extensive among the confederates, it was judged expedient to depute Conrad Weiser, the Pennsylvania interpreter for the Six Nations, to make a tour of friendly observation among them. Weiser was a native of Schoharie, partaking largely of the confidence of the Indians; and it was rightly judged that a mission by him to their several towns and castles would be attended with happy results. Those results were realized. On the twenty-ninth of July the missionary returned, and his journal was laid by Mr. Clinton before his council. After traversing the cantons beyond Onondaga, and soothing their feelings, he was accompanied from the

---

[1] Manuscript journals of the executive council.

Great council fire by a party of the chiefs to Oswego, where free conferences were held. The Indians complained that the English kept them in the dark about the progress of the war, dealing out their news in generals only, whereas they wanted the particulars. They were aware that the governor of New York was displeased with their visits to Canada, but they insisted that they went thither only upon business,—the governor of Canada knowing very well that he could do nothing with them to the detriment of the English.

Returning from Oswego through the Mohawk country, Weiser was received gladly at their castles and treated kindly. The Indians there said they inclined to the English, having always been used well by the governors of New York, Massachusetts, and Pennsylvania. But the people of Albany had not treated them well. They had cheated them, and were yet trying to get their lands and destroy them. They likewise accused the Albanians of being engaged in unlawful commerce with the enemy, to whom they had sold large quantities of powder. In regard to the visits of the Mohawk chiefs to the French in the winter, they admitted that they had gone thither because they were displeased with the Albanians, and in order to let them know that they would act as they pleased.

At Dyiondarogon, the Indians convened a council to hear Mr. Weiser on the subject of their late alarm in consequence of the rumored invasion from Albany. He assured them that the whole story which had caused their panic was false, and told them of the great surprise of the governor on hearing of such an occurrence, at a time, too, when he thought the parties were all so friendly to each other. The Indians, in reply, admitted that their alarm had been very great; but, they said, the matter had all been settled, "and thrown into the bottomless pit." The explanations made to them had been perfectly satisfactory; and they now requested even that no inquiries might be instituted as to the authors of the alarm.[1] But it will presently appear that they did not exactly hold to this resolution themselves.

At the same meeting of the council, letters were received from the commissioners of Indian affairs at Albany, announcing the approach of scalping parties of the Canadian Indians toward the frontier settlements at the north. They also stated that two men had been murdered on the border of New England,—the Indians having plucked out their eyes, torn off their scalps, and cut out their hearts. This last statement was confirmed by a letter from Governor Shirley, who spoke of it as a violation of the treaty of neutrality between the Canadian Indians and the Six Nations, and urging as a proper measure that the latter should now forthwith take up the hatchet. Upon these representations, the council advised that an interpreter be immediately dispatched to the Six Nations, with a request that they should ascertain to what tribe or nation the offending Indians belonged; and also whether the murders were approved by their tribe. If so, then the Six Nations were requested to consider what was to be their own line of duty. If not,—if the murders were disapproved,—then it was left to the Six Nations to say whether they ought not to demand the surrender of the murderers,—the outrage having been altogether unprovoked.[2]

The cruelties just set forth, were committed upon the frontier of New Hampshire; but others equally atrocious were committed shortly afterward in the border settlements even of Connecticut, of which information was given to Mr. Clinton by Governor Low of that colony. Nor were these all. It was discovered in August, that while the Canadian Indians had thus been let loose upon the New England frontiers,—crossing even the province of Massachusetts in order to strike Connecticut,—the French

---

[1] Manuscript journals of the executive council.

[2] Manuscript proceedings of the executive council.

had become yet more earnest in their solicitations for the Iroquois to join them against the English. Certain of the Mohawk and Tuscarora chiefs, moreover, had made still another visit to the governor of Canada, in connection, as there was but too much reason, to believe, with these solicitations. At all events, the return of those chiefs was preceded by a state of feeling among the people, that deterred the Indian commissioners at Albany from sending a messenger among them, with the overture from the governor and council as directed on the twenty-ninth of July. Meantime a letter was received from Mr. Phipps, acting governor of Massachusetts during the absence of Governor Shirley at Louisburg, announcing that by the advice of his majesty's council of that province, war had been formally proclaimed against the Eastern and Canadian Indians.[1] The alarm had therefore become very general before the special attention of the assembly was called to the subject by the message from the governor of the twentieth of August. That body saw the necessity of immediate and efficient action, and an appropriation of six hundred pounds, in addition to an unexpended balance of four hundred pounds yet in the hands of the executive, was made to defray the expenses of a treaty with the Indians at Albany. The assembly thereupon adjourned over by permission, from the twenty-ninth of August to the fifteenth of October; and the necessary measures were concerted for holding a general council with the Indians without unnecessary delay.

The negotiations were opened on the fifth day of October, Governor Clinton being attended by Messrs. Philip Livingston, Daniel Horsmanden, Joseph Murray and John Rutherford, members of the executive council. Delegates were also in attendance from the provinces of Massachusetts, Connecticut, and Pennsylvania.[2] About four hun-

---

[1] Manuscript journals of the executive council.

[2] The commissioners from Massachusetts, were, Colonel John Stoddard, Jacob Wendell, Thomas Berry, John Choate and Thomas Hutchinson. From

dred and sixty Indians were present, representing all the confederates excepting the Senecas, who had been detained by a distressing malady, which was sweeping off many of their members. The first interview between the parties was brief,—the Indians retiring immediately after they had been presented to the governor and drunk the king's health. A consultation was then held among the commissioners as to the arrangement of their subsequent proceedings, at which it was determined that in order to impress the Indians with an idea of the harmonious action and consequent strength of the English, Governor Clinton should speak the united voice of the whole,—that is, of New York and New England. The Pennsylvania commissioners, being members of the Friends' society, preferred to make an address by themselves, in their own peculiar way. It was likewise determined that Mr. Clinton should present the chiefs with the hatchet to strike the French, and the Indians in their alliance, for the infraction of their treaty of neutrality with the Six Nations, unconditionally,—leaving it with the Indians themselves to suggest, should they elect to do so, some other measure for obtaining satisfaction for the barbarities that had been committed.[1]

Before proceeding to the main business for which the council had been convened, however, the governor having heard that notwithstanding their message by Conrad Weiser, the Indians had never been altogether satisfied in regard to the affair of the panic, heretofore described, determined upon having a full explanation of that mysterious affair;—and two days or more were occupied upon that subject. Hendrik, chief sachem of the Mohawks, made a long speech. He said their distrust of the designs of the English, but especially of the people of Albany, had

---

Connecticut, Roger Wolcott, lieutenant-governor, and Colonel Stanley. From Pennsylvania, Messrs. Thomas Lawrence, John Kinsley, and Isaac Norris.

[1] Manuscript journals of the executive council.

been originally awakened by Jean Cœur, a French interpreter, residing principally among the Senecas. This man had long been regarded by the English as a dangerous neighbor, and they had endeavored to persuade the Senecas to send him away,—but in vain. Hendrik now informed Mr. Clinton that Cœur, on returning from a visit to Canada, had told the Indians that the governor of New York had been proposing to the governor of Canada to unite for the entire destruction of their people. The tale sank deep into their minds. They knew that the Albany people had treated them badly, and when they came to reflect upon the project, and thought of the condition to which the River Indians had been reduced, and of the fact that the people of Connecticut and Massachusetts had taken all *their* land away, they began to ponder whether such might not be the design of the English against themselves —the Six Nations. "You," said Hendrik, pointing to Colonel Stoddard, "have got our land, and driven us away from Westfield, where my father lived formerly."[1] When they thought of these things, he repeated, we feared that " the Mohawks would be brought to the same pass," and rendered " as poor " as the River Indians were. " This," he said, "had remained in their hearts some years, and now, as the governor would have them open their minds, they had done it, and they hoped it would have a good effect."[2]

A long discussion followed the harangue of Hendrik, in regard to the authors of the claim, and several persons were to a greater or less extent implicated. Next to Jean Cœur, a man named Philip Van Patten, was charged as the chief agent in getting up the mischievous alarm, and a

---

[1] This remark will be the better understood on the statement of the fact that the family of Hendrik was Mohegan, and only Mohawk by adoption. Yet Hendrik and his brothers were chiefs of the first influence—Hendrik himself being the principal chief of the tribe, and was known as King Hendrik.

[2] Manuscript journals of the executive council.

negro wench of Schenectady was likewise compromised. But the statements of the Indians were contradictory; Van Patten purged himself on oath, and the Indians were evidently opposed to any very rigid investigation being made.[1] Indeed before the close of this branch of the proceedings, it came to be justly doubted whether the whole affair had not been a contrivance of a few of the Indians to excite sympathy, and perhaps extort from the government an increased amount of presents,—a lame and impotent conclusion of the touching and dramatic scene brought to the contemplation of Conrad Weiser.

The council was opened for the transaction of the proper business upon which it had been summoned, on the tenth of October. After the usual preliminary salutations, in which the Indians were told as a matter of course, that the council had been invited for the purpose of "rendering, strengthening, and brightening the covenant chain," and after condoling with them for the absence of the Senecas, because of the grievous sickness their people were suffering, the governor spoke to them directly, and in a tone of disapprobation of the late visit of some of their chiefs to Montreal, where they had met the French governor. It had been asserted in justification of that visit, that they had gone thither to protest against any invasion of Oswego by the French—the Six Nations desiring that that post might be suffered to remain as "a place of trade and peace," and pretending that they were determined to defend it if attacked. But at the very time when their chiefs were in Montreal, the Canada Indians had been breaking their treaty, and murdering the English. Not only so, but the governor assured them he had been informed that while pretending that their mission was thus pacific, they had so far accepted the hatchet from the French, as to agree to bring it home, and consider whether they would strike their English friends with it or not. This story, however,

---

[1] Manuscript journals of the executive council.

the English could hardly believe to be true, unless they should hear it from their own lips. A full and plain answer was expected, "that all stains might be wiped from the covenant chain."

Mr. Clinton next proceeded to relate to the chiefs the progress of the war—informing them of the action of the French the preceding year upon Annapolis Royal, and giving them an account of the fall of Louisburg, and the conquest of Cape Breton. In this part of the country, the English had lain still; but they had last year informed the governor of Canada, that unless the war should be conducted in a Christian-like manner,—unless the Canada Indians were restrained from murdering the English,—the Six Nations would immediately join the latter and strike upon the settlements of Canada. Yet the French seemed determined not to be at peace with us, and their Indians had not only killed some of the English, but had left a hatchet by the side of one of the dead,—thus defying the English and the Six Nations to take it up. The most solemn and sacred engagements were broken by them, and they had shown that even belts of wampum would not bind them to their promises. The English had been slighted, and the Six Nations treated as though they were not worthy to be regarded. They think you will not perform what you have threatened, and they fear not your displeasure. Thus they reflect dishonor upon you.

The chiefs were next told that it was high time both the English and the Six Nations should exert themselves to vindicate their honor. The English desired not the destruction of their fellow creatures, yet they felt that they ought not any longer to bear these insults and this evil treatment from the French. "Therefore, since neither our peaceable disposition nor examples, nor any methods we have been able to use, have sufficed to prevail upon them to forbear their barbarous treatment of us, but on the contrary, they seem determined to provoke our resentment,—

in the name of God we are resolved not only to defend ourselves, but by all possible methods to put it out of their power to misuse and evil-entreat us as they have heretofore done. And we doubt not of your ready and cheerful concurrence with us, agreeable to the solemn promise you made us in this place last summer, in joining with us against the French, and such Indians as are or may be instigated by them to commit hostilities against us." This passage of the governor's speech was followed by the presentation of a large belt of wampum, with a hatchet hung to it.[1]

Having taken two days for consideration, the Indians replied, renewing the covenant chain, which they said they were determined should never rust again, " because they would daily wipe off the dust, and keep it clean." In regard to the visit of their chiefs to Montreal, they denied peremptorily, the truth of the report of their having consented to receive the hatchet from the French governor, even for the purpose of consideration. Upon this and some other points of less importance, the chiefs answered without embarrasment. But on the subject of consenting to go upon the war-path against the French, they spoke warily. They thanked the governor for the information he had given of the progress of the war; but touching the direct appeal to them to engage in the contest, they cautiously said:—"you desire, as we are of one flesh with you, that we would also take up the hatchet against the French, and the Indians under their influence, with you. We the Six Nations, accept of the hatchet,—*and will put it in our bosoms!* We are in alliance with a great many of the far Indians, and if we should so suddenly lift up the hatchet without acquainting our allies with it, they would perhaps take offence at it. We will therefore before we make use of the hatchet against the French or their Indians, send four of our people, who are now ready to go, to Canada, to demand satisfaction for the wrongs they have done our

---

[1] Manuscript journals of executive council.

brethren, and if they refuse to make satisfaction, then we will be ready to use the hatchet against them, whenever our brother the governor of New York orders us to do it." Two months, they said, in reply to a question from the governor, would be time enough for them to ascertain whether the aggressors would make the requisite satisfaction; and in the event of their not doing so, they repeated their declaration to use the hatchet at the command of his excellency.[1]

In subsequent sections of their speech, the Indians took occasion to remind the governor that the original design of their alliance with the English was the advantages they hoped to derive from a reciprocal trade; but goods had been sold very high to them of late. They were now destitute of clothes, powder, and lead; "and people who are to go to war ought to be well provided with ammunition. This, however, should their request be now denied, was the last time they should speak upon the subject." In his rejoinder, the governor explained to them the causes of the high prices of goods at that time. They were occasioned by the war; but he would see that goods should be sold to them at as reasonable rates as possible. The presents to be distributed among them were then announced,—the governor enjoining it upon the chiefs to reserve for the absent Senecas their due proportion.[2] The discussions were concluded by a few words of wholesome advice addressed to the red chieftains now about returning again to their own beloved wilds.

Thus far the proceedings of the conference had been marked by apparant harmony. But Mr. Clinton had no sooner ended his closing address, than the Massachusetts

---

[1] Here the Indians requested his excellency, that, as they had given the war-shout upon his delivering the hatchet to them, that their brethren would now signify their approbation of this article (or avowal) in their usual method. Whereupon his excellency and most of the company joined in shouts with three hurrahs."—*Ms. records of the council recorded in the executive journals.*

[2] Manuscript journals of the executive council.

commissioners rose to express their disapprobation of that part of the speech of the sachems in which they had declared that for the present instead of using the hatchet they should "put it in their bosoms." The commissioners stated that when the Indians first arrived in Albany, they came with a good heart to enter into the war at once; and they attributed their change of purpose and desire of delay, to the intrigues of the people of Albany. The Albanians, the commissioners said they well knew, were opposed to having the Six Nations engaged in the contest, and they doubted not that the hesitancy which the chiefs had manifested, was altogether owing to their influence. On the subject of the proposed mission to obtain satisfaction from the red men in Canada, the Massachusetts gentlemen regarded the proposition as a mere pretext for delay. If satisfaction were given at all, as pretended to be given, it would probably consist of a small bundle of skins, of no substantial value, and would be no atonement at all. They were therefore greatly dissappointed with the turn the negotiation had taken.[1]

It would not be safe to affirm that this suspicion of the Massachusetts gentlemen was indulged without cause. The Albanians, at that time, regardless of the higher obligations of patriotism, were engaged in a lucrative contraband trade with Montreal, through the agency, probably, of the Caughnawagas, as in former years. Of this trade the Six Nations themselves had complained, because of the supplies of ammunition thus furnished to the French; and the governor, in his last preceding message to the assembly, had recommended strong measures for its suppression. Nevertheless, from a motive of policy,—for it could have been prompted by nothing else,—Mr. Clinton affected surprise at the suggestions of the Massachusetts gentlemen, inasmuch, he urged, as it had been the declared opinion of Governor Shirley himself, that it would

---

[1] Manuscript journals of the executive council.

be in every view sufficient were the entire neutrality of the Indians to be preserved. That neutrality it was the strong desire of the Six Nations to maintain unbroken; and it was to this end, as Mr. Clinton now insisted to the Massachusetts gentlemen, that some of their chiefs were in Canada at the very time when the directions for holding the present council were issued. And yet before it was possible for them to ascertain the disposition of the Canada Indians, or to reap the fruits of their pacific endeavors, greatly to his surprise, Massachusetts had actually declared war against the Indians living under the jurisdiction of the French. It was moreover urged as an additional reason why the Six Nations sought the delay, that many of their own people were in Canada and their safety would be compromised should their friends at home take up the hatchet at once.[1] Thus closed the council; but the vail which Mr. Clinton had attempted thus adroitly to throw over the subject-matter of the complaints of the Massachusetts gentlemen, was quite too transparent to be satisfactory.

A new aspect was imparted to the case in the course of the ensuing night, by the arrival of an express from Massachusetts with intelligence that a body of French and Indians had fallen upon one of the block-houses on the New England frontier, — situated at Great meadow, on the Connecticut river. On the next morning, therefore, the Massachusetts gentlemen applied to Governor Clinton upon the subject, urging that by this attack of the French and their Indians upon one of the king's forts, the case had substantially arisen, in which he might, under the express agreement of the Six Nations two days before, order them forthwith upon the war-path, and that they would be bound to go. They had said, that if before the expiration of the two months delay for which they asked, further acts of hostility should be committed by the enemy, at the orders

---

[1] Manuscript journals of the executive council.

of the governor they would "strike with the hatchet."[1] The exigency had already occurred, and the commissioners now requested that the order might be given,—stipulating at the same time, that they would supply the Indians with the necessary munitions of war for the campaign, at their own expense, provided they could be led forth against the enemy at once. But this request, after full advisement in council, was not acceded to by Mr. Clinton. The Indians were not inclined to immediate war; nor had the case provided for actually arisen, inasmuch as the attack upon the block-house must have been made before the Six Nations had entered into the engagement referred to. Those nations, moreover, were the only existing barrier between the frontiers of New York and the enemy; and the withdrawal of that barrier, while the frontier of New York was thus naked and exposed, would be subjecting the settlements to infinite peril. The governor, therefore, could not consent to the proposition, until he had consulted the assembly, and given that body time to place the frontier of New York in a posture of defence. While, however, for these and other reasons that were stated, Mr. Clinton declined allowing the commissioners the immediate aid of the Six Nations, he nevertheless offered a detachment of militia for their assistance at the expense of this province.[2] This proffer was declined, and the Commissioners departed—not, it is to be presumed, in the best possible humor.

Returning to the city of New York, where the general assembly, after a short recess, had resumed its sittings, the governor, on the second of November, communicated the results of his mission to Albany, by a special message, in which he took occasion to speak of the aggressions of the French and their Indian allies upon the border settlements

---

[1] So the Massachusetts commissioners insisted, but the fact does not appear exactly thus in the formal speech preserved in the records of the council.

[2] Manuscript journals of the executive council.

of New England, and urged the importance of making immediate and adequate provision for the defence of the northern frontier of New York. It was not known how strong was the combined French and Indian force that had attacked the fort at Great meadow, nor how soon it might fall upon some of the exposed settlements of this province. Such an attack was certainly to be apprehended; and the governor pressed home with earnestness upon the assembly the absolute necessity of erecting fortifications at the exposed points, not only for the security of the out-settlements, but for the purpose of giving encouragement and confidence to the Indians, that they might be induced, with the greater cheerfulness, to join in the war. For the Mohawks, always brave themselves, "felt a very allowable repugnance to expose the lives of their warriors in defence of those who made no effort to defend themselves; who were neither protected by the arms of their sovereign, nor by their own courage."[1]

These admonitions received not that immediate attention which the exigency of the case demanded; and but two short weeks intervened before the war-whoop, and the reddened sky at the north, startled the assembly from its inaction, and taught it that earlier and more earnest heed ought to have been given to his excellency's repeated recommendations. Fort St. Frederick, at Crown Point, was at that period garrisoned with sufficient strength to enable its commander, M. Vaudreuil, to send out strong detachments to annoy the English settlements at his pleasure. One of these had fallen, as already stated, upon the Great meadow settlement in Massachusetts; and at break of day, on the morning of November seventeenth, a combined force of four hundred French and two hundred and twenty Indians, invaded the flourishing settlement of Saratoga, overcame the garrison, killed and took nearly the entire population prisoners, and laid every building in ashes, excepting a new mill standing out of their course. The affair is represent-

---
[1] Mrs. Grant's Memoirs of Madame Schuyler.

ed as having been "barbarous," in the only contemporaneous written account of it which I have been able to find; the number of persons killed, however, is not stated.[1] But the slaughter must have been considerable, since Governor Clinton, in a speech to the assembly several weeks afterward, says, "many of our people were murdered." Among the slain was the brave Captain Schuyler, a brother of Colonel Phillip Schuyler. More than one hundred prisoners were taken away, a majority of whom were blacks,—slaves, it is presumed. Thirty families were sacrificed in the massacre; a description of the horrors of which would be but a repetition of the story of Schenectady, fifty-five years before.[2] So adroitly had the enemy concerted their plans, that every house must have been attacked at nearly the same instant of time. One family only escaped, the footsteps of whose flight were lighted by the conflagration.

From Saratoga the invaders crossed the Hudson, and swept with equal desolation the village of Hoosic. A small fort at this place, commanded by Col. Hawks, made a spirited defence, but was compelled to surrender. These events laid the settlements naked and open to the ravages of the enemy down to the very gates of Albany, spreading general consternation through the interior of the province. The inhabitants in the settlements most exposed rushed into Albany for security; and the males of that city capable of bearing arms, were obliged to go upon the watch in the environs, each in his turn every other night.[3]

Immediately on the receipt of these unwelcome tidings in New York, the governor transmitted a message announcing the facts to the general assembly, written under the

---

[1] Ms. letter from Robert Sanders, of Albany, to "Mr. William Johnson, merchant at Mount Johnson,"

The reader must bear in mind that this is not the Saratoga watering place of modern days, but the old town of Saratoga lying upon the margin of the Hudson river, rendered yet more famous in history by the surrender of General Burgoyne upon its plains in 1777.

[2] Dunlop's History of New York.

[3] Sanders's letter.

strong excitement of the moment, and upbraiding that body for its disregard of those measures of defence which had so frequently been urged upon its consideration. "The like was never known," he said, "that one part of a government should be left to be butchered by the enemy, without assistance from the other." The high road from Crown Point to Albany, was now open to the enemy, and he again called upon the assembly for means to enable him to erect a proper fort at the carrying-place, and such other defences as might be necessary for the protection of the settlements in the neighborhood of the places that had been destroyed. Further provision was also demanded for the Indian service, the exigence having now occurred which would authorize the governor to call the Six Nations forthwith into the service. Supplies were moreover indispensable for subsisting the troops and militia from the city, and the lower counties which must be detailed to the north for its protection. The sharp tone of the message gave offence. And yet it was very natural that the governor, who certainly was chargeable with no neglect of duty himself, should speak to those who were, in terms of earnestness, if not of reproof.[1]

Suppressing their resentment at the governor's tartness, for the moment, however, the assembly declared its readiness at all times, " to concur, cheerfully, in every reasonable measure for the honor of his majesty, and for the welfare and security of this colony; for the assistance, also, of our neighbors, and for any well-concerted plan, consistent with the circumstances of the colony, for distressing and harrassing the enemy." As an earnest of their sincerity in this declaration, bills were passed making liberal appropriations for the service, accompanied by a resolution for building the oft-recommended fortress at the carrying-place,

---

[1] It is asserted by Smith, that the governor's irritation with the assembly had been excited a few days before the receipt of the news from Saratoga, by its proceedings in the case of the contested election of Edward Holland, to which transaction I shall have occasion again to advert.

CHAP. IV.
1745.

and for rebuilding the fort at Saratoga. A resolution was also adopted authorizing bounties to be given for scalps, taken either by white men or Indians, provided that that barbarous mode of warfare should be resorted to in the first instance by the enemy. Having done thus much for the military service, and passed the annual salary and supply bills, the assembly adjourned over from the twenty-eighth of November to the seventeenth of December, "then to meet at the house of Rear Admiral Warren, in Greenwich."[1]

Early in December an important letter was laid before the privy council from Colonel Philip Schuyler, requesting the governor to send up three hundred men from the militia of the lower counties for the defence of Albany and Schenectady, and also asking for the immediate rebuilding of the fort at Saratoga where his brother had been slain. These requests had been in part anticipated by the governor, the two companies of independent fusileers stationed in New York having been ordered upon that service, who were then on their way. Yet, notwithstanding the pressing nature of the emergency, the removal of these troops from the metropolis caused dissatisfaction, and the local militia refused to perform duty as sentinels at the governor's residence, or at any other place save within the walls of the fort. Conceiving this conduct a high personal indignity, the attention of the executive council was called to the subject, by whom an order was passed directing that the refractory conscripts should be compelled to perform the duty required.[2] In addition to the fusileers, a competent number of the militia were drafted for the frontier service, which was not very desirable to the yeomanry of the counties, especially in winter; and a spirit of insubordination among

[1] See journals of the colonial assembly. The prevalence of the small-pox in the city,—the simple antidote to that terrible disease of Dr. Jenner not having been discovered until nearly half a century afterward—rendering the change expedient.

[2] Manuscript journals of the executive council.

them, manifested in several respects, but particularly in their refusal to aid in building the fort at Saratoga, gave Colonel Schuyler no small amount of trouble.[1] There was probably cause for dissatisfaction among these levies, to some extent, arising not only from an ill-supplied commissariat, and the consequent absence of many things necessary for their comfort in a rigorous winter climate, but also from the want of a hospital for the sick, there being none at Albany. Nevertheless the work at Saratoga went slowly forward, by such assistance as could be obtained from the people in that part of the country, covered by patrols of a few militia and about forty Indians upon whom Schuyler had prevailed to engage in that service.

On the whole, therefore, the winter set in gloomily. The entire frontier of New England and New York was exposed to the incursions of an agile and subtle enemy, certain to strike if opportunity presented, and yet equally certain to conceal the point of attack until the fall of the blow. On the eleventh of December, Mr. Low, governor of Connecticut, wrote to Mr. Clinton that a force of six hundred Frenchmen and Indians was investing Stockbridge, against whom he had ordered a force to march with all possible alacrity. Several months previously, the governor of Georgia had written that he had been advised through the Chickasaws of a general movement against the northern colonies, by the Indians as remote even as the Mississippi valley acting in alliance with those upon the great lakes,—all of whom had been instigated against the English by the French governor at New Orleans. This rumor was now received through a different channel, with the additional statement that these distant Indians were to join the French from Canada, and strike from the westward upon the settlements of Orange, Ulster, and Albany counties,—especially upon the towns of Esopus and Mini-

---
[1] Manuscript journals of executiue council, correspondence of Colonel Schuyler.

[2] Letter from a surgeon to the executive council.

CHAP. IV.
1745.

sink,—and also upon the frontiers of New Jersey and Pennsylvania; while certain suspicious movements among the clans of Indians yet remaining in Orange and Ulster, who had withdrawn themselves suddenly from their hunting-grounds, served to strengthen the apprehension. But in regard to these latter clans, the alarm was allayed in a short time by a communication from Colonel DeKay, of Orange, who had induced them to come back and renew the chain of their covenant. The colonel was actually bound to some of their chiefs by a chain, for an hour or more, at their request, as an evidence that the two peoples were fast bound to each other.[1]

Meantime the general assembly met again on the seventeenth of December, the session being opened by a speech, short and to the purpose. After a brief statement of the measures he had adopted for the public defence during the recess, and asking for such an appropriation as would enable him to build a fort of stone, "large and strong," at the locality so often designated north of Albany, to guard the carrying-place between the Hudson river and Lake Champlain, the governor again urged the adoption of such measures as would enable him to form a union for the more efficient prosecution of the war with the other colonies, a proposition which had again been pressed upon his consideration by the government of Massachusetts. Some action of this kind had become the more necessary, inasmuch as there was reason to believe that the French were organizing a powerful force in Canada, with the design of penetrating into the heart of New York. Among the documents communicated with the speech, was a letter from Doctor Colden, dated at Coldenham, in the county of Orange, stating that the French had now a considerable party among the Six Nations, industriously engaged in sowing the seeds of disaffection, and in promoting their own interests. Certain it was, that

[1] Manuscript journals of the executive council.

by means of some adverse influence, the Confederates were again occupying a doubtful position. This appears from the fact, that immediately after the disaster at Saratoga, the governor had directed the Indian commissioners at Albany, to send an interpreter into the Iroquois country, requiring of them a compliance with their engagements in such a contingency, made at the treaty. The order for them to "draw the hatchet from their bosoms," and proceed immediately against the enemy, was peremptory. But the chiefs refused a compliance with the mandate; and the commissioners, in announcing the result of the mission, suggested the calling of another council larger than the former, at which they thought it would be necessary to send the Indians off upon some expedition before they should return to their castles.[1] This unexpected information was announced to the general assembly by a special message; and the dispatch from the commissioners was referred to a committee of the executive council for consideration.

But notwithstanding the irritation which the faithlessness of the Indians was so well calculated to produce, Mr. Horsmanden, chairman of the committee of reference, made an able and humane report, going so far in extenuation of their conduct as almost to justify their sullen refusal to enter into the war. It was considered that they were a scattered people, and their cantons remote from each other; and whatever other plausible pretexts they might themselves assign for their conduct, it could not be doubted that they were under terrible apprehensions for the safety of their own wives and children, should they engage in the contest, since in the absence of their warriors, who were to protect their own country from the French and *their* Indians? The committee therefore recommended that forts and garrisons should be established in the country of the Confederates, as places of security for the women and children, and the old men, in

---

[1] Manuscript journals of the executive council.

case of invasion. This measure would give confidence to the chiefs; and the committee therefore recommended a correspondence with the other colonies upon the subject, with a view of obtaining assistance in the erection of the works proposed.[1]

The importance of an alliance with the New England colonies, both for mutual security, and for offensive and defensive operations, was by this time becoming more obvious, and the recommendations of the governor began now to be received with greater favor by the assembly than previous to this threatened Indian defection. Accordingly, on the twenty-fourth of January the house asked of the council its concurrence in a resolution for the appointment of a joint committee upon the state of the colony. The proposition was acceded to; and the result of their deliberations, after their action had been again quickened by an Indian alarm, was the sanction, in the spring, of the project which had been so long and so much desired by the executive, and so blindly resisted by the representatives of the people.[2] The commissioners appointed to confer with those from New England, were Philip Livingston, Daniel Horsmanden, and Joseph Murray, of the council; Philip Verplanck and William Nicholl, of the assembly.

An improved spirit of liberality was likewise evinced as to appropriations for the public defence, and for other branches of the service. Yet the proceedings of the Assembly, upon some of these measures at least, were not characterized by the greatest harmony. There was an increasing hostility in the lower house against the governor; the assembly and council were at odds upon a question of parliamentary law, involving, indirectly, the royal preroga-

---

[1] Manuscript journals of the executive council.

[2] The committee on the part of the council, recommending this course, consisted of Chief Justice DeLancey, Joseph Murray, Daniel Horsmanden, and John Moore. On the part of the house, the committee consisted of Mr. Clarkson, Captain Richards, Major Van Horne, Mr. Cruger, Mr. Verplanck, Colonel Beekman, Captain Livingston, and Colonel Chambers.

tive, and finally, the members of the assembly fell into discreditable feuds among themselves touching the distribution of the public burdens among their respective counties.[1] The mixed question of parliamentary law and prerogative, arose on a disagreement between the legislative council and the assembly, upon the details of a bill authorizing an emission of bills of credit to the amount of ten thousand pounds. Before the introduction of the bill, the assembly had inquired of the governor whether he had any objection to an emission of paper money to meet the exigencies of the country; to which question the proper answer was given by Mr. Clinton, that "when the bill came to him he would declare his opinion."[2] The bill was therefore introduced and passed by the assembly; but the council, disapproving of certain of its provisions, requested a conference. The assembly, however, declared that inasmuch as it was a money bill, they would consent to no such course upon the subject. The council thereupon summarily rejected the bill, and sent up an address to the governor, written by the chief justice, DeLancey, setting forth their reasons, by which their course had been governed. One of the objections to the bill, according to this representation, was found in the fact, "that the money proposed to be raised by the bill was not granted to his majesty, or to be issued by warrants in council, as it ought to have been, and as has usually been done." This objection involved the old question of the royal prerogative—nothing more. On the subject of the right claimed by the assembly of exclusive power over the details of money bills, the address asserted "the equal right of the council to exercise their judgments upon these bills." Various other objections of detail were suggested; but the two points specified above, were the only grounds of principle upon which the council relied in justification of its course. Yet the unreasonableness of the assumption of the house, that the

---

[1] Smith's *History of New York*, vol. ii, p. 94.
[2] Ibid. p. 96.

CHAP. IV.
1746.
council should not be allowed even to point out and rectify the defects of anything which they chose to call a money bill, was argued at considerable length.[1]

Just at this point of collision, the small pox, which had driven the assembly from the city, appeared in Greenwich, producing a panic that for several days entirely arrested the course of business. The assembly prayed for a recess from the ninth of March to the twelfth of April, and also for leave to adjourn their sittings to some other place. Jamaica and Brooklyn were suggested; but in the opinion of the governor the demands of the public service forbade so long an interregnum, and he therefore directed their adjournment for a week, then to meet in the borough of Westchester. They convened there accordingly; but the inconvenience of the locality was such that the members begged permission to adjourn, even back to the infected city again, rather than remain where they were. In the end the governor directed them to adjourn to Brooklyn, at which place the transaction of business was resumed on the twentieth of March, on which day an address to the governor was ordered to be prepared, in answer to that of the council respecting the rejection of the before mentioned revenue bill.

Whether such an address was prepared or not, the journals of the assembly afford no information; but the bill appears to have died between the two houses. Still, the dangers and necessities of the country were such as to forbid inaction, whatever might become of questions of prerogative, or of legislative etiquette. Letters from the interior were pouring in upon the governor and council full of alarming reports, and asking for assistance at various points. The inhabitants of Kinderhook and Claverack, now that the fort at Hoosic had been destroyed, and the settlement deserted, petitioned for the erection of a couple of block-houses for their security; large parties of

---

[1] Journals of the legislative council, from the proceedings at length.

the enemy were traversing the country about Saratoga, the garrison of which, weak and uneasy, threatened desertion; parties both of French and Indians were infesting the environs of Albany and Schenectady, destroying property, and killing and scalping, or snatching into captivity such of the inhabitants as ventured beyond the walls; the emissaries of the French, of whom the Jesuit priest, Jean Cœur, was the leader, were holding the Six Nations in check, and preventing them from going upon the war-path, while advices were received from the Canajoharie castle that the governor of Canada had invited the Confederates to a meeting with him at Onondaga, which invitation had been accepted.[1] The settlements in the interior, not excepting the considerable towns of Albany and Schenectady, were, therefore, in a state of general panic. A stronger principle than that of prerogative, if not than that of political liberty, demanded, with irresistible emphasis, some efficient action from the legislature. Before the close of the session, therefore, another revenue bill, originating in a spirit of compromise, and yet making no essential concession on the part of the representatives of the people, was passed by both houses, and received the signature of the governor.

This bill provided for raising a supply of thirteen thousand pounds, by a tax on estates, real and personal, and for emitting bills of credit to the same amount for the public

---

[1] Ms. journals and correspondence of the executive council. Among the letters written about this time was one from the Indian commissioners stating that certain persons for a suitable compensation were willing to undertake to bring Jean Cœur from the Seneca country to Albany. The commissioners thought it an important object, but it seems not to have been acted upon. A letter was also received from Arent Stevens, a landholder residing at the Canajoharie castle, announcing that the Caughnawaga Indians had sent a belt from Canada, desiring to come back to reside in their native valley. On the same day a communication was received from John Henry Lydius, who had an intimate knowledge of the Caughnawagas, proposing a scheme for persuading them to the same course. But these suggestions came to nothing.

service, and creating a sinking fund for their redemption.[1] But though the bill was passed by the council without amendment, it did not get through wholly without opposition. Chief Justice DeLancey, usually among the most strenuous supporters of the prerogatives of the crown, it is true, yielded his hostility to the popular demand; but Mr. Rutherford recorded his protest upon the journals of the council at length. His objections were manifold as to the details of the bill, but the objection in chief was one of principle. The bill, he contended, proposed a method of raising a revenue which should be resorted to only in case of extreme necessity; the amount proposed to be raised, was to be applied wholly to the object set forth in the bill;—the points of defence designated would be entirely insufficient for the protection of Albany county;—but above, and more than all, the Assembly had in the bill encroached upon the royal prerogative by nominating officers to receive and apply the money to be raised, and by designating the sites of the defences to be constructed,—duties properly belonging to the commander-in-chief.

On the other hand, the majority of the council caused to be entered upon the journals, the reasons which impelled them to vote for the bill. These were, in chief, the exigencies of the country at large, and especially the perilous condition of the frontier,—the enemy having appeared in the environs both of Albany and Schenectady, where several bloody outrages had been committed. In answer to Mr. Rutherford's objections touching the prerogative, the majority of the council said that the provisions objected to had been inserted, and the officers designated in the bill

---

[1] The annual tax by which it was proposed that the bills should be redeemed in three years, amounted to the sum of £4,331. 10s. 8d The apportionment was as follows:—New York £1,444 8s. 11d. ;—Albany, £622. 3s. 9½ ;—Kings, £254. 18s. 0½d ;—Queens, £487. 9s. 5½d ;—Suffolk, £433. 6s. 8d. ;—Richmond, £131. 6s. 3½d. ;—Westchester, £240. 14s. 8½d. ;—Ulster, £393. 18s. 9½d ;—Orange, £144. 8s. 10½d ;—Dutchess, £180. 11s. 1¼d ;—Total, £4,331. 10s. 8d.

named, with the consent of the governor. It will be at once perceived that this arrangement with the executive was a mere subterfuge. The victory was with the representatives of the people. And it was signal; deserving of special note as marking the progress of the great principles of popular liberty.[1]

The general assembly had now been in session, with a very few brief intermissions, for nearly a twelvemonth, and although it had done much, yet the fruits of its labors were not altogether satisfactory. In addition to the passage of the revenue bill as already rehearsed, a resolution had been adopted directing the construction of six strong blockhouses, three of the number to be planted between the south-west frontier garrison of Massachusetts, and the post at Saratoga; and the other three between Saratoga and Fort William in the upper Mohawk country. The appropriation for these objects, however, had been diverted from the greater and more essential projects of a substantial fortress at the carrying-place,—orders for the construction of which had been given by the governor early in the preceding winter, and without which there could be no security against invasions from Crown Point at the pleasure of its commander. One hundred and fifty pounds were voted for repairing the works at Oswego; three thousand three hundred and seventy-five pounds were directed to be raised by lottery, to be applied to the defences of the city and harbor of New York;—the fort at Schenectady was directed to be repaired;—a corps of rangers were to be organized for the protection of the western lines of Ulster and Orange counties;—the militia laws were amended with a view to their greater vigor, in conformity with the wishes of the governor;—and the resolution of the preceding session, offering a bounty upon scalps, was enacted into a law. But although the fortress of Louisburg was threatened with a formidable attack from France, and although Governor Shirley, Sir William Pepperell, and Admiral

---

[1] See the proceedings at large in the journals of the legislative council.

CHAP. IV.
1746.

Warren had been pressing Mr. Clinton for months to send forward the quota of reinforcements which New York had been required to supply, yet the assembly peremptorily refused a compliance with the demand. They would not even provide a convoy to guard a transport ship then in the harbor of New York, destined to the assistance of that garrison, which had been greatly weakened by fever and other causes. There had indeed been from the first a reluctance in the assembly to coöperate with the New England colonies in regard to the conquest of Cape Breton, not wholly susceptible of explanation; but for their present course at least a plausible excuse was found in the weak and exposed condition of their own colony.

CHAPTER V.

1746.

The period is now approached at which the long, arduous, and in many respects brilliant public career of Sir William Johnson commenced. During the stirring scenes rehearsed in the two preceding chapters, Mr. Johnson had been pushing his fortunes as a private citizen, with a degree of discernment and energy that marked him as no common man. His removal from the south to the north side of the Mohawk river has already been noted. In the year 1744 he erected a valuable flouring mill upon the brisk stream falling into the Mohawk about two miles west of the Chucktanunda creek, in the town of Amsterdam,—where he also built an elegant stone mansion for his own residence; conferring upon the estate the name of Mount Johnson. Not only thus early had he become known to Governor Clinton, but a correspondence was shortly afterward commenced between them which soon became close and confidential; and their acquaintance ultimately ripened into the relations of cordial intimacy. It is very probable that Johnson's introduction to the new governor at so early a period of his administration, was effected by Mr. DeLancey, the chief justice, whose sister it will be remembered was the wife of Sir Peter Warren, and consequently the aunt, by marriage, of the young adventurer. Mr. Clinton, almost immediately on coming to the government, had resigned himself passively into the hands of the chief justice;[1] and that sagacious jurisconsult, would scarce be slow to advance the fortunes of a family connexion, whose talents, sagacity, and enter-

---

[1] Vide *Mass. Hist. Collections*, vol. xiii, p. 79.

prise pointed him out as a man who might one day be of importance in sustaining his own interests. Political friendships, however, are seldom constant or enduring; and it will be seen hereafter that the subsequent relations — at least for a time — between DeLancey and Johnson, form no exception to the remark.

During the years 1744 and 1745, Mr. Johnson's attention must have been closely applied to his own commercial affairs, already widely extended. From his correspondence it appears that he was in both those years often shipping furs to London, and was likewise engaged in the flour trade with the West India islands,—making shipments also to Curracoa and Halifax.[1] Still his time was not thus exclusively occupied, since it appears that in the month of April, 1745, he was commissioned one of his majesty's justices of the peace for the county of Albany—being the first official appointment conferred upon him.[2] He was moreover beginning to participate actively in the political concerns of the colony, his influence being put in requisition in the autumn of the last mentioned year, to aid in the return of his friend Mr. Holland to the general assembly for the township of Schenectady. The election of this gentleman was strongly desired by the governor,— a reason of itself sufficient to enlist the exertions of Johnson. Holland was returned; but in order to annoy the governor, the assembly, upon a flimsy pretext, insufficient in law, and in every other respect entirely indefensible, excluded him from his seat, as has been mentioned in a note upon a preceding page. Justly indignant at this unjustifiable procedure toward his favorite, Mr. Clinton manifested his feelings by the acrimony of his message terminating the session. The rejection of Mr. Holland was nevertheless the making of his political fortunes, inasmuch as it procured for him the mayoralty of the city of New York and a seat at the council board.

---

[1] Private correspondence in manuscript.

[2] Manuscript letter of Edward Holland enclosing the commission.

As I have not been able to ascertain the date of Mr. Johnson's marriage, so likewise have I found it impossible to ascertain the time of his wife's decease. It has always been understood that she died young; but a few years after their union; and before her husband had acquired either civil or military renown; yet not until after she had given birth to a son,—afterward Sir John Johnson,—and to two daughters,—Mary and Nancy. But although the exact time of her death cannot be determined, there is reason to believe that it took place at least as early as the summer of 1745. It has already been noted, more than once, that it was Mr. Johnson's policy to cultivate an intimate acquaintance with the Indians. Being largely engaged in commerce with them, his facilities to that end were great; and no white man perhaps, ever succeded in more entirely winning their confidence. He mingled with them freely; joined in their sports; and at pleasure assumed both their costumes and their manners, and cast them aside, as circumstances might require. He was consequently fast gaining an ascendency over them upon which the French looked with exceeding jealousy. It became therefore an object with the latter either to cut, or to *take* him off—an object which it will presently appear was seriously meditated in the autumn of 1745. Among the private letters of Mr. Johnson escaping the ravages of time and chance, is one from Mr. James Wilson, of Albany, addressed to "William Johnson Esquire," and dated "November 26th, 1745," from which the following passage is extracted:—" Mother desires you to come down and live here this winter, until these troublesome times are a little over. They have kept a room on purpose for you, and they beg that you will send down the best of your things directly. There is room enough for your servants, if you will bring them down. I would not have you stay at your own house, for the French have told our Indians that they will have you dead or alive, because you are a relation of Captain Warren, their great adversary.

Therefore I beg you will not be too resolute and stay. If you will not come yourself, I beg you will send your books and papers, and the best of your things." The entire silence of this letter in regard to Mrs. Johnson, and the appropriation of only a single room for his occupancy, induces the supposition that she must have died previous to the time when it was written. Still this conclusion is merely conjectural; and to say the truth, but little can be ascertained respecting Mr. Johnson's domestic relations for several years of this portion of his life.

Resuming then, the course of public events, the views of Governor Shirley were comprehensive, and in planning the expedition against Cape Breton, they had by no means been confined to the reduction of that island. His design comprehended nothing short of another effort for the entire subjugation of Canada,—an object that had several times been attempted, but always without success. The conquest of Louisburg by the provincials, aided by the fleet, afforded strong encouragement for attempting the larger enterprise. With this great design uppermost in his mind, Shirley made a visit to Louisburg after its fall, to confer upon the project with Pepperell and Warren. In the flush of their late brilliant success, his views were warmly seconded by those officers; and such representations were made to the ministers at home as prevailed upon them to approve the undertaking. A circular was accordingly issued by the duke of Newcastle, on the ninth of April, 1746, directed to the governors of all the British American colonies, south to Virginia inclusive, requiring them to raise as many men as they could spare, and form them into companies of one hundred each, to be in readiness for taking the field. The design was to attack the enemy's territory simultaneously from two directions. The New England troops, to be first in motion, were to proceed to Louisburg, there to be joined by a squadron of ships of war with a large body of land forces from England. These combined forces were then to proceed south and ascend the St. Lawrence against

Quebec; while the provincial troops of New York and the other colonies upon which the requisition had been made, together with the Iroquois Indians, provided they could be brought heartily into the service, after being concentrated at Albany, were to make a descent upon Crown Point and Montreal. The expedition from Louisburg was to be commanded by General Sir John St. Clair, acting in conjunction with Sir Peter Warren and Governor Shirley. The command of the other division was committed to Brigadier General Gooch, the lieutenant-governor of Virginia, who, six years before, had signalized himself in the unsuccessful expedition against Carthagena. Sir William Pepperell and Sir Peter Warren both visited Boston early in the spring, to confer jointly with Shirley upon the business of the enterprise;[1] but Warren was shortly ordered home, where, on the fourteenth day of July he was advanced to the rank of rear admiral of the white.[2] His successor in the command of the American squadron, was Commodore Knowles. But this officer proposed remaining at Louisburg, so that all the preparatory arrangements devolved upon Shirley.[3]

The project of this formidable enterprise had been communicated to the government of New York by Mr. Shirley, as early as the second week in January, and was received with high favor.[4] The general assembly met again on the third day of June, in Brooklyn, being deterred from sitting in the city by the small-pox. A message from the governor informed them that during the recess such had been the alarming state of affairs at the north, that an additional force of three hundred men had been drafted from the several counties, and ordered to Albany for the protection of

---

[1] Belknap

[2] Charnock.

[3] Belknap.

[4] Smith's *History* says it was approved by the general assembly on the twenty-fifth of February, for which statement the author had the authority of a message from Governor Clinton of June six; but the legislative journals do not sustain the assertion.

the frontier. The exigency had fully warranted such an exercise of discretionary power on the part of the governor; for the records of the privy council disclose the fact that the most urgent letters for assistance had been received from the Indian commissioners at Albany, in consequence of the murders and scalpings perpetrated in that neighborhood; and on the very day when the legislature reassembled, an account was transmitted from the commissioners of a skirmish between some of the northern settlers and a party of French and Indians, in which one of the latter was killed. The assembly readily voted the necessary supplies for the exigency, increasing the amount for the support of two hundred levies more than had previously been called into service, thirty of whom were to be stationed in Kinderhook, and the residue between Albany and Schenectady. Fifty Indians were likewise to be employed if they could be raised for the better security of the last mentioned town. But the assistance of the Indians was doubtful,— the commissioners having ascertained at an interview with several of their chiefs that they were reluctant to any belligerent action until after a grand council of their warriors could be held at Onondaga.[1]

On the sixth day of June, a message by the hand of Mr. Goldsborow Banyar, who, four days previously, had been appointed deputy secretary to the colony, required the presence of the assembly in the council-chamber, where the governor announced in a speech the receipt of the before-mentioned circular from the duke of Newcastle, and requested the coöperation of the legislature in all measures necessary for a prompt and efficient prosecution of the intended campaign. An outline of the plan of the intended double invasion of the French possessions, has already been given. All needful information was imparted to the assembly upon the subject, and a long letter from the duke of Newcastle was also laid before the council, stating that General St. Clair would sail from England with five bat-

---

[1] **Manuscript records of the council board.**

tallions of regulars, who were to be joined at Louisburg by two regiments more from Gibraltar, and urging it upon the colony of New York not only to put forth its utmost strength upon the occasion, but if possible to obtain the active coöperation of the Indians.[1]

These communications were received in the best possible spirit, both by the legislature and the people. There was indeed universal rejoicing at the prospect of speedily crushing the power of France in America,—it being evident to all that there could be no permanent repose until that work should be accomplished. In the council, Mr. Justice Horsmanden moved the address, and Mr. Clarkson in the assembly, both of which breathed a dutiful degree of loyalty, and a lofty spirit of patriotism. Especially did the assembly pledge itself that hearts and hands should be employed in the great work proposed, and that its proceedings should be conducted with such unanimity and despatch as should attest their duty, loyalty, and gratitude to his majesty. A kindred feeling prevailed in every direction, both with the local government, and the people. True indeed, the legislature of Massachusetts had in the outset manifested some disinclination to participate in the enterprise, burdened as she was with the debt incurred by the Louisburg expedition, not yet reimbursed by the parent government;[2] but the arguments of Shirley, strengthened by the out-breaks of the Canadian Indians upon their frontiers, overcame their reluctance, and all was now enthusiasm among the people,— the New England colonies directing their energies toward the eastern division of the expedition. Governor Hamilton, of New Jersey, wrote on the second of July, that that little colony had voted to raise five hundred men for the enterprise, and a contribution of two thousand pounds for the military chest. General Gooch wrote from Virginia, enclosing a bill of exchange of three hundred pounds, with

---

[1] Graham's *History of North America.*

[2] Manuscript records of the council board.

directions that it be applied to the purchase of presents for the Indians.[1]

Mr. Horsmanden, from a committee of the privy council, appointed to consider and report as to the best measures to be adopted in furtherance of the great enterprise, made an elaborate report on the thirteenth of June. The active coöperation of the Six Nations was regarded by the committee as an object of high moment; to secure which the commissioners at Albany were advised to dispatch an interpreter, with two assistants, into the Indian country, to dance the war dance among them by way of rekindling a military spirit, especially with the young warriors; and also to invite the chiefs and prominent warriors of the entire confederacy to meet the governor in a grand council, to be holden at an early day in Albany. Presents were likewise recommended upon a liberal scale, to be given, not as compensation, but as incentives to action,—the Indians always fighting for honor, and scouting the idea of going upon the war-path for pay.[2]

Four days afterward, the house of assembly asked of the council a committee of conference for the purpose of joint deliberation upon the condition of the colony. The request was acceded to; and every branch of the government united heart and hand in every possible measure for advancing the grand design.[3] An act was promptly passed the more effectually to prevent the exportation of provisions and warlike stores. In order to the descent upon Crown Point and Montreal, a fleet of bateaux was essential for the navigation of Lakes George and Champlain. Stephen Bayard and Edward Holland, members of the council, were deputed to superintend the building of the bateaux. They reported on the sixth of July that the ship-builders had all refused

---

[1] Manuscript council minutes.
[2] Ibid.
[3] The committee on the part of the council consisted of Chief Justice De Lancey, and Messrs. Van Courtlandt, Horsmanden, Murray, and More. The chief justice, however, seems to have acted no very efficient part during the whole year,—for reasons which will appear hereafter.

to perform the work, under the pretext that they were employed in the execution of prior engagements. This conduct of the naval architects formed an exception to the general disposition of the people; and a bill was forthwith introduced, and expeditiously passed into a law, authorizing the impressment into the public service, of all ship and house-carpenters, joiners, sawyers, and their several servants, and all other artificers and laborers whose assistance might be required for the state, together with horses, wagons, and whatsoever else might be required to forward the expedition.[1] Resolutions were adopted allowing a bounty of six pounds for the enlistment of each able-bodied man into the king's service, over and above his pay; six thousand pounds were appropriated for the purchase of provisions for the colony's levies; three hundred men were by law directed to be detached for the army from the city of Albany; and to cover the expense of these and other appropriations demanded by the exigence, a tax of forty thousand pounds was imposed upon the real and personal estate of the colony, and an emission of bills of credit authorized to enable the government to anticipate the avails of the tax. Indeed the general assembly hesitated at no appropriation that was required, save for the Indian service, and for *the transportation* of troops and military stores. In respect to the latter, they refused to advance money to the crown, even upon loan, preferring to raise it by bills of exchange,—"a hint which Mr. Clinton improved greatly to his own emolument."[2] With respect to the Indian service, they conceived that inasmuch as the grand council which the governor had already summoned at Albany, pursuant to the recommendation of his privy council, was to be convened for the common benefit of all the exposed colonies, they ought all to contribute toward the heavy expenses to be incurred, not in presents only, but for their clothing, arms and subsistence. Toward these objects Virginia had

---

[1] Journals of the legislative council.

[2] Smith, vol. ii, p. 99.

CHAP. already made a handsome remittance; but Connecticut and
V. Pennsylvania had declined making any contribution; and by
1746. a message of the ninth of July, Governor Clinton informed
the assembly that no answers had been received from the
other colonies to the applications addressed to them upon
the subject.

Nevertheless the means for holding the council were not
wanting; and having in these matters discharged its duties
to the public service, the assembly closed its session on the
fifteenth of July. Not, however, until after a joint address
of the two houses had been voted to the king, congratulating
his majesty upon the defeat of the rebels engaged in the
cause of the Pretender, by the army under the duke of
Cumberland.[1] The mover of the resolution for this address
was the chief justice; but the journals disclose the unusual
circumstance, that he was not placed at the head of the
committee, which was organized thus—Philip Livingston,
Chief Justice DeLancey, and Mr. Justice Horsmanden.
The active labor seems to have been performed by the latter.

Meantime great apprehension prevailed in New England
at the inaction of the parent government, from which much
had been promised, and more was expected, and without
whose powerful coöperation an enterprise so vast as that

---

[1] The battle of Culloden. The young Prince, Charles Edward, called the
Pretender, having defeated the royal forces under Sir John Cope at Preston-
pans, had penetrated a short distance into England; but finding the people
unanimous against him, he was compelled to fall back rapidly into Scotland.
On his return he routed General Hawley at Falkirk, but the approach of the
duke of Cumberland put an end to his triumph. He retreated before the
royal army, and at last the hostile forces met in the field of Culloden to de-
cide the fate of the kingdom. The Scotch fought with accustomed bravery,
but the English prevailed, and the unfortunate youth escaped with difficulty
from the battle where he left three thousand of his misguided adherents
dead. Though a large reward was offered for the head of the illustrious
fugitive, who had thus to combat against want and temptation, yet the
peasants of Scotland pitied his misfortunes, and even those of his enemies
who were acquainted with his retreat, kept inviolate the fatal secret, and
while they condemned his ambition, commiserated his distresses. He at last
escaped to St. Maloes, and never again revisited the British dominions,—
dying at Florence in 1788.

which had been projected, could not within themselves be carried forward by the colonies. It has been already stated that eight battalions of regular troops had been promised by the parent government, to rendezvous at Louisburg. The ministers had not specified the contingent of troops required from the respective colonies, contenting themselves by announcing the wish of the king that the total levies should not fall short of five thousand men;[1] but, fired with ambition to preserve the laurels they had won at Cape Breton, the provinces vied with each other in putting forth their strength for the achievement of a yet greater exploit, and the forces embodied with alacrity exceeded by far the expectations entertained at home. New Hampshire voted to raise one thousand men, and more if they could be enlisted—with a bounty of thirty pounds currency and a blanket to each recruit.[2] Of this number eight hundred were ready for embarkation by the first of July. Massachusetts voted three thousand five hundred men; Connecticut one thousand; and Rhode Island three hundred. But such was the spirit of the people that a yet larger number were actually enlisted. These all were destined for Louisburg, and thence for the assault of Quebec. For the forces to be directed upon Crown Point and Montreal, New York raised sixteen hundred men; New Jersey five hundred; Pennsylvania four hundred, though not by the act of its Quaker government, but by a popular act unsanctioned by its executive; Maryland three hundred; and Virginia one hundred;—making the grand total of provincials eight thousand two hundred. But of the promised assistance from England, two regiments only were sent; and these from Gibraltar, to relieve the New England men who had garrisoned Louisburg from the day of the conquest. Of other reinforcements none came; neither the general who was to command; nor fleet; nor orders. The New Eng-

---

[1] Grahame.

[2] Belknap states the number thus; but Hutchinson, in a note, affirms that New Hampshire voted to raise only five hundred.

land levies were mustered and prepared for embarkation,— the transport vessels, moreover, being in readiness to receive them. But their ardor, after weeks of cruel suspense, was doomed to a sad disappointment by the inaction of ministers. Admiral Warren, after his visit with Pepperell to Boston for consultation with Mr. Shirley, had sailed for England. It was now mid-summer, and neither troops nor tidings arriving from home, it was evident that the season was already too far advanced to allow the farther prosecution of that branch of the expedition destined against Quebec; since it was impossible that a fleet could now reach Louisburg from England in season to justify an attempt to ascend the St. Lawrence. Under these circumstances, although not without deep chagrin, that important feature of the enterprise was abandoned. The strange inaction of the parent government on that occasion, has been variously, though never satisfactorily accounted for. That a feeling of jealousy at the growing strength of the colonies, was awakened in England by the conquest of Louisburg, had been apparent almost from the moment of its fall; and cotemporary politicians were not wanting, who attributed the inaction of 1746 to a feeling on the part of ministers, that it might after all be as well to allow Canada unconquered to remain as a check upon its young and vigorous Anglo-Saxon neighbor. The excuse offered, has been, that ministers had reason to suspect that the armament which the French were ostensibly preparing for the reconquest of Cape Breton, and possibly for the invasion of some of the English colonies, was in reality intended for the invasion of Great Britain itself.[1] Be all this as it may, it was still believed that by uniting the Eastern levies with the forces collecting in New York for a descent upon Crown Point, a combined movement might be made in that direction which could not well fail of success. The New England forces were accordingly directed to hold themselves in readiness to concentrate upon Albany.

---

[1] Grahame.

But this scheme in its turn, was disconcerted, and the anticipated march for Albany was arrested by serious alarms from the opposite direction. It was known that France had been making great preparations,—not, as some have affected to believe, for the invasion of England, but for the recovery of Louisburg, and the conquest of Nova Scotia,—with the ulterior design, as was apprehended, of ravaging the sea coasts of the English colonies, from Annapolis-Royal to Georgia.[1] The vigilance with which Rochelle, where the preparations were making, had been watched by the English, had not prevented the enemy's fleet from getting to sea, which it succeeded in accomplishing on the twenty-second of June. And although the English fleet, destined for the interception of the French, and also for Louisburg, had put to sea several times, it had been driven back as many, being utterly unable to get to the westward. It was commanded by Lestock, an admiral in whom, certainly, no great confidence ought to have been reposed. The fleet of the French was commanded by the Count D'Anville, numbering, as it was affirmed, seventy sail, fourteen of which were ships of the line; thirty were men of war of a smaller size; the remainder of the force, consisting of fire-ships, bombs, tenders, and transports for eight thousand troops,[2] "and a formidable apparatus of artillery and military stores."[3] In anticipation of D'Anville's arrival, accounts were received in Boston that a French officer named Ramsay, had collected a force of seventeen hundred Canadian troops and Indians, to coöperate with the French admiral, which force was even then threatening Annapolis-Royal, while the Acadians were also known to be rife for a revolt. In order, therefore, to prevent the loss of Nova Scotia, the orders for marching to Albany were countermanded, and the troops directed

---

[1] Hutchinson.

[2] Ibid.

[3] Grahame. This author greatly reduces the number of disciplined troops on board D'Anville's fleet, from the statement of Hutchinson and other provincial historians—making it no more than three thousand.

to embark for Annapolis. Before, however, the embarkation had actually taken place, news of D'Anville's arrival at Chebucto Bay in Nova Scotia was received, and the whole country was thereby thrown into a state of consternation. "England was not more alarmed by the Spanish Armada in 1588, than Boston and the other North American sea ports were by the arrival of this fleet in their neighborhood."[1] It was not supposed that so formidable an armament as that of D'Anville, to equip which the whole power of France had been exerted for many months, could be destined alone against Louisburg. A recapture of that important post would only be the prelude to a sweeping attack upon the entire sea-board; and feeling themselves neglected, if not deserted by the parent government, as though willing to see the colonies sacrificed, all thoughts of sending away any of their forces were at once abandoned. Shirley was a man of energy, enjoying in a high degree the confidence of the people; and he bore himself in the crisis in a manner worthy of his position and his character. The first intelligence of D'Anville's arrival upon the coast, had filled the public mind, wearied and discouraged by the disappointments of the season, with dismay. But the elasticity of the New England character was soon manifested by the return of all the courage and resolution necessary to enable its possessors to look danger in the face and to meet it. Under the lead of Shirley, therefore, inspired by his example, the whole energies of New England were immediately directed to the now paramount object of self-defence,—to which end all hands were at once engaged in putting the country in the most commanding attitude. The troops which had been destined, first for a descent upon Canada and next for the defence of Nova Scotia, found sufficient employment at home, as a matter of course, in strengthening the defences of the coast, by repairing dilapidated forts and building new ones. Nor were they left to labor with unaugmented

---

[1] Hutchinson.

numbers. The militia spontaneously left their homes, and their ripening harvests, seized their arms, and within a few days, to the number of more than six thousand, marched into Boston, while an additional six thousand more were promised from Connecticut in the event of an actual invasion.[1]

Governor Clinton had appointed the twentieth of July as the day for meeting the Six Nations in council at Albany. He arrived there himself on the twenty-first; but as the city was afflicted with small-pox, and also at the same time with a malignant bilious fever, his excellency, not having had the former disease, deferred his landing until the following day,—not making it then in the town but at the fort. Whether the governor's quarrel with De-Lancey, had or had not served to alienate from him any other members of the council, does not appear; and the fact that the latter could prevail upon none of its members to accompany him to Albany, excepting Doctor Colden and Mr. Livingston, is left unexplained. Major Rutherford of the council being already at Albany in the discharge of his military duties, enabled the governor, though with the smallest number allowed by his majesty's commission, to form a council board for the transaction of business.

The cause of DeLancey's quarrel with the governor has been attributed to his own native arrogance; to an overweening family pride, engendered by the elevation of his brother-in-law, Sir Peter Warren; and also to his reliance upon the patronage of his former tutor, Doctor Harris, bishop of York, who was soon afterward elevated to the archbishopric of Canterbury.[1] On his arrival in the colony, Mr. Clinton had found the chief justice omnipotent with the assembly, and being himself fond of his ease, and caring more for the emoluments than for the glory of official station, the governor had to a great

---

[2] Smith,—who makes Doctor Harris at this time archbishop of Canterbury, which is not correct. Dr. H. was not advanced to the primacy until the following year, 1747.

extent yeilded the direction of the government to this ambitious minister. Every thing went smoothly enough between them, until after the governor in a moment of incaution, had renewed DeLancy's commission as chief justice, during good behavior,—or, in other words, for life. " He now began to dictate rather than to advise. Dining one day with Mr. Clinton, and insisting upon some favorite point with great imperiousness, the governor, who had so long suffered himself to be led, refused on this occasion to be driven. The chief justice then arose and left him; declaring, with an oath, that he would make his administration uneasy for the future. His excellency replied he might do his worst. Thus they parted, nor were they ever afterward reconciled."[1] The governor's confidence was immediately transferred to Doctor Colden, in whom it was reposed to the end of his administration.

But notwithstanding the preparations made in anticipation of his arrival, the governor found no Indians at Albany to meet him, save two straggling Onondagas, and one Oneida warrior; all three of whom had arrived on the same day with his excellency, from the north, bringing with them two French scalps which they had boldly taken at the very gate of Fort St. Frederick—Crown Point. On presenting these trophies to the governor, the leader of the party made a formal speech, as belligerent as could be desired, declaring that the murders committed by the French had been suffered to remain unavenged until his

---

[1] See *Letter to a Nobleman*, being a review of the military operations in North America from 1753 to 1756, the authorship of which was attributed to Governor Livingston, of New Jersey, and his friends Messrs. Smith and Scott, lawyers, of New York. Smith has since been known as the historian of New York; and the coincidences between portions of this letter and passages of his history, are so numerous and striking, as to warrant the conclusion that he must have shared in writing the former. The letter, which is long, may be found in the fourth volume of *Mass. Hist. Collections*.

Still in forming an estimate of the character of Mr. DeLancey, as well as of other individuals mentioned in this letter, great allowance should be made for the intense political rancor which its authors cherished against the **personages** therein assailed.

heart could bear it no longer; and he had therefore himself determined to open for his brethren the path of revenge. The scalps had been taken at noon-day, within two hundred steps of the fort. The report of their guns startled the garrison, and a party of soldiers sallied forth in pursuit; but having forgotten their arms in their haste, and being consequently obliged to run back after them, the Indians were enabled to make good their retreat. They were each rewarded with strouds and a laced hat,— the leader receiving in addition a fine laced coat and a silver breast-plate. The governor at the chief warrior's suggestion favored him with a new name, signifying *The-opener-of-the-path*. Proud of his distinction, the warrior then informed his excellency that his two associates, together with a River Indian, were going upon the war-path again; and were it not that he supposed he could render better service in the council, he should go against the enemy with them.[1] No other Indians having arrived to meet the governor, and the reports from the interpreters who had been sent to the cantons of the Six Nations being exceedingly discouraging, the Path-opener, who proved to be a very faithful fellow, volunteered upon an embassy to bring the Indians to the council himself, not doubting that he should to a considerable extent be successful.

For nearly a month the prospect of procuring a general attendance of the Indians, was discouraging. Within a day or two of the incident just recorded, another party of six or seven Indians, previously sent by the commissioners of Indian affairs to lurk about in the vicinity of Crown Point, returned without having met with any success, and with the loss of two of their number, made prisoners by the enemy. One of these, however, had been released through the interposition of the Caughnawagas in the service of the French. It was the impression of these spies that the enemy was strong at Fort St. Frederick, both in

---
[1] Minutes of the council board.

regular troops and Indians. This unpleasant intelligence was confirmed very soon afterward by the return from the same region, of a party of sixteen Mohawks, who had been sent thither to reconnoitre the enemy's works by Mr. Johnson,—whose active agency in the Indian department was now about first to be brought into requisition. These Indians added the expression of their belief, from the extent of the enemy's preparations at Crown Point, that an expedition was on foot against Schenectady and the white settlements farther up the Mohawk valley, and possibly against Albany itself. These reports were strengthened by letters from Mr. Johnson to the governor, and also by advices from the officer commanding the small English garrison kept in the Mohawk country. Mr. Clinton, however, attached less importance to these reports than those did who communicated them; believing them to have been sent abroad by the French to deter the Indians from gathering in the council at Albany. He thus wrote to Johnson; endeavoring at the same time, by the offer of liberal rewards, to persuade the last mentioned Indian party to return to the neighborhood of Crown Point, but without success,—the Indians insisting that they must return to their homes, to inform their relatives and friends of what they had heard and seen. Mr. Johnson likewise thought there were serious grounds for alarm; writing to the governor that the white settlers for twenty miles above him, and below to Schenectady, had deserted the country. Of his own property in jeopardy, he had eleven thousand bushels of wheat and other grain; and he asked the favor of a small detachment of troops for his protection. A lieutenant and thirty men were immediately sent to him; and a company of militia was likewise added to the upper Mohawk castle to assist the Indians in adding to the strength of that defence.[1] It will appear in the course of the present chapter that the apprehensions of an invasion from Fort St. Frede-

---

[1] Manuscript correspondence of Clinton and Johnson.

rick, were not altogether idle, although it did not take exactly the anticipated direction.

But the Six Nations came not to the council, and the summer was wearing rapidly away; while, to increase the embarrassment of Mr. Clinton, the proposition from Governor Shirley for an immediate expedition against Crown Point had been acceded to on the fourth of August, and the information of a change in Shirley's purpose, rendered imperative by the threatened invasion of the seaboard by the French, had not been received at Albany. The prospect was indeed far from cheering in many respects. The storm of war lowered darkly in the northern horizon. A company of rangers, belonging to Albany, enrolled for the express purpose of traversing the frontier to watch the movements of the enemy, notwithstanding the danger that threatened their own fire-sides, refused to go again upon duty unless the governor would become personally responsible for their pay, at the rate of three shillings each per diem, and also for their subsistence. Indignant at their conduct, and believing that men thus mercenary, when even their own family altars were in jeopardy, could not be safely trusted, Mr. Clinton accepted the services, voluntarily tendered, of Captains Langdon and Tiebout, with their respective companies of new levies. A few of the reluctant Albanians were taken as guides for these generous volunteers; but whenever any signs of hostile Indians were discovered, the heroic guides were sure, either by discharging their guns, or by making other noises, to give the alarm and enable the foe to escape;—thus avoiding the danger themselves, but at the same time defeating the purpose in view. The temper of the Six Nations, with a few individual exceptions, was bad, and apparently growing worse.[1] Notwithstanding the unwearied efforts of the English to

---

[1] Dunlop in quoting Colden, in regard to the discontents among the Six Nations at this time, says: "It was owing to the misconduct of those who were entrusted by the government with the management of Indian affairs;" adding: "The Indian agent was Mr. Johnson." It was not so. Johnson's appointment to that agency took place afterward.

CHAP. V.
1746.

counteract the influence of the Jesuit missionaries among them, yet those crafty ecclesiastics had obtained a hold upon their affections, which it seemed all but impossible to break; and fresh evidences were received by the governor, almost daily, disclosing the unwelcome fact that the Iroquois, if not again balancing which side of the contest to espouse, were more strongly than ever resolved upon maintaining an attitude of neutrality. The messengers dispatched to the Indian country, to persuade them to attend the council, had met with very indifferent success. One of them had fallen sick by the way. Several of the influential chiefs had again been visiting Canada, and were in full communication with the Caughnawagas of the St. Lawrence. These were active in preventing the convocation. The messengers had passed thirteen days among the Oneidas without making any perceptible impression; and the Cayugas met the governor's invitation at first with a flat refusal. The Mohawks, living in the closest proximity to the English, were for a considerable time equally reluctant to join in the council, and several of the chiefs at the upper castle peremptorily refused; nor in all candor can it be denied that their reasons at once attested their political sagacity and the soundness of their judgment. "It was," they said, "a war between the Englsh and the French, in which the Indians had no interest. Those nations could at any time make peace; but it was not so with the Indians. Once involved in the war, they could not make up the quarrel among themselves, but must continue the contest until one or the other party was destroyed." These views were encouraged by the emissaries of the French, who, entertaining little expectation of being able to engage the Iroquois upon their own side, were content to urge them strongly to neutrality. "It is your interest," artfully said the Jesuits, "not to suffer either the French or the English to be absolute masters, for in that case, your slavery to one or the other, will be inevitable." Yet it was not doubted that some of the chiefs had been gained entirely to the French, and were even then ready to strike the heads of the English.

It was in this critical exigency that Mr. Clinton determined to avail himself, in the Indian department, of the services of Mr. Johnson,—services, for the discharge of which he was already exceedingly well qualified from the intimate knowledge he had acquired of their language, their character and customs, and also from the confidence they reposed in him, and his consequent extensive popularity among them. These qualifications of Mr. Johnson for that delicate branch of the public service were well known to Mr. Clinton; and inasmuch as Colonel Schuyler, son of the celebrated *Quider*, and head of the board of Indian commissioners at Albany, had espoused the side of DeLancey in his opposition to the governor, while Johnson had manifested a disposition to sustain the latter, the road to preferment was already open.[1] Indeed there seems to have been a serious misunderstanding between the governor and the Indian commissioners several months before, the latter having written to his excellency on the seventeenth of the previous April, that "as their proceedings give so little satisfaction to him, they beg to be excused from any farther trouble."[2] Mr. Johnson, therefore, already a correspondent and a favorite of the governor, now succeeded Colonel Schuyler in the management of the Indians; although the sincere affection of the latter for the family of their old friend *Quider*, continued long afterward. It is from this point, that the long official career of the young Irish adventurer, William Johnson,—a career equally brilliant and honorable,—takes its date.

The commissioners having neglected to send messages to the Æsopus and Minisink Indians—tribes inconsiderable and not very reliable,—and also to the clans dispersed along the upper Susquehanna and its tributaries,—on the

---
[1] Smith.
[2] Manuscript letter preserved in the minutes of the council.

CHAP. fourth of August interpreters with suitable belts were dis-
V.
patched to those scattered peoples. Meantime a change
1746. favorable to the wishes of the English had been produced
among the Senecas from an unexpected quarter. It happened that while the messengers of the governor were
among the Senecas, a party of twenty Chickasaws arrived
at their castle, with a request " that the Senecas would
show them the way into Canada." The Chickasaws had
always been enemies to the French ; and an expedition of
five hundred men sent against them from Canada, four
years before, had been defeated in the Chickasaw country,
almost to annihilation. These young envoys referred to
the subject in a manner characteristic of the race. Addressing the Senecas, they said :—" Four years ago the
French had been so kind as to visit their country, and
leave among them four hundred muskets. Those muskets
however, by constant use, had been worn out ; and as their
friends the French had not thought proper to bring them
any more, the Chickasaws had determined to go to Canada
and bring away some new ones." It was their desire
that the Senecas would show them the way, and if they
would promise to do so, the young men said they would
return home and bring back about four hundred of their
stout-hearted fellows to find the new guns and bring them
away. Encouraged by this unlooked for alliance from
the south, and also by assurances that other remote nations of the forest were in no good humor with the French,
the Senecas, in considerable numbers, changed their
minds, and determined to meet the governor in Albany.

Mr. Johnson was at the same time exerting himself with
the utmost activity to dispel the clouds resting upon the
moody brows of the Mohawks, and to revive their obviously waning friendship for the English. Familiar with their
language and manners, he assumed their garb, and mingled
among them as one of their own people. He entered
readily into their athletic exercises, their games, and all
the varieties of their pastimes,—prompted, it is likely, in

part, by his love of the picturesque and of wild adventure, and in part, it is but just to believe, by the sincere affection he had imbibed for the race. Flattered by his association with them upon terms of such generous equality,—not for an instant dreaming that there could be ought of simulation in his conduct toward them, as perhaps there was not,—the Mohawks adopted him as a member of their nation, and invested him with the rank of a war-chief.[1] In this capacity he assembled them at festivals, and appointed frequent war-dances, by way of exciting them to engage actively in the war. His success, considering the sourness of their temper, and the spirit of uneasiness that had prevailed among them for so many months, was far greater than had been anticipated by the commissioners; for he not only persuaded numbers of the war-chiefs and sachems to repair to Albany and hear what the governor had to say, but he likewise engaged many of their young warriors unreservedly to join the army in the proposed campaign.

Thus stood matters at the Mohawk castles when the interpreters from the more distant members of the Confederacy arrived with such of the sachems and warriors of those nations as they had succeeded in bringing to attend the council. But here a new difficulty arose. A political feud had existed among the Confederates for a length of time, causing a division into two distinct parties,—the Mohawks, Onondagas and Senecas forming one division, and the Oneidas, Cayugas and Tuscaroras the other,—the last mentioned being numerically the weaker. On the arrival of the warriors and counsellors of the latter, it appeared that they had by no means determined to espouse the cause of the English, and they censured the Mohawks for having committed themselves so far without the previous consent of the other Confederates. The Mohawks replied with warmth. They were less numerous than the other nations, it was true; but they declared that their warriors were all

---

[1] In connection with this custom of adoption, see Appendix, No. 1, to this volume.

men;[1] and in the event of a trial of strength, the Mohawks might not be found in reality the weakest. Chafed at the rebuke of their fellows, they moreover now boldly avowed that their hearts were truly English; and the contention at length became so sharp, that the opposing factions would not consent to move in company to Albany,—the Mohawks marching by themselves on one side of the river, while their opponents took the other. Both divisions entered Albany on the eighth of August,—the Mohawks in full panoply, at the head of whom marched their new war-captain, Johnson, upon whom they had conferred the name of WAR-RAGH-I-YA-GEY, signifying, it is believed, *Superintendent of affairs*[2]—dressed, painted and plumed as required by the dignity of his rank. In passing Fort Frederick at Albany, salutes were exchanged, the Indians firing their muskets, and the fort its artillery. The chiefs and sachems were then received in the hall of the fortress, and served with refreshments.

All the Mohawk sachems but three, had been persuaded by Mr. Johnson heartily to engage in the cause. One of these dissentients was Aaron, of the Lower castle, who, with others, had made a visit in the preceding spring to the French governor in Canada. The two others were of the Canajoharie, or Upper castle. Both were sachems of influence, one belonging to the *Bear tribe*, and the other to the *Tortoise*,—the latter being first in dignity. Great pains were taken at private interviews with these sachems, to bring them into the cause of the English. The task, though difficult, was ultimately accomplished through the instrumentality of the Rev. Mr. Barclay, an English missionary residing among the Mohawks, and the exertions of Doctor

---

[1] The Six Nations reckoned all other Indian nations women in comparison with themselves.

[2] The signification of Johnson's Indian name is not known with certainty. Some authorities have given as its meaning—"one who unites two peoples together." The interpretation however given in the text, reasoning from the analysis or the supposed analysis of the word, appears to be nearer the truth.

Colden, who, during former visits to the Canajoharie castle, had contracted an acquaintance with those reluctant sachems. The doctor had indeed some twenty years before, been adopted into their clan, and invested with a new name. Still, there were other difficulties to be adjusted, and it was not until the nineteenth day of August that a public council could be safely opened. Meantime Governor Clinton had been attacked by fever, and the duty of conducting the council devolved upon Dr. Colden. The commissioners in attendance from Massachusetts, were Colonel Wendell and Mr. Welles. Connecticut was not represented.

The opening speech delivered by Mr. Colden, had been prepared to be spoken by the governor. After announcing, in the usual form, that the council had been called to confirm the covenant chain, and all former treaties and engagements, it recapitulated the history of the war, referring to the cruelties of the enemy, and reminding the Indians of their stipulation the year before, that if satisfaction for those cruelties should not be promptly rendered, they would take up the hatchet and make immediate use of it. But the enemy, so far from having made the least reparation for their wrongs, had repeated their cruelties on the frontiers of New England, by the destruction and massacre of Saratoga, and by barbarous murders in the very precincts of Albany. Yet, knowing these facts, the Six Nations had not fulfilled their promises, an immediate compliance with which was now necessary, if they would show that those promises came when made from the bottom of their hearts.

The speech next announced the determination of "the king their father," to effect the subjugation of Canada, and informed the Indians of the preparations making for that object. They were assured in the most confident terms, that forces sufficient for effecting the conquest at a blow, had been levied and were already in motion. Those from Virginia, Maryland, Pennsylvania, New Jersey and New York, destined to proceed to Montreal, they would soon see in Albany; while the governor was in the hourly expectation of hearing of the arrival of the promised ships and troops from England;—" a great army of experienced soldiers,—who, with the New England levies, were to assemble at Cape Breton;—after which the attack upon Canada would be made on all sides, both by sea and land."[1]

Yet, in order to complete the preparations for so great an enterprise, the Six Nations were required to join all their forces with the English, in doing which they would have a glorious opportunity of increasing their renown by aiding in the conquest of the French,—a perfidious people, who were even caressing the enemies of the Six Nations, desiring nothing so much as to see their name obliterated.

They were next reminded of the many injuries they themselves had received at the hands of the French, especially by their repeated invasions of their territory, as at Onondaga, and the Seneca country. The mischiefs inflicted by them upon the Mohawks in their successive invasions were recounted; the story of the massacre of their warriors at Cadaracqui, was rehearsed; while the cruel burnings of some of their braves at Montreal, was not forgotten. Having thus kindled a spirit of vengeance in their bosoms, as could be read in the flashing eye, and the distended nostril, the ambition of the warriors was next artfully excited by a recital of their own brave exploits when carrying their arms into Canada:—" If your fathers," said the speech, " could now rise out of their graves, how would their hearts leap for joy to see this day, when so glorious an opportunity is put into your hands to revenge all the injuries your country has received from the French, and be never more exposed to their treachery and deceit." As the true sons of such renowned and brave ancestors, animated by the same spirit for their country's glory, and the same desire of revenge, they were invited to share in

---

[1] So ignorant was the governor of the true state of things at the moment in New England, where all expectation of the grand combined attack had been relinquished; Boston not more than two hundred miles distant, and yet the governor of New York was left in ignorance to make these fallacious promises to the Indians.

the honor of vanquishing the enemies alike of themselves and the English; provisions, arms, clothing, being promised in abundance, and ample protection for their wives and children during their absence. They were farther reminded of several murders of their white brethren by the enemy's Indians, committed even since their arrival at the council-fire. These additional insults they were called upon to avenge; and in conclusion a belt was given as an assurance of the intention of the English to live and die with their red brethren.

The speech was well received. At the end of each sentence one of the chiefs called out—" YO-HAY ;"—"*do you hear?*" and the response of approbation was general. When, moreover, after its close, the war-belt was thrown down, the significant act was followed by a war-shout, unanimous and hearty. The council-fire was then raked up to give the forest counsellors time for deliberation. Three days afterward they announced that their answer was ready; and on the following day, August twenty-fourth, the governor himself was able to meet them in council for its reception.

The fire having been rekindled at the appointed time, an Onondaga sachem spoke to the following effect—the speech of course abounding in the figurative expressions inseparable from Indian eloquence and diplomacy. It opened by informing the council that the Missesagues had united with them for the purposes immediately in hand, as a seventh nation. The Six Nations were rejoiced that the English were wiping away their sorrowful tears, opening their throats, and washing clean the bloody bed. They also spoke of the silver covenant chain formed of old, which both were holding fast. They acknowledged having received the hatchet the year before, and their pledge to use it in the event of further provocations and murders by the French;—admitted that the bloody affair of Saratoga, and other acts of hostility, demanded the fulfilment of the pledge; and they farther declared their readiness "from the bottom of their hearts," to use their hatchets against the French and their children,—the Canada Indians meaning,—from that day forward. As an earnest of their sincerity in this declaration, the war-belt was thrown down with great emphasis both of attitude and expression. They assured the governor of the entire union of their clans in this declaration, and hoped the governors of the different English colonies would be as closely united in the prosecution of the war as themselves. In regard to the wiles of the French priests against which they had been admonished, they averred that their blood boiled at the manner in which they had formely been treated by them, and being now at war with their nation, those priests would no more dare to come. The Six Nations would have no further use for them than to roast them. As to the Missesagues, whom they now commended to the English as their allies, they numbered eight hundred warriors, all being determined to join in the common cause.[1] In conclusion the chiefs said they would leave some of their warriors with the troops of the governor, while they themselves returned to their castles to send down a greater number.

With this speech closed the proceedings of that day, and the next was appointed for the delivery of the presents sent to them from the king, and also by the governors of Virginia and Massachusetts. When on the twenty-fifth the presents were brought forth for delivery, the Albanians remarked that they were much more valuable than any that had been previously given to the Indians. So, also, thought the recipients, a Mohawk chieftain, of his own volition, addressing his brethren thus :—" You see how you are here treated,—really like brethren. The governor of Canada treats not his Indians so, but sets them on like dogs, and they run without thought or consideration. You see what a noble present is made to you. If the governor of Canada should sieze all the goods in that country, he could not

---

[1] The Missesagues then lived at Detroit, between Lakes Erie and Huron.

make such a present."[1] In the division of the presents among the nations represented, two-eighths thereof were voluntarily assigned to the Missesagues. On the day following, being the twenty-sixth, the war-kettle was put over the fire, and in the evening the solemn war-dance was performed, in presence of the governor and many other gentlemen. The warriors were all painted for the occasion, and the appropriate songs were sung with affecting pathos.

Before the Indians dispersed, the governor had private conferences with the leading chiefs, and rendered the covenant chain yet brighter by making further presents. The two Missesagues present were particularly friendly. One of them assured his excellency that among the Indians yet farther than themselves in the interior, there was a growing dislike to the French, reporting a transaction strongly corroborating his assertion. It was to the effect that a party of sixty Frenchmen had lately been sent to one of those distant nations to persuade them to take up the hatchet against the English. They accepted the hatchet,—and immediately put the whole party presenting it to death. In conclusion, the Missesagues promised on returning home to bring as many of those distant nations as they could upon the war-path. Unfortunately, however, both sickened of the small-pox and died,—one of them not being able to depart for the fair hunting grounds with resignation until the governor had promised to send his mother the first French scalp that should be taken. His companion at the council died on his way home,—the Six Nations at once providing for their wives and children, who had accompanied them to Albany.

---

[1] This account of the Indian negotiations of 1746, I have drawn from the copious details of Doctor Colden. Smith, the historian, intimates that the presents actually given by the governor, were small and unsatisfactory: and charges that Colden wrote a partial account for his patron's vindication—his excellency having been accused of embezzling large portions of the presents. This imputation is unwarrantable. Colden's account was published in the course of a few weeks after the council closed, and, had it been untrue, and the Indian's speech a fiction, the dishonesty would have been exposed at the time.

The alliance, offensive and defensive with the Iroquois, having thus been satisfactorily renewed, Mr. Clinton next turned his attention to the Muh-he-ka-neok, or River Indians,—a small nation residing at Stockbridge, in the colony of Massachusetts,—composed of remnants of the Mohegans, Narragansetts and Schaghticokes, together with various other smaller clans and tribes from Connecticut, who had been formed into a community some ten years before by a philanthropic clergyman,—the Rev. Mr. Sergeant. With these remnants of various peoples who had been peeled and scattered in New England, a council was also holden, the result of which was satisfactory to all. They readily consented to engage in the war, concluding their speech, however, in words equivalent to a condition that they were not to be forgotten on the conclusion of a peace: "When you Christians," said they, "are at war, you make peace with one another; but it is not so with us. Therefore we depend upon you to take care of us; in confidence of which we now take up the hatchet, and will make use of it."[1] They were dismissed with presents.

Lingering in Albany yet a full month longer, Mr. Clinton was enabled to receive in person the Indians from the Susquehanna country, whose principal town was at Oghquago. These Indians to the number of sixty warriors, exclusive of the usual train of old men, women and children,—never-failing attendants upon important councils,—arrived in charge of Captains Vrooman and Staats, about the tenth of September, and sent the governor on the next day. They had responded to the summons with alacrity,—complaining nevertheless at the lateness of their invitation, and regretting that the negotiations with the Six Nations should have been concluded before their arrival. Toward the Six

---

[1] Smith very improperly classes the River Indians—called by him after the Dutch orthography Mohickanders,—with the Esopus and Susquehanna Indians, and denounces them as "dastardly tribes," to whom Governor Clinton "gave presents for promises which they never meant to perform." Toward the Muh-kuk-kan-cok, their denunciation is most unjust. They were always true to the English, and poured out their blood freely for them.

Nations they appeared to entertain feelings bordering upon jealousy. It was a shame, they said, that these Indians had not sooner used the hatchet placed in their hands a year before. They had themselves sometimes been deceived as to the progress of the war, but they were now ready to join in the contest,—adding " We know several roads to Canada, and we want to see the hatchet that we may grasp it." Whereupon the governor threw down a cutlass, which was eagerly seized by one of the chiefs, and they all commenced the war-dance,—declaring that "they should keep firmly hold of the hatchet, and were resolved to use it." A sudden alarm, caused by an incursion of the enemy's Indians, and the murder of a non-commissioned officer in the very suburbs of Albany, served to test both the fidelity and the courage of these Indians, by the alertness with which they spontaneously went in pursuit of the hostile party. Several of their number remained in Albany to act as scouts or guides, as occasion might require; the residue being dismissed with presents—having promised the services of six hundred braves to the governor whenever he should summon them to the field. The governor did not question the sincerity of their professions; but wrote to Mr. Johnson the sixteenth of September, that "they looked as though they were determined to be hearty in our cause," and "he expected their warriors to join him in about ten days." It is astonishing, nay, inexplicable, how completely Mr. Clinton and his counsellors were left in the dark, down even to the date of the letter just cited, as to the situation of affairs in New England. In this letter he tells Johnson that he talked to the Indians "in no other light than that of going immediately to fighting," and adds : " Five hundred troops from the Jersies, and four hundred from Philadelphia, have arrived here, besides several more companies from New York, which amount to over two thousand men. More are expected; and as I hear that the fleet was seen off the banks of Newfoundland, I conclude they are before now at Louisburg,—having sent, some time since, an express to Boston not yet returned, and I think he must be detained on that account."[1] The governor also in the same letter informs Johnson that he has sent the fourteen Susquehanna warriors who had remained behind, against the enemy, attached to a company of sixty men under the command of Captain Staats, and from whom he hoped to hear a good account.

The Canadian governor had not been an inattentive observer of Mr. Clinton's preparations for meeting the Indians. He had indeed adroitly attempted to prevent the gathering, by sending a number of Caughnawaga emissaries among them, with pacific overtures.[2] The Onondaga captain, taken, as already related, at Crown Point, in July, was to accompany them, charged with a message from the governor to the effect, that although the warriors of the Six Nations had killed some of his people, yet he was willing to overlook the past, and "as an evidence of his love for them, he had sent back one of their people instead of eating his flesh." At the same time the Caughnawagas were charged "not to spill any more blood from Albany upward, but to turn their arms toward their inveterate enemies in New England. "There," said the French governor, "There is the place for you to gain honor now." But much to the surprise of the governor, the Caughnawagas declined the honor of the proposed mission, either as the bearers of intelligence, or menaces. "Such a course," they replied, "would only stir up the Six Nations, and bring them and all their allies to destroy you at once. They are not to be bullied by your words or arms; wherefore, father, we must leave you to go through this work by yourself." These sudden scruples of his allies, but that the French governor was doubtless well acquainted with the unstable and impulsive character of the Indians, must well nigh have confounded him. But the Caughnawagas nevertheless dispatched one of their number in company

---

[1] Manuscript letter, Clinton to Johnson.

[2] Idem in reply to a letter from Johnson.

with the returning captain, as the bearer of a message, not from the governor, but from themselves, to their former brethren, conjuring them by all their ancient ties of friendship, not to embark in a war against them, and begging them to give information of any plottings of Governor Clinton against them. They invited the Six Nations to visit them in council again at their seat on the St. Lawrence in the spring; and requested them to inform Governor Clinton that the French had eighteen hundred soldiers at Crown Point, ready for battle, but in which number were included eight castles of Ottawa Indians. It was on the return of the Mohawks from the council at Albany, that they were met by six of their own people as the bearers of this message, which they had received from the returning Onondaga prisoners,—the Caughnawaga messenger having ventured no farther than the confines of the Mohawk territory. But neither the message from their former brethren, nor the desires of the French governor, made the slightest impression upon the Six Nations, since they communicated both to their new war-captain, Johnson, without reserve or delay,—giving every desirable evidence of the good faith in which they had revived their English alliance.

It was suggested by some contemporary writers, that inasmuch as the governor of Canada asked only for the neutrality of the Six Nations, the dictates of humanity required an acquiescence on the part of the English. But whoever has studied the character of this remarkable variety of the human family,—especially of the Iroquois,—must be aware how difficult, if not how utterly impossible, it would have been *to keep them neutral*. The Iroquois were the aboriginals of all others, whose friendship and alliance was most strongly desired by both the principal belligerents, and whose possible hostility was anticipated with the greatest apprehension by both. Their position, stretching from the western shore of Lake Champlain to Lake Erie, placed them like a barrier between the French and English colonies, and enabled them to strike with sudden fury upon the borders of either, as they might elect. The most formidable in numbers, the most compactly disposed in their cantons, and the best governed of the savage race,—inured to war, and accustomed to conquest,—their name was a terror to the Indians from the country of the Natchez to the gulf of St. Lawrence. Their trade was war; and although they had for a season evinced a strong reluctance to engage in the contest then raging, yet the French were continually tampering with them, and their clergy had for a long period exercised great influence over them. They were themselves by no means ignorant of the importance of their position, nor of the important fact, that, as between the French and English colonies, they held the balance of power. How desirous they might be of making the most of their position, the English could not tell; nor had they any warrant, in the event of neglecting to secure their services beyond a peradventure themselves, that when the contest should become fierce, and the Indians should scent blood upon the breeze, they might not, in a moment of impulse, throw off their neutrality and strike suddenly in behalf of the French. Hence it is maintained that the English were by no means bound passively to allow the French to secure the advantage of a neutrality on the part of the Iroquois, the maintenance of which would be so extremely uncertain, and the benefits of which would enure solely to the party proposing and so strenuously urging it.

CHAPTER VI.
1746.

The governor of Canada was prompt in executing the purpose suggested to the Caughnawagas, of striking upon the borders of New England, the people of which he had designated as their most inveterate foes. Indeed the Indians in the French service had not waited for that suggestion, since from the opening of the spring, the whole New England frontier from the eastern border of New York, had been kept in a continuous state of alarm; their hamlets were often in flames; and their fields reddened with blood.

The New Hampshire border being the most exposed, was full of danger at every point. On the thirteenth of April, the Indians appeared at a township called Number-Four,[1] and took three men prisoners, and killed their cattle. Four days afterward a larger party of fifty attempted to surprise the fort at Upper Ashuelot,[2] hiding themselves in a swamp near by with the design of marching into the fort on the departure of the men to their field labors in the morning. But their ambuscade was discovered by a man who went forth very early in the morning, and their purpose frustrated. A skirmish took place in which a man and a woman were killed, and another man taken prisoner. On retreating, the Indians burned several houses and barns. Three days afterward a party of savages came to New Hopkinton, where was a block house guarded by several men. One of these going out very early to hunt, leaving his companions asleep, also left the door open,—a

---
[1] Since named Charlestown.
[2] Keene.

very convenient instance of carelessness,—for the lurking savages, who thereupon rushed in and made eight prisoners—four men, one woman and three children. On the second of May, Number-Four was revisited, and a party of women milking some cows, guarded by several soldiers, were fired upon. One man was killed, and two of the Indians mortally wounded by the return fire. Two days afterward, Contoocook[1] was visited by the enemy, by whom two men were killed, and a third taken prisoner. The same hostile party made two prisoners two days afterward at Lower Ashuelot,[2] but lost one of their number in another attempt upon the little fort at Upper Ashuelot. About the same time, a party of savages made an incursion into Bernardstown, in Massachusetts. They attacked a house garrisoned by only three men, but the duty of these was performed so effectively, that the enemy retreated with two of their warriors mortally wounded. On their way through Coleraine they ambuscaded a road near one of the forts, and fired upon a party consisting of a man, his wife and daughter, and two soldiers. The first was killed; and the woman and her daughter wounded. But on losing one of their number by the fire of the soldiers, the enemy made off.[3] On the twenty-fourth of May, a company of troops sent for the defence of the inhabitants, was drawn into an ambuscade in Number-Four, and in a smart skirmish which ensued five men were killed on each side—the Indians gaining the advantage of making a prisoner. A month afterward another spirited affair occurred at the same place. In this instance the dogs were the most vigilant sentinels, but for whom, Captains Stevens and Baker would probably have been drawn into a fatal ambuscade. The Indians having been discovered, the provincial detachment had the advantage of the first fire. After a brisk encounter, the Indians were driven

---

[1] Boscawen.
[2] Swansey.
[3] Hoyt's *Antiquities.*

away—leaving evidences of considerable loss. Only one of the provincials was killed, but there were five wounded. The bodies of several Indians were afterwards discovered, concealed in a swamp. Guns, hatchets, spears, and other warlike articles, were left by the Indians, the sale of which produced to the victors between seventy and eighty pounds.[1] On the twenty-fourth of June, two men were killed, and two taken prisoners at Fort Dummer. One of the prisoners killed an Indian before he was taken. Three days afterward a party of laborers were attacked in a field in Rochester, only twenty miles from Portsmouth. The men were unarmed. Four of them were killed, and the fifth, wounded, was made prisoner. He was taken into Canada, as the other prisoners had been, being carefully attended to on the way until his wounds were healed. A lad was likewise made prisoner in another part of the town—the men with whom he was at work, making their escape. Yet another man was killed in Rochester soon afterward. On the third of July, an ambuscade was discovered in Hinsdale, but the Indians were put to flight. One month afterward, they again revisited Number-Four, and killed two men and several cattle. Two men were surprised and taken on the sixth of August, at Contoocook; and a large party visited Penacook,[2] and formed an ambuscade for the purpose of attacking a congregation while at worship in their church. But observing that the men were well armed with carnal weapons, they delayed an attack until the next morning, when five were killed, and two taken prisoners.[3] Murders were also committed again in the neighborhood of Fort Dummer; at Hinsdale; in Winchester, Poquaig,[4] Greenfield; at Penacook, and in several other places. At Pen-

---

[1] Manuscript journal of Deacon Noah Webster.

[2] Concord.

[3] Belknap is the authority for several of these accounts of the border skirmishes of 1746. See also Hoyt's *Antiquities*.

[4] Afterward called Athol.

acook five persons were killed.[1] These hostile parties chiefly came from the St. Francis country, through Lake Memphremagog. The prisoners taken were carried into Canada, where some of them died, but the greater number were subsequently redeemed or exchanged.

But in addition to these partizan operations, painful to neighborhoods, yet more irritating than important in their influence upon the war, there was one of a more formidable character. It has already been seen that the French were concentrating a strong force at Crown Point; and it happened that at the very time when Governor Clinton was opening his conferences with the Six Nations,—a combined force of French and Indians was within so short a distance of Albany, that had the officers and citizens there assembled been aware of the fact, they would most likely have felt rather uneasy in their seats. On the breaking out of the war, the New England colonies had erected a chain of small works—stockades and block houses—along the frontiers of Maine and New Hampshire, from Saco to Charlestown,—thence down the Connecticut river to Greenfield. The old defences at the place last mentioned, and at Northfield, were repaired; and another cordon of similar works was extended from the Connecticut across the Hoosic mountain, to the territory now forming the towns of Adams and Williamstown; thence south through Pittsfield, Stockbridge and Sheffield, at each of which points stockades were erected, and also at Blanford, for the purpose of guarding the principal road from the east to Kinderhook and Albany. The general command of this territory, belonged to Colonel John Stoddart, of the Hampshire militia regiment; but the immediate command of the posts west of Hoosic mountain, was confided to Captain Ephraim Williams, whose headquarters were in a work of considerable strength, called Fort Massachusetts, upon the Hoosic river, within the bounds of what is now the town of Adams. Small but

---

[1] Hoyt's *Antiquities*.

active scouting parties were kept ranging from post to post; and such was their vigilance that the Massachusetts border suffered but little during the years 1744 and 1745, save by the two successive incursions of the enemy upon the Great Meadow settlement above Fort Dummer; in both of which a few persons were killed, and a few others carried into captivity. Irritated, however, by the loss of Louisburg, the French, with their dusky allies, became more active, as well as more savage, along the whole border, as the reader has seen in the rapid account just given of their incursions.

CHAP. VI.

1746.

But the largest demonstration of the enemy that season, was the descent of Rigaud de Vaudreuil from Crown Point, upon the post already described as Fort Massachusetts, which was invested by that officer about the middle of August, with a force of regular troops and Indians numbering nine hundred and sixty-five men. This was the extreme northwestern post belonging to the colony, whose name it bore, and was commanded, as heretofore stated, by Captain Ephraim Williams. This excellent officer, however, with the greater part of the force under his immediate command, was at Albany at the time of the invasion, having been ordered to join the proposed expedition so long in preparation for the conquest of Canada. Meantime the fort was left in charge of John Hawks, a soldier of approved courage and discretion, but whose rank was no higher than a sergeant. But higher honors were in reserve for him as the progress of history will disclose. The number of men in the garrison, was no more than thirty-five, eleven of whom were sick. This small force moreover was yet farther weakened before it was known that an enemy had arrived to besiege it, by detaching Doctor Thomas Williams, the surgeon, and thirteen men, with directions to make the best of their way through the wilderness to Deerfield on the Connecticut river, for ammunition and other supplies. By this reduction, the sergeant-commander was left with but eleven effective men; and when the great disparity of the respective forces is considered, to say nothing of other untoward circumstances, the defence he made of the post may be regarded as one of the most gallant affairs, of no greater magnitude, upon record. The enemy showed himself before the slender works on the nineteenth of August,—the very day on which Mr. Clinton opened his conferences with the Indians at Albany. The fort was most unfavorably situated for defence, its site having been designated by some one who must have been lamentably deficient in the science of war, since it stood in a low long meadow, commanded by heights in every direction. But although short of ammunition himself, Hawks was aware that the enemy had no artillery, and he determined to defend the post as long as he possibly could, in the expectation that the advance of so large a body of the enemy must be known very soon at Albany, and the possible hope that a competent force might be detailed from the main army to his relief. But the movement of M. de. Vaudreuil had been executed with such profound secrecy, that nothing of it was known at Albany.

The enemy commenced his attack at about nine o'clock in the morning, and continued it briskly until the same hour in the evening—approaching at times, within the range of small shot. The fire was returned with vigor and effect from the fort, until about one o'clock past meridian, when the sergeant discovered that his ammunition was so near exhaustion as to require an order that no man should fire save when a fair opportunity was presented of doing execution. Such an order was disheartening; but it was obeyed with advantage as was soon perceptible from the deliberation of every subsequent shot, and the obvious frequency with which they told. The men were sharp-shooters, and by singling out their objects among their assailants, many were brought down even at long shots,—some of them falling while standing, as they supposed, in perfect security. Two soldiers of the garrison only were wounded on that day. The fort was entirely surrounded during the night following,—the night itself being rendered hideous by the dismal howlings, and the warlike songs and revelries of the Indians. With the return of light the attack was renewed, and in the course of the forenoon, one of the brave fellows in the fort was killed. At twelve o'clock meridian, the assailants ceased firing, and an Indian was sent forward with a flag to request a parley. The invitation was acceded to, and the sergeant, accompanied by two or three of his comrades, repaired to the head quarters of the French commander, who offered honorable terms of capitulation. Hawks returned with the proposal to the fort, and convoked his little army as a council of war. Prayer for wisdom and direction from above was offered by Mr. Norton, their chaplain, whereupon in view of their exhausted magazine, and the fact that their number was reduced to eight effective men, it was resolved to accept the proffered terms and surrender. By those terms they were to be received as prisoners of war, and to be treated with humanity until ransomed or exchanged,—terms, moreover, which the French commander would not probably have granted, had he known either the weakness of the fort, or of the force defending it. There was also a farther stipulation that the prisoners should not be delivered into the hands of the Indians. The enemy took immediate possession of the fort and ran up their colors; but they nevertheless seemed in equal haste to depart, and actually set the works on fire before they had plundered the cellar of its stores.

The articles of capitulation were not strictly observed by M. Vaudreuil, and several of the prisoners were allotted to the savages, by whom one of them was killed. The others were all kindly treated, both by the French and their uncivilized allies. There were in the fort two women and several children,—to the number of the latter one being added on the second day of the march. But mother and child were kindly borne along by the Indians, and the little stranger brought thus rudely into the world, was baptized by the chaplain. The prisoners were taken to Crown Point, and thence to Canada,—the gallant sergeant being every where treated by the French officers as brave men should ever treat the brave. Arriving successively at Chamblee, Montreal and Quebec, they met with numbers of their countrymen in captivity; but they were themselves, for the most part, ultimately redeemed or exchanged, and enabled to return to their own homes. Sergeant Hawks with several of his companions, was shipped from Quebec to Boston. The number of the enemy killed or badly wounded during the siege, was forty-seven. After the capitulation, it was ascertained that the besiegers were lying in ambuscade in the neighborhood of the fort, watching for an opportunity to take it by surprise, at the time of Doctor Williams's departure in quest of supplies on the Connecticut river. They had probably no idea that the doctor's small party of thirteen had constituted more than one-third of the garrison; and they allowed the little platoon to pass without molestation, in order to prevent an alarm that would have discovered their presence and object.[1]

Remarkable was the conduct of the Indians in this affair toward the prisoners. It is a single bright spot of relief in the generally dark and bloody picture of savage warfare. But there was an episode to the siege and capture of the fort, of a deeply tragic character. Vaudreuil's Indians, numbering about fifty, crossed the Hoosic mountain, with the design of falling upon Deerfield. Having reconnoitred the village, however, an open attack was judged to be imprudent. They accordingly withdrew two miles south, and formed an ambuscade upon the margin of a meadow of newly-mown hay, for the purpose of rushing upon the haymakers when they should come out to their work. Their object was rather to make captives than to kill; and but

---

[1] My authority for the facts given in the present account of the chivalrous defence of Fort Massachusetts, is the unassuming manuscript journal of Sergeant Hawks himself, for which I am indebted to Dr. S. W. Williams, of Deerfield, grandson of Surgeon Williams mentioned in the text.

for an accident, that object would probably have been accomplished by the seizure of the laborers of two families, with several children, numbering in all ten persons, who came to the meadow in the morning as the savages had anticipated. Alarmed by the discharge of a gun aimed at a partridge by a fowler who happened to be shooting at no great distance from the place of their concealment, the Indians started up, and first killing the fowler, rushed down upon the laborers in the meadow. Those of the latter who were men, being armed, made a resolute stand for their own lives, and the defence of the children. A struggle, vigorous and fierce, ensued; but the disparity of force was great, and three of the men were killed and scalped. A daughter of one of the slain was likewise severely wounded by a blow from a tomahawk, and left upon the field as dead;—but she recovered, and lived to an advanced age. One of the lads fell into the hands of the Indians and was carried away,—the residue of the party making good their escape.[1]

Meantime the summer had passed away, and with it the best season for active operations against Crown Point and the French. General Gooch, who had been commissioned by the crown for the special service of conducting the expedition, had declined the appointment; and the chief command of the forces at Albany, had thus far devolved upon Governor Clinton.[2] With great pains and labor, the Iroquois Confederacy had finally been prevailed upon to take an efficient part in the contest, but there was not yet an immediate demand for their services in a body; although at this late day it seems strange that large numbers of them were not employed in connection with the rangers who had

---

[1] Hoyt's *Antiquities*.

[2] Major General Sir William Gooch was lieutenant-governor and governor of Virginia from 1727 to 1749. "He sustained an excellent character, and was popular in his administration." He had superior military talents, and commanded a division of the forces in the unsuccessful attack on Carthagena in 1740.

been sent out from Albany to scour the forests, and watch the motions of the enemy at the north. It certainly argues great negligence, somewhere, that so large a force as that led against Fort Massachusetts by M. Vaudreuil, could have made such a movement, approaching as it did within forty miles of Albany, without the fact being known at headquarters until after the invaders had retired. Yet it appears to have been so. Equally in the dark, moreover, was Mr. Clinton in regard to the state of affairs in New England; and on the sixteenth of September, timely advices not having been received from Shirley and Warren, the governor, with his council, came to the reluctant decision that the season for active military operations was so far advanced as to render an expedition, even against Crown Point, impracticable, and that nothing more could then be done than to make the necessary dispositions for the security of the frontiers.[1] Four days afterward letters were received both from Governor Shirley and the admiral, the former announcing that he had appointed General Waldo, of Massachusetts, to the command of the northern expedition, in the place of General Gooch.[2] But it was now too late; and the high hopes of the people were dashed with bitter disappointment. The parent government had entirely failed in every engagement. Neither a fleet of adequate force, nor the promised troops under Sir John Sinclair, had appeared; while the threatened invasion of the New England coast by France, had placed those colonies entirely on the defensive, and it now only remained for New York, instead of attempting a descent upon Crown Point, to prepare winter quarters for her own levies, and to adopt such measures as would afford the best security to her frontiers.

To this end Mr. Johnson was directed, on his return to the Mohawk castle, to organize war parties of the Indians, and send them to harrass the French settlements in Canada.

---

[1] Manuscript proceedings of the council board.
[2] Manuscript journals of the council board.

But his first efforts were discouraging. Many of the Indians had contracted the small-pox at Albany, and a considerable number of their finest young men had died of the pestilence, either while journeying homeward, or after reaching their castles. It was during their affliction from this at that period appalling disease, that Mr. Johnson was pressing them to go against the enemy; and his urgency, on one occasion, drew a rebuke from a sachem of the Canajoharie clan, that was full of feeling :—" You seem to think that we are brutes," said the first chief; " and that we have no sense of the loss of our dearest relations, and some of the bravest men we had in our nation. You must allow us time to bewail our misfortune."

Nevertheless, early in October, a party of seventy warriors, composed of some from each of the cantons, was made up for the purpose of harrassing the Canadian border. Several Englishmen accompanied this party, as well to assist, as to be witnesses of their conduct, under the lead of a son of Captain Butler, of the royal forces. But they had not been out many days before Mr. Butler fell sick of the small-pox, and five of the Indians were obliged to return to carry him back. The residue continued their course, being instructed to avoid the paths and water-courses usually traveled between the English and French colonies, and to thread the woods and cross the mountains in such manner as, if possible, to escape observation. Another small party was sent forth to hover about the precincts of Crown Point for the purpose of gaining intelligence, and rendering such other service as chance and opportunity might require. After the return of Mr. Butler the first party found it expedient to divide,—thirty of the Indians, with ten white men, taking one direction, and the residue striking off in another. The first division fell upon a French settlement on the north side of the St. Lawrence, ten leagues above Montreal; killed and scalped four people, and brought away ten prisoners, one of whom was a captain of militia.

Another party of nine Indians entered Canada still nearer to Montreal, and mingled with the Caughnawagas, under the guise of friendship. Their dissimulation was carried still farther, for they allowed themselves to be taken to Montreal, where they had an interview with the governor, and by whom they were dismissed with presents. So well did they play their part that they were entrusted with official dispatches to the commanding officer at Crown Point, and were also charged with letters from officers to their friends at that post. These communications were all delivered to the commanding officer at Albany on their return. They moreover had the good fortune on their way back to surprise a small French defence, in which they killed five men, bringing away one prisoner and one scalp.[1]

But notwithstanding the mortifying failure of all the plans of the year for such a vigorous prosecution of the war as it was supposed must result in the subjugation of Canada, the immense preparations of the French for the reconquest of Cape Breton, and possibly the invasion of New England, were equally abortive, and her high hopes were likewise overthrown. The grand armament destined upon this service has been described in a former part of the present chapter. Its misfortunes were truly remarkable. Indeed before the summer was entirely gone, such accounts were received in Boston of its distresses, as very materially to lessen their apprehensions of an invasion, even if the promised augmentation of Admiral Townsend's naval force at Cape Breton should not be realized. The number of vessels in the French armament has already been stated. Comprised in that number were eleven ships of the line, thirty smaller vessels carrying from ten to thirty guns each, with transport ships conveying land forces to the number of three thousand one hundred and thirty men. To this force a squadron of four ships, under Admiral Conflours from the West Indies, was to be added,— D'Anville, the commander of the whole, being a nobleman

---

[1] Colden's account of the treaty at Albany.

of high qualities and courage, in whose conduct the utmost confidence was placed. On arriving in Nova Scotia, the land forces were to have been joined by seventeen hundred Canadians and Indians, who were already in arms, awaiting their debarkation. The main squadron of the French, fitted at Rochelle, was ready for sea in the beginning of May, but was prevented by contrary winds from getting out, until the twenty-second of June. This delay seems to have been ominous of the train of adverse circumstances which followed. A series of disasters retarded the progress of the fleet, and weakened its power. The Count did not pass the Western Islands until the fourth of August. On the twenty-fourth, yet distant three hundred leagues from Nova Scotia, one of the ships proving unseaworthy, was burnt. In a storm on the first of September, two ships, one of seventy-four, and the other of sixty-four guns, were so much damaged in their masts, that they were obliged to bear away for the West Indies; and on the fifteenth, the Ardent, also of sixty-four guns, found it necessary to put back to Brest, in consequence of a pestilential fever, which broke out among the crew. D'Anville arrived at Chebucto on the twelfth of September, with but two ships of the line, and only three or four of the transports. One ship only had arrived before him; and after waiting three days, finding himself joined by only three more of the transports,—and having heard by an intercepted dispatch from Shirley, that the English fleet had arrived on the coast in pursuit of him, although Shirley's information was incorrect,—the admiral died suddenly,—by apoplexy, according to the French accounts, and by poison, self-administered, according to the English. Monsieur de la Jonquière, Governor General of Canada, an officer of age and experience, was on board of D'Anville's ship, the Northumberland; and having been created a *chef d'escadre* previous to the sailing of the fleet, by the death of the admiral, he succeeded to the command. Two days afterward the vice admiral D'Estournelle, came up with three or four more of the missing ships, and a council of war was thereupon called to determine what next should be done. Considering the extent to which their forces had been weakened by such a succession of calamities, equally unlooked for and severe, the absence of many of the regular troops who were on board the missing and disabled vessels, and the sickness of many more among whom the fever was raging with violence, the vice-admiral proposed returning to France. Being strenuously opposed, however, in this suggestion by Jonquière, and overruled by the council, D'Estournelle fell upon his own sword and died. Jonquière thought himself yet in a condition to conquer Annapolis-Royal and recover Nova Scotia, and made his dispositions for that object. Most of the sick having died at Chebucto, the fleet sailed thence with the residue on the thirteenth of October; but a violent storm was encountered two days afterward, when off Cape Sable, which continued several days and separated the fleet,—two ships only, one of fifty, and the other of thirty-six guns, remaining in company. These, on approaching Annapolis-Royal, discovered the Chester man of war, the Shirley frigate, and a smaller British vessel, under sail,—whereupon they retired under a press of canvass, to return no more.

Such was the disastrous termination of that memorable expedition from which so much had been expected by France.[1] "Never had so great an armament been dispatched from Europe to North America; and never had any proved more inefficient."[2] The people of New England accustomed to see the hand of Providence in every event of human life, viewed their deliverance as a signal and direct interposition of the deity in their behalf,—by pestilence and storm. "Never was a disappointment more severe on the part of the enemy; nor a deliverance more complete, with-

---

[1] Hutchinson.

[2] Grahame.

out human help, in favor of this country."[1] Not a single honest effort had been put forth by the ministers for their defence beyond the sending of Admiral Townsend with reinforcements for the squadron of Commodore Knowles at Louisburg; "and these two commanders," says Grahame, "doubtless in conformity with orders which they had received, contented themselves with guarding that harbor from attack, without making the slightest demonstration in support of New England."

Governor Clinton returned to New York early in October, meeting his council in that city on the fourteenth of the same month. Before leaving Albany he had made arrangements for a winter camp at that place, and adopted measures which it was supposed would be adequate to the protection of the frontiers. His detention at the north for nearly three months had been unexpected, and his exertions had been arduous and patriotic. The critical state in which he found the Indian affairs, required the exercise of all the prudence and attention in his power to bestow; and in their management he had derived but little assistance from the Board of Indian commissioners. Great dissatisfaction had prevailed respecting the conduct of this board; and knowing that the governor's confidence had been withdrawn from them, several members of the commission refused to attend the council, frankly confessing that they had lost all influence over the Indians.[2]

It was in this posture of that important branch of the public affairs, that the influence and services of Mr. Johnson were invoked; and the management of that department thenceforward devolved chiefly upon him.

In addition to all his other duties, the governor had been likewise compelled by the refusal of Gen. Gooch to serve in the campaign, to assume all the cares and responsibilities of military commander-in-chief; and the cares and

---

[1] Belknap.
[2] Manuscript journals of the council board.

responsibilities, after the arrival of the colonial troops from New Jersey, Pennsylvania and Maryland, irrespective of the Indian administration, were by no means light. Environed by difficulties, and limited in his means, contemporary historians have not awarded him that meed of justice to which he was unquestionably entitled for the zeal with which he labored to discharge his public duties.

The general assembly met on the seventeenth of October; and the governor, being indisposed, instead of opening the session in person, sent for the speaker, and through him transmitted a copy of the speech he had intended to deliver to the house,—a procedure which that body, acting under the influence of De Lancey, and not coming together in the best possible humor, voted to be not only unprecedented, but irregular. De Lancey, it will be remembered, on his rupture with the governor, had sworn that he would thenceforward render his excellency's administration uncomfortable; and he made good his oath. "His uncommon vivacity and ease, his adroitness at a jest, and his condescension to his inferiors, wonderfully facilitated his purposes;" and it took him not long to infuse such a spirit of factious opposition to the governor that the assembly paused not at measures to embarrass him of the most indefensible character. Still the assembly proceeded to the consideration of the public business. The speech opened by rehearsing the history of the governor's mission to Albany,—the difficulties that had attended, and the measure of success which had crowned it. Owing to misconduct on the part of the commissioners, the Indians, who had been tampered with by the French, had well nigh gone over to them; but the governor said he had fortunately secured their alliance, and it remained only by judicious measures to retain their friendship. The events of the summer, as connected with the prosecution of the war,—feeble enough in every respect,—were spoken of; and a call was made for increased appropriations for the Indian service, for the construction of additional defences on the frontiers, and especially for the maintenance of a winter encampment in the neighborhood of Albany, for the shelter of the troops destined against Canada, whenever the time for a decisive movement should arrive. In conclusion the speech exhorted the assembly to union and harmony, interposing a caution against the dangers consequent upon encroachments by either branch of the government upon the constitutional privileges of the others.

The speech was a very fair one, and nothing appears upon its face dictated otherwise than by a very proper spirit. Yet such was the temper of the assembly that the speech was like the dropping of a spark into a magazine. The house was instantly inflamed. His excellency's "persuasions to harmony excited only to discord;" and in the concluding admonitions against encroachments upon the prerogatives of other branches of the government,—the prerogatives of the crown meaning,—the assembly discovered, or affected to discover, a degree of distrust which incensed them exceedingly. They voted, however, the sum of six thousand five hundred pounds for the subsistence of the winter encampment at Albany; but provided for the transportation of supplies to that city, and no farther,—refusing, in effect, the means for conveying those supplies to the several posts at which they were needed. Farther provision for the subsistence of certain detachments of militia which had been ordered to Albany in May and June, was likewise refused. The governor promptly sent in a message rebuking the legislature for its parsimony, and insisting that when at the preceding session they had voted to provision the forces of the province destined against Canada, they had as a consequence pledged themselves to bear all the charges incident thereto. He told them with military truth "that the provisions for an army are so necessary a part of all warlike enterprises, that any defeat or obstruction in the daily supply of them, might defeat the best concerted measures; and that if the provisions of an army are not subject to the orders of the commanding officer, it would

CHAP. VI.
1746.

be in the power of those charged with furnishing the supplies, to frustrate any enterprise." His excellency therefore required a grant for transporting supplies along with the forces, to whatever parts they might be ordered. The assembly was also informed that there were thirteen hundred and sixty men at Albany, to whom but a portion of their promised enlistment bounty had been paid; and the necessity of making up the deficiency was urged in suitable terms, for the prevention of irregularities and desertions.

This message was referred, *nemine contradicente*, to a committe consisting of Colonels Phillipse, Morris and Schuyler, with instructions to prepare an humble representation in reply,—the house meantime voting, in addition to the ordinary civil list, only the deficient bounty money. But before the committee had prepared its report, information was received from the commissioners having in charge the purchasing of provisions for the forces, that Henry Holland, late high sheriff of Albany, by order of Colonel Roberts,[1] had broken open the store-houses in that city, and taken thence a large quantity of provisions in their custody for the public service.

The address reported by the committee, was an answer both to the special message, and to the opening speech of the session. The temper of this document was such as might well try that of the governor. In regard to the Indian service, the committee affected ignorance either of a bad disposition on the part of the Indians, or the causes of such disposition if it existed. They said they had voted liberal supplies for this department, and for the customary presents to that people, adding significantly, "in what manner that service has been performed, your excellency, and those whom you have thought proper to employ,

---

[1] An officer of one of the independent companies, now raised by Mr. Clinton to the rank of colonel in the intended expedition. He had been a cornet of horse at the accession of George I., and was connected, by his first marriage, with the earl of Halifax. His second wife was the daughter of that Mr. Harrison who had so deep a share in the feuds of Cosby and Van Dam.—*Smith.*

can certainly best determine." In respect to the alleged mismanagement of the Indian department, the address avowed the readiness of the assembly to enter upon a full investigation, whenever the governor should communicate to them all the papers and documents connected with that branch of the public service since the commencement of his excellency's administration,—until which time no larger sum than usual would be voted for that department, *lest there should be further misconduct.* The winter encampment was disapproved of, as being calculated to retard rather than facilitate the meditated invasion of Canada. The soldiers could not be made comfortable in the climate of Albany, and sickness and desertion would be the consequences of attempting to keep them there. The address declared that larger appropriations had been voted than even the king had expected. The imputation of parsimony was therefore repelled; as also was the intimation that the most perfect harmony did not exist between the different branches of the legislature. It was farther declared that the assembly was to guard against the private views of any artful or designing men; and they should be sorry to find that any such men could prevail upon his excellency to break that harmony so necessary for the public welfare;—adding, that if any such persons had been infusing such distrust into his excellency's mind, they must have had sinister ends in view, and could be no friends to their country. Disclaiming any designs to encroach upon the prerogatives of others, it was said that although collisions had happened in former times, yet they had arisen from the bad advice given by designing men to the governors, rather than from any wanton stretch of power by the people. In regard to the transportation of the army supplies, the address vindicated the action of the assembly, declaring "the circumstances of the colony would not suffer them to take one step farther;" but the committee nevertheless concluded their report with an assurance that as far as was consistent with the duty they owed his majesty, they would always endeavor to make his excellency's administration easy. This last declaration was a mere flourish of rhetoric, hollow and insincere.

The address was presented to the governor on the fifth of November. Three days afterward the committee to which had been referred the complaints of the commissioners of supplies touching the conduct of Roberts and Holland, in breaking open the stores of the commissariat at Albany, brought in their report. The documentary history of the controversy upon this subject is long. In brief, however, it appeared that in order to supply the deficiency in the number of state levies caused by sickness, desertion, and death, the governor had annexed to these forces four companies of independent fusileers, the supplies for whom did not fall within the precise letter of the act of appropriation. The commissioners of purchases had consequently refused to issue provisions for these four companies, in the face of an express order of the governor. When, moreover, the forces at Albany were ordered to march for the carrying place *en route* to Crown Point, the commissioners refused to convey the provisions to the place designated, and to other frontier points also, for their subsistence. Under these circumstances, having an order from the governor to meet the contingency, issued under a special impressment act of the general assembly, Roberts and Holland took the responsibility of taking the necessary supplies from the store houses themselves,— Doctor Colden, one of the governor's council, having sanctioned the procedure, after in vain threatening the commissioners with removal from office as a punishment for their contumacy. But it has been seen that under the influence of Mr. DeLancey, the assembly was rife for a quarrel with the governor; and a resolution was passed censuring him in the first instance for the warrant that had been issued for the subsistence of the fusileers. A second resolution was adopted approving of the conduct of the commissioners; a third, declaring the warrant of

Colonel Roberts to Holland, directing him to open the stores for supplies to be arbitrary and illegal; a fourth, declaring both Roberts and Holland guilty of a high misdemeanor; a fifth, declaring the breaking of the storehouses, and the seizure of the provisions, to be a manifest violation of the rights and liberties of the subject; a sixth, declaring that Holland was guilty of a high crime and misdemeanor for breaking the store-house; a seventh, declaring it a high misdemeanor for any person in authority to attempt by threats to influence any officers appointed by law to violate their duty; an eighth, applying the last mentioned resolution expressly to Cadwallader Colden, and declaring him guilty of the crime charged; a ninth, declaring that it would be in vain for the assembly to vote farther supplies until an effectual stop should be put to such proceedings; and a tenth, calling upon the governor to direct the attorney-general to prosecute the delinquents.

Mr. Clinton replied to the address of the house of the fifth of November, on the tenth, with firmness and energy,—exhibiting more of dignity, and less of irritability than might have been expected under the circumstances of the case from his choleric temperament. He had supposed the bad feeling of the Six Nations, and the misconduct of the Indian commissioners, matters of too great notoriety to require special averments or commentaries in his opening speech. But in order to the better understanding of the case by the assembly, he had ordered copies of the documents which they had intimated a desire to examine, to be laid before them, whenever it might suit them to make the call. Had they asked for information respecting the military transactions at Albany, before expressing their dissatisfaction with those transactions, the governor suggested that they might possibly have formed different opinions, or arrived at different conclusions in regard to them. His excellency censured the house for having given publicity to their address; expressed his regret that his recommendations for a good agreement among the different branches of the government in times of danger should have given offence; and renewed his protestations of a sincere desire to cultivate a spirit of harmony in his administration. "And now gentlemen," he added, "I think this is an occasion on which I may be allowed to tell you, that within the six months last past, I have gone through with more difficulties, I have had less assistance, and I have done more for this province, than I believe any governor of New York has done before me; I feel in my own heart my zeal for my king and my country's service; and therefore I can with pleasure lay the account of my administration at his majesty's feet. Meantime I shall to the utmost of my power, be careful of the rights and liberties of every man under my government. I shall be more especially careful of the preservation of your privileges; and at the same time to preserve that part of his majesty's authority entrusted to me."

This message, however, having been prepared in answer to the proceedings of the assembly of the fifth of November, formed of course no answer to the resolutions of the eighth, respecting the seizure of the provisions at Albany by Roberts and Holland, and demanding the arrest and trial of those officers. Indeed it is most likely that those resolutions had not been communicated to the governor in form when this message was delivered, the tone of which was not calculated to allay the already excited feelings of the legislature. A recess of ten days, from the fourteenth to the twenty-fourth of November, was allowed; and on reassembling of that body, a message was in readiness to meet them, extended and elaborate, answering the resolutions of the eighth *seriatim*, and justifying the proceedings at Albany, which, his excellency declared, had been directed by himself and his council under the pressure of the utmost necessity.

Viewing the transactions in question at this length of time, although the commissioners entrusted by the assembly with the supplies, whose duty it was to deliver them out, and the assembly which sustained their course, had the advantage of the popular side of the controversy, yet it seems equally certain that those commissioners acted in a manner greatly embarrassing to the public service;—for what substantial reason does not appear. Mr. Clinton, in obedience to the orders of the crown, and in concert with Governor Shirley and Admiral Warren, had planned what was intended to be a final and decisive descent upon Canada, —the conquest of which was indispensable to the security and repose of the English colonies,—for which purpose the forces had been collected at Albany. In October they were ordered to advance to the carrying-place between the Hudson river and Lake Champlain,—to which point the commissioners of subsistence were requested to forward the necessary supplies from the store houses in Albany. The request was refused under the flimsy pretext that they were not in funds that could be applied to that purpose. Those commissioners were John Cuyler and Dirck Ten Broeck. On being demanded by Colonel Roberts whether they would deliver the provisions, should the means of transportation be provided, they refused because they had no power, as they alleged, to comply. The colonel then demanded whether they would deliver the provisions to a commissary, or to the quartermasters, under the warrant of the governor, to be receipted for. This request, right in itself, and reasonable withal, was also refused, upon the mere technical pretext that by the act of the assembly they were allowed to deliver supplies "only to the captains." All these excuses were obviously evasions. The Schuylers, whose interest was powerful, were offended because Mr. Johnson was rising into favor in the Indian department. De Lancey, who had been succeeded in the governor's affections, by Colden, was implacable; and he was omnipotent with the assembly, of which body the commissioners were the agents. Hence it was the policy of each of these interests to embarrass, rather than to strengthen, the commander-in-chief. Yet the frontiers must be protected; and the orders to Colonel Roberts were peremptory to move his forces northward to the carrying-place. A council of war was held after the refusal of the commissioners to move the provisions, consisting of Lieutenant-Colonels Roberts and Marshall, and Majors Clarke and Rutherford,—the latter officer being also one of the executive council,—at which it was determined, as the only alternative in the emergency, to make use of a warrant granted in anticipation of some such act of contumacy, authorizing the impressment of the necessary supplies from the colonial stores, giving a receipt for the same, and taking all proper measures to guard against waste or extravagance. The case was stated with all frankness and candor in the message, yet without asperity. But, although under the circumstances then existing, it is difficult to perceive what other course could have been adopted on the instant of the emergency, the governor's explanations nevertheless gave no satisfaction to the assembly, as was made fully to appear by the resolves passed two days afterward. In addition to the declaration of dissatisfaction, it was resolved that no further supplies should be voted while the abuses of which they complained were openly avowed and encouraged. A thrust was likewise aimed at Doctor Colden, who had concurred in the proceedings of Colonel Roberts, and who had doubtless advised, if he had not prepared, the vindictory message, by a resolution declaring "that whoever had advised the said message, had endeavored to create jealousies and dissensions among the several branches of the legislature; had encouraged a manifest breach of the laws of the colony; and were enemies to the constitution thereof." But notwithstanding the attitude thus assumed, the assembly still avowed its readiness, as soon as proper assurances were given that the alleged abuses should be effectually prevented, to vote an ample allowance for the subsistence of the forces.

Mr. Clinton was either alarmed at the resolutions, or else

he judged it no suitable time for a controversy. His message in reply was conciliatory if not yielding. He only required that for the future, the provisions for the army should be delivered out agreeably to the existing engagements of the assembly, in which case nothing that had happened could or should happen again. He also pledged himself that all possible care should be taken of the provisions, and exact accounts rendered. This advance had the effect of allaying the storm, and the assembly applied itself to its duties in a spirit that encouraged the governor to call for additional supplies for the maintenance of artizans among the Senecas, and also for bounty money for female scalps—bounties being allowed only upon the scalps of males by the existing laws. The immediate cause for preferring this request,—so abhorent to the feelings of the present day,—was the fact that a party of the Six Nations had recently brought in three female prisoners from Canada, and one female scalp. Evidence was thus afforded that the Confederates had at length engaged heartily in the war; and the governor thought they should be encouraged in the manner proposed. The same message also demanded supplies for Oswego, and announced that Mr. Johnson had become the contractor for that post,—with a stipulation that no higher charges should be made in time of war, than it had been usual to pay in time of peace. Heed was taken of these requisitions, and the necessary supply bills both for the civil and military service, were passed.[1] An act was also passed authorizing a lottery to raise two thousand two hundred and fifty pounds for founding a college in the city of New York. This was the first step taken toward the establishment of Kings, now Columbia College,—so far behind the colonists of New England were those of New York, on the great subject of education.[2]

---

[1] Manuscript letter from Johnson to Capt. John Catherwood, acknowledging receipt of advices that the assembly had by resolution approved of the governor's recommendation that he (Johnson) should supply the troops at Oswego. Thanks the governor, and promises to act with energy, &c.

[2] This was at the distance of more than one hundred and twenty years after the discovery and settlement of New York, whereas the colonies of

CHAP. VI.
1746.

It was now the fourth of December, and the general assembly was drawing its session to a close. Mr. DeLancey, however, could not allow the session to terminate without making another demonstration against his rival, Doctor Colden. On the day last mentioned, the chief justice called the attention of the legislative council to a pamphlet giving an account of the Indian negotiations at Albany, of which so much has already been said in the present chapter, wherein it was set forth that although the governor had requested the members of his council to attend and assist in those negotiations, three only had complied with the request, viz: Messrs. Colden, Livingston, and Rutherford. According to that narrative, therefore, his excellency had been left to act with the smallest number of counsellors that could constitutionally form a board. Mr. DeLancey considered this statement a reflection upon the non-attending councilors, and moved that the printer of the pamphlet be summoned to the bar, to answer as to its authorship. An animated debate ensued upon the motion, in the course of which Dr. Colden averred the authorship, and assumed the responsibility of its publication. Messrs. DeLancey, Horsmanden and Murray successively uttered some animadversions upon the pamphlet; and on the motion of the former, a vote of censure was adopted, denouncing the offensive passage as a misrepresentation of the facts, and an invidious reflection upon those members of the council who did not accompany the governor to Albany.

Massachusetts and Connecticut had commenced their institutions of classical learning very soon after planting their colonies. Smith, the historian, states that for many years within his recollection the only academics in the colony of New York, except such as were in holy orders, were Mr. DeLancey a graduate of Cambridge, England, and Mr. Smith, (the historian's father,) who was at the bar. At the time even, now under examination, there were not above thirteen graduates in the colony, excluding the clergy. Except Mr. DeLancey, there was then no graduate of a college upon the bench, or in either of the branches of the legislature. The practice then, even of the most opulent of the citizens, whose attention was generally engrossed with commerce, was to send their sons directly from the writing school to the counting room, and thence to the West Indies.

The session closed on the following day. No events of public or political importance occurred within the province of New York during the residue of December; nor did the enemy after the capture of Fort Massachusetts, harrass the northern border any more during this year.

Meantime, Mr. Johnson was growing rapidly in the favor of the governor, to whom he paid a visit in New York toward the close of the autumn. I have not been able to discover the date of Johnson's elevation to the military rank of colonel; but it must have been at about the period of time now under review. He had a brother, Warren Johnson, a captain in the royal service, who had recruited a company in Boston that year. The captain wrote to his brother William, on the ninth of October, that his uncle Warren, (the admiral,) was on the eve of sailing for Louisburg, and that his lady was preparing to return to New York to pass the winter. On the tenth of December, the captain was in New York on his way to the Mohawk country to visit his brother. By his hand, under the last-mentioned date, governor Clinton addressed a letter " *To Colonel William Johnson, at Albany.*" This is the earliest document I have found among the Johnson manuscripts, superscribed with a military title. The letter, the main purpose of writing which was to request the colonel to purchase for his excellency a pair of black stallions, contained the following passage :—" This comes by your brother. I hope he will find you well. I hear nothing of news but what he will tell you. I have recommended you to his majesty's favor through the duke of Newcastle. I must desire you will keep up the Indians to their promises of keeping out scouts to watch the motions of the French." From this letter, therefore, it is probable that Clinton had just then commissioned Mr. Johnson as a colonel, subject to the approbation of the crown.

The operations of the New Englanders in Nova Scotia, ended disastrously. The French and Indian forces, whose purpose it was to coöperate with the fleet of the Count

D'Anville, did not retire from that peninsula on the dispersion of the fleet, and General Shirley judged it necessary to send a body of provincials, to dislodge them. The levies from Massachusetts, with the exception of those on board of one of the transports which was wrecked, arrived at Annapolis in safety, as also did two hundred of the New Hampshire troops. One of the New Hampshire transports, after a blundering cruise in the Bay of Fundy, was decoyed to a French sloop, and the crew captured. The Rhode Island levies did not reach their place of destination, their vessels being wrecked. In the course of the winter, the Massachusetts forces at Annapolis being inferior in numbers to the enemy, yet deceived as to the extent of the disparity, were drawn into the field by false representations, and defeated, after a severe engagement, in the midst of a driving snow storm at Minas. Col. Arthur Noble, with about sixty men, was killed, and there were fifty wounded. Noble's army did not exceed six hundred men; and the survivors of the battle, unable to escape, were compelled to capitulate. Chevalier Ramsay commanded the French; but notwithstanding his victory, he did not venture to attack Annapolis, nor did the French inhabitants yet move in their meditated revolt.[1] The posts on the western border of New Hampshire, had been guarded by troops from Massachusetts; but inasmuch as those posts were without the jurisdiction of the colony, the garrisons were withdrawn late in the autumn. The settlers along that border, being left thus exposed, fell back upon the larger towns—taking away such of their goods as they could remove, burning such as could not be concealed in the earth without damage, and leaving the residue exposed to the ravages of the enemy. But the enemy was not active during this winter, and its deep repose in the forests of the north was only broken once, by an attack of the Indians upon Fort Hinsdale, occupied only by six families, by the stalwart hands of which the post was successfully defended.

---

[1] Belknap, Grahame, Hutchinson, Hoyt.

CHAPTER VII.
1747.

Impatient of delay, and anxious that the blow so long meditated against Canada might be struck before the French should have power to repel it, the active mind of Shirley conceived the project of a descent upon Crown Point at mid-winter. The legislature of Massachusetts was readily persuaded to second the enterprise; and on the sixteenth of January, Governor Clinton communicated to his council a very long letter from Mr. Shirley, setting forth his plans, and urging the coöperation of New York, and the adoption of immediate and vigorous measures to that end. It was Shirley's intention, while the troops destined directly against Crown Point were concentrating in the neighborhood of Albany, to create a diversion in the enemy's country, by detaching a force of five hundred men, to march through the valley of the Connecticut, and fall upon the villages of the St. Francis Indians, two hundred miles north of the English settlements. A similar movement, for the like object, was urged upon Governor Clinton, to be made against Fort Frontenac by the way of Oswego. Could the French be thus doubly distracted by simultaneous attacks at those distant points, it was presumed that in respect to the grand enterprise against Crown Point and Montreal, there could remain no well-founded doubt of success. Mr. Shirley, therefore, seeming to take it for granted that New York would second the enterprise without hesitation, much less with reluctance, asked for the services of its levies, then in garrison at Albany,[1] and requested that accommodations

---
[1] The New York forces during the winter of 1746—'47, were distributed

for the New England troops might be provided at Saratoga. He desired farther that the Six Nations might be brought into the field, and that forts might be erected by New York, at the heads of Lakes George and Champlain.[1]

The letter was referred to a committee by the council, the report of which was indecisive and unsatisfactory. The committee affected to be in favor of the enterprise, yet doubted the practicability of carrying it into execution before the breaking up of winter. It was alleged that there were sufficient accommodations for the New England levies at Saratoga; the forts could not be built in time to guard the portages at the heads of the two lakes; and as to the proposed design against Fort Frontenac, New York was then in no condition to undertake it. On the whole, therefore, the committee thought "a winter campaign against Crown Point was liable to many difficulties, and would be a hazardous undertaking."[2] Governor Clinton was nevertheless inclined to favor the scheme, wild and impracticable as it seemed to many; and on the second of February he requested a more definite expression of opinion by his council. Two days afterward that opinion was given, in the form of a very decisive report against the whole project. It was urged, not without reason, that the winters in that high northern latitude were at best exceedingly unfavorable for military operations, and it was moreover then too late. The warriors of the Six Nations could not by any possibility be collected in season for the contemplated movement; and besides, more than a fortnight had intervened since a syllable had been heard from the projector of the expedition—Mr. Shirley. It was therefore held, as presented, to be utterly impracti-

---

at various points. Some were posted at Saratoga; others in the Mohawk country; and others again at Schenectady. Three companies were at Schaghticoke; four at Half Moon; two at Niskayuna, and others still at Albany.

[1] Shirley's letter—Minutes of the council board.
[2] Idem.

cable.[1] Belknap adds, as another reason prompting to this conclusion, that the small-pox was prevailing in the settlements north of Albany, through which the forces must necessarily pass,—a disease, the violence of which, at that day, had not been disarmed of its terrors by vaccination, or even mitigated ·by the process of inoculation. The agency of Clinton's council in defeating this darling enterprise of Shirley's, seems not to have been generally or publicly known, and the merit,—if such it may be called,— of defeating it, has been accorded alone to " the more sober discretion of Connecticut," the government of which " deemed the winter an improper season for so important an undertaking," refusing to furnish its quota of troops until spring.[2] Equally effectual was the unfavorable interposition of the New York council board.

An active correspondence was maintained between Governor Clinton and Colonel Johnson, during the winter and spring, having relation to the protection of the frontiers in general, but more especially to the Indian service; and the letters of the governor bear evidence that the colonel was already in the enjoyment of his strongest confidence. The notorious Jean Cœur, one of the most persevering and mischievous of the Jesuit emissaries in the Indian Confederacy, was yet among the Senecas, and it was deemed by Johnson an object of high importance to obtain possession of his person. He communicated his views upon the subject to the governor in February, by whom the project was warmly approved, and the colonel was urged to use his utmost endeavors to effect the object, either by stratagem or force, as circumstances might require. Early in March, moreover, Mr. Clinton wrote to Johnson directing him to send out as many war-parties

---

[1] Council minutes in manuscript

[2] Belknap and Marshall. Smith does not even allude to these winter deliberations.

"of Indians and Christians,¹ to harass the enemy in their own settlements," as he could bring into the service. To carry the war into the enemy's own country, and in his own way, was rightly judged "one of the most effectual means to prevent their daring mischief to us."² The Colonel was yet farther directed to send a party of Indians to the garrison at Saratoga, to act as scouts,—the commanding officer of which post being enjoined to treat the Indians thus coming to his assistance with the utmost kindness.³ In reply to the letter thus abridged, Colonel Johnson wrote as follows:

Colonel Johnson to Governor Clinton.
"MOUNT JOHNSON, March 18, 1747.
"May it please your Excellency:
"This instant I am honored with your's by the express, and by whom I send this in return. In answer to what your excellency says about sending a party as out-scouts to Saratoga, I can only say that I find already that it is not at all agreeable to the Indians, they being now inclined and ready to go against Canada, where they say they can do more execution. Moreover they never like to keep in a garrison among so many Christians. Yesterday a party of twenty-two Christians and Indians returned from Saratoga, where I sent them in hopes to have met and intercepted some of the enemy's out-scouts. But they met none. No

---

[1] The whites at that day were called *Christians* in distinction from the Indians.

[2] Grahame, in his usually acurate, and very excellent history of the United States, falls into an important error respecting these predatory excursions of the Indians, which he maintains, were not encouraged by the English. Such was by no means the fact. The English employed all the Indians they could upon this service. Grahame, however, was probably led into the error by Belknap, who wrote particularly of New England, and evidently in great ignorance of the operations in New York. See Grahame, book x, chap. ii.

[3] Manuscript letter; Clinton to Johnson. At its close, the governor says—"Pray let me know how poor old Hendrick dies. who, I am sorry to hear, is so bad." Hendrick, it will be remembered, was the king of the Mohawks.

one will more readily comply with your excellency's orders than I shall; but at this time I would beg leave to assure your excellency that the consequence of it may be disastrous by keeping the Indians from fighting—they being now inclining that way more and more. I have this week sent out a parcel of Canajoharies, mixed with a few of the Five Nations[1] against the French and their settlements, and am every day busy with fitting out more. I am going to send up Captain Stephens and two of the lieutenants, with a small party of men, and Indian chiefs of the two castles with them, to bring down some of the Five Nations to go a-scalping. I am of opinion we shall make the French smart this spring, by taking, scalping, and burning them and their settlements. But I shall be ruined for want of blankets, linen, paints, guns, cutlasses, &c., for I am almost out of all these, and cannot get them in Albany. I believe your excellency has seen how difficult it was last fall for you to get those things. But how much more so for me, being so envied by them. Wherefore if I cannot have them from New York by the first opportunity, I do not know what I shall do. So I hope your excellency will endeavor to have them procured and sent up,—as also the pay for those belonging to me, about four hundred and thirty pounds. The party now going out were so uneasy that I paid the most of them to encourage them. Old Hendrick is in a pretty fair way of recovering again, which will be of great service to our cause. I hope that your excellency will order it so that my people may be supplied as the rest, with every thing on a march which is requisite. As to the party which you intend to send to Oswego, I shall be ready to transport them a little after the lake opens, which I judge to be in about a fortnight. But be that as it will, I shall always let you know time enough beforehand. We kept St. Patrick's day yesterday and this day, and drank

---

[1] So in the original draught of the letter. Yet the Canajoharies were only a clan of the Mohawks—the head of the original Five Nations.

your health, and that of all friends in Albany, with so many other healths that I can scarce write.

"I am, with great regard, dear sir, your most obedient humble servant,

"WM. JOHNSON."

As a farther encouragement to the Indians, the legislature of Massachusetts voted an additional bounty for scalps; but Johnson opposed the allowance, and suggested that a different direction be given to the appropriation. Inasmuch, he said, as the bounty for scalps allowed by the assembly of New York, was entirely satisfactory to the Indians, and inasmuch also as he had already sent off several war-parties under the promise of that bounty and no more, he proposed applying the Massachusetts funds to the purchase of clothing and subsistence for the Indians and their families, now become very poor from the long time they had been kept from their hunting.[1] The Indians were at this time wretchedly armed, and scantily supplied; but Clinton was doing all in his power, as he wrote to Johnson on the twentieth of March, to remedy these deficiencies. The letters of the latter show that the need was pressing.

It was now the fourth year of the war. Yet, with the exception of the conquest of Louisburg, scarcely anything had been accomplished against the enemy, even in retaliation for the remorseless cruelties visited upon the border settlements of the English along the whole northern frontier. The energies of the colonies had been exerted, seemingly almost to exhaustion, in large preparations ending only in mortifying abortions. Such being the situation of affairs, Colonel Johnson, now at the head of the Indian department, determined to exert himself to the utmost in making the enemy realize the true character of the species of warfare he had adopted, by pouring into the Canadian settlements as many scalping parties as he could command. The contest became, therefore, so far as the colonies were con-

---

[1] Manuscript letter; Colonel Johnson to Colonel John Stoddard, of Northampton.

cerned, ignoble upon both sides; "resembling more the practices of banditti than the operations of civilized warfare, and tending to no other results than obscure individual suffering, and partial havoc and devastation." In order to a better understanding of the manner in which the war was thus waged, and of the activity and energy of Colonel Johnson, even at this early period of his military career, the following letter is inserted at large:

Colonel Johnson to Governor Clinton.
"MOUNT JOHNSON, May 30, 1747.
" May it please your Excellency:

" You cannot conceive the uneasiness your long silence gives me,—not having had the honor of a line from you since the thirtieth of April. It is now the first time that I have wanted money for scalps and prisoners, and instructions most of all. The numbers about me every day going to war, takes abundance of arms, ammunition and clothing, and I am quite bare of most of those things. Your excellency will conceive that what I have received is but a mere trifle with so many as I have to distribute it among, although so sparingly done; and were it not for my own store, and what goods I have been obliged to buy, I should have been obliged to drop the affair some time ago, which would have been very hard after all my trouble to bring them so heartily into our interest. I am quite pestered every day, with parties returning with prisoners and scalps, and without a penny to pay them with, it comes very hard upon me, and is displeasing to them, I can assnre you, for they expect their pay, and demand it of me as soon as they return, as I mentioned to your excellency in my last of the twenty-fifth instant. Now that they find the money is not ready, they tell me this was but a draw to encourage them. Therefore I wish your excellency would only consider of it shortly. I thank God there is nothing wanting or backward in my affairs, wherefore hope your excellency will not let me suffer, or the cause drag for want of things requisite to carry it on. If your excellency intends soon to come up to Albany, I should be glad to receive your orders concerning the Indians coming down, for they certainly expect to be called, or invited, down this summer by you, or else by me. I am positive I could do more with them here, by far, than if they went to Albany, without going to above a quarter the expense; because there they are corrupted by evil people, and drink all the goods they get, whereas here they have not that opportunity, but can carry them home and show their families what they have had of you,—which would encourage them much. Moreover here I have all my counsellors, the Mohawks and Canajoharies, with whose assistance I could bring them to do anything. There is nothing more requisite at present than some blue camlet, red shalloon, good lace and white metal buttons, to make up a parcel of coats for some chief warriors from the Senecas, and for others who are daily expected. Wherefore I wish your excellency would send me up these things by the first opportunity, and also about thirty good castor hats, with scallop lace for them all; white lace, if to be had, if not some yellow with it. This I assure your excellency goes a great way with them. They have been gained so mostly by the French always, and of consequence they expect it from us, and we have promised it. There is three months pay due to my officers and people the first of June, and as they are all upon hard service with the Indians daily, they require their pay, which I hope your excellency will please pay unto Mr. Anthony Duane, merchant of New York, who will give your excellency a receipt for it. I also should be glad your excellency would advise me how I shall get the money for the enclosed account, being now a year due almost, and by your orders. Just as I was finishing my letter, arrived another party of mine, consisting of only six Mohawks, who brought with them seven prisoners and three scalps, which is very great for so small a party. I have my house, &c., now all full of the Five Nations,—some going out to-morrow against the French. Others go for news, which, when furnished, I shall let your excellency know. My people's success is now the talk of the whole country. I expect in a short time several more parties home from Canada. I believe Hendrick will be the first, who, I dare say, will bring a great many with him, dead or alive—so that we shall need a great deal of money among them all. They have brought in this spring as follows:

First, by Lieut. Walter Butler and his party, from Crown Point, the scalps of men,	6
By Lieut. Thomas Butler and party, prisoners,	8
By a Canajoharie party, prisoners,	3
Scalps,	2
By Gingegoe and party, prisoners,	7
Scalps,	3
Total this spring,	29

"If the money is sent up to me for this use, I shall give certificates of age, and render a clear account thereof, and the Indians shall receive it all in dollars, and not be cheated, as they would be by others, who would only give them some trifles of goods, rum, &c., for their bounty,—which usage has ruined our Indians mostly.

I am, with the greatest respect, your excellency's much obliged humble servant, &c.

"WM. JOHNSON."

Petty details of a petty warfare; but the record is essential to a just understanding of the border history of those times, for it was in this manner only that active hostilities were prosecuted during the entire open season. Neither the inhabitants of the English nor of the French borders were left to the enjoyment of a moment's security or repose. Exposed every hour to these hostile and often bloody incursions, they were compelled to fortify their houses by night, and go armed while performing the labors of the field by day.

One of the most considerable of these hostile incursions during the spring of this year, was an attack upon a small fort in Charlestown, New Hampshire, by a large body of French and Indians, under the command of M. Debeline. This post had been unoccupied during the winter; but toward the close of March, captain Phineas Stevens, an officer who had been in command of it the year before, returned to the station, at the head of a body of thirty Massachusetts rangers, and no more. The enemy came stealthily into the immediate neighborhood of the fort, as it was called,—being, however, nothing but a small picketted stockade,—and lay in concealment, watching, doubtless, for an opportunity when the gate should be opened, to rush in and carry the work by a sudden assault unawares. Uneasiness, however, on the part of the dogs in the fort, created a suspicion that all was not right without. The little garrison being thus upon the *qui vive*, one of the men, desirous of ascertaining the cause of this canine inquietude, left the fort, and creeping cautiously to the distance of thirty rods, discharged his gun. Supposing themselves to have been discovered, a party of the enemy sprang up and fired at the adventurous ranger, slightly wounding him. Not with sufficient severity, however, to prevent his regaining the fort, though hotly pursued by the enemy, who, no longer affecting concealment, rushed forward with savage yells as though determined at once to carry the defence. But their courage was unequal to the attempt; and for a considerable time nothing more was done than to keep up a general fire, brisk, but ineffectual. The rangers were well covered, and small arms could of course make no sensible impression upon the stockade; but the fire was nevertheless returned with spirit. Finding the garrison bent upon a resolute defence, and perceiving that the work was constructed of combustible materials, the enemy next attempted to set on fire, and thus summarily to compel a surrender. To this end the torch was applied to the neighboring fences, and also to a log-house standing about forty rods to windward. A brisk wind favored the design, and the flames approached, enveloping the fort in a dense body of smoke, and eclipsing the view of the enemy,—but of whose continued presence, the hideous yells of the savages, and the incessant rattle of musketry, gave ample evidence. There was indeed immediate danger from the approach of the devouring element, and it is quite probable that through its agency the enemy would have been successful but for a lucky expedient devised by captain Stevens, and bravely executed by his men. The soil being favorable for rapid excavation, several subterranean passages or galleries were carried under the parapet, deep enough to allow the men to stand in them at the foot of the stockades on the outside, yet completely covered from the enemy. Buckets of water from the well within were then passed rapidly to the men standing in the trenches without, which being dashed upward upon the timbers, they were moistened sufficiently to prevent ignition. Failing in this first effort to produce a conflagration, M. Debeline next prepared a sort of *mantalet*, loaded with faggots, which were fired and forced down upon the fort. Showers of burning arrows were also shot into the defence,—a device which was alike abortive. The exertions of one-half the thirty preserved the work from the fire, while the other half lost no opportunity of firing upon the enemy, as often as he could be discovered through the intervening clouds of smoke. On the second day of the seige the French commander proposed a cessation of hostilities, until sunrise of the following morning,—a proposition readily acceded to by Captain Stevens, but the object of which does not appear. But no matter: just before the expiration of the armistice, Debeline, himself, bearing a flag, with fifty of his men, approached within fifty rods of the stockade, and a parley ensued,—Stevens receiving a lieutenant and two of the enemy into the fort as hostages, while the same number proceeded to a conference with the French commander. His demand was a surrender of the fort, the garrison to be conducted to Montreal as prisoners of war, with a request that Captain Stevens should meet him and reply to the summons in person. Ascertaining that his men would stand by him in defending their little work to the last, Stevens proceeded to meet the Frenchman as requested, but was received roughly. Without pausing for an interchange even of the ordinary courtesies required by good breeding, Debeline threatened that if his terms were rejected, he would take the fort by storm;—adding, that in the event of the death of any of his men in the assault, he would put every man of the garrison to the sword. Under a menace like that, Stevens at once declined further negotiations,—declaring his purpose to listen to no overtures of surrender whatever, until his means of defence should be exhausted. "Do as you please," replied Debeline;—"I am resolved to have the fort or die. Go and see if your men dare fight any longer, and give me a speedy answer." Returning to the stockade, the hostages were interchanged, and at about twelve o'clock meridian, hostilities were recommenced, the firing being continued all that day, and the night following. Just at the peep of dawn on the third day, Stevens was addressed from the ranks of the enemy with the friendly salutation "Good morning," to which was added a proposition for a second armistice of two hours. It was granted; and shortly before its expiration, two Indians approached with a flag, proclaiming that if the English would sell them some provisions, they would withdraw without offering further molestation. The negotiation was declined upon the basis proposed;—Stevens, however, offering to supply them with provisions at the rate of five bushels of corn for every prisoner the enemy would stipulate to release at Montreal, hostages to be left to secure a faithful performance of the agreement. This proposition was in turn rejected; but the fire of the enemy gradually fell away, and before nightfall the seige was raised and the foe departed, deeply chagrined, beyond all doubt, at the failure of his enterprise, especially of the boastful confidence with which it had been commenced. The attack continued three days, during which thousands of balls were discharged into the fort, yet not a man of the garrison was killed, and but two of them wounded, and those slightly. Commodore Sir Charles Knowles, then with his squadron lying at Boston, was so highly gratified with the conduct of Captain Stevens, that he sent him an elegant sword, bearing a suitable inscription. The bravery of Stevens, and the mental resources which he discovered, were subjects of high praise in other quarters; yet he has been criticised for his imprudence in admitting the hostages retained by him during the negotiations, *into* the fort,—thus necessarily disclosing his weakness,—while it has also been suggested that he ought not to have risked his own person by placing himself within the power of a perfidious enemy, when he might rather have sent a subaltern to meet the French commander.

Debeline did not retire from the country at once, but on raising the siege of the stockade he divided his motley forces into several small parties, by which the border settlements of New Hampshire were infested for weeks thereafter. Skirmishes were frequent, houses were burnt, and individuals were killed from day to day. All the dwellings in the two settlements of Winchester and Upper Ashuelot were destroyed by fire. Yet nearer to Albany the enemy was hovering about in considerable numbers.

In May, the government of Massachusetts commenced rebuilding the fort of that name which had been destroyed the year before by M. Vaudreuil. A party of one hundred men having been detached to Albany for provisions, on its return discovered the enemy in ambuscade in the very environs of the works. The discovery was timely. An engagement ensued, and the enemy, attacked upon both sides,—both by the returning party and the garrison,—was soon obliged to flee to the woods, whence he did not again emerge. The loss to the English was trifling, two men only being wounded, and one killed,—the latter an Indian ally of the Stockbridge tribe.

While the border-men were engaged in these predatory affairs,—prolific of individual suffering, but, though illustrated by many acts of personal conduct worthy of all praise, productive of no important results,—Governor Clinton was again involved in hostilities with his legislature. In the reasonable expectation of receiving instructions from ministers touching the prosecution of the war, the governor had delayed summoning the general assembly until the twenty-fifth of March. But no instructions came; and the season was already so far advanced as to require very active dispositions of the forces already in service for guarding the exposed points of the frontiers, even were offensive operations not in contemplation. The assembly was told in the speech that Colonel Roberts had been sent to Boston to confer with Governor Shirley, and that the Mohawks had been detained from their hunting expeditions that they might be in readiness to act in the war as circumstances might require. For the purpose of yet farther cultivating the friendship of the Six Nations, the governor proposed another voyage to counsel with them at Albany, for which object he required an appropriation. The long proposed expedition against Crown Point was again presented for legislative consideration; and, in the absence both of the advices and supplies expected from England, appropriations were required for the construction of the forts so long talked of at the carrying-places between the Hudson river and Lake Champlain. The forces likewise for the expedition, were to be levied and paid by the colonies embarking therein, upon all which points a full and cordial understanding existed between Governors Clinton and Shirley. Provision having only been made for victualing the levies then in the service until the first of May, farther supplies were required for that object. A week afterward a special message was sent down asking an appropriation for maintaining scouts, and a corps of rangers upon the frontiers. These requests were judged the more reasonable, inasmuch as all the expenses of the Indian service, and for the rangers, had been defrayed during the preceding year by the crown. No other business was presented to the consideration of the assembly, whose session, the governor suggested, must be short.

Justice Horsmanden reported the address of the council in answer to the speech. It contained the following passage embodying a reflection upon the integrity of the Indians, which, judging from the correspondence of Colonel Johnson, seems not at that time at least to have been deserved.

"It cannot but occasion great uneasiness in us to observe, that our Indians employed in the barbarous method of scalping, (only justifiable by the precedent practices of our enemies,) industriously avoid attacking, or meeting the French Indians; or when they meet, treat each other as friends; whereby they are encouraged in their cruel practice of butchering those who are not in arms, and even those who are unable to bear arms—women and children."

The assembly, determined to continue its quarrel with the governor, neglected the customary civility of voting an address. But the situation of the country forbade entire inaction, and a petition from the inhabitants of Kinderhook, accompanying the special message, contained a pathetic appeal to the assembly for a garrison of fifty men for their defence, and a like number of rangers to traverse the woods to the northward and eastward. Moved by this appeal, resolutions were passed directing the employment of one hundred rangers, one-half of whom were to be stationed upon the east, and the other upon the west side of the river in the county of Albany. Supplies were also voted for victualling the levies for the term of three months beyond the twenty-fourth of May. But the house at the same time reaffirmed its declaration of the preceding November, that it would make no provision for the transportation of any supplies beyond Albany. In regard to his excellency's proposed conference with the Indians, it farther manifested its temper by voting the beggarly allowance of one hundred and fifty pounds. Nor was this all. After passing the bill in form, pursuant to the resolutions,

CHAP. VII.
1747.

and before it had received the assent of the representative of the crown, the assembly adopted yet another resolution setting forth that the levies then in service, so long maintained at very great expense, had thus far been unemployed, and praying that the hundred men authorized in compliance with the Kinderhook memorial, should be detached from those levies—from the little army destined against Canada! The pay proposed in the bill was one shilling per diem, over and above the wages allowed and paid by the crown. Eight days afterward, the governor not yet having approved the bill, the assembly, availing itself of a memorial from Albany giving a melancholy representation of the suffering and defenceless situation of that country, as if purposely to chafe his excellency by farther insult, sent up an address of affected tenderness and solicitude for the condition of the frontier settlers, and praying him no longer to withhold his assent from the measure they had been so prompt to enact.

In his reply to this address, the governor went into a full and elaborate vindication of his conduct during the last eventful year of his administration,—rehearsing his labors and exertions in the public service, for which he had been so unworthily requited. In regard to the bill presented for his approbation, his excellency said he looked upon the allowance of the extra shilling per diem, as altogether inadequate, considering the character and severity of the service, the extra expenses to which the rangers were subject by the wear and tear of their clothes when plunging into morasses, climbing mountains, or threading the deep-tangled woods. He denied that the levies had been inactive, and gave an account of the dispositions that had been made of them. The invasion of Canada having been necessarily deferred, the next object of the executive had been to make an advanced movement in that direction, for the purpose of forming a winter encampment at the carrying-place, and for the construction of fortifications at the heads of the two lakes, Champlain and St. Sacrament,—

measures of the first importance, and of the greatest efficiency in affording protection to the frontiers against the predatory bands so frequently issuing from Crown Point. But his purposes had been frustrated by the conduct of the assembly respecting the provisions at Albany; and also by reason of a waste of time, the consequence of which was, that the levies, instead of advancing to the designated point, had been compelled to halt and winter at Saratoga,—an ill-chosen and unsafe locality for a military position. In all these proceedings his excellency said he had had the concurrence of Governor Shirley, as well as of the other colonies uniting in the prosecution of the war. They had all evinced a willingness to share the expense, but in the expectation, of course, that as New York was the most immediately interested in the result of the contest, she would set a cheerful example in meeting the exigency. After reciting various measures that had been adopted for the common security, his excellency intimated that points other than those enumerated, would have been occupied and fortified, but for the obstinate refusal of the assembly to appropriate even the sums necessary for their own safety. He upbraided them for the disrespect with which they had treated his speech at the opening of the session, although in the preparation of that speech he had carefully avoided everything which he supposed could have a tendency to revive the unpleasant difficulties of the former session. Referring to the many difficulties he had been obliged to encounter, especially at Albany, he did not conceal his belief that they had been fomented by the opulent traders of that city, who had grown rich by their trade with Canada, and who were desirous of preserving the neutrality of the Six Nations. He likewise intimated a suspicion that there were Roman Catholic emissaries in the colony,—artful and cunning men,—engaged in treasonable practices,—" dangerous instruments for the destruction of the religion and liberty of the land." In conclusion he said, that notwithstanding the opposition they had made to his measures, there was nothing in his power which he would not cheerfully do "for the security of the frontiers, and to preserve the inhabitants from the incursions of a cruel and barbarous enemy."

On the subject of the suspected disloyalty of some of the people of Albany, to which reference had been made in the message,—charging them in effect with leaguing with the enemy to obstruct the operations against Canada, the governor wrote to Colonel Johnson as follows:

Governor Clinton to Colonel Johnson.

"NEW YORK, April 25th, 1747.

"Sir:

"You will find by a paragraph of a message I sent to the assembly yesterday, that I have taken notice of the endeavors which I suspect some people of Albany have used for to obtain a kind of neutrality between them and Canada.

"You told me of some private messages you heard had been sent by Indians for the purpose. Send me a particular account of what you know and have heard on that subject, and of what you can now, or at any time after this, learn by farther inquiry. I expect you will use all the diligence possible to discover every part of this scheme, and in what manner it has been carried on. I long much to hear from you, for we have most villainous reports spread. I hope the Indians all remain steadfast and in good health.

"In the bill I am going to pass, the council did not think it proper to put rewards for scalping or taking poor women or children prisoners in it; but the assembly has assured me the money shall be paid when it so happens, if the Indians insist upon it.

"I am, Sir,
"Your very humble serv't,
"G. CLINTON."

"To Colonel Johnson."

Those portions of the message alledging that the house had treated his excellency with disrespect, and charging it with neglecting to provide for the safety of the colony, as also the paragraph containing the imputation upon the Albany traders, were received with high displeasure,—real or affected,—and a committee was appointed by resolution with instructions to prepare an answer.[1] The appointment of this committee was made on the twenty-fourth of April; and for several days immediately subsequent, the assembly met but only to adjourn, without proceeding to business. At length, in order to give the members time to abate their choler, the house was adjourned from the second of May to the twelfth, and again to the nineteenth of May.

While these disputes between the executive and his assembly were in progress in the city of New York, affairs at the north were in a sad condition. The levies who had been kept in service during the winter, clamorous for their pay, were almost in a state of mutiny. The officers wrote from Saratoga that they were fearful the garrison would desert in a body. Colonel Roberts wrote to colonel Johnson, announcing the desertion of thirty-four men from a single company; the garrison at Saratoga had become so much weakened, as to create apprehensions that the post would be lost; while the officers wrote to the governor from Albany, that they could not persuade the designated quotas of the northern militia companies to march for the defence of that jeoparded position. During the months of April and May, the communications spread before the executive council upon the subject, were of the most urgent

---

[1] The gentlemen forming this committee were, David Clarkson, Cornelius Van Horne, Paul Richard, Henry Cruger, Frederick Phillipse, John Thomas, Lewis Morris, David Pierson, and William Nicholl Smith, in a note, suggests that the reflection upon the Albany traders, was intended by the governor as a cut at DeLancey, whose father, many years before, during the administration of Governor Burnett, had been largely benefitted by the Indian trade with Canada through Lake Champlain. But Clinton's private letter to Johnson, now first brought to light, shows that he was acting in perfect good faith—having reason to believe the imputation just.

character. Funds for the payment of the troops in part, were remitted; but partial payments by no means sufficed; the discontents became more impatient; and on the thirty-first of May, a dispatch was received from Colonel Roberts, announcing that the levies upon all the frontier stations had united in a solemn resolution that unless their *whole* pay should be immediately forthcoming, they would desert *en masse*, and pay themselves by the plunder of the city and county of Albany. Additional remittances were made with all possible alacrity; but Mr. Clinton nevertheless cautioned the officers against paying at once *all* that was due, lest from the prevailing spirit of insubordination they might still desert the moment their pockets should be filled. Not long before this, two Mohawk Indians had been discovered in an attempt to kill and scalp some of Captain Tiebout's company, stationed at Schenectady. They were lying in wait for that object, and had wounded one man. Roberts wrote to Johnson upon the matter, and as the offenders had been secured, the latter advised that they should be surrendered to their own people for punishment.[1]

The committee charged with the preparation of an address to the governor, made their report on the nineteenth of May. It was very long, extending to nearly eight large folio printed pages; and as it was read to the house, approved, engrossed, and presented to his excellency all on the same afternoon, it must have been evident that its terms, even to a letter, had been previously settled by what is in modern times designated a caucus, and the labor of engrossing performed in anticipation. The spirit of the address was very bitter, though sweetened by terms of ill-dissembled courtesy. They protested with the utmost gravity that it had been far from the intention of the house to give his excellency the least occasion of offence by their former resolutions. The suggestion for the employment of one hundred men to be taken from the levies as rangers, had been made, they averred, in compliance with applica-

---

[1] Journals of the council board.

tions to that effect from the people of Albany; and a precedent for the adoption of that course had been found in the course of his excellency's own proceedings at Albany the year before. By the remark that "the levies had hitherto been unemployed," they meant no more than to say what was known to all, that they had not been employed in the Canada expedition. They were "much concerned that this misconstruction of their innocent intentions," should have induced his excellency to give so full a history as he had done, of his conduct in defence of the country during the preceding year, since in doing so he "had taken the trouble of relating many particulars well known before." They acknowledged the importance of preserving the friendship of the Six Nations, and rehearsed their own proceedings to that end during the entire period of his administration. It was admitted that the crown had defrayed the charges of the great council at Albany of the preceding year; but for the expenses of the council of the year before that, they had voted one thousand pounds, besides appropriations for his excellency's own personal expenses; and they intimated an opinion that while they had not been informed what sums had been actually disbursed for presents to the Indians, there were not wanting individuals who had profited largely in that branch of the service. Yet, notwithstanding all the expenditures upon the Indians, and the pains that had been taken to secure their friendship, they had not joined in the war to any considerable extent. In regard to the governor himself, they had received him with distinguished consideration on his arrival; and in consequence of the efforts he was understood to have made in behalf of the colony before his embarkation for his government, they had voted him a gratuity of a thousand pounds, and had moreover, ill as the colony could bear the expense, caused a new and elegant house to be built for his residence, in conformity to his own plans, besides raising as much for his support as had been allowed to any of his predecessors. In reviewing

CHAP. VII.
1747.

the events of the war and their own acts for sustaining the public service, they recurred to the destruction of Saratoga, two years before, as an event that might not have happened but for the withdrawing of the independent companies from that post. Afterward, at the governor's request, they had appropriated money for rebuilding that fort, which was done, and the works garrisoned by the militia, at the expense of the colony. In addition to this they had also at the governor's request, made appropriations for building other forts to guard the frontier passes. Yet again, the plan of defence having been changed, they had voted money for building a chain of block-houses from the New England border to the castles of the Mohawks; but this plan being in turn abandoned, the money was diverted to the payment and subsistence of detachments of the militia posted upon the frontiers by the governor during the recess of the assembly. They admitted the importance of guarding the passes of the great carrying-place by suitable fortifications, but shrunk from the expense, both for the building, and for the maintenance of garrisons. The other exposed colonies had an equal interest with New York in building and sustaining those defences, and they thought the expense should be shared among them,—intimating a doubt, however, notwithstanding the assurances of his excellency upon that point, whether the colonies referred to would in fact be willing to bear a portion of the burden. Touching his excellency's complaint that his projected northern encampment had been frustrated, and the division of levies destined upon that service compelled by the climate to fall back upon Saratoga for winter quarters, knowing the severity of that climate as they did, they had anticipated as much; and as to the unsuitableness of the locality, as now averred by his excellency, it had at least been rebuilt there by his own directions. His excellency's reference to the difficulties at Albany, the previous autumn, in regard to the delivery and transportation of provisions, whereby as was alleged, his plans had been defeated, was tartly answered. "If," they said, "your excellency means thereby the refusal of "the commissioners to deliver the provisions contrary to "the law you were pleased to pass but a little before, the "house had occasion to give your excellency their thoughts "upon it in their resolves of the seventeenth of November "last, which were by order of the house laid before your "excellency, to which we beg leave to refer." Rehearsing, next, in reply to the charge of the governor that they had not shown a disposition even " to take care of themselves," they pointed to the previous measures they had adopted for the public defence, and the appropriations, among which was one of forty thousand pounds for the northern expedition, as irrefragable proofs of the reality and sincerity of their intentions,—suggesting that if his excellency, on cool reflection did not think them so, " they must be so unhappy "as to despair of giving him satisfaction on that head." They said the appropriations they had made of nine pounds per man for the enlistment of sixteen companies of one hundred men each, and the provisioning of those companies, were nearly exhausted; and they intimated a belief that in the erection of fortifications, great waste had been indulged, and much needless expense incurred for the want of competent engineers. Whenever they should have reason to believe that their money would not be advanced in vain for this department of the public service, and whenever they should have an earnest that the other colonies were prepared to coöperate in the work of mutual protection, they would be found ready to vote for such additional fortifications as might be judged necessary. In regard to the statement in the governor's opening speech, that an agreement had been made with the commissioners of Massachusetts for building the two forts so often recommended, at the passes of the carrying-place, and also in respect to the forces to be raised by the several colonies expected to coöperate in the Canadian invasion, and the rates of expense for each, the assembly was surprised, inasmuch as the governor had but three members of his council with him, while Massachusetts alone of the other colonies was represented at the conference, that his excellency should have entered upon any such agreement. Moreover as they were in the daily expectation of advices from England, hoping withal for the speedy arrival of experienced officers, they trusted his excellency would excuse the house for its opinion, "that they could not in conscience provide for schemes the "execution of which would be very hazardous, and put "the colony to great expense." They told the governor plainly, that "ever since he had thought fit to place his confidence in a person obnoxious to, and censured by the house, the public affairs had been much perplexed, and had not been attended with the steadiness and good conduct which their importance required. They attributed several of his excellency's late speeches to that person, declaring that until the day when he was taken into favor the utmost harmony had existed between all the branches of the government. These thrusts were aimed at Doctor Colden, the lance having been barbed by DeLancey, the master-spirit in fomenting these dissensions. Respecting the charges against the people of Albany, entire disbelief in the justice of the imputation was expressed,—the mind of his excellency having probably been poisoned upon that subject by the individual to whom reference had already been made as an abuser of his confidence. If the people of Albany were indeed engaged in treasonable practices, they marvelled that none of them had been arrested and brought to trial. In answer to his excellency's apprehension that Popish emissaries had been engaged in sowing dissensions and kindling every spark of discontent, the house seized upon the suggestion and applied it to a person then in great favor with Mr. Clinton in the Indian service—Mr. John Henry Lydius, son of a former Dutch minister in Albany, and of course bred a Protestant; who had resided several years in Canada; married a wife there of the Romish church, after having abjured his own religion; and whom they declared to be a person of desperate fortunes. They admitted the great skill of this man "in all the weaknesses of human nature, but wondered how he could have secured his excellency's favor. To him, and his intrigues in Albany, and among the Indians, the assembly attributed many of the difficulties that had arisen. He had been the means of undermining the influence of the Indian commissioners, and distracting the affairs of that department. They nevertheless admitted that there might possibly be some Popish emissaries in the province; but at the same time there was equal reason to believe that there were other men screening themselves behind the curtain, and answering all the ends of such emissaries,—men of wrong heads and worse hearts, who were doing infinite evil by infusing groundless jealousies into his excellency's mind. They next told the governor that although they were not disposed to listen to every idle tale, yet they had hoped that before that period the report might have reached his ears that there had been a large embezzlement of the funds appropriated for Indian presents in 1745,—one thousand pounds having been voted, while not more than three hundred pounds worth of goods had reached the hands of those for whom they were designed. So at least it was said by persons who saw the goods delivered. They also informed the governor,—for the benovolent purpose of enabling him to bring the authors of the scandal to justice,—that a report was current to the effect that French and Spanish prisoners had been sold under the authority of his name, for a pistole a head, to owners and captains of flags of truce. The concluding paragraph contained another pungent reference to Doctor Colden, whose designing artifices and private views, "although they had hitherto been providentially blasted, "it was still feared might at length spring up again, and "bear a greater increase, which God forbid."

Mr. Clinton's reply to the address, which was presented on the twenty-sixth of May, was brief and emphatic. He remarked upon the rapidity with which the address had been hurried through the house,—two hours only having elapsed from the time when it was reported by the committee until its presentation all engrossed! "You shall have," said the governor, "the best answer to this representation "you can expect. I shall take all possible care that it be "laid before his majesty and his ministers, who are the "proper judges of my conduct. I doubt not that the min-"istry will discern with what spirit it is made, and for what "purposes." Commanding an adjournment for a week, the indomitable sailor-governor then dismissed his refractory little parliament.

Reassembling on the second of June, they were met by an executive message calling their attention to the distractions prevailing among the levies at the north, for want of their pay. The governor informed them that thus far these levies had been paid by the crown, he himself having provided the means by drawing bills of exchange. The amount thus drawn was then nine thousand pounds, the whole of which he declared should be applied to the payment of the new levies. Although these bills had all been drawn by the advice of his council, yet his excellency began to fear, or pretended to fear, that they might not all be honored, in which event his private fortune might be involved. Though willing to draw yet farther for that object, yet he was not willing to jeopard his own estate,—believing, as he did, that every man in the province was as much bound as himself to contribute from his private means for the safety of the people. Indemnification against the consequences of a protest of his bills, should he be required to draw any more of them, was therefore demanded in justice to his own family.

The house, in answer, referred to a letter from the duke of Newcastle of April, 1746, authorizing the necessary preparations for the long-projected expedition, with an assurance that the forces to be raised, officers as well as rank and file, should be taken into his majesty's pay. It was therefore clearly not intended by the crown that the payment of these forces should in any event be devolved upon the people of the colony; and the refusal of the governor to continue his drafts would imply a distrust of the king, and render himself personally answerable for the lives and estates of his subjects. Entertaining these views, the assembly peremptorily refused the act of guaranty,—declaring at the same time that as his excellency had the means of paying the forces in his own hands, should he refuse to use them, and should the lives and estates of the people be endangered by the threatened desertion of the levies, "his excellency alone would be to blame."

From the fourth of June to the same day of August, the assembly only met to adjourn. Meantime the governor replenished his exchequer by the usual resort to bills of exchange, and on the nineteenth of June embarked for Albany, in order, if possible, to put an end to the troubles with the levies.

I must not lose sight of Sir Peter Warren, whose name, as an adopted citizen of New York, belongs to its history. France, smarting under the loss of Cape Breton, and mortified at the disastrous failure of D'Anville's armada, determined again to put forth her energies for the recovery of Louisburg, and the resuscitation of her naval character —of late so deeply compromised. To these ends, therefore, another fleet was equipped, at Brest, destined against Louisburg early in the spring, under the command of M. de la Jonquiere. The duty of watching the motions, and, if possible, of intercepting this fleet, was assigned to Vice Admiral Anson,—a widely different man from Admiral Lestock, whose equivocal conduct, on the French coast, when engaged in the like service, has already been recorded. It has already been said that Sir Peter Warren returned to England in the autumn of 1746. In the beginning of the year following he was appointed second in command under Mr. Anson, hoisting his pennant on board the Devonshire, of sixty-six guns. The Brest fleet, uniting a large convoy of Indiamen, and numbering, in all, thirty-eight ships, proceeded to sea about the last of April. It was fallen in with by Admiral Anson, on the third of May, off Cape Finisterre. When descried, nine of the ships,—men of war, mounting from eighteen to seventy-four guns,—were shortening sail and drawing into a line of battle, while the remainder of the fleet, consisting of the vessels under convoy, stretched to the west with all the sails they could set. Anson immediately formed his fleet into a line; but observing by the manœuvres of the enemy that his object was to gain time, for the purpose, probably, of escaping under favor of the night, then approaching, he made signal for the whole fleet to close and engage the enemy, without any regard to the line of battle.[1] In the course of the action that ensued, Warren had an opportunity which he failed not to improve, of signalizing and covering himself with glory. He ran his ship, the Devonshire, up with *Le Sérieux*, the flag-ship of M. de la Jonquiere, and after receiving his fire, which was well-directed, closed within pistol-shot, and continued to engage in the most daring and brilliant style, until the enemy struck. Having silenced his antagonist, Warren proceeded next to encounter the Invincible, seventy-four, commanded by M. de St. George, the second officer of the enemy's squadron. Being seconded by the Bristol, Captain Montague, the Invincible was in a short time dismasted and taken by Warren. The general action was short and brilliant, resulting in the capture of the whole French squadron, consisting of six ships of two decks, including the Gloire, of forty-four guns, and four frigates.[2] It is true that Anson's fleet was greatly superior in the appointment of ships and guns. Three of his ships, however, participated in the action but a very few moments, —having been detached as soon as the Frenchmen were so far crippled as probably to render them unable to get away, with all the sail they could press, after the enemy's flying Indiamen.[3] The loss of the English was not severe,—Cap-

---

[1] Admiralty official report, May 16, 1747.
[2] Charnock.
[3] Admiralty report.

tain Grenville being the only officer of note who was killed. The French were greater sufferers,—M. de la Jonquiere himself was shot under the blade bones of both his shoulders, but the wounds were not mortal. In the month of July following this memorable engagement, being stationed with a squadron off Cape Finisterre, Sir Peter fell in with four valuable merchant ships of the enemy, convoyed by two men of war, which ran into a bay on the island of Sisarga, and being closely pursued they all ran on shore. One of the men of war, mounting forty-four guns, was fired by the crew and blown up before Warren's boats could board her; but the merchantmen were all got off and brought into Plymouth the next day, being the twenty-second of July. Warren was now floating in the tide of fortune, for very shortly after taking these noble prizes at Sisarga, he fell in with and captured a considerable fleet of French West Indiamen. According to one account, this fleet consisted of a very large number of ships, though Charnock, in his biography of Warren, makes no mention of this affair.[1] Sir Peter's gallantry on these occasions, was rewarded by his farther promotion to the rank of admiral of the white. He sailed again from Spithead on a cruise, on the second of September, but falling sick was compelled to relinquish his command and go on shore. But glory had not been the only reward of his splendid career. The number of his captures had produced an ample fortune, which he invested in part, by purchasing a country-seat in Westbury, Hampshire county, to which he now retired. His circumstances must indeed have been affluent. At least so thought some of his relatives, as appears from the following extract from a letter from his nephew, Captain Warren Johnson, to his brother the colonel. This letter also corroborates the preceding account of the last great capture of West India merchantmen, not mentioned by Charnock:

---

[1] Gentleman's Magazine.

Captain Warren Johnson to his Brother.

"NEW YORK, September 13, 1747.

"Dear Brother:

"Last evening I arrived here from Louisburg, in order to go to England in the Scarborough man of war.

* * * * * * * * *

"I make no doubt you have heard of my uncle Warren's great success in his two cruises, the first with Admiral Anson, and the second with a squadron of which he was commander-in-chief—part of which fell in with the St. Domingo fleet, and took sixty-two sail of them. He had taken several rich ships before. He must now be one of the richest men in England, and not one has done his country so much service. He must be worth three or four hundred thousand pounds sterling. He is now vice admiral of the white, and a member of parliament from Westminster, and I have no doubt in a very short time he will be a peer of England, there being no person better able to maintain that dignity.

* * * * * * * * *

"Your most affectionate Brother,
"WARREN JOHNSON."

"Colonel Johnson."

In the autumn of this year, Sir Peter was returned to parliament. He was likewise at about the same time presented with a large silver monteth, of curious workmanship, by the inhabitants of Barbadoes, in acknowledgment of his services in the cruise of that season.[1] The exultation of Sir Peter's relatives at his good fortune was justifiable, for they had been bravely won.

---

[1] Gentleman's Magazine.

CHAPTER VIII.
1747.

Governor Clinton, who, as already observed in the last chapter, had departed for Albany on the nineteenth of June, did not leave an hour too early, for the military affairs in that quarter were in a deplorable condition. Instead of increasing them, for the purpose of offensive operations, the forces were diminished by sickness and desertion, and the thousand mischances incident to an army of irregulars kept in the field contrary to their own inclinations. In such numbers did they desert, that a party of thirty-eight in a body were fired upon by the officers at Æsopus, and retaken,—two of them being wounded. They were marched back to Albany.[1] The road from Mount Johnson to Oswego, was infested by the enemy; murders were committed at Burnetsfield;[2] so that Colonel Johnson could not forward supplies without a strong guard, thus materially enhancing the expense of executing his contract for that post;[3] while in addition to all, as if grown weary of awaiting an invasion at Crown Point, the French, with their Indians, were again showing themselves in formidable numbers in the vicinity of Saratoga. Colonel Johnson was advised, on the sixteenth of June, by the return of an unsuccessful war-party of the Schoharies,[4] of the approach upon Lake Champlain, of a fleet of three hundred canoes, and admonished to be on his guard against a surprise.[5] Im-

---

[1] Manuscript letter: John H. Lydius to Colonel Johnson.
[2] The present village of Herkimer.
[3] Manuscript Letter: Johnson to Clinton.
[4] A clan of the Mohawks.
[5] Manuscript Letter: Lydius to Johnson.

mediately on the arrival of this intelligence at Saratoga, Captain Chew was ordered forth with a detachment of one hundred men to reconnoitre the country between that post and the head of Lake Champlain. Falling in with the enemy on the nineteenth of June, an action ensued in which fifteen of his men were killed, and forty-seven more, with himself, taken prisoners. The detachment encountered by Chew was commanded by M. Lacose, who immediately fell back upon a much larger force, occupying the path of communication between the Hudson and the lake. But Lacose did not fall back without leaving a detachment of three hundred men, under M. Laquel, to lurk about Saratoga, and cut off approaching supplies. According to the representation of one of the enemy's Indians, who deserted and came into Saratoga, the main force of the French at the carrying-place consisted of twelve companies. The Indian informed farther, that Lacose was to advance again immediately with artillery and mining tools, to lay seige to the fort. Meantime the three hundred who had been left in the environs of the fort, under M. Laquel, performed bold service by appearing openly and attempting to fire a block-house, used, as they supposed, as a magazine, by shooting burning arrows against its walls. "The person "appointed to perform this duty," said the commander of the fort in a letter written to Colonel Johnson, "had a "blanket carried before him that he might not discover the "fire upon the points of the arrows.[1]" The main body of the enemy soon moved down to Fish Creek, a few miles north of Saratoga, and a detachment of his troops was thrown between that post and Albany. Colonel Schuyler immediately marched with his regiment, and such other forces as he could raise on the instant, to meet the invader; who, however, though greatly superior in numbers, retired at his approach and fell back to Crown Point.

The Indian allies of the English were again becoming

---

[1] Letter to Colonel Johnson, copied in his own hand, but the signature of which is omitted.

much dissatisfied with the languor pervading the service. After having, though with great reluctance, been incited to engage in the war, they were desirous of seeing it prosecuted with vigor. A number of their chiefs now met Colonel Schuyler and complained bitterly of the continued and most discouraging delays. They had been chiefly induced to take the war-path against the French by the extraordinary preparations they had marked as in progress for the invasion, and they had not themselves been backward in annoying the enemy; but as they were convinced from the present inactivity of the English, that the design of an invasion must have been laid aside,—a conviction strengthened by the daily and rapid decrease of the new levies,—they said they should be necessitated to make peace with the French for themselves, on the best terms they could. Still, if the English would immediately march against Crown Point, they would cheerfully assist them with one thousand of their best warriors.[1]

I have found no record of Mr. Clinton's doings at Albany during this visit, save a single sentence in a letter written by him to the duke of Newcastle upon his return to the city, to the effect that while at Albany, he had prevailed upon two powerful Indian natives—formerly in the French interest—to join the English. The visit, however, was probably a short one, since he was at the council board again in July. But from the letters of Colonel Johnson it appears that he met the governor and concerted arrangements for relieving Oswego,—Lieutenant Visscher having been dispatched thither with a cargo of goods, provisions, and ammunition.

Meantime notwithstanding the loss of so great a portion of the open season, and the utter neglect of the contest by the ministers, so far at least as the colonies were concerned, Governor Shirley was pushing his design of an attack upon Crown Point, with all the zeal and energy of his character, and all the means at his command. There could be no

[1] Gentleman's Magazine, September, 1747.

security for the frontiers either of New York or New England from the devastations of the enemy, until Crown Point, the grand rendezvous of the numerous war-parties continually harrassing the border, should be wrested from him; and in order to unity of action, and the organization and concentration of a force adequate to the undertaking, Shirley wrote to Clinton in July, proposing a congress of the colonies from New Hampshire to Virginia, both inclusive, to consult for the common defence, and render their efforts for the prosecution of the war more effective. He informed Mr. Clinton that he had summoned a meeting of the Massachusetts legislature to consider the subject, and he urged a similar course upon New York. He said he had made like communications to the colonies included in the project, urging them all to coöperate,—Massachusetts, at all events, being determined to exert her utmost power in the enterprise. He was very anxious that the Six Nations should be persuaded to greater exertions than they had hitherto made; and for the better security of the northwestern settlements of Massachusetts, he asked that one hundred rangers might be employed by New York between Saratoga and the New England border.[1]

The general assembly of New York came together again for the transaction of business on the fourth of August, when Shirley's letter was laid before them by the governor, accompanied by a message informing them that by the advice of his council he had acceded to the proposal contained in that letter, and that the forces of the province were to be put into action in conjunction with those of Massachusetts and Connecticut. The season for offensive operations, however, was already too far advanced to allow of a meeting of commissioners to make estimates of the expense, and to adjust the proportions which each colony respectively should bear. But on a rough calculation it was thought that fourteen thousand pounds would cover the charges of the intended movement, and his excellency

---

[1] See Shirley's letter in the minutes of the council board.

trusted that neither of the colonies would be backward in meeting its just share of the amount. Indeed, he thought New York might venture to assume more than its quota, both Massachusetts and Connecticut having advanced considerable sums to stimulate the Six Nations in continuing their incursions against the enemy. The governor said he had received the renewed assurances of the good feelings of the Six Nations, with pledges of their most vigorous assistance; and he had likewise reason to expect the aid of several more distant tribes, heretofore in the interests of the French. He would bring no other subject to the attention of the assembly then, wishing their immediate action upon this important matter, that he might communicate their determination to the other governments forthwith, and thus prevent further loss of time.

The message was not met in a corresponding spirit by the assembly, but on the contrary, the first action was the adoption of a series of resolutions insulting the governor, and evasive as to the object specially pressed upon their consideration. They cautiously declared their willingness to come into any "well-concerted" scheme for annoying the common enemy, but they would not consent to raise moneys upon the "pretence" contained in the message, without a better knowledge of the "grounds" and "reasons." They doubted whether Massachusetts and Connecticut had ever contributed any "considerable sums" for the Indian service, and even if they had done so, New York had paid more than both of them put together,—adding to the sentence the significant insinuation—"and his excellency knows how these sums have been applied." Still, for the promotion of any "well concerted scheme" against the enemy by the three colonies named in the message, they would consent to bear one-third of the expense; believing, however, that the other colonies, not mentioned, ought to contribute to the cause. These negative resolves were adopted on the sixth of August. From that day until the thirty-first, not the least attention was paid by the assembly to the state of the colony,—its time being occupied upon bills of comparatively trifling moment, such as for farming out the excise,—for raising a farther sum by lottery toward founding a college,—and for the examination of the public accounts for the year 1713; for preventing desertions from the forces, &c., &c.

But if the assembly was idle, the enemy was not, and the people of the northern settlements, even of Albany itself, were in a high state of alarm, and that not without reason. Parties of the enemy had penetrated south of the Mohawk, into the valley of the Schohariekil, where a number of men had been killed and scalped. Saratoga was also once more nearly if not quite surrounded by the foeman, and several persons had likewise been killed in that vicinity. How Colonel Johnson was engaged at this time, will appear by the following extracts from a letter addressed by him to the governor:

Colonel Johnson to Governor Clinton.

"MOUNT JOHNSON, August 13, 1747.

"May it please your excellency:

"I enclose the message sent by the New England Indians to their uncles, the Mohawks, and their answer to it, by which all people may see that the Indians are in earnest, and resolved to proceed in the war. I this day had an account by an Indian express from Oswego, that there were a great number of Senecas, and some of the foreign Indians with them, (called the Flat Heads,) coming down to me with several belts of wampum,—one whereof is a vast large one,—almost like the one your excellency gave the Six Nations last summer,—which belt must purport a great deal of news. I expect them here in two days, and am making everything ready for their reception. As soon as I have heard the news, and have done with them, I shall let your excellency know the purport.

* * * * * * * * * *

"I spoke to your excellency when in Albany, about necessaries for the men destined for the Indian service, but find nothing done about it. I have not one pair of Indian shoes for them, without which they cannot go through the woods. I proposed doing great service with these men, and the Indians together, but it seems I may not have the opportunity; for there is not even one of the companies which were ordered for that service moved up here yet, which makes the Indians think worse and worse of us, after assuring them they should be up very shortly. I lead a most miserable life among them at present, occasioned by so many disappointments.

* * * * * * * * * *

"There is one thing which I wish your excellency to consider of, which is my extraordinary expense in keeping several hands employed to attend the numbers of Indians I have daily had at my house these twelve months past; as also of a clerk, who, with myself, has more work than men can well bear. This the country is very sensible of. So I shall leave it to your excellency's consideration what to do in it."[1]

* * * * * * * * * *

On the twenty-fourth of August, information was received by the governor from Albany, that the forces stationed there had been withdrawn from the city, and posted on the east side of the Hudson, a mile below, by which movement the city was left defenceless, greatly exposed, and the people much alarmed. Several gentlemen from Albany were examined upon the subject before the legislative council, who confirmed the statement. It farther appeared that depredations had been committed by the enemy in the very precincts of Albany; that there were not more than three hundred of its citizens, old and young, capable of bearing arms; and that all were compelled, from the aged judge of the court to the stripling, to mount guard in turn each one every fourth night,—whereupon an address was presented to the governor praying that the levies at the north be ordered to move into the city and remain there for its pro-

---

[1] Manuscript Letter.

tection until otherwise directed. The cause of this movement of the troops from Albany nowhere appears. It seems, however, to have been of a piece with the bustling, yet strangely inefficient conduct of the war in this quarter from the beginning.

Impatient, and not without reason, at the inaction of the assembly, the governor sent them a message on the thirty-first of August, informing them explicitly that he would no longer furnish provisions for the four independent companies stationed at Albany, at the expense of the crown, nor for the levies from the southern counties, destined for the Canadian expedition. Neither would he draw any longer upon the crown for the support of the Indian department, although he could not disguise the fact that a failure of supplies for the Indian war-parties, might be followed by frightful consequences. He therefore requested a vote of supplies for those objects of the public service for two months,—by the end of which time he hoped to receive definite information as to his majesty's pleasure respecting the forces at Albany, and also to learn whether the neighboring colonies would contribute toward the defence of the country. He informed them that since the invasion of the enemy at Burnetsfield, Colonel Johnson could no longer supply the post at Oswego, save at double the former expense, nor even then unless furnished with a guard to escort the stores. A vote of supplies for this object, and also to defray the cost of transporting provisions to Saratoga, was necessary, since these expenses could no longer be borne by the crown. Accompanying the message was an extract from a letter from Colonel Johnson, informing the governor that he was about to set out at the head of a considerable party of Christians and Indians in quest of a large body of the enemy and his allies who had been discovered between Saratoga and Crown Point. This letter was dated on the nineteenth of August. Two days afterward another dispatch from the colonel, dated the twenty-eighth, was communicated to the assembly upon the same subject.

The assembly replied by resolutions declaring that neither the crown nor the colony need be at the expense of supporting the four companies of independent fusileers stationed at Albany, they having always subsisted themselves, out of their own pay, save when detached to distant posts, as at Oswego, for example, in which cases the colony had always furnished the supplies, as of course they ought. The colony, it was said, had from time to time, and sometimes even without his excellency's recommendation, provisioned the sixteen companies of one hundred levies each; and it appeared to the assembly unreasonable that they should be burdened with the farther expense of supporting the forces from the more southern colonies, which ought each to provide for their own. In regard to the Indian service, inasmuch as the crown had authorized the making of such presents to them in 1746, as would secure their hearty coöperation in the war, they urged that his excellency ought to continue drawing upon that source, for that object, at least until his majesty's pleasure should be signified to the contrary,—hoping at the same time—for the house lost no opportunity of renewing, at least by implication, the charge of a former embezzlement of Indian presents,—that his excellency had made such use of the means placed in his hands by the crown for that object, as had been for the advantage of his majesty's service. So of supplying Saratoga, as his excellency's bills for supplying that post had thus far been borne by the crown, he should continue to draw until instructed to the contrary. Respecting the hardship of Colonel Johnson's case, it was held that according to his excellency's own message of December second, 1746, that gentleman had contracted to supply the garrison at Oswego upon the same terms in war as in peace. No additional allowance ought therefore to be made to him for that service, even for defraying the expenses of guards. The pressure of the enemy upon the northern settlements, however, awakened the assembly to a partial sense of duty in the emergency; and having thus cavalierly discussed those subjects of the message, it had the grace to resolve that provision ought to be made for the pay and subsistence of three companies of rangers, of fifty men each, for the protection of the inhabitants against the skulking parties of the enemy,—one for the defence of Albany, one for Schenectady, and one for Kinderhook. The feelings of Mr. Clinton in regard to these resolutions, may be inferred from the subjoined letter communicating a copy thereof to Colonel Johnson: It also shows the high estimate which Clinton placed upon the services which Johnson was then rendering to the country:

Governor Clinton to Colonel Johnson.
NEW YORK, September 7, 1747.

"Sir:

My last letter to you was dated the twentieth of August. Soon after I received yours of the fourteenth, seventeenth, and nineteenth, acquainting me of your intention of going out with a party of Indians and Christians; and very uneasy I have been ever since, afraid lest that letter should be the means of your laying aside such a glorious design, which must always redound to your honored reputation. You ought to receive the thanks of the whole province for what you have already done for it, but am sorry to say, instead of public thanks, you have the frowns of an inveterate assembly, as you will see by the inclosed resolves. But I hope you will receive thanks from their superiors.

"I must now acknowledge the receipt of yours of the twenty-eighth of August, which I immediately communicated to the council and assembly, in hopes it would have touched their souls.[1] But notwithstanding it was delivered to them before their resolve about the provisions for

---

[1] Johnson was very careful in preserving the original draughts of his letters. But the letter we have spoken of, with many hundreds of others, has not survived the ravages of time and chance. According to the entry of its substance in the minutes of the council board, however, the force the colonel was now preparing to lead against the enemy, consisted of "four hundred Christians and about the same number of Indians."

Oswego, it had no effect on them. But I will venture to say, that though these stubborn Dutchmen won't do you the justice they ought, yet when I represent to his majesty the vast progress you have made, (beyond any reasonable expectation,) by your good management, and most extraordinary influence with the Indians, which you surprisingly cultivate continually, your conduct and behavior will be greatly approved by his majesty, and in such a manner as may show these wretches you have merited your royal master's favor, in a great measure preserving not only this but all the northern colonies from ruin.

"I acquainted governor Shirley what you desired in relation to Lydius, who desired I would acquaint you he was sorry you had taken umbrage at Lydius's being concerned with you in what has been done by his government towards securing the Indians of the Six Nations in our interest. He would not have you imagine that himself, or any part of his government, puts Lydius's services in the least computation with your own, or that the Indians have been engaged in acts of hostility against the French, by any person's influence but your own, under my directions; and your uncle Sir Peter, to whom his letters on that head, and the duke of Newcastle, have been shown, can inform you that he has done your merit all the justice in his power.

"For my part I think this expedition you have now undertaken, to be of such infinite service to this and the neighboring colonies, that though I was determined to be at no more charges for the Indians at the expense of the crown, yet I can't avoid doing it again in justice to you and the brave Indians who are on this party with you; for which reason, whatever goods and expense you are at, for satisfying the Indians, on your return I will give you my bills on the treasury therefor. But then I must desire you to give it out, (and to let nobody know to the contrary) that you take this expense upon yourself from the faith you have in the assembly, which can't refuse to pay you for service that is so absolutely necessary for the safety of the people of this province.

"I would send you up money, but as I writ you word in my letter of the twentieth, I could not get a farthing, on account of a man-of-war going to England. I should therefore be glad if you would take bills for the account you sent me, and add this to it, your uncle can solicit it, and I promise to do all in my power, both with the duke of Newcastle and Mr. Pelham, to get them immediately paid; and I can assure you you may depend on Mr. Shirley's interest in it entirely. I think you had best come down, and we can together settle things to the satisfaction of both of us.

"Commissioners are come from Boston to negotiate a scheme for securing the Indians and frontiers, and I expect others.[1] It will not be amiss to acquaint the Indians of it. I hope Mr. Shirley and I shall soon agree upon something to keep the Indians steadfast in our interest.

"You have several friends on the spot who heartily wish you well, and a great deal of success; and I do assure you nobody does it more heartily than, dear sir,

"Your faithful friend and serv't,

G. CLINTON.

"P. S. I must caution you to be on your guard, for some people who ought to bear a greater regard for you than they ever showed, considering the alliance between them and Sir Peter, have some designs not to save you, take my word, but themselves. I wait with great impatience to hear from you.[2]

"Colonel Johnson."

---

[1] These commissioners were Samuel Wells, Robert Hale, and Oliver Partridge. Shirley's letter announcing their appointment, was received and laid before Governor Clinton's council on the fourth of September. On the eleventh, Roger Wolcott, Thomas Fitch, and Benjamin Hall, were announced as the commissioners from Connecticut. On the twenty-second, Philip Livingston, and Joseph Murray, of the executive council, and William Nicholl, Philip Verplanck, and Harry Cruger, of the assembly, were appointed commissioners to the congress on the part of New York.

[2] Manuscript letter.

The sailor-governor, who certainly wrote his own letters, although Colden had the credit of preparing his state-papers, was not the best rhetorician of his day. Still, he could write well enough to make himself understood. Colonel Johnson was now evidently in high favor with his excellency, while the members of the assembly were denounced with emphasis, though in a private letter, as "wretches." The character of Lydius was questionable, and there was probable cause for the jealousy of Johnson toward him. Lydius had visited Boston during the preceding month of May, and from the tenor of a letter addressed to him soon after his return to Albany, by Colonel Stoddard, of Northampton, which I find among the Johnson papers, he must have succeeded in imposing himself upon Governor Shirley and his counsellors as a man of no mean consideration. The postscript to the foregoing letter of Mr. Clinton, referred, of course, to DeLancey, now become the master-spirit of the assembly, and who had probably moved the house to the hostile resolution against Johnson. But the chief justice was too wary to commit himself upon paper,—using Mr. Horsmanden, his associate upon the bench, as his amanuensis. The resolutions and addresses of the assembly during this stormy period were understood to have been written by him, and the day on which he was to be punished for these labors, was now rapidly drawing nigh. Having invested the chief justice with a commission irrevocable during good behavior, and therefore being unable to visit him with his resentment, the governor determined to bestow the full measure of his vengeance upon his instrument. Accordingly, on the twelfth day of September, Mr. Horsmanden was suspended from his majesty's service as a member of the council, and a note of his suspension was directed to be entered upon the journals. The reasons for this procedure the governor said he would cause to be laid before his majesty. Having also been previously named as one of the commissioners to meet the representatives from the other colonies in con-

CHAP. VIII.
1747.

gress, Mr. Horsmanden's name was ordered to be stricken from that commission.[1] Nor was his degradation completed until his removal from the bench, and from the recordership of the city,—measures that followed in quick succession. Yet he continued to hold the pen for the assembly for a considerable time afterward. Being poor, however, he was compelled to rely upon the private bounty of his friends and partisans; and those who know the selfishness and ingratitude of politicians, in all ages, and almost without an exception, may well judge how he fared. In the emphatic language of Smith, he was "employed, applauded,—and ruined.[2]"

The return of Colonel Johnson from his expedition toward Crown Point in search of the enemy, whom he was not able to find, was announced to the governor by express on the thirteenth of September. Very unpleasant intelligence, however, had been received from that direction a few days before, filling the assembly and the people with alarm. The fort at Saratoga was garrisoned by the New Jersey levies, commanded by Colonel Peter Schuyler; but as Mr. Clinton was inflexible in his purpose of drawing no more upon the crown, there was danger of a speedy evacuation of the post for want of provisions. Indeed, information to that effect from Colonel Schuyler himself, caused the assembly, without waiting for his excellency's answer to their resolutions of the second of September, to address him on the ninth, praying earnestly for the adoption of such

---

[1] Minutes of the council board.

[2] "Such was his condition, until he raised himself by an advantageous match, and, by forsaking his associates, reconciled himself to Mr. Clinton, when that governor broke with the man whose indiscretion and vehemence the chief justice had improved, to expose both to the general odium of the colony. Until his marriage with Mrs. Vesey, Mr. Horsmanden was an object of pity; toasted indeed as the man who dared to be honest in the worst of times, but at a loss for his meals, and, by the importunity of his creditors, hourly exposed to the horrors of a jail; and hence his irreconcilable enmity to Doctor Colden, by whose advice he fell, and to Mr. DeLancey, whose ambitious politics exposed him to the vengeance of that minister."—*Smith*, vol. ii. page 139.

measures as would prevent the destruction of the forces, and preserve the fortress from falling into the hands of the enemy, with its heavy cannon and stores. In the event of the desertion of the Jerseymen, the house suggested that the post might be regarrisoned by a detachment from the new levies destined against Canada. Or, if these levies were not still within his excellency's command, they prayed that a portion of the independent fusileers might be sent thither, the assembly pledging the necessary supplies for that service. But before this address had been presented, the governor had rendered any answer thereto unnecessary by a message of a very decided character in reply to the resolutions of the house of the preceding week, in which all the demands for supplies contained in his last preceding message, were reiterated, with a threat that unless the house should revoke its determination not to provide for the transportation of supplies to the outposts, together with its refusal to allow Colonel Johnson a guard to convey the supplies for Oswego, he should be under the necessity of withdrawing the garrisons both from the last mentioned post, and from Saratoga,—points which would of course be immediately occupied by the enemy. Recapitulating again the history of his own successful negotiations with the Indians, and extolling the services of Colonel Johnson, his excellency reminded the assembly of the great expense to which the crown had been put in bringing the Indians into their present amicable state of feeling toward the English, and insisted that the colony ought in justice to defray the future charge of maintaining those relations. In any event, he demanded appropriations to cover the demands of the service for at least two months, admonishing the assembly that if this demand should again be refused, the responsibility for every calamity that might consequently ensue, would rest upon them. "If," said his excellency in closing, "you deny me the necessary supplies, all my endeavors must become ineffectual and fruitless; I must wash my hands, and leave at your doors the blood of the innocent people that may be shed by a cruel and merciless enemy." This message was received by the house on the tenth, and referred to a committee. One day after, the committee deputed to wait upon his excellency with the resolutions of the ninth, reported that they had discharged their duty, but that the governor had declined answering them. Whereupon it was forthwith resolved that his excellency be again addressed to the same effect as before in regard to the perilous condition of Saratoga; and on the sixteenth another series of resolutions was adopted, embodying the exact substance of those of the ninth, save that the assembly now avowed a willingness, should Colonel Johnson, by any unforseen accident, be a sufferer in the execution of his contract for supplying the garrison at Oswego, to take his case into consideration, and do for him whatever might appear to be reasonable. But upon every other point the house insisted upon its former positions.

This vexatious game of cross purposes was interrupted by successive adjournments, by command of the governor, until the fifth of October,—not, however, without a remonstrance by the assembly against these interruptions, and a vote of censure for the inconvenience to which his excellency was subjecting the members. Yet Mr. Clinton deserved not the censure, being engaged during the recess in active negotiations with the commissioners from the several colonies then in session, and not desiring the presence of the assembly until the results of those negotiations could be communicated. Meantime, as volunteers could not be obtained for recruiting the garrison at Oswego, Colonel Philip Schuyler was ordered to draft the requisite number of men for that service from his own regiment; and Colonel Roberts was directed to send three companies of levies to Saratoga, with instructions that should it be found impossible to maintain that post, the fort and blockhouses must be destroyed, and the cannon and military stores removed to Albany.[1] Very shortly afterward advices

---
[1] Journals of the council board.

were received that the latter clause of the instructions had been obeyed to the letter. The fort had been burnt and the stores removed as directed,—by which measure of questionable necessity the northern frontiers was left entirely uncovered.[2]

At the earnest solicitation of the governor, Colonel Johnson had now arrived in New York for consultation respecting the condition of the colony at large; and on the third of October, a committee of the executive council was directed to summon the colonel before them for examination, with special relation to Indian affairs and the measures proper to be pursued in their immediate administration. The examination was held on the ninth. The colonel's advice was, that an agent should be dispatched to Oswego without delay, with suitable presents for distribution among the Indians, in order to preserve their existing good disposition. He stated that when he first engaged in the management of the affairs of that department their sachems were chiefly in the French interest, and had actually received belts from them which they had since given up, receiving belts from him in their stead, in behalf of the English. He believed that unless proper measures were taken to secure them in their present favorable mood, there would be great dissatisfaction and danger resulting from repeated disappointments. He stated that the Indians had been detained from hunting during the whole year, by the directions of the governor, and were consequently in a state of destitution,—actually suffering for many necessaries for themselves and their families. Should not the necessary measures be taken for their relief, he felt that he himself would be obliged to leave his Mohawk settlement, and his removal would of course be the signal for a general flight of the people from that valley also. He furthermore thought it of importance that the English should build a fort in the Oneida country, and another among the Senecas. The Indians would be gratified at the adoption of

---

Journals of the council board.

measures like these, which in themselves would go far to secure their confidence. At the close of his examination the colonel made a complaint on oath against several persons for selling rum to the Indians, and the attorney-general was instructed to institute prosecutions for the offence.[1]

The commissioners of Massachusetts, Connecticut and New York having closed their deliberations, Mr. Clinton communicated the result of their conferences to the general assembly on the sixth of October. Long and tedious as had been the procrastination, the expedition against Crown Point and the invasion of Canada, was still uppermost in the minds of Shirley and Governor Clinton; and the message announced a compact agreed upon by the commissioners, for the immediate prosecution of the long-deferred enterprise. By the terms of that compact, New York was bound to have a certain number of men in readiness to march on a certain day; and supplies were demanded for raising and paying the levies, and for covering all other expenses connected with that service, save for arms, ammunition, and camp equipage, which were to be provided by the crown. But the season for warlike operations in the north had again so nearly passed away, that it was yet again found necessary to defer the expedition until the ensuing spring. Nevertheless, contrary to Mr. Clinton's wishes, and indeed against his earnest entreaties, the commissioners had concerted nothing for the security of the frontiers of New York, nor for the equally important object of preserving the friendship of the fitful Indians. For both these objects, therefore, supplies were needed. Mr. Clinton again reviewed the history of his own labors in the Indian department;—taking care to mention that since the treaty of the preceding year, Massachusetts had given presents to the Six Nations to the amount of one thousand pounds, and Connecticut to the amount of three hundred; while neither at the treaty referred to, nor since, had New York been put to any expense for that service,—the whole having

---

[1] Minutes of the council board.

been borne by the crown. "But," said his excellency, "I can no longer, and will no longer, continue this charge on the crown." The views of Colonel Johnson were enforced, especially his suggestions that forts should be erected in the several cantons of the Six Nations. The Indians were yet friendly; but they had been so frequently disappointed in their expectation that Canada would before now have been strongly invaded by sea and land, that the most wise and efficient measures would be necessary for preserving their confidence. Although the entire charge of the Indian service, and the defence of the frontiers, would henceforward devolve upon the colony, yet his excellency said he intended to make an appeal to the governments of the colonies south, as far as, and including Virginia, to contribute to the expense—the public defence being an object common to all. In conclusion, after a variety of suggestions as to the best method of raising and sustaining the quota of levies falling upon New York, the message stated that the sachems of the Six Nations were then in the city, awaiting the determination of the house, concerning themselves and what was to be done for them. They had been accompanied by Colonel Johnson, "whose name," said the governor, "I cannot mention without grateful remembrances of the services he has done his country." These sachems were impatient to be gone; and the message strongly urged upon the assembly the immediate adoption of such measures as would soothe their feelings, and send them away with presents so liberal as to be satisfactory.

According to the articles of the compact founded by the commissioners, Crown Point was first to be reduced. The number of troops to be raised for the expedition, was four thousand, exclusive of all the Indians who could be brought into the service. Of these four thousand levies, New York was to furnish twelve hundred from its own territory, and four hundred more, to be drawn from Massachusetts, and paid for by New York,—bounties, wages and supplies. For the Indian service of the campaign, Massachusetts stipulated to pay nine-twentieths of the expense, New York eight-twentieths, and Connecticut three. Every Indian warrior was to be equipped to the value of five pounds, and at the close of the expedition, a present to the same amount. The three colonies were to appoint and commission the three general officers who were to conduct the expedition. Applications are to be made to the other colonies, from New Hampshire to Virginia inclusive, to exert themselves to the extent of their ability in the prosecution of the war, and generally for the common defence. They were also to be invited to send delegates to meet in a grand committee of conference at Middletown, in Connecticut, in December. Meantime an application was to be made to the crown to create a diversion in Canada by sending a large fleet into the St. Lawrence, to attack the citadel of Quebec in accordance with the plan concerted two years before. In the event of a refusal on the part of ministers thus to coöperate in the grand design, the colonies were to create the diversion themselves, by fitting out such a fleet as they might, to act in concert with such ships of war as might chance to be cruising upon the American station. In case of a failure of both branches of the enterprise, the first three parties to the agreement, were each to employ a corps of rangers to harrass the border settlements of the enemy, and make war upon their allies, as best they could —the other colonies being invited to aid in this description of service likewise. In the event of an invasion of either of the colonies, parties to the agreement, the others were to march to their assistance. The forces to be directed against Crown Point, were to rendezvous at Albany as early as the fifteenth of April then ensuing,—1748. The concluding article of the compact set forth as a reason for this alliance the utter inability of the colonies, singly, to maintain a sufficient force to guard so extensive a frontier,—it being five hundred miles in length. Already they had suffered severely from the repeated and frequent incursions of the enemy, the loss of life, and the destruction of their towns and hamlets. To put an end to such a harrassing species of warfare, the reduction of Crown Point was indispensable; and the commissioners strongly appealed to the other colonies, less exposed only because guarded and protected by them, and who were in fact better able to defray the charges of this war than themselves, to come to their assistance. Nothing could have been more reasonable than such an appeal, but its reception was more cold than redounded to the credit of the parties directly appealed to, either for their patriotism or liberality.

Mr. Clinton had requested a speedy answer to his message communicating these important arrangements, and it was given two days afterward in a series of resolutions, in part, at least, very little to his liking. Although the assembly voted with alacrity for everything essential to the Canadian invasion, for the defence of the frontier during the intervening winter, and supplies for making suitable presents to the Indians chiefs brought to the city by Colonel Johnson, yet among the resolutions were some breathing a spirit of rank and bitter hostility. Of this description was one setting forth that although his excellency had made large drafts upon the crown for the Indian service during the preceding summer, no disposition of the avails had been heard of. But the importance of preserving the alliance of the Six Nations was so great that they would nevertheless vote for the sum of eight hundred pounds for that object, *to be placed in the hands of proper persons for disbursement.* This proviso was but a thinly disguised impeachment of the executive integrity. In reference to the building of forts in the Indian country, for the security of the women and children and old men while the warriors were absent in the service, the vote was conditional that the other colonies must share the expense. The forces at Albany destined for the defence of that section of the frontier during the approaching winter, the house was not inclined to take into pay unless their discharge should be directed by his majesty. News of the destruction of the fort at

Saratoga not having yet reached the ears of the assembly, it was voted that that post should be preserved at all events; and a resolution of censure was added because the governor had not responded to the proceedings of the house in respect to that fortress, on the ninth and eleventh of September.

The wrath of the governor was kindled by these resolutions to vehemence as will sufficiently appear by the following laconic reply:

"Gentlemen:

By your votes I understand you are going upon things very foreign to what I recommended to you: I will receive nothing from you at this critical juncture, but what relates to the message I last sent you, viz: By all means immediately to take the preservation of your frontiers, and the fidelity of the Indians into consideration. The loss of a day may have fatal consequences; when that is over, you may have time enough to go upon other matters.

G. CLINTON."

The effect of this message was like the casting of a live coal into a magazine of gun-powder. In its consideration the doors of the assembly were shut, locked, and the key laid upon the table in the due and ancient form in cases of alleged breaches of privilege; and a series of resolutions was passed, *nemine contradicente*, wherein it was declared to be the undoubted right and privilege of the house to proceed upon all proper subjects for their consideration, in such order, method and manner as to themselves should seem most convenient;—that any attempt to direct or prescribe to the house the manner in which they must proceed in their discussions of public affairs, was a manifest breach of the rights of the house and the people;—that the declaration of the governor that he would receive nothing from the house at that time but what had been recommended in his message, was irregular and unprecedented—tending to the subversion of the rights, liberties and privileges of the house and the people;—and that whoever had *advised* that message had attempted to undermine those rights and privileges, and to subvert the constitution of the colony, and was moreover an enemy to its inhabitants. The resolutions were followed up immediately by an address, or remonstrance to his excellency, extending to the great length of eight printed folio pages, conceived in the same acrimonious spirit which had indeed characterized the proceedings of both parties for many months. It professed to review the whole controversy between the governor and themselves from its inception, being his excellency's message of June sixth, 1746. Down to that period, the remonstrance declared that the utmost harmony had existed between them, and their distractions had only arisen since his excellency "had thought fit to place his sole confidence in that person who styles himself the next in administration, and been pleased to submit himself to his direction and influence." This individual, Dr. Colden, was bitterly denounced. In reviewing the late proceedings both of the governor and themselves, in connexion specially, with the Indian affairs, the executive was severely censured for taking the management of those affairs from the hands of the Indian commissioners at Albany, and confiding them to other individuals, the chief of whom, of course, was Colonel Johnson. Much of the ill-feeling of the Indians, prior to the treaty of 1746, was attributed to the intrigues of designing men, seeking to supplant the commissioners for interested and mercenary purposes. Instead of the course the governor had pursued by the summary employment of individuals, if dissatisfied with the conduct of old commissioners, he should have caused them to be suspended by new appointments issued in a regular manner.

This attack upon Colonel Johnson showed very conclusively that he was at that time in no favor with his relative, Mr. DeLancey. His excellency had repeatedly advocated, in his late messages, not, indeed without an air of self-complacency, to his successful diplomacy with the Indians, whereby he had changed their policy, and defeated the designs of the people of Albany, whose aim it was to keep the Indians from the war-path, and allow them to maintain the position of neutrals. Upon this point the address avowed the opinion, distinctly, that it would have been far better had the Indians been left in that position. His excellency had indeed told them that the Six Nations had engaged heartily in the war; but the house was yet in ignorance touching any *engagement* in which they had participated. All the evidence of their prowess, which they had seen, consisted in the exhibition in the city, by a small party of Indians, of three scalps, and a few French prisoners. Again, on the subject of Indian expenditures, they hinted at the misapplication of funds *said* to have been laid out for presents; and considering the heavy drafts upon the crown for this service during the late summer, they intimated a belief that notwithstanding his excellency's call for appropriations, he must have already a considerable sum in bank. They treated his excellency's frequent expressions of concern for the welfare of the people with ridicule, charging upon him and his adviser the guilt of the massacre of Saratoga in the autumn of 1745, which event, they alleged, could not have taken place but for the rash withdrawal of the garrison from that place. Many other charges of faults and official delinquencies, civil and military, were set forth and commented upon with biting irony. They declared that from a very early time of his administration, he had treated with contempt the people of the colony in general, and the members of the house in particular; and that he had applied to them in terms so opprobrious as to render them unfit for publication. They complained of the many short and inconvenient adjournments to which they had been subjected, and were particularly displeased that they had not been kept in session during the recent negotiations with the Massachusetts and Connecticut commissioners, "that they might have been daily advised with, and their opinions consulted from time to time as to the matters under consideration,"—forgetting, probably, in the ardor of their patriotism, that the house of assembly was not exactly the executive council, and that by the English constitution the treaty-making power resides not in the house of commons. They thought it very likely his excellency had been advised that the best way to manage an assembly was to harrass them by frequent and short adjournments; but they assured him that with them, such a course would be vain and fruitless. "No treatment your excellency can use toward us, no inconveniences how great soever that we may suffer in our own persons, shall ever prevail on us to abandon or deter us from steadily preserving the interest of our country."

This address was reported by Mr. Clarkson, from a committee previously appointed upon the subject, on the ninth of October. Immediately upon its reading, the speaker, David Jones, was directed to sign, and a committee consisting of Messrs. Clarkson, Phillipse, Thomas, Cruger, Beekman, Lott and Chambers, were designated as a committee to present it to his excellency. This duty was promptly discharged; but the irascible governor would neither allow the chairman to read it to him, nor leave it in his chamber.

Three days afterward, before the assembly had taken any farther action in the controversy,—unless a request for information as to the state and condition of the forts and garrisons of Saratoga and Oswego might be considered of that character,—the governor sent down a message in answer to the assembly's resolutions of the eighth, almost as long, and if possible, even more vituperative than the address of the house. In the first place, however, the governor expressed the pleasure he felt at the ready approbation which the house had given to the compact of the commissioners for the invasion of Canada. The scheme contemplated by that compact closely resembled the *project* between himself, Mr. Shirley and Sir Peter Warren, the year before; and had it then been executed it would have been at the expense of the crown. Now, however, it must be done entirely at the charge of the colonies. His excellency was also pleased at being able to announce that one or more forts, by the arrangement of the commissioners, sanctioned by the unanimous vote of his council, were to be erected at the carrying-place. This expense also, would fall exclusively upon the colonies;—whereas but for the conduct of the commissioners appointed by the house, in regard to the transportation of provisions and general supplies for the forces, those defences would likewise have been constructed at the cost of the crown.

His excellency next proceeded to vindicate his own conduct from the aspersions so frequently cast upon it in connection with his management of the Indian department, and the oft-repeated insinuation of a misapplication of the money drawn from the crown for that branch of the service. The house had asserted, in one of its resolutions respecting this money, "that no disposition thereof for the purpose intended had yet been heard of." In this resolution, Mr. Clinton now charged the house with uttering "as bold a falsehood as ever came from a body of men." In vindication of himself, and in refutation of the assertion, the message pointed to a long chain of operations in the Indian department, known to them all, and sufficient to absorb a very large sum, but for which not a shilling had been paid by the colony. The Indians had all been armed, clothed, and provisioned by him; numerous war-parties had been kept in constant motion, and at one time as many as six hundred warriors were marching together.

The services of Colonel Johnson in that department, were adverted to in terms of high praise. Before the governor's interview with the Indians at Albany the previous year, it was a difficult matter to prevail upon a dozen or twenty of them even to go forth upon a scout. Now, however, Colonel Johnson engages to bring a thousand warriors into the field upon any reasonable notice. Through his influence the chiefs had been weaned from their intimacy with the French, and many distant Indian nations were now courting the friendship of the English. As to the money he had received from the crown for this service, the governor said he was in no way accountable to the house for its application. Not having supplied a penny of it, they had nothing to do with it. In this connection he inveighed against the proviso of the resolution appropriating eight hundred pounds for the Indian service, to be placed for disbursement in other hands than those of the executive. This condition disclosed the motive for the slander against him, it being nothing less than a determination to violate an undisputed prerogative of the crown, and to wrest his majesty's authority from the executive hands.

The conditional resolve concerning the supplies for the forces at Albany, was likewise denounced as an interference with the military prerogative of his majesty; in connection with which his excellency tauntingly inquired whether the house had received any advices or orders from his majesty, or his ministers, upon the subject of the army regulations. "The forces at Albany are under my command only," said he; "and you will never know anything of his majesty's pleasure about these forces, but from me, or from my successor." * * * "His majesty will not part with the least branch of his military prerogative; nor dare I, nor will I, give up the least branch of it on any consideration, however desirous you may be to share it, or to bear the whole command." In this spirit the crown had sent him orders relating to Saratoga; and while they knew that he was heartily inclined to do what they desired of him in that matter, they, also, some of them, knew it was impracticable.

He had formerly told them that the fort at Saratoga was inadequate for the security of that section of the frontier; and of what has happened to it they had been forewarned, unless proper assistance should be afforded for its preservation. The position of that fort was unfavorable; it had been maintained at great expense, and more lives had been lost by reason of its disadvantageous situation, than by any other cause since the war. It had been placed there by commissioners recommended by his council; but it had since been discovered that their object in selecting that site was not the protection of the country, but of quantities of wheat growing in its neighborhood. The work itself being of no substantial use as a military position, and finding it impossible longer to maintain it without hazarding the total dissolution of the forces at Albany, the cannon and stores had been withdrawn and the fortification destroyed. In addition to all which, the conduct of the assembly itself had compelled him to abandon the place by their opposition to every measure proposed by him for its preservation.

On the subject of his endeavors to confine the action of the house exclusively to his recommendations for the welfare and protection of the colony, especially in regard to his brief message of the eighth, his excellency attempted a justification. His design was simply to secure in the first instance, such action as would guaranty the safety of the province. There would afterward be time enough for the consideration of as many other subjects as they could desire. He taunted them sharply for what he called the farce of locking the door and laying the key with solemn form upon the table,—asking them whether there were any suspicious people without the doors of whom they were afraid, and whether they apprehended that any of their own members were intent upon running away. If not,—it was really an attempt to shut him out so that he could not communicate by message,—then the act was a high insult to the royal authority, and for the time being a withdrawal of their allegiance. He declared that by their resolutions of the ninth, they had assumed all the rights and privileges of the house of commons of Great Britain. Such an assumption was nothing less than claiming to be a branch of the legislature of the kingdom, or in other words a denial of subjection to the crown and parliament. He reasoned the point to show that it could not be so; the supreme power had a right to put limitations upon their proceedings; and he told them not only that these and some subjects which they had no right to discuss, but that "he had his majesty's express command not to suffer them to bring some matters into the house, nor to debate upon them." It was for that reason that the clerk of the house was required every day to lay before the governor the minutes of their proceedings, that the governor may put a stop to them when they become disorderly or undutiful.

He reproved them for having recently adopted the disrespectful and unmannerly practice of ordering resolutions to be served upon him from time to time; and censured them severely for their rudeness on a late occasion, when, within a quarter of an hour after they had served him with a copy of their resolutions of the ninth, several of the members of their body thrust themselves upon him in an apartment of his own house, without previous notice of, to read "a large bundle of papers," which they called a remonstrance from the house. Every private man in the country considered his own house his castle, and his excellency demanded whether their governor was not entitled to the same privilege? Whether he must be thus intruded upon, and bear it with patience? Under the circumstances of the case, he had but too much reason to refuse to receive the remonstrance ;—and he then gave them warning that he would never again receive from them a document in public, which had not first been communicated to him in private.

He reminded them of another act of incivility. At the opening of the session, they had not, as usual, acquainted him with their organization,—an omission without precedent, and evidently by design. They had resolved forthwith to enter upon the consideration of the state of the province, without having received any information as to what its condition was. They also resolved to make a remonstrance upon the condition of the colony, without resolving what should be the subject matter of the document,—ordering their committee to draw it up without instructions. That committee presented the report so soon, and the house adopted it so hastily, as to preclude the exercise of any rational judgment upon the subject. No precedents could be found for their conduct, save in the course taken by the house of commons when they had determined to take away the king's life, and overthrow the established government. This allusion was certainly not *malapropos*. The same leaven was doubtless at work in Clinton's little parliament, which, in the greater, had sent the unhappy Stuart to the block.

Various other points of the controversy were passed in review. The house had been insolent toward him, and forgotten all kind of decency and regard for the authority vested in him by his majesty. They had endeavored to deprive him of the esteem of the people. They had witholden supplies for the public service; and for the purpose of justifying themselves to their constituents, had endeavored to induce a belief that he had applied the public money to his own use. To refute this idea he now stated that during the few years of his administration no more than one thousand eight hundred pounds currency of the colony had passed into his hands for the Indian service; and the account he then gave of the uses to which the money had been applied, and the benefits secured by its expenditure, when viewed at this distance of time, proves very clearly that the expenditure was made with wisdom, prudence and economy. Upon this point his excellency insisted that if they had really entertained any suspicions of his integrity, they should have instituted an investigation. But they had not done so, although they had seemed to act as though he was the only man in the province who could misapply the public revenues; for more than sixty thousand pounds had passed through the hands of their own commissioners, while no reports as to the manner of its disbursement had been exacted, nor any inquiry made.

In a word all the charges and insinuations of the house against the governor, were pronounced to be false, and their conduct toward those who had endeavored to support his administration against their opposition, was declared to be malicious. Their long-continued unbecoming conduct, in the view of his excellency, could arise but from one of the following causes:

I. A firm principle of disloyalty, with a desire to deliver the country up to the king's enemies:

II. The desire of some individuals for such a shameful neutrality as was established in the war of Queen Anne's time.

III. A design to overturn the constitution, and throw everything into confusion:

IV. The gratification of the pride and private malice and rancor of a few men, at the hazard of the lives and estates of their constituents. It was added—"That there *are* such men in this country, is no secret, nor what share they have in your private consultations."

The governor then drew a contrast showing how widely different had been his conduct from their's. When he discovered that they had fallen into a state of unreasonable heat and passion, he had adjourned or prorogued them, that they might have time to cool down. And on their reassembling, although he had endeavored to forget past differences, they would strive by every means to revive them. Even now, although they had every just reason to expect the manifestation of strong resentment from him, yet he was resolved to disappoint them. He therefore in conclusion again exhorted them to make the proper provisions for the care and safety of the province,—admonishing them, however, to beware of attempting any measures that might clash with his instructions from the crown, or infringe upon the royal prerogative. "The ill effects of the condescensions of former governors of the province," were now too sensibly felt to justify any further concessions.

It appears by the assembly's journal, that after referring the message to a committee, the house entered upon the consideration of public affairs with a commendable degree of diligence. On the fifteenth day of October they

CHAP. VIII.
1747.

requested the governor to execute one of the projects agreed upon by the commissioners, by sending gun-smiths and assistant artizans into the country of the Six Nations among all the tribes beyond the Mohawks, pledging the ways and means, in the full confidence, however, that Massachusetts and Connecticut would defray their respective proportions of the expense. On the next day the governor communicated a table of estimates requiring appropriations for the winter service,—stating that it was his intention to invite the coöperation of the colonies south to the Carolinas, for the common defence. Having ordered the proper arrangements for the security of the colony during the repose of winter, it was thought the assembly might be safely adjourned—to be aroused into action again in the spring, when the bugle should sound to arms for the actual invasion of Canada.

But the hopes and the high expectations of the colonies, especially those of New York and New England, were again dashed by disappointment alike mortifying and severe. On the nineteenth of October, orders were received from the duke of Newcastle, signifying the royal approbation of the preparations made jointly by Shirley and Clinton, for the intended expedition, but nevertheless directing them to desist from that expedition, and to disband all the levies engaged for that service, retaining such a number of the New England forces as might be judged necessary for the protection of Nova Scotia. The colonies were directed to pay off the levies, and transmit the accounts to be reimbursed by parliament. Mr. Clinton immediately transmitted these disheartening orders by message to the assembly, with a recommendation that so many of the levies at Albany as might be deemed necessary for the defence of the north might still be retained in the service, and provision be made for their subsistence. This suggestion was followed by a vote of the assembly to retain eight full companies at Albany until the ensuing month of August, if their service should so long be necessary; but in view of the heavy expenses to which the colony had already been subjected by the war, and the almost ruined condition of the colony, the house felt itself obliged to decline advancing either money or credit for the payment of the forces in arrears. With this exception, the assembly proceeded with apparent calmness to make just and proper appropriations for various objects, such as the employment of a corps of rangers to traverse the northern border, and for repairing sundry forts. Appropriations were also voted for divers other matters, among which was one for the completion of the governor's house. But the calm was short, if not delusive, and the storm directed against the executive broke out on the twenty-sixth of October with unabated violence. It appears that two days before that date, it being on Saturday, the governor, by a written order under his own hand, had forbidden Mr. James Parker, printer to the assembly, to publish in the journals of that body the celebrated remonstrance of the ninth, of which a copious analysis has already been given. Parker had refused to recognize the validity of a verbal order to the same effect, communicated by his excellency's secretary, Mr. Catherwood; and this written mandate he was required to publish in his newspaper, which he accordingly did on Monday morning,—together with the paragraph contained in the governor's message of the thirteenth, wherein his excellency had charged the committee of the house, bearing the said remonstrance, with obtruding themselves rudely into a private apartment of his domicil. Chafed at this arbitrary mandate to Parker, and smarting yet from the imputation cast by the governor upon the committee, Mr. Clarkson rose in his place on Monday, and called the attention of the house to the contents of the newspaper. The publication having been read, Mr. C. proceeded to relate, and his colleagues of the committee to confirm, the history of the transaction in question. The committee "knocked at the outward door, and told the servant who attended, that they had a message. Retiring into an inner room, the servant soon returned, accompanied by a gentleman, who showed them into the presence of the governor, by whom they were received without any manifestation of displeasure. They informed his excellency that they came as a committee of the house with a remonstrance, which they offered to read; but his excellency refused either to hear it, or even to allow them to read it, upon the ground that such a procedure, without the presence of the speaker, was not parliamentary. The next step was to order the attendance of Parker at the bar of the house, to produce the original order from the governor, a copy of which had been published in his newspaper. This being done, resolutions were passed declaring that the attempt to prevent the publication of their proceedings, was a violation of the rights and liberties of the people, and an infringement of their privileges; that the remonstrance was a regular proceeding; that the governor's order was unwarrantable, arbitrary and illegal, a violation of their privileges, and of the liberty of the press, and tending to the utter subversion of all the rights and liberties of the colony; and that the speaker's order for printing the remonstrance, was regular and consistent with his duty."[1] Parker preferred to identify his fortunes with those of the popular party, rather than to obey the behest of the crown, as expressed by its representative. The governor's order was therefore disregarded, and the remonstrance printed as directed by the house. The controversy was maintained with increasing intensity, for many days; in the course of which the house, in order, doubtless, as much to reassert its own power as to annoy the governor, directed Parker to reprint the offensive document, and furnish each member with two copies thereof,—"that their constituents might know it was their firm resolution to preserve the liberty of the press."

But while these proceedings were yet in progress, the governor startled the assembly by a message announcing that he might find it necessary to detach large bodies of

---

[1] Smith, vol. ii. pp. 132, 133. Vide also journals of the colonial assembly.

the militia for the defence of the frontiers, and requiring a contingent appropriation to meet the expense. This species of service was not only burdensome, but particularly irksome to the people, and the house was thrown into fermentation by the requisition. The message was referred to a committee which a week afterward reported in substance, that they were amazed that his excellency should have sent them such a message, since he had so recently given them to understand that he should rely upon the levies already at Albany for the public defence; for the pay and subsistence of whom the house was even then taking the necessary measures. In conclusion the committee avowed the belief that while his excellency was governed by such unsteady and ever-varying counsels, and while he continued to send them messages conceived in such doubtful and ambiguous terms as had of late marked his communications to them, it would be difficult to make such provision for the defence of the frontiers as seemed necessary. Nevertheless it was acknowledged to be their duty to adopt such measures as the exigency of the case appeared to require.

This report had no sooner caught the eye of the governor while examining the copy of the assembly's journal as presented for his inspection by the clerk, than he turned the tables upon his opponents, and demonstrated beyond doubt the factiousness of their cause. He first reminded them of their vote upon his message of the nineteenth of October, refusing to pay the arrears of the levies. They had indeed voted to retain eight companies of the levies at the north, but not upon the terms suggested in his message, viz: the continuance of full pay; instead of which they had cut the officers and subalterns down to less than one half of the compensation allowed upon the regular military establishment. Upon these terms it was not to be expected that the levies would remain in the service. Indeed men fit to serve ought not to remain. And he begged the assembly to consider what would be the condition of things, were the levies to disband themselves and return to their homes, unpaid and without clothes,—leaving the nothern frontier entirely uncovered. As to the charge of vascillation in his councils, the governor said they must necessarily vary with changes of circumstances; but in the present instance it was the conduct of the assembly alone that had caused the variation. Still duty required him to do all in his power to avert the mischiefs arising from their conduct, and also to take care of the people.

The assembly rejoined in a bad spirit, reiterating the charge of inconsistency against the governor, and accusing him of pursuing measures purposely intended to cause the disaffection and desertion of the levies, that a plausible pretext might thereby be afforded for wantonly harrassing the poor people of the colony by dragging them into the military service. Under all the circumstances of the case, therefore, they had arrived at the conclusion that to retain the levies would now be impossible, and that as a consequence immediate provision must be made for raising a sufficient number of volunteers for the public defence. The committee's report was concurred in *nemine contradicente;* and on the fifth of November resolutions were passed directing the employment of eight hundred volunteers, for two hundred and seventy days service, and appropriating the sum of eighteen thousand pounds for their subsistence. Contemporaneously with this procedure, the house was notified by the legislative council that they had passed its bill for the supply of the eight full companies of levies already at Albany, as heretofore mentioned. This scheme however, having been virtually abandoned by the house, a resolution was adopted, declaring the impracticability of retaining those eight full companies of levies in the service, and praying the governor to issue warrants for raising thirteen companies of volunteers of sixty men each, with the promise of commissions to those who should actually recruit them, at the reduced rates of compensation to which his excellency, in respect to the retention of the levies, had objected, as being altogether inadequate to the employment of respectable men. A committee of which Colonel Schuyler was chairman, waited upon his excellency with this resolution, but he declined answering it. Three days afterward, to wit on the tenth of November, the assembly deputed another committee to wait upon his excellency, and inform him of their apprehensions that the river navigation to Albany would close before the necessary winter supplies for the forces at the north could now be sent up, and praying his assent to the subsistence bill, which, having passed both houses, now awaited only his signature to become a law. But his excellency, like Richard, was "busy,"—preparing despatches as he alleged, for Boston,—and would receive no message from the house otherwise than at the hand of their speaker. On the thirteenth, the request was renewed by a formal address presented by the house in a body—the speaker of course being at their head. From the reply of his excellency, it appeared that his reluctance to sign the bill in question, had arisen from an objectionable principle involved therein. He had on two previous occasions given his assent to bills involving the same principle, and had been censured at home for so doing. His excuse to the crown had been the pressing necessity of the public service, and he hoped the same excuse would avail again, as he had made up his mind to sign the bill. He took occasion, moreover, to admonish the house in regard to the bill for the pay of the forces to be raised, then pending, not to incorporate in its provisions any thing that might in anywise interfere with the prerogatives of the crown. The bill thus specially referred to, authorized the raising of the sum of twenty-eight thousand pounds, by a direct tax, for the military service, and the like sum by an issue of bills of credit, with provisions for sinking and cancelling the same. In closing his reply, the governor farther informed the house that the officers of the four companies of fusileers stationed at Albany had notified him that for the want of supplies they were on the point of dissolution.

On the twenty-fifth of November his excellency commanded the attendance of the house in the council chamber, when he approved the bill for victualling the forces and also the important revenue bill just spoken of. Two other bills of minor importance, likewise received his excellency's signature; whereupon, finding that the controversy in which he had so long been engaged with the assembly had evidently become past healing,—indeed that on the contrary the breach was daily becoming wider and yet wider,—the general assembly was dissolved. His excellency commenced his speech announcing the dissolution, by referring to the votes of the house in the case of Parker. He maintained that their remonstrance, of which he had forbidden the republication from the journals in Parker's newspaper, was a false, scandalous, and malicious libel upon him throughout; and he therefore had a right, for the protection of his own character, to inhibit the publication of a document surcharged with falsehood, as they very well knew it to be. As to the popular out-cry which they had attempted to raise about the liberty of the press, he said it was a liberty very liable to be abused, and against which there ought to be a remedy. Nor could the application of a proper remedy be considered a restraint upon a just degree of liberty. He charged them with a design, as was obvious from their whole course, to usurp the supreme authority of the government, and in support of the charge the governor again entered upon a summary review of the conduct of the assembly, rehearsing its sins both of omission and commission. Among the former, he observed that notwithstanding the frequency and earnestness of his appeals to them for the Indian service, and the importance of preserving the existing amicable relations with the Confederates, the assembly had not made the slightest provision for that object. The house had complained that he had kept secret from them the orders he had received for discharging the forces intended for the Canada expedition until the hour had arrived for their execution. His reply to this charge was an ample justification of his course. It was necessary to keep those orders from the knowledge of the enemy lest advantage should be taken of them, and the frontiers invaded, before the necessary preperations could be made for their defence. He had, however, given them timely notice of what was to happen; and had the suggestions he had made to them been seasonably acted upon, the object of security could have been attained at an expense forty thousand pounds less than what would now be the cost to the colony. In reviewing his own exertions for the public defence, and his endeavors to preserve a force at Albany so large as to render drafts upon the militia unnecessary, his excellency charged upon the assembly the design of usurping the command of the militia, and with having passed resolutions calculated to produce disobedience to orders, and which, in fact, had produced such disobedience. Their refusal to pay the arrears of the forces on the credit of the king, showed what little regard they had either for his majesty's pleasure, or for the interests of those who had willingly exposed their lives for the defence of the country. It was now well known, that had his advice been followed in the first instance, a sufficient number of the levies might have been retained at Albany. Equally well was it now known that the necessary force could not now be readily obtained. The consequence was that by the advice of his council he should now be obliged to apply to some of the other colonies for assistance. Other points were raised in the speech which have become familiar in the history of this protracted controversy. Even now, in one of the bills to which he had just placed his signature, they had inserted a clause that would very likely defeat its object. He referred to a section placing the provisions and ammunition for the public service under the exclusive control of persons of their own nomination, without consulting the governor in the appointment of those persons,—they, too, having it in their power to control any order which the governor might give! He had been compelled by the public danger, to sign that bill, though contrary to the express instructions of the crown. In a word, they had done all they could to traduce his character; to encourage disobedience; to inflame the passions of the people; and to paralyze his exertions for the safety of the province. Near the close of the speech the following passage occurs, which was true beyond a doubt:

"Your continued grasping for power, with an evident tendency to the weakening of the dependency of the province on Great Britain, accompanied with such notorious and public disrespect to the character of your governor, and contempt of the king's authority intrusted with him, cannot be hid longer from your superiors, but must come under their observation, and is of most dangerous example to your neighbors."

Knowing, therefore, that great numbers of the inhabitants disapproved of their proceedings, and for the purpose of giving them an opportunity of vindicating their loyalty to their prince, as well as their love of country, his excellency declared the general assembly to be dissolved.

This act appears to have come somewhat suddenly upon the assembly, a committee having at the time been engaged in the preparation of another address to his excellency, similar in tone and character to the late remonstrance, but much larger, and more elaborate. The dissolution having prevented the house from giving an official impress to the document, it was shortly afterward published in the form of "A letter from some of the representatives in the late general assembly to his excellency the governor, in answer to his message of October thirteenth, and to his dissolution speech." This document comprised a very extended review of the whole controversy between the parties, dwelling upon each and every particular point with exceeding minuteness, and evidencing considerable powers of reasoning and analysis. There was no abatement in the bitterness of its tone, either toward the governor, or his chief confidential adviser, Doctor Colden. But from the historical sketch already given of the controversy, no necessity exists for a synopsis of this formidable paper—sufficient, of itself, to fill one hundred pages of an ordinary octavo. Smith attributes the authorship to Judge Horsmanden,—Doctor Colden being also charged with the composition of his excellency's state papers. These suppositions were probably correct. Indeed Mr. Horsmanden had been summarily degraded from his station for his officiousness in this respect; and Doctor Colden had entered several protests upon the journals of the legislative council, bearing strong family resemblances to the papers bearing the signature of Mr. Clinton. Among these was a protest against a bill from the assembly, which passed the council on the third of November, instituting a committee to examine the public accounts of the colony from the year 1713. The doctor protested against this bill, first, as being an infringement upon the royal prerogative. The moneys, he asserted, had been raised for the service of the king, and his majesty, or his representative, had therefore an undoubted right to appoint the persons charged with the proposed examination, especially in regard to their expenditure, whereas the governor had not even been consulted as to the persons constituting the commission. Secondly, the commissioners named were merchants. As the revenues were in a great measure raised from duties and imposts, he held that a mercantile commission was improper. The revenues from those sources were not half as much as they would be if honestly collected. These commissioners, if merchants, could connive with their friends for the concealment of frauds. Other exceptions were taken to the details of the bill; but those just mentioned are the most important. The doctor also protested against a bill from the assembly cancelling certain bills of credit, together with the special revenue bill for the prosecution of the war, upon the old ground of collision with the kingly prerogative. The last mentioned bill it was averred was specially objectionable because it usurped the executive power for the appointment of troops and officers, and provided for the disbursement of money from the treasury without the governor's warrant.

Although from a very early date in the history of this protracted controversy, it became inexcusably personal, yet it is not difficult to perceive that it was in reality one of principle. On the one hand, the infant Hercules, though still in his cradle, was becoming impatient of restraint. The yoke of colonial servitude chafed the necks, if not of the people, at least of their representatives. The royal governor was not slow to perceive what kind of leaven was fermenting the body politic; and hence he became perhaps over-jealous in asserting and defending the prerogatives of his master. Doubtless in the progress of the quarrel there were faults on both sides. Of an irascible and overbearing temperament, and accustomed in his profession to command rather than to persuade, he was ill qualified to exercise a limited or concurrent power with a popular assembly equally jealous of its own privileges and of the liberties of the people; watching with sleepless vigilance for every opportunity to circumscribe the influence of the crown; and ready at every moment to resist the encroachments of arbitrary power. Still, however patriotic the motives, under the promptings of DeLancey, their opposition to Mr. Clinton became factious; and it is not difficult even for a republican to believe that he was treated not only with harshness, but with great injustice, especially in regard to his measures, and his personal exertions for the public defence and the prosecution of the war.

But the principles for which Hambden bled, and Sidney

died on the scaffold, were striking deeper root in British America every day,—an additional proof of which fact, not easily to be misunderstood, was manifested about this time by a transaction at Boston. Time immemorial the crown had claimed the right in periods of war, of raising and equipping its fleets by impressing the ships of merchants, and seamen to man them. In the feudal ages, indeed, the claim had been asserted much farther, and the right of impressment exerted in respect to every description of force, as the public service required, including even the members of the medical profession.[1] But with the growth of a permanent national marine, the impressment of merchant ships could only be necessary as transports, and the practice had been narrowed down to the employment of press-gangs for the procurement of common sailors. Fortified by the opinions of the law-officers of the crown, the ministers had repeatedly asserted the right of extending the right of this odious practice to the colonies. The claim, however, had been uniformly resisted by the people, and nowhere more strenuously than in Virginia,—held at the time to be the most loyal of the provinces. Indeed it was in Virginia, that the first act of resistance to the practice was made, and in every instance in which the right was attempted to be put in exercise, the officers of the crown were defeated by popular interposition.[2] No experiment of the kind, however, had as yet been made in New England; and the honor of the first attempt, and of experiencing a signal defeat, was

---

[1] It appears from Rymer's *Fœdera*, that king Henry V, in 1417, authorized John Morstede, to press as many surgeons as he thought necessary for the French expedition, together with persons to make their instruments. It is also true, and appears in the same book of records, that with the army which won the day at Agincourt, there had landed *only one surgeon*, the same John Morstede, who indeed did engage to send fifteen more for the army, three of which, however, were to act as archers! With such a professional scarcity, what must have been the state of the wounded on the day of battle?— *Andrews's Great Britain*.

[2] Grahame,—who says that Franklin was the first writer by whom its indefensible injustice was demonstrated.

reserved for Commodore Knowles, then governor of Cape Breton, and the successor of Sir Peter Warren in the naval command of the American station. Visiting the waters of Massachusetts with his squadron, and lying at Nantasket about the middle of November, the commodore lost a number of his sailors by desertion, the places of whom he determined to supply by a vigorous act of impressment in Boston. Detaching a number of boats to the town at an early hour in the morning, a sweep was made of all the seamen found on board the vessels lying at the wharves, and also of a number of ship carpenters, with their apprentices, together with several landsmen. The act was executed with such suddenness that the men were far down the bay on their way to the fleet, when the transaction had become generally known to the people. But *when* known, such a popular fermentation ensued as had never before taken place in Boston. All classes of the people were greatly excited; but the rage of the lower classes knew no bounds. Siezing whatever arms they could find, spears, clubs, pitchforks and guns, the mob rushed together, determined upon vengeance, or a rescue, or both. A lieutenant of the fleet falling first within their power, was siezed, and would have been treated with violence but for the interposition of the speaker of the provincial legislature, then in session, who assured the multitude that this officer had not been concerned in the transaction. The next movement of the mob was directed against the house of the governor, Shirley, who was at the very time entertaining several captains of the fleet. Of these officers the rioters resolved to demand satisfaction, and the house was speedily surrounded by the infuriated legion. The officers within doors being supplied with fire-arms, determined to defend themselves, and there would doubtless have been a serious effusion of blood, had not a number of the more considerate citizens insinuated themselves among the rioters, and dissuaded them from the commission of actual violence. Among the peace-officers on duty was a deputy sheriff, who was irreverently siezed and borne off to the stocks, with the practical use of which invention he was made acquainted, both his legs being made fast therein. There was a dash of the ludicrous in this exploit, of the "sovereigns," creating merriment, and serving for a while to moderate, though it did not appease their anger. The deepening of the twilight into night, however, was a signal for renewed outrages, and the deliberations of the legislature, or general court, as it was called, were disturbed by the breaking of their windows, and other riotous proceedings. The governor, with several distinguished gentlemen and counsellors, ascended to the balcony, whence they addressed the people in the most soothing and considerate manner,—rebuking their turbulence, it is true, but at the same time expressing strong disapprobation of the outrage of which they complained, and promising their utmost exertions to obtain the discharge of every man who had been kidnapped and carried away. But the tempest was not to be thus easily hushed, and the arrest and detention of every officer of the squadron in town, was demanded as the only measure that would answer the purpose. Such being the temper of the populace, it was judged advisable that the governor should withdraw from the scene of tumult to his own house,—to which he was accompanied by several officers, civil and military, and also by a small party of personal friends. Meantime it was bruited that a barge had come up to the town from the fleet, whereupon the rioters rushed headlong to the wharf to sieze it. The report was not true, for no such barge had arrived. Yet the populace thought otherwise, and a huge boat, lying at the dock, belonging to a Scotch merchantman, was taken by mistake, and drawn through the street, as though no heavier than a birchen canoe. It was at first resolved to kindle a bonfire with this unlucky craft in front of the governor's house; but a suggestion that lighting a fire there would jeopard the town, the mob drew away, and indulged their heated design in a place of greater security. Thus ended the proceedings of the first day. On the next, the governor ordered the militia under arms for the preservation of the peace; but the drummers were interrupted in beating to arms, and the militia, with a surprising degree of unanimity, refused to parade. Several of the British officers on shore had been siezed by the populace, by whom they were retained as hostages. Of this number was Captain Erskine, of the Canterbury. He was taken in Roxbury, but was speedily liberated on giving his parole not to go on board until the difficulty should be adjusted. Such being the temper of the people,—the entire militia refusing obedience to their officers,—it was thought expedient, as well for the personal security, as for the power, of the governor, whose authority was thus virtually suspended, that he should retire to the castle—Fort William. From this place Mr. Shirley wrote to Commodore Knowles, informing him of the high exasperation into which the people had been thrown by his proceedings, and urging an immediate release of the persons impressed, as the only means of restoring the public tranquility. But the commodore declined even to entertain the proposition until those of his officers who had been caught on shore should be liberated. The first suggestion of Knowles was to land a body of marines to aid the governor in quelling the disturbances; but Shirley was too wise a man, and understood too well the character of the New England people to second such a proposition. The commodore thereupon became enraged, and threatened to burn the town,—directing at the same time certain movements of his ships which for a few hours caused much uneasiness. During the eighteenth and nineteenth days of the month the town was under the entire control of the mob,—the general court feeling reluctant to interpose, even for the preservation of order, lest their action should be construed as favoring the conduct of Knowles. The provocation had been great; and although the prevailing spirit of insubordination was indefensible, yet it was regarded by every American with greatly mitigated displeasure. Still, the danger of allowing the town longer to remain under the sway of an infuriated populace, and the impropriety of leaving the governor, whose conduct had not only been wise and patriotic, but blameless, thus unsupported, was perceived before the close of the day last mentioned, and a series of resolutions was adopted by the house of representatives, strongly condemning the tumultuous proceedings of the people; pledging themselves, their lives and estates, to sustain the executive authority; but at the same time declaring that they should put forth their utmost exertions to redress the grievances which had provoked the riots. Simultaneously with this procedure the council passed an order for restoring Captain Erskine and the other officers in actual custody, to their liberty, and declaring them to be under the protection of the government,—which order was concurred in by the house of representatives. These measures had the effect of allaying the excitement, and the rioters soon began to disperse. A town meeting was holden in the afternoon; and although it was urged by the less discreet portion of the assemblage that a suppression of the tumults would have the effect of encouraging his majesty's naval commanders in the commission of similar outrages in future, yet the counsels of the more prudent prevailed, and the town, by solemn vote, condemned alike the riotous proceedings of the people, and the injury and insult by which those proceedings had been provoked. Not anticipating so favorable a turn of affairs, so soon, the governor had made preparations for calling to his assistance the provincial troops of the circumjacent towns, horse and foot; but on the following morning the militia of Boston paraded spontaneously, and many citizens were in arms who had seldom been seen in arms before. In the course of the day the governor was escorted from the castle back to his house with great parade, and law and order resumed their wonted sway. Commodore Knowles dismissed all, or nearly all, the subjects of the impress, and sailed for Louisburg, to the great and irrepressible joy of the people.[1] But his sovereign had little cause to thank him for an act which awoke a spirit that slumbered not until the richest jewel was torn from his diadem.

There remains little more to be written of the border troubles of New York during the year 1747. Small parties of the enemy continued to hover about the new settlements until the depth of winter, and several additional murders were committed. One of their autumnal forays was melancholy and bloody. A party of woodmen, engaged in cutting timber, about four miles west of Schenectady, was fallen upon, and thirty-nine of their number killed. Along the confines of Massachusetts and New Hampshire these murders or assassinations were yet more frequent during the autumn than in New York. Skirmishes between the enemy and the borderers, were common, and in one of these a French officer of some consideration, named Pierre Ramboert, was wounded and taken.[2]

Late in November, Governor Clinton pressed the command of the northern frontier upon Colonel Johnson. The people were strongly in favor of that appointment[3] and it was ultimately accepted. But aside from this command, the colonel had full employment upon his hands for the winter, independently of his Indian charge. The militia of Albany county, then embracing all the northern and western settlements beyond Ulster and Dutchess, had fallen into a state of sad demoralization; and to Colonel Johnson Mr. Clinton entrusted the duty of effecting a complete reorganization. All confidence was reposed in him; and in the removal of incompetent officers, and the appointment of new ones, his word was law. "Send down a list immediately, of those you think proper, and look upon it as done."[4]

---

[1] Hutchinson. Grahame.

[2] Hoyt's Antiquities.

[3] Manuscript letter of Jacob Glen.

[4] Manuscript letter; Major Rutherford, of the executive council, to Colonel Johnson.

CHAPTER IX.

1748.

Colonel Johnson had now become, through his own tact and the influence of Governor Clinton, a prominent man in the affairs of the colony. In February, he accepted the command of the New York colonial troops for the defence of the frontiers—a circumstance which affords another proof of the high favor in which he was held by the governor. Though still continuing the traffic in furs, and by no means neglecting his mercantile pursuits, he devoted himself more assiduously, not only to political matters, but also to the management of the Indian department over which he had for the last two years had the control. Becoming favorably known both to the colony and the British government, he now assumed, as better suited to his improved standing, more dignity in his appointments, his manner of living, and his intercourse with the Indians.

It was about this period, although I have not been able to learn the exact date, that Colonel Johnson employed as his housekeeper, Mary Brant, or Miss Molly, as she was called, a sister of the celebrated Indian chief Thayendanegea, with whom he lived until his decease, and by whom he had several children.[1] This circumstance is thus mentioned

---

[1] That Molly Brant was not the *wife* of the Baronet, is fully proved by his last will, (published in appendix to vol. ii.) in which, after desiring to have the "remains of his beloved wife Catherine," interred beside him, he speaks of the "children of my present housekeeper, Mary Brant," as his "*natural* children." It is, however, but justice to Molly Brant, to state that she always regarded herself as married to the Baronet after the Indian fashion.

The traditions of the Mohawk valley state that the acquaintance of Colonel Johnson with Molly, had a rather wild and romantic commencement. The story is, that she was a very sprightly and a very beautiful Indian girl of about sixteen, when he first saw her. It was at a regimental militia

by Mrs. Grant in her entertaining book. "Becoming a widower in the prime of life, he connected himself with an Indian maiden, daughter to a sachem, who possessed an uncommonly agreeable person and good understanding; and whether ever formally married to him according to our usage or not, continued to live with him in great union and affection all his life." Colonel Johnson himself repeatedly speaks of this Indian lady in his private journal. During his expedition to Detroit entries occur in which he speaks of having received news from home, and of having written to Molly. He always mentioned her kindly. Thus under date of *Wednesday, October 21st*, 1759, he writes:

"Met Sir Robert Davis and Captain Etherington, who gave me a packet of letters from General Amherst. Captain Etherington told me Molly was delivered of a girl and all were well at my house, where they stayed ten days."

Molly, as has already been stated, was the sister of Thayendanegea, and both, according to the account in the London Magazine of 1776, the earliest printed testimony upon the subject, were the grand-children of one of the Mohawk chiefs, who visited England half a century before. That her father was a chief, several authorities have likewise been cited to show; to which may be added Allen's Biographical Dictionary, where the fact is positively asserted.[1]

By thus forming an alliance with the family of an influ-

---

muster, where Molly was one of a multitude of spectators. One of the field officers coming near her upon a prancing steed, by way of banter she asked permission to mount behind him. Not supposing she could perform the exploit, he said she might. At the word she leaped upon the crupper with the agility of a gazelle. The horse sprang off at full speed, and, clinging to the officer, her blanket flying, and her dark tresses streaming in the wind, she flew about the parade ground swift as an arrow, to the infinite merriment of the collected multitude. The colonel, who was a witness of the spectacle, admiring the spirit of the young squaw, and becoming enamored of her person, brought her to his house.

[1] President Allen was connected by marriage with the family of the late President Wheelock, and has had excellent opportunities for arriving at the probable truth.

ential and powerful chieftain, Colonel Johnson evidently aimed at a more extended influence over the Indians. Nor did the result disappoint him; for in this alliance and in his custom of mingling among them in his familiar way, is doubtless to be found the secret of his extraordinary ascendency over the fickle red men of the forest.

Meantime a new assembly had been chosen, which the governor met upon the twelfth of February. The election, however, had made but few changes in the composition of that body; all the former leaders being returned, and Mr. Jones consequently again presented for his excellency's approbation as speaker. The opening speech of the governor was conciliatory. He announced that the convention agreed upon between the commissioners of New York, Massachusetts and Connecticut, had been ratified by the first and last mentioned of those colonies, and by the legislature of Massachusetts, with the exception of a single article, which his excellency did not conceive to be very material. The place of the cordon of rangers provided for by that article, the governor thought, could be supplied by strong parties of Indians. Notwithstanding the abortive efforts of the two preceding years to achieve the invasion of Canada, and the strangely vascillating conduct of the ministry upon this important subject, measures to that end were again proposed, and the necessary means suggested, with as much confidence as though there had been no disappointment. The disbanding of the forces at Albany had necessarily discouraged the Indians, who had regarded the measure as a want either of courage or strength, and the French had not been slow to avail themselves of the opportunity again to sow the seeds of disaffection among them— particularly the Senecas and Onondagas. Measures were therefore advised for regaining the hearty coöperation of their people. The death of Mr. Bleecker, long the government interpreter in its intercourse with the Indians, and the appointment of Arent Stevens in his place were announced. The government was indebted to Colonel Johnson for various advances of money, and he had given notice that such was the increased cost of provisioning the garrison of Oswego, that he could no longer perform that service without an advance upon the terms of his contract of two hundred pounds per annum. The fortifications of Albany needed repairs, and several of the forts were short of ammunition. The attention of the assembly was also called to the fact that no provision had been made at the last session for paying the salaries of the officers of the government. Other suggestions connected with the public service were made in the speech, one of which was the employment of a smith for the benefit of the Indians at Oswego. Finally he recommended that they should make immediate provision for rewarding those Indians who had acted as scouts for transporting the new levies to Albany, victualing them in the Mohawk's country, removing cannon from Saratoga to Albany, and also for the salary of a commanding officer to the troops raised by the province.

It would appear that the dissolution of the assembly had, for a time, at least, produced a better state of feeling in the new assembly than in the previous one. The answer of the council was moved by Chief Justice DeLancey; that of the assembly was reported by Mr. Clarkson; and both were conceived in a better spirit, and couched in much more respectful language than had been usual for some time past. In the address of the house to the governor upon the eighteenth, the assembly assured his excellency of their readiness to enter immediately upon the consideration of the different matters which he had submitted to them, and to make provision for such supplies as were essential to the well being and security of the colony. Two days afterward, however, as if they feared that they had conceded too much, and wished therefore to counteract it by thwarting the favorite scheme of the governor, the committee of the whole on his speech, reported it as their opinion, that to follow out the plan proposed by Massachusetts, would be contrary to the purposes of the agreement, and therefore that the house ought not to accede to the alteration.

The temper of the assembly, however, as before remarked, was much more tractable; and at this sitting, several resolutions were passed in favor of repairing the different fortifications along the frontiers, stationing a larger garrison at Oswego, defraying the expenses of the gunsmiths stationed among the Indians, paying the rangers employed as scouts, building block houses, and other plans of a like character. Two hundred pounds were also voted to Colonel Johnson, for the extraordinary charges to which he had been subjected in supplying the garrison of Oswego with provisions, and an appropriation made for the payment of the salaries of the officers of the government, but to which was attached "a reward of one hundred and fifty pounds to Mr. Horsmanden, for his late controversial labors, under the pretext of drafting their bills, and other public service."[1]

The most important act of the session, however, was an appropriation of two hundred pounds per annum for the compensation of an agent, to reside in the parent capital, to solicit in the concerns of the colony. The appointment of such an agent had been previously recommended; and though successful at last by a unanimous vote, it might not have been, but from the design of the house to employ an agent who should be under its own direction, and whose office, at least in part, should be to thwart the views of the governor at home. The enactment was so shaped as cautiously to deprive the governor even of a concurrent power in making the appointment; and indeed the agent, Robert Charles, was named and his first instructions actually given, a few hours before the house was summoned into the presence of the governor to witness, previous to the adjournment, his assent to the bills that had been passed. These instructions are in part inscribed upon the journals of the assembly; while another portion may be found in

---

[1] Journals of the colonial assembly, Smith Hist. New York.

the appendix to the second volume of Smith, being a letter to Charles from the speaker, Jones. They will be found to sustain the opinion already advanced, viz: that the agent was to be the instrument of the assembly against the governor.

This course of action has been attributed to a desire on the part of the DeLancey family to supplant Mr. Clinton with the view of bringing Sir Peter Warren into the executive chair; and color is given to the suggestion by the fact that Mr. Charles was enjoined "in the execution of his instructions, always to take the advice of Sir Peter Warren if in England."[1] DeLancey, the chief justice, was likewise ambitious; and it is not unlikely that he might have cherished such a design in favor of his brother-in-law; but I have found no evidence that Sir Peter Warren himself was a party to any such intrigue. Why should he have been? The measure of his naval glory was full. He was now a member of the imperial parliament, in the enjoyment of a princely estate, and withal in a bad state of health. The governorship of the colony of New York, therefore, could have been no object with him, even should he be able to compete with success against the Newcastle interest by which Mr. Clinton was sustained.

Meanwhile the Indians of the Six Nations, true to their wavering character, upon hearing that the expedition against Canada had been given up, had become exceedingly discontented. Added to this, an express arrived at New York on the seventeenth of February, bearing advices to the governor from Colonel Johnson of an alarming nature. Intelligence had been recently brought in by scouts, so Johnson wrote, that an expedition was fitting out in Canada against the settlements, but whether the blow was to fall upon Albany, Schenectady, or the Mohawks, could not be ascertained. Advices were also received on the twenty-second, from Lieutenant Lindesay, the commanding officer

---

[1] Letter of Speaker Jones to Mr. Charles, April 9th, 1748.

at Oswego, stating that his scouts reported that a French army was marching to attack that post. The whole country, but especially the border, was kept in a state of great terror for several days. Nor was the panic confined to the sparsely peopled settlements. It extended to Albany, and so great was the fear of the inhabitants, that Colonel Schuyler ordered into the city for its defence, several companies of the militia, who were quartered in the neighboring districts.[1] While affairs were in this harrassing state, Colonel Johnson wrote to Governor Clinton that the governor of Canada, through the instrumentality of the Jesuit missionaries, was pressing upon the Six Nations warm invitations to visit him in Montreal, and by every means in his power was endeavoring to seduce those Indians from their alliance with the English. Nor had these artifices been entirely without effect, for the Indians, especially the Onondagas, were already wavering, and were even now manifesting alarming symptoms of defection.

In this exigency, the governor, at the suggestion of Shirley, immediately wrote to Colonel Johnson, directing him to proceed forthwith into the Indian country attended by a strong guard. The note of preparation for this visit is given in the following letter:

Colonel Johnson to Captain Catherwood—(Extract.)

"ALBANY, April 9, 1748.

"* * * * * I am so much hurried with settling my affairs before I go, that I declare I have not time to write a line. I intend to set off next Thursday from my house, with a guard of fifty men, Captain Thomas Butler, and Lieutenant Laurie, officers. We shall have a fatiguing journey of it, and I reckon pretty dangerous; for I am informed by Hendrik's son, that the French at Cadaracqui, having heard of my intention by Jean Cœur, were quite uneasy at the news, and said they would prevent it—an

---

[2] Manuscript letter Colonel Schuyler to Governor Clinton.

CHAP. IX.
1748.

attempt which I think very likely, as it would be of great consequence to them. The worst of it is, we must march for above one hundred miles on foot to go through all their castles by the way, in order to talk to some of the most obstinate of them privately before the meeting, which is the only way I could ever find to gain a point with this sort of people. I reckon I shall have a great deal of trouble to overset all that the French have been doing since last fall. However, I shall leave no stone unturned to accomplish what I go at, either by fair or foul means, for if they are obstinate,—I mean the Onondagas,—I shall certainly talk very harsh to them, and try what that will do. I hope to return in about three weeks, (if nothing extraordinary happens,) when I trust I shall be able to give his excellency an agreeable account of my progress. I also hope his excellency will not omit writing to me if anything of consequence occurs. It will be the time to hear good news when among them all,—especially of an expedition going on, which would cheer up all their drooping spirits. If the governor and Governor Shirley intend to come soon, it would be very proper to give me timely notice, in order to prepare the Indians for a meeting. I hope the assembly will not be so unconscionable as to expect I should take the command of these companies without a salary. But I leave that, and the affair of the regiment entirely to his excellency and you, to do as you think proper against I come back. As to the latter, I assure you it is in a bad way, as also is the watch of Albany."

The orders given to Colonel Johnson were, to erect forts for the protection of the Indian women and children; and by the judicious distribution of presents, to arrest this defection, and thus counteract the insidious influence of the Jesuit priests. The governor farther directed him " to keep the Indians with some Christians continually engaged in skirmishing and in hostile acts against the enemy;" hoping that in this manner the Indians might be led to forget their dissappointment.[1] But these were not the only objects aimed at in this journey. Colonel Johnson was moreover particularly instructed to ascertain the temper of the Six Nations towards the English; and if possible persuade their sachems to attend a grand council to be held shortly at Albany at a time not as yet designated.

Upon the reception of these orders, a council of all the chiefs and warriors of the Six Nations was summoned by Colonel Johnson to meet him around the central council fire at Onondaga; and it appears to have been pretty well attended. Whatever of doubt or distrust, moreover, the colonel might have previously entertained as to his probable reception, he certainly had no cause of complaint upon that head. Being the bearer of presents to a considerable amount, in goods and provisions, which were necessarily transported by bateaux, his advance was slow. Indeed the assemblage at Onondaga, had been well nigh dissolved the day before his arrival, from sheer hunger. But the colonel was well received at all the castles on the route, and his arrival at Onondaga, on the twenty-fourth of April, was greeted by the display of English colors and a salute of fire-arms, which was returned by his guards. He was attended by the principal chiefs to a large house prepared for his reception, spread with new mats, and three others of their bark houses, were appropriated to his attendants. In about an hour afterwards all the sachems of the Confederacy waited upon the colonel in a body, and welcomed him in a general speech, delivered by an Onondaga sachem named Gan-ugh-sa-dea-gah,— "thanking the Great Spirit that he had been spared to come among them at this bloody time." They apologized for the "miserable poor condition" in which he had found them, owing to the fact that by the directions of the English they had now been kept two years from their hunting, in the expectation of being employed upon the

---

[1] Manuscript letter from Governor Clinton to Colonel Johnson.

war-path,—" and that" said the sachem, " all for nothing, as we see no sign of your doing anything with your army as we expected." They had now assembled, pursuant to a belt which he had sent them, " in their present hungry condition having nothing to eat," to hear what he had to say, and to thank him for the supplies they had brought, " although the day before," being quite out of patience and hungered," they had resolved to break up and go home." Colonel Johnson thanked them for the kind welcome they had given him, but being too much fatigued to enter upon business then, he deferred them until the next day, adding—" So I hope you will be easy in your minds, and content yourselves so long, and I will this night provide a feast for your sachems, and another for the warriors and dancers, who I hope will be merry, as it will be my greatest pleasure to see them and make them so."

On the following day the colonel met them in grand council, and imparted the business which had called him thither in a general speech, prepared after the usual pattern of Indian diplomacy. He told them that he had found in some of the old writings of our forefathers which were thought to have been lost, an old and valuable record, containing an account of the manner in which the first friendship between their respective ancestors had commenced on the arrival of " the first great canoe" at Albany. As that canoe contained many things that pleased the Indians, they resolved to tie it fast to the strongest tree on the bank of the river, by a great rope, that the greatest care might be taken of it. But on farther consideration, fearing that the tree might be blown down, it was thought safest to make a long rope and tie it fast at Onondaga, and the rope put under their feet, that in case of any danger to the canoe, by the shaking of the rope, they might all rise as one man, and see what the matter was. Afterward, that their covenant of friendship might be the stronger, the governor had provided a long silver chain instead of the rope, that it might never break, or slip, or rust. This chain was to bind both peoples together, as of one head, one heart, one blood; and whenever it became rusty, it was to be immediately brightened up again, that the covenant might be perpetual. Having thus figuratively rehearsed the history of the ancient alliance, Colonel Johnson proceeded with directness to the object of his visit. He told them that the French had emissaries among them, who were endeavoring to blindfold them, and persuade them to slip their hands out of that chain, which, as their wise forefathers had told them would certainly be the destruction of them all. He conjured them therefore to listen no longer to their deceitful enemies, whose object in the end, would be to destroy them all. In answer to their complaint that for two days all their roads had been stopped by the orders of the English—in other words that they had been kept from hunting,—the colonel told them they had misunderstood the belt he had sent them. He had only meant to stop the road leading to Canada. He informed them that the governors of New York and Massachusetts, to their great concern, had heard of their determination soon to go that way again, contrary to their engagements, and he told them explicitly, that he had been sent by those governors to stop their going. It was the wish, both of the governors and himself, that they should act for their own interests, and go in whatever direction they pleased excepting to Canada. On no consideration whatever should they offer to go there.

The plea of the Indians for their present desire to send a mission to Canada was, that several of their "flesh and blood" were in Montreal, chained and imprisoned, 'and they wished to go thither " and get them back;" but the colonel told them they had better leave that matter to their brethren the English, who would be most likely to succeed. He then rebuked them sharply for a transaction of the preceding year. They had then expressed a strong desire to send an embassy to Canada, to persuade their "flesh and blood," the Caughnawagas, to leave the French, and return to their own country and kindred; and at their solicitation, hostilities were to be suspended during their absence—they promising to return within a month. But instead of that, they staid in Canada the whole summer, and brought back none of their "flesh and blood" when they finally returned. True to his engagement the colonel had kept all the warriors of the Six Nations at home during their absence, and the consequence was that the lives of several of his people had been lost by the incursions of the Canada Indians, and he told the Onondagas plainly that he had no doubt they had seen their scalps. Indeed he charged them with having feigned the errand to the Caughnawagas, for the purpose of giving them an opportunity to talk with the French governor; but he warned them not to set their faces that way again.

Thus far Colonel Johnson told them, the Six Nations had not hurt the Caughnawagas during the war; and yet some of their principal men had lately been murdered in the open fields by the Caughnawagas and the French. "The Frenchman's axe is therefore sticking fast in our heads day after day." By this barbarous act, it was rendered very plain that the French aimed at nothing short of their destruction, which, he insisted, had ever been their design, "as you all," said he, "by sorrowful experience have formerly seen and felt, when they used to destroy your castles, and sacrifice such numbers of your predecessors, that large heaps of their bones yet lie scattered over your whole country. This consideration alone ought to be sufficient to stir up everlasting resentment in your bosoms against such a barbarous people; and it would, if there was the least spark of that Great Spirit in you, for which your brave ancestors were noted through the world. If you are worthy of those ancestors you will now use the axe against them which you have had so long in your hands.

Before closing his speech, the colonel repeated his suspisions of their friendly intentions toward the French, and warned them against any farther duplicity. They must either drop the French entirely and stand by their own brothers, or declare themselves at once and explicitly, if the contrary was their determination. In conclusion, however, he informed them of the liberal disposition entertained toward them by the governor, and by their great father the king. He had now orders to build forts in their country for the defence of their towns and castles while their braves were absent in the war; and he had the pleasure farther to inform them that the king had sent a quantity of goods as presents for those of them who were hearty in his cause. These presents were expected shortly to arrive, and it was his desire that their nations should meet the governor at Albany, there to receive them.

The council-fire was then raked up until the next day, when the sachems delivered their answer; and even if they had been meditating treachery, either the decided tone in which Colonel Johnson had spoken, or the promised presents, or perhaps the influence of both, had wrought sa favorable change in their temper as could have been desired. They admitted that they had been tampered with by the French, "who had used a great deal of art," but promised that their friendship for the English, should never be dropped. They nevertheless thought it hard and cruel that they should not be allowed to go to Canada for their "flesh and blood," rotting and dying in irons, when their release had been offered if they would go for them. "Had you," they said, "got them from thence as you did your own people, we should not have thought of going to Canada as friends, but in another manner." However, as the colonel promised that efforts should be made to procure the release of the Indian captives in exchange for French prisoners, they would not look that way any longer. Yet they begged earnestly that their brother would make haste in this matter. They explained the reason of their long detention when on a mission to

Canada, the summer before. While they were in Montreal, news came that the Six Nations had killed and taken several French people, upon which they were ordered to Quebec to be imprisoned. They were detained ninety-two days, at the end of which they were permitted to return, but with only two of their warriors who were prisoners. The governor would release no more, but told them he would give them all up if they would come again this spring, unless in the meantime the Six Nations should make war, in which event he would put them all to death. "Now," said the governor "as we have told you all about this affair, we hope you will not blame us as you have done, but be assured our resolution is to live and die by you. We listen to you with open ears and mind what you say, you may depend upon it. And we hope you will not make a doubt of it that our firm resolution is, to keep up in every step, to the rules laid down by our forefathers. And as we have your axe so long in hand, we assure you that we have been, ever since we last took it up, always ready to make use of it in conjunction with you and will ever continue so." Recurring in the course of their speech to the same idea of having had the axe so long in their heads again, the sachem proceeded as follows:

"*Brother*, we were in hopes to have used the axe before now to some purpose, as you told us two years ago that you were then ready to march with your army against Canada. But instead of an army you only sent out small parties, several of whom were by that means cut to pieces. Had you gone on with your army and ships, as you told us you would, and assisted us properly to get over the foreign Indians to our interest, who offered their service, then we should have been able with the loss of a few men to have driven the French and his allies into the great lakes and drowned them. But as you have not done that, which we are sorry for, we tell you now, brother, according to your desire, we used what interest we could that way, and have gained a considerable number of the foreign

Indians who were ready to join you, and us. But there is no sign of an army now, nor the encouragement given to them which they expected. We cannot pretend to say now what they will do."

This rebuke of the English for the feeble manner in which the war had been conducted, notwithstanding all the bustling preparations of the two preceding years, was not undeserved.

The sachems closed their address by warm expressions of thanks to Colonel Johnson for his care over them, and for the presents he had brought. They also promised to meet the governor at his call; and in conclusion, the colonel assured them that he should inform the governor of what had taken place "with a cheerful heart."[1]

Yet in transmitting the proceedings to the governor, the colonel avowed his decided belief that no restraint that should be at once wholesome and permanent, could be imposed upon the Indians, unless by strong legislation, unprincipled white men could be prevented from hastening their destruction by the "accursed traffic of rum."

The idea of a grand council, to be held at Albany the ensuing summer, had been long in contemplation both by Governor Clinton and Governor Shirley.[2] Strangely enough, moreover, considering the course of the ministers in terminating the military demonstrations of the preceding autumn, and ordering the disbanding of the troops, a letter was received from the Duke of Newcastle, in February, addressed to Governors Shirley and Clinton, urging in the strongest terms, the importance of destroying the French settlement at Crown Point—an object, it need not be here repeated, long entertained by the colonies, and the achievement of which, had only been prevented by the indecision, if not the weakness of ministers. They were also directed in the same despatch, to do everything in their power to

---

[1] For a full account of the proceedings of this council, see journals of the council board.

[2] Letter from Governor Shirley to Governor Clinton—London documents xxx.

secure the steady attachment of the Six Nations to the king's interests—to which end the necessary presents were to be provided at the expense of the crown. This communication from the ministers only hastened the carrying out of the proposed council; and on the twenty-eighth of March, Governor Clinton being indisposed, Chief Justice De Lancey, by his order, laid before the council the duke of Newcastle's letter. The letter having been referred to a committee, the suggestions contained in it were fully approved, and an expedition against Crown Point recommended as best calculated to secure the Six Nations in the interests of the crown. The committee farther seconded, without a dissenting voice, the project of holding a council with the Indians during the ensuing summer, and suggested that the governor should send down a message to the house asking for its cheerful acquiescence in these plans. In accordance, therefore, with this advice, the governor sent a message to the assembly, urging upon its consideration these suggestions of the council, and asking for immediate action. On the next day a committee of the whole house reported favorably upon the message. They acknowledged the kindness of his majesty in directing that the Indians should be protected at the expense of the crown; they proposed that the provinces should unite with each other in every well concerted scheme for defence; and suggested that provision should be made to enable the commissioners of the different provinces to meet together and determine upon suitable measures. This report met the entire approval of the assembly, and on the same day it further brought in a bill for reimbursing the governor for the money which he had advanced out of his own funds to Colonel Johnson as pay for the scalps which had been brought in by the Indians.

But notwithstanding this seeming disposition on the part of the assembly to acquiese in the wishes of the governor, all his efforts to second governor Shirley's favorite plan for an expedition against Crown Point were fruitless.

Although the new assembly had not openly opposed the governor thus far, yet its apathy showed plainly how little it was its purpose to second vigorously his efforts. In a letter from Governor Clinton to the lords of trade, under date of April of this year, the writer complains bitterly of this indisposition to second him in his endeavors to promote the welfare of the colony; and alludes in no gentle spirit to the continued encroachments of the house on the crown, particularly as shown in the appointment of Robert Charles as agent for the province without his privity or consent. This appointment by the assembly without reference to the wishes of the governor, was well calculated to exasperate a far less choleric temperament than his; and accustomed as he had been all his life to command, he could ill brook the growing spirit of insubordination in his legislature. Indeed, this is but another evidence of the tendency which was everywhere manifesting itself in the colonies, to assert their entire independence of the crown in the government of their home affairs.

The general assembly again met on the sixth of June, but was adjourned until the twenty-first. The session was opened by a message from the governor, transmitting, among other papers, Colonel Johnson's report of the proceedings at the Onondaga council. Favorable, however, as these proceedings appeared, his excellency said he had little hope of preventing their ultimate defection to the French, unless some enterprise against the enemy should be speedily and resolutely undertaken. He therefore again urged an expedition against Crown Point, conjointly with the colonies of Massachusetts and Connecticut, who were ready to unite immediately in an attempt for the reduction of that post. On the subject of intercourse between the traders and the Indians, a strong enactment to prevent the sale to the latter of spirituous liquors, and the purchase from them of arms, ammunition and clothing, was recommended. The message farther announced that his excellency was preparing to meet the Indians at Albany in the course of the ensuing month; but particularly it called the attention of the assembly to the disaffection of the Indians on account of the detention of their braves in Canada; urging in view of this, that immediate provision be made for the exchange of these prisoners.

Upon the last mentioned suggestion the assembly acted with promptitude; and a resolution was passed, requesting the governor to send a flag of truce to Canada with twenty-five French prisoners then confined in New York, together with all the prisoners detained at Albany, to be exchanged for such of the inhabitants of the colony, and Indians of the Six Nations, as were held in captivity by the French,—the house pledging itself to defray the expense. But as to the other recommendations of the message, a decided spirit of reluctance was manifested. The house refused to engage with Massachusetts and Connecticut in the proposed united expedition against Crown Point;—instead of which they recommended merely that the governor should unite with Governor Shirley, and the other governors on the continent, in humbly representing to his majesty the distressed state of the colonies by reason of the French in Canada, and imploring his assistance.

There had as yet been no collision between Mr. Clinton and his new assembly—rendered new only by the process of an election,—but however smooth the surface, the elements of an outbreak were smouldering beneath. And these had well nigh been called into action by a very small affair, during the present short session. On the twenty-fourth of June, Colonel Beekman, one of the representatives from the county of Dutchess, brought forward with all possible solemnity, a charge against the governor, "of such a violation of the laws, and such a grievance upon the people,—such an attempt upon their rights and properties, —as called loudly for redress." The facts adduced by Colonel Beekman to sustain this very grievous charge, were these: Some of the late levies from Dutchess county, who had served on the northern frontier, had sued, and others were preparing to sue, their captain for their pay; upon which the governor had written to the judge, and Mr. Catherwood, his secretary, to the clerk of the court, and also to the sheriff, desiring them to put a stop to the proceedings. Upon this representation, a committee of inquiry was raised, with power to send for persons and papers. No sooner, however, had the governor seen the entry of these proceedings upon the journals, than he transmitted a message of explanation to the house, from which it appeared that the suits in question had been instituted by sundry deserters who had gone off with his majesty's arms and clothing, by reason of which they had fortified all pay due them from the crown; and the letters written to the officers of the court, merely recommended that a stop should be put to the claims of those deserters. "If," said the governor, "such a step taken, can, in the most extensive light, be construed any violation of the laws, or a grievance upon the people, it was done through inadvertency; as I never had an intention to infringe upon any man's right or property; and if the people have received any damage thereby, I am ready to redress it." No farther action was had in the case, and the assembly adjourned on the first of July,—not, however, without complying with the suggestion of Colonel Johnson, by passing an act more effectually to cut off the pernicious traffic in rum with the Indians.

Mr. Clinton's attention was next occupied in preparations for his approaching interview with the Indians, at which Governor Shirley proposed to be present. Just as he was on the point of starting for Albany, however, tidings though unofficial, were received from Europe, the nature of which would be at once to change the character of the negotiations with the Indians, and of which the governor wrote thus to Colonel Johnson:

Governor Clinton to Colonel Johnson.

NEW YORK, July 5, 1748.

Sir:

I have just this moment received yours of the first instant, which I have but time to acknowledge by Lieutenant Cleavland, and send you the enclosed piece of news, which I believe will startle you, as it does everybody else; though I think if the Parliament had agreed to the preliminaries, we must have had orders before this. Upon this news I received a letter from Governor Shirley last Saturday, to desire I would postpone my meeting the Indians for eight or ten days. Upon that I have sent an express to know the difficulty I shall meet in complying, besides the danger of making them angry if I don't meet them at or about the time appointed. Therefore I was obliged to set out, but would defer speaking to them till the twentieth instant, in the hope of his being there by that time. I set out on Thursday, and expect an answer to my express at the manor of Livingston this day sènnight,— having given him positive orders to be there in the morning, and written to Mr. Shirley to despatch him for that end. One reason Governor Shirley gives for postponing the conference, is, that we may expect some directions from home in regard to the Indians, and what it would be proper to say to them on this occasion. Adieu in great haste.

"Yours most sincerely,
"GEO. CLINTON."

"To Colonel Johnson."[1]

The report proved to be true—the preliminaries of a general peace having been signed by the ministers of the great powers, at Aix-la-Chapelle in May, as announced by the king in closing the session of parliament on the thirteenth of that month. The truth was, that all parties had become tired of the war,—England, because of the prodigious expense she was compelled to incur, not only in keeping up her own fleets and armies, but in subsidizing

---
[1] Manuscript Letter.

the northern powers of Europe,—an expense so great as not to be countermanded by the splendid series of victories which her arms had achieved at sea, and by the glory which the Duke of Cumberland had won upon the continent. The king of France, too, had in the preceding autumn, expressed his desire of a pacification in a personal conversation with Sir John Ligonier, made prisoner by the French in the battle of Laffeldt; and his minister at the Hague had subsequently presented a declaration to the same effect to the deputies of the States General.[1] Nor is it strange that the French monarch should have been desirous of peace. For notwithstanding the successes of his arms in the Netherlands, the victory of Marshall Saxe over the confederates at Laffeldt, was accidental, and withal had been dearly purchased, while the Marshal de Belleisle, though at first successful in Italy, had been checked, and his brother, the chevalier, slain in Piedmont, and his large army defeated. Everywhere upon the seas the English had been victorious. In addition to the loss of the expensive armament under the Duke D'Anville, occasioned by sickness, tempest, and the death of the commander, and the victories of Anson and Warren, of which an account has already been given in a former chapter, Commodore Fox had, in the month of June of the preceding year, taken above forty ships richly laden from St. Domingo, and in October following, Admiral Hawke had achieved his splendid victory over the French fleet commanded by Monsieur Letendeur, in the latitude of Belleisle. Letendeur's fleet consisted of nine ships of the line, besides frigates, in convoy of a numerous fleet of merchant ships bound from the West Indies. A large number of the merchantmen were intercepted before their arrival at Martinique, and taken. The number of prizes captured by the British cruisers that year from the French and Spaniards, was six hundred and forty-four—the loss of the English during the same period not exceeding four hundred and fifty.[2]

---
[1] Smollett.
[2] Smollett.

CHAP. IX.
1748.

These results had been sufficiently discouraging to the French monarch, who now knew in addition, that Great Britain had at length succeeded in subsidizing the Czarina of Russia, who had a large army then on the march to join the Duke of Cumberland and the Confederates in the Lowlands. Every day France was becoming more and more impoverished by the expenses, and the losses of the war, while her statesmen were amazed at the resources of England, enabling her not only to maintain invincible armies and navies, but to subsidize all Europe.[1] Hence the desire of the French monarch for peace, the preliminaries of which were signed in May of the present year, as already stated, although there was no cessation of hostilities until the conclusion of the treaty in October.

The time for holding the grand council—so earnestly desired by the royal governors, and so long looked for by the Indians—had now arrived. Preparations for this event had been made upon a large scale, and everything which would render it attractive to the Indians had been thought of and prepared. Accordingly, on the twentieth of July, Governor Clinton, accompanied by Doctor Colden and other members of his council, arrived in Albany. Here they found waiting them, Governor Shirley and the commissioners of Massachusetts Bay, who had arrived a day or two previously. Nor had the Indians been less prompt in their attendance. The representations from the Six Nations, the River Indians, and some of the far off tribes, were unprecedented in the history of any former council. So large, indeed, was the number of Indians assembled upon this occasion, that the oldest of the inhabitants declared that Albany had never before witnessed such a large concourse within her precincts. The exertions of Colonel Johnson, which had been unremitting to secure a full delegation from each of the different tribes, undoubtedly contributed much to this result. Indeed, such had

---

[1] Smollett.

been his influence, that numbers of those Indians, who had hitherto leaned toward the French interest, came flocking in from the surrounding country, anxious to show their allegiance to the British crown.

The old Dutch city had in fact seldom witnessed such a sight. Here were gathered Indians from the far West, many of whom at a later period were destined to redden their tomahawks in the blood of so many brave garrisons, under the great Pontiac. Here were many of the River Indians,—remnants of once powerful tribes,—whose grandsires had followed the brave Uncas and Miantonomo to battle, and had taken their last stand with the noble but ill-fated King Philip. In one spot, a painted and tattooed warrior might have been seen smoking his pipe, as he recounted to his wondering companions the sights seen in his morning's stroll; while everywhere groups of picturesquely attired Indians, with nodding plumes and variegated blankets, wandered through the streets, gazing with curious eye upon the novelties of civilization.

The proceedings of the council, however, contrary to expectation, were not important. The governor's speech was but another rehearsal, in substance, and in metaphor, of former ones. The old "covenant chain" was again "brightened," and the Indians were again admonished against the wiles of the French. They were requested to keep "the axe in their hands," and to restrain their young men still longer from their hunting. They were cautioned against allowing their people, under any pretext whatesover, to be seduced by the invitations of the French into Canada, and they were peremptorily directed to arrest the celebrated Jean Cœur, so long the arch enemy of the English residing among the Senecas at the Niagara carrying-place, and deliver him to the colonial authorities, and likewise to banish every French emissary from their territory. They were furthermore requested to desist from a war-expedition which they were about to undertake against the Flathead Indians, residing far in the northwest, who were claimed by the governor as his majesty's allies. The following is the concluding paragraph of the speech, which is quoted *in hæc verba,* for the reason that it refers to a massacre of which the particulars are not known.

"*Brethren:* You have since you came to this place, given a new and strong proof of your love to your brethren and fidelity to the king your father, by so cheerfully and speedily sending out a number of your warriors with our troops in quest of the enemy, who a few days since surprised and killed many of our brethren at Schenectady, and although those who earnestly pursued the enemy, had not the good fortune to meet with them, you may assure yourselves that this instance of your affection and readiness to join in our cause, shall always be remembered by me, and made known to the king your father."

No printed or official record of the affair here referred to is believed to exist. Among the Johnson manuscripts, however, I have discovered a very confused and unsatisfactory account of it, contained in a letter to Colonel Johnson from Albert Van Slyck, dated Schenectady, July twenty-first, 1748. From the details preserved in this letter, it appears that a party of men from Schenectady, the leader of whom was Daniel Toll, had been dispatched to some place in the vicinity to bring in a number of horses, which was surprised by a party of the enemy, whose presence in the neighborhood was neither known nor suspected. The firing being heard by Adrian Van Slyck, a brother of the writer of the account, who seems to have resided at a distance from the town; he sent a negro man to the latter place to give the alarm, and obtain reinforcements. Four parties of armed men successivly repaired to the scene of action, the first of which was composed of "the New England lieutenant with some of his men, and five or six young lads," accompanied by Daniel Van Slyck,—another brother. The second party was led by Angus Van Slyck, "and some men"—how many of either party is not stated. Adrian Van Slyck followed next, at the head of a party of New York levies; but on reaching the scene of action, where Angus, with inferior numbers, was holding the enemy at bay, the levies all fled, in the most cowardly manner. The fourth party, was composed of Albert Van Slyck, (the writer of the letter,) Jacob Glen, " and several others," on the approach of whom the enemy drew off, leaving Adrian Van Slyck among the dead. The letter adds—" It grieves me, I not being commander, that when we went, Garret VanAntwerp would suffer no more to accompany the party."

Having taken three days for consideration, the Indians replied on the twenty-sixth, Onnasdego, an Onondaga sachem, and orator of renown being the speaker. But the occasion was not such as to kindle the fire of his genius, or to elicit a single glowing period. His oration was therefore a commonplace answer, in their exact order, to the various topics of the speech addressed to them by the governor. In the outset all their ancient covenants with the English were renewed; and while they "freely acknowledged that the French were continually using artifices to induce them to break the covenant chain," they nevertheless were resolved to hold it fast. They promised that none of their people should be allowed to visit the French; declared that no French interpreter should be longer allowed to reside among them; and announced that Jean Cœur had already been delivered up by the Senecas—but of this fact there seems to be no good evidence. Their war-kettle, they said, was yet over the fire, and the hatchet in their hands. They would grasp it still, and be ready to use it when summoned to the path. They promised to desist from the prosecution of hostilities against the Flatheads; thanked the governor for his efforts to procure an exchange of prisoners; expressed their grief for the people who had been slain at Schenectady, and their regret that their wariors had not been able to overtake the enemy, "who had gone a different road from what they used to go." But they would "wipe up the blood of the slain," and "dry up the tears of their friends."

The council fire was then raked up, and the conferences were closed by a dance of the young warriors in the evening, the governor giving them five barrels of beer wherewith to drink his majesty's health.

On the following day the River Indians presented themselves, and were thus welcomed by the governor:—

"*Brethren:* I am glad to see you here and do give you thanks for the fidelity you have always shown to this government, and I do assure you, you shall never want my protection as long as you behave yourselves with duty and obedience to his majesty. And as a token of the king your father's affection, he has directed me to make you a present which I have ordered to be given you."

To which the chief addressing himself to the governors both of New York and Massachusetts, replied:—

"*Fathers:* We wipe off your tears you had for the loss of your people who have been murdered since the commencement of this war.

"*Fathers:* We are very much rejoiced for the regard our father the king of Great Britain has for us by ordering a present which you assure shall be given us.

"*Fathers:* Our forefathers told us that before any white people came among them, they saw a vessel in the river. For some time they were afraid to go to it. But at last they ventured on board and found them to be white men who treated them civilly and exchanged mutually presents to each other, with promise that they would return the next year, which accordingly happened. When they came again the white people and they entered into a covenant together that they should live on their lands, which they did. And they also promised to take us under their arms and protect us which they have done to this day.

"*Fathers:* When you came first to this country you were but a small people and we very numerous. We then assisted and protected you, and now we are few in number, you become multitudes like a large tree, whose roots and branches are very extensive, under whose branches we take our shelter as we have heretofore done.

"*Fathers:* It is now almost three years since the war first began. You have had a very numerous army together. We were ready to join you in hopes that Canada would have been in possession of the English before now. We have been always ready and have still our hands on the cocks of our guns to go against our common enemy whenever we shall be commanded.

"*Fathers:* We thank you for your kind expressions toward us, and are very sorry we were not here the other day, when the enemy murdered a number of our brethren at Schenectady, which if we had we would have readily and cheerfully joined in the pursuit of them, even to the gates of Crown Point."

While this council was sitting, the rumor that the preliminaries for a general pacification had actually been agreed upon by the great powers of Europe, became general, and was soon the topic of conversation among Indians, as well as among whites. To the Indians of the Six Nations, who had hoped by a continuance of the war to have avenged their slaughtered relatives, the rumor of a peace was a severe blow. All the clans of the Confederacy had lost some of their braves, but the Mohawks upon whom the loss naturally fell with greater force, now that they had at last gone upon the war-path, were loth to relinquish it. They recalled, too, with bitterness the justice of the remark made by them to Colonel Johnson, when urged by him to take up the hatchet. "You and the French can make peace whenever you choose, but with us when the hatchet is once dug up, it cannot be so easily buried, but the war must be one of extermination."

Still the result of this council, so far as the colonies were concerned, was all that the most sanguine could desire. The Six Nations promised, either to drive all the

French emissaries who had privately resided among them, out of their country, or to deliver them up to Governor Clinton. They agreed farther to send no deputations to the Canadian governor, and to keep their warriors in constant readiness to obey the commands of Mr. Clinton. Indeed so strong had been the desire of the Confederates to send a deputation into Canada—Galissonière having represented that this was the condition alone upon which their braves detained by him would be given up—that Governor Shirley thought it best to bring with him fourteen French prisoners to be immediately sent into Canada as an exchange for an equal number of Indians detained there in captivity.

The tragedy at Schenectady, was not the only one enacted upon the northern border of the colony during the summer of 1748. Another, of a most heart rending description, was perpetrated at about the same time, in the town of Hoosic, twenty-five miles north of Albany, by a party of Indians from St. Francis, which, from its peculiar barbarity, and the character of the victims, deserves a more extended record than is usually awarded to these incidents of the border. Indeed among all the scenes of blood, written or traditionary, in the early history of this country, none surpass in cruelty the one now about to be related.

Maria Keith, whose name is identified with this savage transaction, was born in 1721, of highly respectable parents, on the banks of the Hudson, about eighteen miles above Albany. Of her infancy and early life, it is sufficient to say, that she gave decided promise of no ordinary qualities of mind, evincing an unusual attachment for books, and devoting to reading the greater part of that, which her contemporaries in childhood spent in play. By seizing thus upon every opportunity of improving her mind, she acquired much information, and laid up a considerable amount of knowledge, though the expression of her biographer, from whom the leading facts of the narrative are drawn, that "she had informed her opening mind with the principles of every useful science," is probably somewhat exaggerated.[1] But be this as it may, it is evident that her mind was well cultivated. To this excellence may be added another, which though of less importance, yet deserves notice, that her manners were elegant, and her person uncommonly attractive. Her beauty became so celebrated that her fame reached Albany, and drew thence several admirers who visited Miss Keith, and solicited her hand. This she refused to all her Albanian suitors, reserving her affections for a relative of the same name. The latter, though not handsome, yet having an engaging address, and being mutually and morally such as suited her tastes, won her heart, in preference to other lovers, who might have been considered in a worldly point of view, more eligible. She was married at the youthful age of fifteen, her nuptials being celebrated under the most favorable auspices.

Immediately after her marriage, Mr. Keith erected a beautiful mansion on the banks of the Touhannock, a tributary of the Hoosic river, whither they removed, and where they were surrounded by everything necessary to happiness and tranquil enjoyment. Among the neighbors they were both very popular, winning golden opinions by their kindness to the sick, their generosity to the poor and needy, and their hospitality to all of every grade in life who entered within their peaceful doors. In this way they passed twelve years of uninterrupted happiness, during which time Mrs. Keith gave birth to a daughter and a son, between whose ages there was a difference of nearly eleven years,—this latter having been born in the spring of the year now under review. In every hour of alarm, therefore, Mrs. Keith felt increased anxiety on account of the helpless infant which she held in her arms. Indulging the feelings of a devoted and an attached mother, she listened with breathless solicitude, to all the rumors which were spread concerning the

---

[1] Works of Ann Maria Bleecker.

marauding bands of Indians, sent out from Canada by the French, for the purpose of ruthless devastation upon the property, and merciless cruelty upon the persons of the borderers. Rumor with her thousand tongues, many of which spake but too truly in this case, soon repeated the nearer and nearer approach of another band of the dreaded ministers of French and savage vengeance. When it was ascertained that the Indians had arrived within the vicinity of Fort Edward, and were seen prowling about that place, Mr. Keith dispatched a messenger to bring his brothers who resided there, to his house on the Touharna,—deeming his residence a safer sanctuary, on account of its being more interior. One of his brothers had been married several months before, and his wife at the time of their flight from Fort Edward, was in a peculiarly delicate situation.

Not long after Mr. Keith had thus collected his relations around him, and under his roof, his family were visited by some Indians of the St. Francis tribe, who had pitched their wigwams a small distance from the village of Schaghticoke. These were hospitably entertained, and were permitted to pass several hours in eating and drinking; during which time much conversation passed between Mrs. Keith and her savage visitors. To soothe her apprehensions, an old Indian who was spokesman, assured her that the family might dismiss their fear, and solemnly promised that in case of any danger she should be seasonably informed, and the means afforded her for escape. To enforce his "glozing lies," he presented her with a belt of wampum, saying, "There, receive my token of friendship. We go to dig up the hatchet, to sink it in the heads of your enemies. We shall guard this word with a rail of fire. You shall be safe." Still farther to quiet her fears, he added in apparent anger that she should suspect his fidelity, "No Maria, I am a true man. I shoot the arrow up to the Great Captain every new moon; depend upon it, I will trample down the briars round your dwelling that you do not hurt your feet."

These bland words seem to have satisfied Mrs. Keith, though her husband, with greater sagacity, suspected and feared that beneath was concealed a plan for their destruction.

The next morning after the ominous visit of the savages, perhaps for the purpose of dispelling the anxiety of his mind, Mr. Keith proposed a hunting excursion to his brother Peter, which was accepted, and they sallied forth with their guns in quest of game. Musing upon the perils that surrounded their families, they had gone several miles from home, before they became aware of the distance they had traveled. At that moment their eye caught sight of a fine doe, at which Peter leveled his piece, and brought her to the ground. But scarcely had the echo of the explosion died away among the the hills, when they heard a rustling, followed by the crack of a rifle, and Peter fell forward pierced by two balls in his heart. This was rapidly followed by the rushing of two savages upon them, one of whom prepared to scalp his victim, while the other aimed his gun at Mr. Keith. Quick as thought Mr. Keith shot his antagonist dead on the spot, and assailing the other Indian with the butt of his rifle, prostrated him on the ground. Leaving his foes for dead, he placed the bleeding corpse of his brother upon his horse, and hastened home with the dire intelligence.

It is not necessary to describe the scene of woe that followed his arrival, bearing with him the dead body of a brother, who a few hours before, had been in the enjoyment of life and health. Suffice it to say, that after having washed the body from its gore, and prepared it for the grave, they laid it in an upper room, designing to have the obsequies performed the following day. Under circumstances calculated to excite no great alarm, Mr. Keith resolved to set out that night for Schaghticoke, to procure a couple of wagons, and convey his family to Albany. Though dissuaded by his wife from going, yet he persisted in his design, and accordingly went, leaving an affectionate circle behind him, which he fondly hoped to see again in the course of a few hours, and greet them with tidings of his success, and the certainty of being soon placed beyond the reach of danger. But he had not been gone long, when at the hour of midnight, the inmates of Mr. Keith's mansion were startled by voices and yells of savages surrounding the house, and clamoring for admission. Blow after blow was made upon the doors. Every moment increased the violence of the assailants, who were bent upon deeds of blood. Mrs. Keith pressed her children more closely to her heaving bosom, and all stood petrified with terror. At length the brother of Mr. Keith, who, as I have already mentioned, had been lately married, advanced as if in frantic despair, and unbarred the door. Instantly it flew open, and he fell pierced with balls, and weltering in his blood. In rushed the savages, and immediately began the work of death. They seized the prostrate husband of Cornelia, and tore off his scalp before her eyes. While this deed was perpetrating, an Indian, hideously painted, strode up to Cornelia, and buried his tomahawk in her forehead. Her eyes just opened as the blow descended, and then closed forever. Perceiving her near approach to being a mother, they ripped her body open, and tearing the unborn child from her womb, dashed it against the wall.

While this horrid carnage was going on, another Indian, —the same one who had with Punic faith presented the belt of wampum as a token of peace,—approached Mrs. Keith, who sat circling her children in her arms, and uttering the most piteous entreaties for mercy. She drew forth and showed to her treacherous foe, the belt, and appealed to his promise made when he gave it to her. But she might as well have remonstrated with the ferocious tiger, when hungry for prey. He only replied that *she* should be spared, and "dance with him around the council fire in Canada"—and then with a sardonic smile, expressing the fear that her infant son would only incumber her on the journey, he seized the child by the wrists, and tore it from her embrace. Enraged apparently at her resistance, he dashed its forehead against the wall, and hurled its reeking body some distance from the house. Frenzied by the sight she rushed to the mangled remains of her loved infant, redoubling her cries of anguish, casting herself upon its body, wiping the blood from its ghastly countenance, and pressing it to her bosom.

The savages having plundered the house of everything that was portable, forced those who had escaped their vengeance, to quit the house, consisting of Mrs. Keith, her daughter Anna, a lovely girl in her twelfth year, and a brother of Mr. Keith. They then completed the work of destruction by firing the building, which was soon enveloped in flames. But Mrs. Keith's cup of sorrow was not yet full. Anna, acting as if she thought that death in any shape was to be preferred to being in the hands of ruthless barbarians, to whom pity was a stranger, fled precipitately back to the house, though the flames were bursting forth in every direction, and entering in, secreted herself in a closet, where she remained until her escape became impossible, and perished in the devouring fire. The excruciating feelings of Mrs. Keith, on being compelled to behold this funeral pile of her only daughter, can readily be imagined. Words fail to express the horror which must have filled her bosom, when seeing at her feet the mangled remains of one child, and witnessing the raging flames that were consuming the other, by a most agonizing death. She continued calling the name of her daughter with loud cries, till the Indians, impatient at her delay, compelled her and her brother, the only survivors in this fearful tragedy, to set out with them in their journey to Canada.

The remainder of the story is soon told. On her wearisome journey with the savages, nothing remarkable occurred that deserves a particular mention. As might be supposed, she suffered various privations, and was exposed to great fatigue. Unaccustomed to their mode of living, she would have been starved, had not her brother prepared her food, and ministered to her necessities. After enduring numerous perils and hardships, she at last reached Canada. When in the Indian village, to which her captors hastened, she narrowly escaped having her brains dashed out by an old hag, who seemed determined to glut her vengeance upon the prisoners. But on reaching Montreal, bating some painful circumstances which, to the disgrace of civilization were allowed, she was kindly provided for by some charitable ladies, one of whom received her into her house, and treated her with the kindness of a sister.

Thus she remained in the house of this charitable Samaritan, till she was at last found by her husband. The morning after the deed of cruelty which has been described, was perpetrated, he returned with two wagons to carry his family to Albany. But what was his horror, on beholding his house burned to the ground, and the scene of ruin which on every side met his eye! By exploring the ruins, however, he found the bones of those who had been murdered, and also, which touched his heart to the quick, the half consumed remains of his infant, bearing yet the marks of savage violence. Collecting these charred bones, and depositing them in a box, he returned with them to Schaghticoke, where they were decently buried. Resigning himself to despair, and supposing that Indian vengeance had spared not a single object of his affections, he joined the colonial army, resolving to seek death by placing himself in the front of the battle, and courting places of the greatest exposure. But the bullets passed harmlessly by him, nor could he find the death he sought. At length the thought occurred to him that he might yet find his brother, who possibly had not fallen a victim. Cherishing the idea, he set off for Canada, availing himself of the opportunity of accompanying some prisoners, who were returning to Quebec. In Canada he pursued the object of his journey with indefatigable ardor, inquiring of every officer the names of prisoners who had been captured during the war.

On arriving at Montreal, he was immediately introduced to the general officer, who patiently heard his story, and treated him with great clemency. Having obtained permission to remain in town a few days, he respectfully withdrew, and turning down a street inquired of a man where lodgings were to be let. The stranger turned about and civilly took off his hat, when whom should Mr. Keith recognize in the stranger, but his brother Henry? By him Mr. Keith received the delightful intelligence of his wife's preservation, and of her being then in Montreal. He speedily flew to her embrace. The rapture of the reunion was greater than she could endure. She fainted in his arms, but soon recovered, and felt that the joy of meeting compensated her for the wearisome months of sadness, grief and distraction which she had endured.

Nor were the borders of Massachusetts and New Hampshire unmolested during the spring and summer of this year. Unable to obtain assistance from their own government, the inhabitants of the exposed settlements of New Hampshire upon the Connecticut river, applied to Massachusetts, by the legislature of which a garrison of one hundred men was placed in the fort at Charlestown, called Number Four, under the command of the gallant Captain Stevens, who had signalized himself by his bravery in that position before. His second in command was Captain Humphrey Hobbs. Fort Massachusetts having been rebuilt, was also garrisoned by one hundred men, and entrusted again to its former commander, Captain Ephraim Williams—Colonel John Stoddard of Northampton, having the general command of the northern and western frontiers of that colony. Dying, however, in the month of June, that eminent man was succeeded by Colonel Israel Williams, of Hartford.

But it was not garrison duty alone which the officers and soldiers of Number Four were required to perform. They had a wide extent of territory to guard against the irruptions of the enemy, extending from the upper Merrimac country to Lake Champlain, and a suitable number of men, from both forts, were required to be constantly employed in ranging the forests to intercept the enemy in their sallies from Crown Point, and the great Indian rendezvous of St. Francis. The enemy first appeared at Charlestown about the middle of March, when a party of thirty Indians attacked eight of Stevens's men, at a short distance from the fort. Captain Stevens sallied forth for their rescue, and brought them in after a sharp skirmish, with the loss of two men, one of whom was killed, and the other taken prisoner. A third was wounded. A yet larger party, consisting of eighteen men under Captain Melvin, from the same garrison, had a narrower escape in the month of May. Melvin having crossed the woods to the shore of Lake Champlain opposite Crown Point, imprudently disclosed himself to the enemy in that fortress by firing upon two canoes of Indians. A party was immediately sent out from the fort to intercept him on his return, which by a rapid march gained his front. Having crossed the enemy's trail, and thereby discovered his design, Melvin endeavored to circumvent him by changing his course from Charlestown, and striking down in the direction of Fort Dummer.[1] But the enemy was soon upon his path, and in close pursuit, though without his knowledge. Arriving at West river, Melvin incautiously allowed his men to halt and amuse themselves by shooting the salmon which were passing up a shoal of that stream. The consequence had well nigh been fatal to the whole party, since the enemy, thus apprized of their halt, and by stealthy observation of their amusement, rushed upon them unawares, and killed six of the most valuable men,—the residue, after vainly attempting to make a stand against superior numbers, making their escape to Fort Dummer. A month afterward a party of thirteen men on the route from Hinsdale to Fort Dummer,

---

[1] Fort Dummer, frequently spoken of in the early border wars, was first built in 1723. It was situated on the Connecticut river, forty miles below Charlestown, or Number Four.

fell into an Indian ambuscade, and were all but three either killed or taken prisoners.[1]

The history of this feebly conducted contest shows that in a large majority of these border affairs, the enemy was successful—a fact, perhaps, that should create no wonder, when it is considered that his movements were always by stealth, and his attacks by surprise,—he having the selection of time and place, and the option of fighting or not, according to circumstances. But fortune was not always turning in their favor. It happened that on the twenty-sixth of June, while Captain Hobbs, at the head of forty men from the garrison of Number Four, was ranging the woods west of the Connecticut river, when about twelve miles from Fort Dummer, he was attacked by a strong body of Indians, under a resolute half-breed chief named Sackett. Hobbs and his men were regaling themselves at their knapsacks at the moment of the attack, in an opening upon a rivulet hedged with alders, and covered with large and towering trees. The precaution of posting sentinels, however, had not been omitted, so that the surprise was less complete than otherwise it would have been. At the instant of alarm, each man selected a tree for his cover, and the Indians rushing upon the heels of the sentinels, were in the onset so warmly received as to check their advance. The Indians, in like manner, selected trees for their protection; and an irregular battle succeeded which lasted four hours. The two captains were both men of coolness and courage. They were personal acquaintances, and had been friends before the war, and frequently called out to each other in the course of the fight—Sackett claiming—as he had—a large superiority of force, and demanding a surrender, on pain of the indiscriminate use of the tomahawk in case of refusal. Hobbs, with stentorian voice, refused and bade defiance. Less cautious than the English, the Indians several times exposed themselves by attempting to advance to a hand to hand contest, but were as often

---

[1] Hoyt.

repulsed, with severe loss. Discouraged, at length, by the unyielding courage of Hobbs and his men, and probably forming an erroneous estimate of their strength, the Indians at length drew off—dragging off, also, their dead, by reason of which their loss was not known.[1] Many Indians, however, were seen to fall, and the battle ground was deeply sanguine. But notwithstanding the duration of the fight, only three of the English were killed, and the same number wounded.[2] The strength of the Indians was estimated at one hundred and sixty. Still, the expedition of Sackett was not altogether bootless, since, a fortnight afterward he surprised a party of seventeen men between Hinsdale and Fort Dummer, killed two and wounded the same number, and made nine of the residue prisoners. Four escaped. In these enterprises it seems to have been the desire of the enemy to take captives rather than to kill. There was sound policy in this; the large amounts received from the friends of the captives for their ransom, going far toward defraying the expenses of the war.

Fort Massachusetts was not molested until past midsummer. But on the second of August, a party of four men being engaged at some distance from the fort, were fired upon by an enemy whose presence had not been suspected. Captain Williams immediately sallied forth for their rescue with Lieutenant Hawley and thirty men. The attacking party, apparently small, were soon driven back; but in the moment of fancied safety, an ambuscade of thirty Indians rose and poured in a fire upon Williams's right, moving with the design of intercepting his return to the

---

[1] "In all battles the Indians endeavor to conceal their loss, and in effecting this, they sometimes expose themselves more than in combat with the enemy. When one falls, his nearest comrade crawls up, under cover of the trees and brush, and fixing a *tump line* to the dead body, cautiously drags it to the rear. Hobbs's men related that in this action they often saw the dead bodies of the Indians sliding along the ground, as if by enchantment."
—*Hoyt*.

[2] Hoyt's *Antiquities*.

fort. The celerity of Williams's movements, however, frustrated this manœuvre, and the fort was reached with the loss of only one man killed and two wounded—one of whom was the lieutenant. It soon appeared that the escape of Williams was most fortunate. Indeed it must be confessed that he had exhibited singular absence of military precaution in hazarding a sortie with so small a party, while ignorant of the strength of his enemy; three hundred of whom, including thirty Frenchmen, followed close upon his heels as he regained the fort, and commenced a general attack. The fire was sustained on both sides about two hours; but having no artillery, the enemy was unable to make any impression upon the works, and drew off with a loss, the amount of which was not ascertained. The enemy was shortly afterward more successful in the neighborhood of Fort Dummer, where a party of seven under Lieutenant John Sargeants, was defeated, the commander being among the killed, and the survivors made prisoners.[1]

Meanwhile serious trouble began to manifest itself among the troops stationed at Albany and along the frontiers, in consequence of the scarcity of supplies. Many of the men deserted, and some of the officers resigned their commissions, flatly refusing to serve longer.[2] The assembly was not to meet until October, and the commissioners refused to execute the orders which the governor, by the advice of his council, had given them for supplying the troops,—urging as an excuse that they had not been so authorized by the assembly. The governor was exceedingly chafed by this refusal of the commissioners to act. This appears in all of his correspondence at this time, but especially in his correspondence with Colonel Johnson, with whom he was now on terms of intimacy. In a letter

---

[1] Hoyt's *Antiquities*.
[2] Manuscript letter, Johnson to Clinton; also manuscript letter to Johnson from Captain Stoddard, then in command at Schenectady.

CHAP. IX.
1748.

under date of October fifth, the following passage occurs: "By a letter I have from Captain Stoddard that no provisions are gone up, I conclude it was designedly neglected by the commissioners in order to distress the service and disband the troops sooner than I thought it necessary; and with a great deal of assurance, declared that even if they were served with an order from the council they would not obey it! What a low ebb is the governor and council of New York driven to, that their orders are refused for three weeks provisions for a few men. * * * * Formerly the governor and council had the disposal of every shilling, and did it all in council by warrant, without consulting the assembly or anybody."[1]

Those persons have read little, and have thought still less, who suppose that the revolt of the colonies was the result of a moment. The controversies between the assembly and the executive; the seeming apathy of the house to provide for the safety of the frontiers, and its general indifference in providing the needed supplies of which Mr. Clinton so bitterly complains, had in fact their rise not so much in an unconcern for the welfare of the colonies as in a fixed determination to resist the encroachments of the crown. Still it must be frankly admitted, that the assembly were often in the wrong, and that much of their treatment of the governor was harsh and ill-judged.

In the assembly, which met upon the twelfth of October, the governor determined to reassert the prerogative in the strongest terms by bringing the subject of a permanent supply to direct issue; choosing as an able writer has remarked, New York "as the opening scene in the final contest that led to independence."[2] Accordingly on the fourteenth Mr. Clinton sent down his message to the house, in which, after congratulating them upon the near prospect of a general peace, he demanded a permanent support for five years. The message stated that on coming

---

[1] Manuscript letter.
[2] Bancroft.

to the administration of the government, he had been disposed to do all he could, consistently with his duty to the king, for the care and satisfaction of the people. Hence, reposing confidence in the advice then given him, he had given his assent to various acts of the assembly, the tendency of which, as experience had taught him, was to weaken the authority of his majesty's government. Still, as the country was very soon afterward involved in war, he had forborne to take that attitude in the premises which duty to his sovereign seemed to require. But with the return of peace, he deemed it to be his indispensable duty to put a stop to such innovations. Prominent among these was the practice which had been growing up, of making only *an annual* provision for the payment of the officers of the government. He also alluded to the modern practice of naming the officers, for whose benefit the appropriations were made, in the act—thus interfering with the prerogative in the appointing honor. He admonished the assembly that he should give his assent to no acts of that character for the future; and demanded an appropriation for the payment of the governor's, secretaries, judges and other salaried officers, for the term of five years, according to the practice that had prevailed during the administration of his four immediate predecessors, namely, Governors Hunter, Burnett, Montgomery, and Cosby. The inconveniences of these annual grants of salaries and allowances, was adverted to, and objections farther urged against the recent method of intermixing matters of an entirely different nature with the provisions of the salary bills, and tacking new grants for other purposes to the governor's own support. The governor desired them farther to make immediate provision for the payment of the troops at Albany, and on the frontier; recommended that the troops should be continued at Albany; and concluded by calling the attention of the assembly to a debt of two thousand one hundred and thirty-eight pounds, due to Colonel Johnson for disbursements made by that gentleman in the public service, and which had been allowed and ordered to be paid by an act of the preceeding session. Owing to a deficiency in the funds, upon which it was directed to be charged, the money had not been paid; and the inconvenience of being kept so long out of so large a sum of money, was so great, that it was only with much difficulty that he had been enabled to persuade the colonel to undertake again the supplying of the important garrison at Oswego.

The assembly, in its reply, justly regarding the request for a permanent supply as a direct attempt to render the crown independent of the people, with great indignation, refused to grant it. As to the more recent practice of naming the officers provided for in the salary bills, it not only justified it, but intimated that if this course had been adopted at an earlier day, his excellency would not have been able to remove the third justice of the supreme court "without any color of misconduct" on his part—who was "a gentleman of learning and experience in the law."[1] Respecting the other matters in the message, it replied, that it saw no reason for burdening the colony with the troops in Albany, declaring that the troops at Oswego were quite sufficient in time of peace for the protection of the province. It passed however, a bill granting three thousand six hundred pounds for the pay of the troops on the frontier, but ignored entirely the claim of Colonel Johnson. The result can readily be seen. After continual bickerings for several weeks, Mr. Clinton, in great wrath, prorogued the assembly.

Thus the parties separated, and thus again commenced that great struggle between the republican and the monarchal principle, which in the onward progress of the former was destined at a day not even then far distant, to work such mighty results in the western hemisphere.

---

[1] Alluding to the removal, the year before, of Justice Horsmanden. This act was again imputed to the influence of "a person of a mean and despicable character"—meaning, as it was well understood, Doctor Colden.

Although hostilities were suspended between the belligerents, whose armies were contending in the Netherlands, immediately after the preliminaries were signed at Aix La Chapelle, yet it was long before the forces at sea were apprized of the fact. Meantime Admiral Boscawen, in the East Indies, having invested Pondicherry by land and water, was compelled to retire with signal discomfiture. Rear Admiral Knowles, too,—the same who had rendered himself so deservedly unpopular at Boston the year before,—continued to prosecute the contest in the West Indies with various success. With a squadron of eight ships he attacked fort St. Louis, on the south side of St. Domingo, which after a warm action of three hours was surrendered on capitulation and dismantled. But he afterward made an abortive attempt upon St. Iago de Cuba, at the result of which he was greatly chagrined.[1] Early in October Admiral Knowles, while cruising in the neighborhood of Havana, with eight ships of the line, fell in with a Spanish squadron of nearly equal force, commanded by Admiral Reggio, and a severe engagement ensued, which lasted six hours, commencing at two o'clock in the afternoon, and ending at eight. Knowles himself began the action in gallant style, but being seriously disabled, his ship was compelled to drop astern of the squadron, and was not afterward engaged in the line; but being borne down upon by the enemy, and another ship coming to his assistance, a struggle sharp and bloody ensued. The Spanish commander, notwithstanding the inferiority of his force, was at one time confident of victory;[2] but the fortunes of the day were against him, and he was compelled to put into the Havana with the loss of two ships; and a third was destroyed the next day to prevent her from falling into the hands of the English. Admiral Knowles taxed some of his men with misbehavior in this affair, and he was accused in turn. Several of the officers were

[1] Smollett.
[2] Spanish official account in the Gentleman's Magazine for April 1749.

tried by a court martial, and reprimanded, and Knowles himself was tried in December, 1749. The court acquitted him of the charge of cowardice; awarding him on the contrary, the merit of great personal bravery. But he was nevertheless found guilty of negligence in his arrangements, in several particulars, and ordered to be reprimanded.[1] High feelings of animosity arose among the officers, who either took sides with or against the admiral, and several duels were the consequence, in one of which a Captain Jarvis was mortally wounded by his antagonist Captain Clark.[2] But according to both English and Spanish accounts the action was bravely fought on both sides. As it proved it was a needless waste of life.

The definite treaty of peace was concluded and signed on the seventh day of October at Aix La Chapelle; and considering the circumstances under which it was concluded, and the relative strength of the parties and the condition of the alliance at the head of which was England, for a farther prosecution of the contest, it was a most inglorious peace.[3] Thus ended the "old French war," produced by the wickedness of Frederick, "the evils of which were felt in lands where the name of Prussia was unknown; and, in order that he might rob a neighbor whom he had promised to defend, black men fought on the coast of Coromandel, and red men scalped by the great lakes of North America."[4]

---

[1] Proceedings of the court martial, vide Gentleman's Magazine,

[2] Smollett.

[3] This contest was called "the old French war." It was in fact begun by Frederick the Great, by an unjust and rapacious attack upon the Empress-Queen Maria Theresa, for the purpose of wresting Siberia from her. It involved the world in arms. The respective alliances on the one side, were the king of Great Britain, the empress-queen, the states-governors of the United Provinces, and the king of Sardinia, with several smaller princes as auxiliaries On the other side, was the alliance of France, Spain, (claiming the Austriain succession,) the infant Don Philip, brother of the king of Spain and son-in-law of the king of France, with the republic of Genoa and the duke of Madrid.

[4] Macauley's life of Frederick the Great.

Meanwhile the Confederates were again becoming solicitous for those of their warriors who were still languishing in chains in Canada.¹ The promises made to them, at the council at Albany, by Clinton and Johnson, of the speedy release of their brethren, had quieted them for a time. But now, as month after month passed away and nothing was acomplished, they doubted the power of the English to bring this about, and thought seriously of taking the matter into their own hands. Johnson feared this himself, for in a letter written at this time to Governor Clinton upon the subject, he says:—"There is not one of our Indians suffered to come, nor any of the Christians who were taken with them, which is very hard, and will be the means, I reckon, of all the Five Nations going down now to Canada to get them." There was indeed cause for alarm; and it required the most strenuous exertions of Colonel Johnson to keep the Mohawks quietly at their castles, until the terms of the exchange of prisoners could be settled. This was no easy matter; and throughout the remainder of the year the attention of Mr. Clinton was chiefly occupied in successive negotiations with Galissonière, for an exchange of prisoners. But notwithstanding the evident approach of peace, and an arrangement for a cessation of arms in Europe, the French governor opposed various obstacles in the way of an equitable and prompt exchange. Mr. Clinton had sent two flags of truce without success, particularly in reference to the captive warriors of the Six Nations, who, as before hinted, were becoming exceedingly restive under the delay,—so much so, indeed, as to lead them to send a special deputation of their chiefs to New York at the close of September, to plead with the governor upon the subject.² There were likewise many prisoners in Canada, males and females, inhabitants of the frontiers, who had been carried away, and who were of course, with their friends, anxious

---

¹ Manuscript letter; J. Williams to Major Lydius.
² See journals of the council.

for their return.[1] But the difficulty was not so much in relation to the exchange of the English for the French prisoners, as it was in reference to the exchange of the Mohawks for an equal number of the French held as prisoners in New York. La Galissonière, claimed that the Mohawks were an independent nation, and as such, qualified to treat alone with him upon the subject; while Clinton justly maintained that by the treaty of Utrecht, the Mohawks were the dependants and subjects of the British crown.

Instead therefore, of meeting the views of Mr. Clinton and proceeding at once to a general exchange, Galissonière released only a few, sending a return flag, with seven officers, eighteen privates, and four Canadian Indians, accompanied by some propositions to which the governor of New York refused to accede. On the arrival of this formidable company at Albany, Colonel Johnson's suspicions were aroused that all was not right; and he would not allow them to proceed to New York, until permission to that effect had been received.[2] That permission having been given, the French party, the leader of whom was M. Francis Marie, proceeded at once to New York. The embassy was, however, bootless as appears by the following passage taken from a long manuscript letter upon this and other subjects, addressed by Mr. Clinton to Colonel Johnson on the fifth of October:—" As the commandant of this party is a very pretty gentleman, it grieves me much that I can't send any of his people back with him, as it might be of great service in recommending him to the governor. But his letter is so haughty, and indeed rather insolent, that I am obliged to stick on punctilios. His detaining our Christian prisoners from us in time of peace, is not right. Yet if he had sent one or two of the Indians

---

[1] Manuscript letter from Peter Van Schaick to Colonel Johnson,—written at this time, while a prisoner in Canada,—begging that the latter would use his earnest efforts to obtain his speedy release.

[2] Manuscript letter; Colonel Johnson to Governor Clinton.

back in room of the five of his I sent, something might have been done. But the poor gentleman must go back as he came, and thank his own governor's indiscretion for putting things on a wrong footing."

Thus matters stood until the end of the year. Nothing definite was arrived at in relation to the exchange; and although there were no active hostilities, yet the year closed, leaving all parties mutually dissatisfied, and equally suspicious of the designs of each other.

CHAPTER X.
1749—1750.

The exchange of prisoners still continued to be the subject of a lengthy correspondence between the royal governors. The Six Nations yet retained in their possession several of the French, uncertain—as in turn they were influenced by the French emissaries, or by Colonel Johnson—to which of the governors to yield them up. To the Confederates at least, the final disposition of their prisoners was a subject of grave consideration. Should they treat directly with La Galissonière, they were fearful of incurring the displeasure of Governor Clinton; while on the other hand, should they yield up their prisoners to Colonel Johnson, they feared that by so doing, they would lose the power to redeem their braves from their captivity.

To Colonel Johnson this delicate matter of effecting a transfer of the prisoners into his hands, was entrusted; and after considerable negotiation, rendered necessary by their vascillating course, the Mohawks were induced to yield up twelve of their prisoners. This transfer, however, was accompanied by a request, on the part of the Mohawks, that the colonel would not allow the Frenchmen to return home, until those of their warriors, who yet languished in the jail at Quebec, should be brought down to Crown Point, and delivered into his hands. The success of his negotiations, the colonel immediately communicated to Mr. Clinton in a letter, which the latter at once laid before his council for its action. Several months elapsed before farther orders touching the final disposition of the prisoners were received from the governor; during which interval, the colonel received them into his own house, treating them with much kindness and consideration.

Meanwhile the Mohawks, always suspicious, and not understanding the delays and forms of diplomatic intercourse, began to be apprehensive lest the object they had in delivering up their prisoners might not be attained. These apprehensions were likewise increased by messages which the wily La Galissonière, with artful tact, continued to send to the Mohawks, inviting them to come to Quebec, and treat in person for their braves. This, as it was designed, only increased their ill temper,—conscious that they had lost the power to do this, when they allowed the Frenchmen to go out of their hands. Their discontent at first manifested itself in angry looks and dark hints, until finally, unequivocal symptoms showed that they designed taking the matter into their own hands, by wresting back by force that which they had so unwillingly granted. So deeply rooted had their disaffection become, and so widely had it spread, that the colonel himself feared that even his influence would not much longer avail for the protection of the prisoners. In this strait, he at once wrote to Mr. Clinton, stating the situation of affairs and his own fears. The governor immediately replied as follows:

"NEW YORK June 7, 1749.
"Sir.
"I have the favor of yours of twenty-sixth of last month, and am well pleased with the accounts you give me of your conduct with the Indians. You may assure the Mohawks that the reason of my not sending back the French prisoners which you have in your hands, is in order to secure the return of their people who are prisoners in Canada, and that their people shall not have their liberty on any conditions but that of the liberty of the Indians who are prisoners in Canada; that all these messages from the governor of Canada are only an artifice to draw them to Canada in order to make mean and shameful submissions to him there. And in order to prevent any of their people making such a shameful step, so disgraceful to their nation, you must endeavor to persuade them to deliver

the remaining prisoners into your hands that they may be kept safe till the liberty of the Indians be secured. And for this purpose, if you have any apprehensions that the French now at your house cannot be safely kept there, you are to send them to Albany to the sheriff, there to be kept in jail till such time as he shall receive my orders for their liberty. If you think it may be attended with any inconvenience to keep the French in prison at Albany, then you may send them down to New York where I shall take care to have them secured.

Inclosed is an order to the sheriff to receive the prisoners from you, and to keep them in safe custody.

"But as the Indians are frequently very humorsome, and there must be some regard had to it, you are allowed to take some latitude in the execution of these orders, by delaying the full execution of them, till you inform me of any inconvenience which you may apprehend may attend the strict observance of them. I have received no orders from court relating to the liberty of prisoners, and I delay sending to Canada for their liberty in expectation of receiving such, and am,

"Sir, Your very humble servant,
"G. CLINTON."

On the reception of this letter Colonel Johnson summoned both of the Mohawk castles together, and used all his influence to divest them of their suspicions, and persuade them to leave the exchange of the prisoners entirely with Mr. Clinton. In this he succeeded; but only after great effort, and by the payment to the Indians of large sums of money out of his own purse. The Mohawks were also induced at the same time to deliver up to him the remainder of their captives, thus increasing the number under his protection to nineteen.

Scarcely had this affair been amicably arranged, when another difficulty arose, which for a little while threatened to mar the harmony between the Indians and the

English. This time, however, the trouble had its origin in the indiscreet conduct of a few whites. It seems that some traders from Albany and the adjacent settlements, in going their yearly rounds among the different cantons of the Confederacy, had taken several Indian children as pawns or pledges for the payment of the goods sold to the parents. Notwithstanding the latter came at the appointed time to redeem their children, the traders refused to deliver them up,—designing to keep them as security for future purchases. The chiefs of the several tribes, justly indignant at this breach of faith, came in a body to Mount Johnson, and laid their grievances before the colonel, who thereupon informed Mr. Clinton of these facts. The result was a proclamation from the governor directing that the children should at once be restored to their homes. Most of the traders forthwith obeyed, but a few were obstinate and refused compliance. The French, ever ready to seize upon anything which might be turned to their advantage, used this circumstance to inflame the minds of the Indians, adducing this as a proof that the English wished only to reduce them to slavery. Finally, however, through the exertions of the colonel all the children were restored and the wound healed, though not until several council fires had been rekindled and many belts of wampum exchanged.

It was not until the following year that a general exchange of prisoners was effected. During the interval Colonel Johnson was chiefly occupied in soothing the temper of the Six Nations, and in preventing them from committing themselves to the French. This was not an easy task. The Jesuit priests were busy among them endeavoring to undermine their attachment to the English; for notwithstanding the solemn assurances given by the Indians that these emissaries should be given up, a few continued to reside at the different castles. The colonel, however, was not discouraged. Well aware of the character of his opponents he was not satisfied with pursuing merely a negative policy, but set himself vigorously to work to thwart the machinations going on around him. He therefore labored more earnestly than ever to strengthen his influence over the Indians. At times I find him taking part in their ceremonies and condoling with them upon the death of some chief: at another, he is wearing their dress, dancing and smoking their pipes, and entering with seeming zest into their games: while again he is found addressing their chiefs in council, and instigating an incursion upon one of the French settlements. Yet with all this adaptation to their habits, there was withal a certain dignity of mien which ever commanded respect, and secured him from that familiarity which with the red, as well as with the white race, always breeds contempt.[1]

The energy of Colonel Johnson—always remarkable—was perhaps never more displayed than at this period of his life. A few years later he relinquished business and devoted himself entirely to the service of the crown. At this time, however, beside the duties incident to the care of the Indian department, he was assiduous in the prosecution of his private business relations. Numerous letters to his agents in London, filled with orders for goods, are still in existence, copies of which were filed away with that accuracy which was so characteristic of him during his entire life. On the same day he is found ordering from London lead for the roof of his house; dispatching a load of goods to Oswego; bartering with the Indians for furs; and writing to Governor Clinton at length on the encroachments of the French—doing everything with neatness and dispatch. Yet amid all the cares incident to his mercantile business, which had now grown very exten-

---

[1] It was in this year that Kalm, the distinguished Swedish naturalist, visited Mount Johnson bearing a letter of introduction from Cadwallader Colden. Johnson received his visitor with warm and courtly hospitality, and on his departure gave him a letter to Captain Lindesay at Oswego and furnished him with a guide to Niagara. Kalm wrote to Johnson from Oswego thanking him warmly for his kindness.

sive, he still retained his contract for supplying the garrison at Oswego; while at the same time he superintended the militia, attended to the affairs of the Six Nations, and as "ranger of the woods" for Albany county—an office conferred on him by Mr. Clinton—kept a diligent watch upon those who were disposed to cut down and carry off by stealth the king's timber.

It will readily be seen, however, that with all this energy, it required great tact to maintain an ascendency over the Iroquois. Any one other than Johnson would have failed; nor was it an ordinary mind that could so successfully baffle the whole power and influence of La Galissonière and his wily priests. Indeed had it not been for his influence, it is difficult to see how the Six Nations at this period could have withstood the seductive allurements of the French. By every appliance in their power the latter strove to shake their confidence in the English—by presents; by the influence of priests; by stories circulated among them of English treachery; by stirring up petty jealousies,—in short nothing which cunning or strategy could devise was neglected. Yet all these arts, through the vigilance of the colonel, signally failed; and the Iroquois still continued the firm allies of the English crown.

The autumn of this year was marked by the encroachments of the French in Nova Scotia, which were soon to plunge the colonies into another bloody and disastrous war. La Jonquière, the successor of Galissonière, had watched the English settlement at Halifax with considerable solicitude; and in November, he dispatched a party of the St. John and River Indians against Minas, with no other effect however, than the killing and capturing of eighteen men. At the same time, La Corne, a bloody and desperate soldier of fortune, was ordered to the isthmus of the peninsula, which position he occupied during the winter, making his head-quarters at the village of Chiegnecto.

CHAP. X.
1750.

Anxious to dislodge these intruders, Cornwallis, the governor of Nova Scotia, sent Major Lawrence in April with a force of four hundred regulars and rangers upon this service. Scarcely had the fleet appeared in sight, when La Corne burned the town, and, retreating across the river with the inhabitants, planted upon its dykes the lilies of France. This position was too strong to be attacked with any prospect of success. Major Lawrence, after holding an interview with the French commander, in which the latter avowed his intention to defend himself to the last extremity, turned the prows of his vessels toward Halifax. A swift vessel conveyed the intelligence of this event to the parent government, and simultaneously a messenger was dispatched to the colonies of New Hampshire and Massachusetts to inform them " of the audacious proceedings of the French, and to invite them to join in punishing La Corne as a public incendiary."[1]

England, however, reaped, in the lukewarm reception of these tidings by the New England colonies, the first fruits of her pusillanimous surrender of Cape Breton. Those colonies already saw the folly of spending so much blood and treasure in aid of a government which had shown itself so incapable of profiting by their victories, and consequently they took no measures for the defense of Nova Scotia. In midsummer another expedition was planned at Halifax to retake Chiegnecto. The attack was successful, though several of the English were killed; and thus was the first blood shed of that sanguinary contest, which was soon to involve the continents of the old and new world in such long and deadly strife.[2]

In May of this year, Colonel Johnson took his first step toward the prominent and influential position which he was destined to occupy in later years. This was no less than his appointment by the crown to a seat in his majesty's council for the province of New York in the room of

---

[1] Bancroft.
[2] Minot.

Philip Livingston deceased.[1] A new phase of life was now to open upon him, in which a wider scope was to be given to his peculiar and extraordinary talents. Hitherto, although he had been appointed in 1748 to the command of the New York colonial troops with the commission of colonel, yet he still occupied the position of a private citizen, fast rising, nevertheless, in influence, by a steady attention to his business. Henceforward he is no longer a citizen, but a public man. From a trader in furs, daily bartering for pelts in a country store, he is soon to become the most prominent man in his majesty's colonies.

To Johnson, this appointment, though unsought, was by no means a surprise. Mr. Catherwood, in April of this year, had written him from London, stating that Governor Clinton had recommended and urged his appointment to the council in place of Colonel Moore;—"I urged your appointment," Mr. Catherwood writes, " to be in the room of Mr. Livingston, as you seemed desirous to take place next to Mr. Holland; but Sir Peter Warren secretly asked it as a favor to place you before Mr. Holland, which was not your own desire, nor do I think it just, wherefore I have been under a necessity of praying that Mr. Holland may take place according to his appointment at New York." Although Mr. Clinton's recommendation undoubtedly arose in part from a personal attachment and a desire to advance the interests of his young friend, yet selfish considerations entered into it in a large measure. The faction in the assembly, far from growing weaker by frequent dissolutions, had, under the lead of the chief justice, waxed more powerful, until the executive was fast verging into a subordinate position. The governor, secure in the friendship of Johnson, hoped by this measure to bind the latter still more firmly to his interests and thus

---

[1] Mr. Dunlop in his History of New York, makes the date of Johnson's appointment to the council two years later. This is incorrect. Johnson, it is true, was not sworn in till the next year.

strengthen his own hands at the council board.[1] Still Mr. Clinton, though an unlettered man, possessed considerable sagacity, and had he not seen in the colonel the promise of ability which would be of service to the crown, he would not have recommended him for this important position merely to sustain his own interests.[2]

Meanwhile the wranglings between the governor and his assembly continued. The former, it will be remembered, rather than yield to the wishes of the faction, had in great wrath prorogued that body in 1748; and by successive prorogations, he had prevented it from sitting for nearly two years, until the affairs of the colony, from lack of funds, were now in an alarming condition. The executive during this entire period, had been wholly destitute of money with which to carry on the government. The post at Oswego was in danger of being given up, from its garrison having threatened to disband through lack of pay; and the public credit, by means of which funds had been obtained for the defense of the frontiers, was nearly if not quite exhausted. In this critical juncture, the governor did not think it advisable to longer delay calling his legislature together. He therefore declared his old assembly dissolved on the twenty-first of July, and issued writs for a new one returnable on the fourth of September. In his opening speech to the house, Mr. Clinton recommended that immediate provision should be made for meeting the arrearages of the pay now long due to the garrison at Oswego, and for the expenses incurred in meeting and con-

---

[1] Thus in a letter from Catherwood to Johnson in May of this year informing him of his appointment, the former writes;—"I have the pleasure to tell you that you are appointed a councillor for the province of New York pursuant to his excellency's recommendation, and as he is very ready upon all occasions to oblige his friends, I hope nothing will move you to drop your attachment inviolable to him; but that you will try now as a member of the legislature to serve him and yourself with the assembly."

[2] In the same way, Governor Fletcher had raised Schuyler to the council board, on account of his like judicious Indian service.

gratulating the Indians upon the conclusion of peace. He informed it of the rapid advances the French were making in the affections of the Confederates, and the urgent necessity there was for making larger presents to the Indians if these advances were to be successfully met. He then urged it to provide for the payment of the salaries of government officers long since due; and concluded by reminding it of the colony's debt to Colonel Johnson still unpaid. The assembly responded to this address by immediately voting the sum of 800 pounds for presents to the Indians; and by passing two acts—one for the payment of the debts of the colony, and the other for the payment of the government salaries. It also allowed the sum of £686 11s. to Mr. Johnson, for provisions supplied by him to the militia and regular troops posted at Oswego during the previous year from September 1748 to 1751. To these acts the governor gave his consent, although they were all passed in the same irregular manner as formerly, and in such a way as to encroach upon the prerogative. Still Mr. Clinton dared not refuse his assent, dreading lest his refusal should cause the loss of the post at Oswego, which on account of its trade with the Indians would have been equivalent to the loss of the friendship of the Six Nations.[1] The assembly shortly after the passage of these acts was prorogued to the second day of the following April.

It will be noticed, however, that with the exception of the £686 11s. allowed for provisioning the Oswego garrison the assembly during their session never once alluded to the debt now so long due Colonel Johnson. So cautious was the assembly, as we have already seen, of doing anything which could be construed into yielding to the wishes of the governor, that it was led into an act of great injustice, not to say ingratitude, in thus allowing this claim to pass unrecognized. Especially was this the case, since the greater part of the debt was not for services rendered,

---

[1] Governor Clinton to the board of trade, published in *N. Y. Col. Doc.*, vol vi.

CHAP. X.
1750.

but for private advances made in treating with the Indians, and in the defense of the frontiers. It was in vain that for nearly three years Governor Clinton in turn entreated and besought. It was to no purpose that he represented the injustice of allowing Johnson's *services* to be so poorly requited, to say nothing of the moneys advanced by him from his own funds for the protection of the colony. The assembly, instigated by the De Lancey faction, were stubborn and would not yield. There was also another influence at work, which to a great extent was the cause of this injustice. It will be remembered that previous to the colonel assuming the supervision of the Six Nations, their affairs had for a long time been entrusted to a board of commissioners at Albany. The commissioners were mostly Dutch; and in the love of gain so characteristic of that nation, they had used their office chiefly to monopolize the Indian trade, and thus make it a source of great private profit. Having finally through their grasping disposition, lost all influence over the Indians, the governor committed the whole management of Indian affairs to Mr. Johnson. The commissioners inflamed with resentment at the loss of authority which they had so long held, and the consequent loss of their trade—no inconsiderable source of emolument,—joined the faction against Clinton. Instigated by petty jealousy of the man by whom they had been supplanted, they used every artifice to prevent his claims from being recognized.[1] Various were the expedients resorted to by the assembly for deferring action upon this matter, many of them frivolous, all of them contemptible. Sometimes it was by directing that payments should be made out of funds which it well knew were exhausted; and again it was by cutting down his accounts, without assigning any reason for so doing.[2] It even charged him with peculation, and accused him of bringing in bills for provisions for the Oswego garrison

---

[1] Manuscript letter; Doctor Cadwallader Colden to Colonel Johnson.
[2] Manuscript letter; Colonel Johnson to Governor Clinton.

which were never sent. To such a length did the spirit of faction lead.¹ Colonel Johnson was thus placed in an exceedingly embarrassing position. For nearly three years past he had himself advanced almost all the money needed for the defense of the frontiers and for treating with the Indians, until there was now due him the sum of £2000. Fearing therefore that his private fortune would be ruined should this draft upon his funds continue, and there being no prospect of having his claims and services recognized, he sent in to the council his resignation as superintendent of Indian affairs,²—dispatching, at the same time, belts to the different Indian castles informing them that he no longer had the charge of their affairs. To Governor Clinton this step was not entirely unexpected, but among the Confederates the announcement, as was natural, carried surprise and consternation; so much so that that they made it the subject of a special belt at the next council, held at Albany the following summer.³

---

[1] Manuscript letter; David Jones (at this time speaker of the house) to Colonel Johnson.

[2] Colonel Johnson to Governor Clinton.

[3] It is true that Cadwallader Colden in a letter to Governor Clinton (published in the *N. Y. Col. Doc.* vi, 139) seems to hint that this action on the part of Johnson, was unexpected; yet in a manuscript letter before me from the latter to Mr. Clinton, he clearly notifies the governor that he will not advance money longer and must soon resign. In the course of this letter, after suggesting that Colonel Lydius should be appointed in his place, and giving some information in relation to the Indians, Johnson adds, "as this is perhaps the last item of Indian news I shall ever have occasion to trouble your excellency with, I should be very glad if it were made the best use of." In another letter to Governor Clinton, also, Johnson writes, "there will be some expense attending my resignation which I think should not be borne by me." Mr. Colden must therefore be mistaken.

CHAPTER XI.
1750—1751.

Peace had once more spread her wings over the American Colonies. The farmer, hanging his trusty rifle over the fireplace, could again sow his fields without fear of the whistling bullet or the reeking tomahawk. The little child, clinging no longer to its mother's breast in frantic terror as the savage warwhoop was borne past on the midnight air, slumbered peacefully in its cradle. And the plowman, as he trudged home at nightfall from a weary day's work, looked forward to the greetings of his wife and children, rather than a lonely and desolated hearth.

The treaty of Aix La Chapelle, however, was received by the colonies with less satisfaction than might have been anticipated, from the termination of the bloody war, which had for so long a period desolated her frontiers. By this treaty—a treaty which has been justly characterised, as "the most inglorious and impolitic compact to which Britain had acceded since the revolution of 1688"—it was agreed that all conquests which had been obtained by either side, should be restored. In accordance with this agreement, England surrendered Cape Breton to France, receiving in return only a slight advantage toward the preservation of that mythical idea—the balance of power.[1] After an immense expenditure of

---

[1] The basis of the treaty, as between England, France and Spain, was a mutual release of all prisoners without ransom, and a restoration of all conquests. Silesia was secured to Frederick, and the hereditary dominions of the empress queen were guarantied to her according to the Pragmatic Sanction. With this restoration of conquests, the American colonists had the mortification to see Cape Breton, with the fortress of Louisburg; surrendered back to France as an equivalent for the towns in Flanders taken by the French from the Germans, her allies. England, moreover,

money; and after a bloody and disastrous war, England came from the convocation at Aix La Chapelle, in the eyes of every true hearted Englishman, humbled and abased. The news of the peace was received by New England, with even stronger feelings of indignation than by her sister colonies. She felt that Cape Breton—for the capture of which she expended so much blood and treasure—had been sacrificed merely to gratify and sustain the selfish policy of the mother country. The private correspondence of this period—the surest test, perhaps, of the real state of public opinion in any age—teems with the strong feelings of men, who feel that they have been duped. Especially was this indignation prevalent among those who had served against the French; and who after receiving so many scars in defence of English honor, saw it now sullied and disgraced.[1]

But though the peace between England and France was now formally consummated, it required no prophetic vision to foresee, that in a short time, it would be a peace only in name. In the articles of the treaty, no mention whatever was made of the French encroachments upon the territory of the Iroquois, although the first care of England should have been, to insist upon the removal of Fort Frederick at Crown Point. The boundaries between the English and French possessions, along the rivers Mississippi and St. Lawrence, and the limits even of Nova Scotia, one of the original causes of the war, were left entirely undetermined; it being tacitly understood, that the boundaries should remain as they were before the war.[2]

---

had stooped to send two hostages, persons of rank, to remain in France, as a pledge for this restoration.—*Smollett*; see also *Grahame*.

[1] In a manuscript letter to Colonel Johnson, from an officer who had left the walks of private life for the army, occurs the following passage. "Nothing would give me more pleasure than to have the honor to serve his majesty, but believe me if ever I get into a good way of life again I shall be very cautious how I quit it."

[2] Commissioners, it is true, were appointed to settle these boundaries, but their proceedings were conducted with such asperity, as rendered their proceedings a mere farce.

When these limits were so indefinite as to occasion the dispute, it was not to be supposed that they would give no more trouble, now that the dispute was brought to a close by a hollow peace. The result is readily seen. Each government hastened to occupy as much land as possible in advance of the other; and the formation of the Ohio company, with a grant from the crown of six hundred thousand acres, determined France to push forward with greater alacrity the bold design which she had formed as early as 1731, in erecting Fort Frederick on Lake Champlain. This was no less than the connecting the St. Lawrence with the Gulf of Mexico, by a chain of forts along that river to Detroit, and down the Ohio to the Mississippi. In accordance with this project, La Galissonière, in 1749, deputed Celoron de Bienville to occupy the valley of the Ohio; and that officer, pursuing his instructions, proceeded down the Ohio in a canoe, burying at the mouth of every large creek a plate of lead, with the inscription, that from the rise of the Ohio to its mouth, the country belonged to France.[1]

But the French government, well aware that the possession of the Ohio, would lose much of its value, so long as a free communication was open to the New England colonies, resolved to lose no time in gaining the Iroquois as allies, and thus interpose a formidable barrier against the designs of the English.

In pursuance of this project, Rev. Abbè Picquet, aided by the French government, established, in 1749, a mission school on the St. Lawrence, at the mouth of the Oswegatchie river, called La Presentation.[2]

Francis Picquet, the founder of this mission, was a man peculiarly formed for this undertaking. A zealous priest and a staunch soldier, the crozier and the sword were to him alike familiar. On several occasions, he had accom-

---

[1] Paris Doc. x. 9—"Within a few years, one of these plates, with the inscription partially effaced, has been found near the mouth of the Muskingum." *North American Review* for July, 1839.

[2] Ogdensburgh.

panied the Indians in their incursions upon the English settlements; and was with the party that destroyed the fort at Saratoga, and the Lydius mills.[1] His keen mind had early foreseen the war which was to rage so fiercely between his nation and the English; and he had long urged the policy of receiving the Six Nations as allies. When therefore the necessity was seen of cultivating the friendship of the latter, as a step toward the secure possession of the west, the proposition of Picquet to La Galissonière, to establish a mission for the conversion of the Six Nations, was readily accepted.[2]

The site chosen by Picquet for the mission evinced his sagacity.[3] Situated on the St. Lawrence, between Oswego and Montreal, the passage of the English into Canada by this route could readily be intercepted. Its proximity to Lake Ontario served to aid and protect the posts which had already been erected on that lake by the French; while its fine harbor afforded a secure shelter, for the bateaux that passed up the St. Lawrence from Montreal with supplies for the French traders at the different posts on the lake. The establishment of this mission, was the occasion of much solicitude on the part of the colonies; while its effect upon the minds of the Indians was exceedingly dreaded by Colonel Jonhson.[4] These apprehensions were not unfounded, for in the next war La Presentation formed a rendezvous, from which scalping parties were fitted out; and which committed such depredations along the New York frontier and the

---

[1] Fort Edward.

[2] Picquet was called by the French "the Apostle of the Iroquois;" by the English "the Jesuit of the west."

[3] It is true that in an account of the war from 1749—1760, published under the direction of the Quebec Hist. Soc. in 1835, an anonymous writer calls La Presentation, Picquet's Folly; but the writer evidently bears such a personal enmity against Picquet, that his authority, on this point, is of no value.

[4] Manuscript correspondence between Colonel Johnson and Mr. Clinton.

Mohawk river, as to lead General Gage to destroy the place in 1757.[1]

While the French were thus vigorously at work in the north and west, they were not less active in the south. As by the late treaty, there was no pretense for active hostilities, the policy of the French was now, to stir up dissensions among the different tribes friendly to the English. By fomenting animosities between the Indians, and causing them to prey upon each other, they hoped finally to compass their utter anihilation, and thus deprive their ancient enemy of the aid and support of its dusky allies—a diabolical plan, well worthy of the time of Nero, but scarcely to be credited of the civilization of the eighteenth century! While, therefore, Picquet was exerting his influence upon the Six Nations from La Presentation, on the St. Lawrence, Jean Cœur was sent to the tribes bordering on the Ohio and Mississippi rivers. The indomitable perseverence of these emissaries, was for the time but too successful. Through their influence—obtained by the lavish use of presents—the minds of the Six Nations, and a few of the western tribes, became greatly inflamed against the Catawbas, a small tribe depending chiefly upon Virginia, and residing principally in the Carolinas; and they were again, in violation of their promises to Governor Clinton, preparing for a devastating war upon that people.[2]

Ever alive to the interests of the crown, Johnson, early in the previous year, had written to Clinton, informing him of the growing ill feeling of the Confederates against the Catawbas; and had advised the holding of a council, at some place where the Confederates and the Catawbas could meet, and conclude a treaty of peace.[3] At about

---

[1] *History of St. Lawrence and Franklin Counties*, by Franklin B. Hough.

[2] Manuscript correspondence between Johnson and Clinton.

[3] As far back as the year 1740, it will be remembered, there had been a feud existing between the Catawbas and the Six Nations. It had, however, become almost extinct until it was revived with a thousand fold more intensity by Picquet and Cœur.

the same time, Governor Clinton was also informed by a letter from Governor Glen of South Carolina, that the Senecas had made several attacks upon the Catawbas, which threatened to produce very serious disturbance. Mr. Glen farther wrote, that the northern Indians made the war upon this tribe an excuse for plundering and killing the negroes and whites; and that unless these inroads were stopped, he would be obliged to offer a reward for every northern Indian, who might be killed within the settlement.[1]

Aware of the importance of nipping in the bud a matter which threatened to involve the colonies in such serious complications, Governor Clinton determined to act upon the suggestions of Colonel Johnson, and summon a council. In view, however, of the active efforts which the French were making, to wean the different Indian nations throughout the country, from their old alliance, he determined to have the ends of the council take a wider scope; and have a general meeting of delegates from all the colonies, at which some plan of union might be adopted, to retain in the British interest, all those Indians who were originally included in the covenant chain. He therefore wrote to the several governors, requesting that they would express their views freely upon this subject; and that if the project struck them favorably, they would appoint delegates to meet in June of the next year. All the governors, with the exception of the governor of Virginia who did not vouchsafe any reply, responded favorably. Those of Massachusetts, Connecticut, and South Carolina, were, however, the only ones who entered heartily into the plan. The governors of New Hampshire and Pennsylvania wrote, that they were favorably impressed with the idea, but that their assemblies were not disposed to vote money enough to furnish their delegates with presents for the Indians; while the other governors, likewise hampered by their assemblies, were still more lukewarm, and still less disposed to enter into the arrangement.

---

[1] Governor Glen to Governor Clinton, 7th July, 1750.

CHAP. XI.
1750.

Notwithstanding these discouragements, Governor Clinton announced his intention of meeting the Six Nations at Albany the following year, and so informed Colonel Johnson. The latter immediately summoned both of the Mohawk castles together, and in a speech, informed the Indians of the governor's intention of meeting them in council, the following year at Albany. The object of the council, he told them, was to afford the Six Nations the opportunity of making a peace with the Catawbas, with whom they had been at war for some time. He represented to them, how wrong it was to war against a tribe that they had agreed to be at peace with, according to the treaty of 1740; and closed with a request, that they would choose their delegates to represent them in the approaching council. The Mohawks, in the name of the Confederacy, replied, that they would consent to a treaty, provided that the Catawbas would send six of their sachems to meet and confer with their chiefs at Albany.[1]

Shortly after this preliminary conference, Thomas Lee, president of the council in Virginia, sent a message to the Six Nations, desiring them to meet the Catawbas in Fredricksburgh, and receive the presents, which the governor of Virginia, on the part of his majesty, desired to give them. The Six Nations, however, feeling that they were the aggrieved party, thought the Catawbas ought, instead, to come and meet them; and in their answer, desired the governor of Virginia " to move his council fire to Albany, where they would gladly hear him, and receive the presents sent by his majesty."

1751. The preliminary conferences opened on the twenty-

---

[1] In the treaty of Lancaster, in 1744, between the provinces of Maryland and Virginia and the Six Nations, occurs this passage, spoken by a sachem of the Six Nations: "You charge us with not acting according to our peace with the Catawbas. We will repeat to you truly what was done. The governor of New York, at Albany, gave us several belts of wampum from the Cherokees and Catawbas, and we agreed to a peace, if those nations would send some of their great men to us to confirm it face to face, * * * but they never came."—*Colden's History of the Six Nations.*

eighth of June. Commissioners from the colonies of Massachusetts, Connecticut, and South Carolina were in attendance. Governor Clinton was also present, accompanied by Doctor Colden, James Alexander, James De Lancey and Edward Holland, members of the executive council. William Bull, the commissioner from South Carolina, and one of the counsellors of that province, brought with him the king of the Catawbas, and five of their sachems, who came on behalf of their people to treat with the Six Nations. The first day was chiefly taken up in treating with a party of Michillimackinac and Caughnawaga Indians, who, chancing to be in the vicinity at this time, came in their canoes to Albany, "as a compliment," as they expressed it, "to his excellency;"[1]— while by the Six Nations, this interval was occupied in various forms and ceremonies usual when entering upon a solemn and lasting treaty.

CHAP. XI.

1751.

Early on the following morning, the Six Nations waited upon the governor, and desired a private interview. It was their wish, they said, to speak with him before the general council was opened, upon a matter which had been discussed that morning in their private deliberations. The audience was, of course, granted, and as soon as the delegation was admitted, Hendrik, the Mohawk, proceeded to explain the object of their visit. They had come to consult with their Brother Corlear in relation to Colonel Johnson. When the war broke out, he had been recommended to them by his excellency, who had then told them that whatever the colonel said to them they might rely on as coming from himself. Moreover, as they had no hand in his appointment to the charge of their affairs, so neither had they been instrumental in his resignation; and he might judge therefore how shocked they were, on receiving from Mr. Johnson a belt notifying them of his

---

[1] The Caughnawagas, at the same time, said that they would immediately leave the city; but so dilatory were they, that Mr. Clinton was obliged to send the Sheriff to expedite their departure.

intention to give up the care of their affairs. "We had him," he continued, "in war, when he was like a tree that grew for our use, which now seems to be falling down, though it has many roots. His knowledge of our affairs made us think him an Indian like ourselves; and we are greatly afraid, as he has declined, that your excellency will appoint some person—a stranger both to us and our affairs." They therefore desired the governor to immediately reinstate the colonel, and let them know his decision as soon as possible—"for," added the Mohawk sachem, "he has large ears, and heareth a great deal; and what he hears he tells to us. He has also large eyes, and sees a great way, and conceals nothing from us." In his reply, on the following day, Mr. Clinton stated that the recent action of Colonel Johnson had been taken contrary to his desire, and that his absence at this time was entirely unexpected, inasmuch as he had promised to be present and assist him with his advice. But since he absolutely refused to take any farther charge of their affairs, he could not help it, and he should therefore be obliged to appoint some other in his place. They might, however, rest assured, that in the appointment of a successor, he should be governed solely by a desire to promote their welfare which he had truly at heart. "You have more reason," added Mr. Clinton "to trust me in this, since Colonel Johnson, by whom you have been so well cared for, was my own selection."[1] The answer of the Indians was characteristic. They told the governor that one-half of Colonel Johnson belonged to his excellency, and the other to them; and that since he could not prevail on the colonel to come down, they begged permission to try their influence by sending a message to him with a string of wampum. This request having been granted, provided they were as expeditious as possible, Hendrik immediately dispatched a fleet runner to Mount Johnson, with the remark that "he would go sooner than a horse."

---

[1] Manuscript council minutes.

Colonel Johnson, who was already on his way to the council, met the Indian messenger near Schenectady; and on his arrival in Albany, he was informed by Mr. Clinton of the state of feeling among the Confederates, and in behalf of his majesty's council, earnestly requested to continue in the charge of their affairs. To this request, the colonel, who felt too much hurt at the manner in which he had been treated by the assembly to change his resolution, gave a courteous but decided refusal. At the same time, however, his reasons for this course were given in full. It was impossible, he said, to continue longer in the management of Indian affairs, without great detriment, if not ruin, to his private fortune. It was well known that prior to the third day of November, 1748, he had advanced from his own purse, for the Indian department and the supply of the garrison at Oswego—after others had declined supplying that post because of the war—the sum of £7,177 3s. 2d.; and that of this amount, although the items had all been duly sworn to by him and delivered into the assembly, that body had made provision only for £5,801 7s. 4d., leaving due a balance of £1,375 15s. 10d., for which no provision had as yet been made. He farther stated, that of this £5,801 7s. 4d., for which he had received warrants on the treasurer several years since, there remained £2,401 still unpaid, and that too, although he had good reason to believe that the Oswego duties—the fund out of which those warrants were paid—were amply sufficient to pay all drafts made upon it. This state of things was also the more galling, since he was well aware that warrants to others, of a much later date than his own, had been paid without any hesitation; while at the same time, no steps had been taken to compensate him for this delay in the payment of these advances. He also reminded Mr. Clinton, that in addition to all this, he had advanced, at his excellency's request, since the third day of November 1748, for the same objects, the farther sum of £595 12s. 8d., of which he had received no part, nor did he know of any provision made to meet it. In view therefore of all these considerations, while he entertained the kindest feelings toward the government, he could not, in justice to himself, continue longer in the Indian department—especially since he could have no reason to depend on the assembly to provide for future advances. At the same time, however, he expressed his willingness to render all assistance, in an individual capacity, during the present treaty.[1]

The colonel's answer having been laid before the council, the latter desired the governor to exercise a supervision of Indian affairs during the treaty now in progress. At the same time, it requested him to lay before the crown the "uncommon and great sufferings, which Colonel Johnson had sustained" in its behalf, and recommend that suitable recompense be given him, not only for the money which he had advanced, but likewise for his personal services, for which he had made no charge.

Although the colonel had been appointed to his majesty's council in April of the previous year, yet it had not been convenient for him until now to take the oaths of office. The usual oaths were accordingly administered at this time, and he thereupon took his seat at the council board,—a seat which he continued to fill until his decease.

Everything being now in readiness, Mr. Clinton opened the council on the sixth of July, with a short speech to the Six Nations, in which the object of the present meeting was fully set forth. It was, he said, to brighten and strengthen the covenant chain, that it might endure for all time against the designs of their enemies. The governor of Canada, especially, was endeavoring to break this chain, by obstructing the trade between Albany and those distant Indians who passed through their country. "Another artifice," he continued, "which the enemies of our covenant chain make use of, is, to excite variance and war between the several Indian nations that are united with your

---

[1] Manuscript council minutes.

brethren the English, in the several parts of this great continent. Nothing can so effectually weaken and at last entirely destroy the brethren, as their falling out among themselves, and eventually killing and destroying one another. This is doing the work of your enemies; while they sit looking on and laugh at your folly. If all the Indian Nations, united in friendship with Carolina, Virginia, Maryland, Pennsylvania, this government, Connecticut, Massachusetts Bay and New Hampshire, were truly and firmly united in the same councils, with love and friendship, how great would that power be, what dread must it strike on your enemies, and who would dare attempt to hurt them. In order to accomplish this so much to be desired union, I have prevailed upon the governor of South Carolina to send a gentleman to this place, whom you now see here, and to send with him six of the chiefs of the Catawbas, who are now in this city ready to make peace with you and to become your fast friends, and to unite with you in our common cause—as in your former treaties in this place, you desired and solemnly promised to receive them as one flesh and blood with you on their coming to it. I therefore, by this belt, excite you to lay hold of the proffered peace and friendship with the Catawbas. It must tend to strengthen the covenant chain and the common interest of us all. I can no longer bear to see those who are our brethren, killing and destroying one another, and therefore I cannot doubt of your cheerfully agreeing to what I now propose."

Two days afterward, the Confederates replied that as the commissioners came to renew the covenant chain with the Six Nations, they also were there for the same purpose; and that as it was the wish of their brother Corlear, that they should make peace with the Catawbas, they would see and talk with them upon the subject. Mr. Bull then rose, and read a letter from the governor of South Carolina, expressive of his good will, and of his hopes that they would conclude a treaty with the Catawbas and keep the covenant chain ever bright and free from rust. He followed the reading of the letter by a few remarks in a pleasant strain, closing as follows: "We have heard what his excellency, Governor Clinton has said concerning a peace, and what his excellency, the governor of South Carolina, has written to you, and also what I have now said. You will hear next what the chiefs of the Catawbas, who came here with me will say. They came to this council fire at Albany, to meet you, in order to make peace with you. They know it is the desire of the English that peace should be made between you, and you know it is the desire of the English, also. To open your ears, I give you this belt of wampum."

As soon as the South Carolina commissioner had finished, the Catawba king and his chiefs approached the grand council singing a song of peace; their ensigns, (colored feathers) being borne horizontally. "Every one present admired the decorum and dignity of their behavior, as well as the solemn air of their song. A seat was prepared for them at the right hand of the governor's company. Their two singers, with the two ensigns of feathers, continued their song, half fronting to the centre of the old sachems, to whom they addressed their song, and pointed their feathers, shaking their musical calabashes, while the Catawba king was busily preparing and lighting the calumet of peace. The king first smoked, and presented the calumet to Hendrik, who gracefully accepted it and smoked. The king then passed the pipe to each sachem in the front rank, and several in the second rank reached to receive it from him, to smoke also. The Catawba singers then ceased, and fastened their feathers, calumets, and calabashes to the tent pole; after which the king stood up and advancing, thus addressed the Six Nations"[1]

"*Friends:* I, last year, with the advice of my great men,

---

[1] This description is taken from Drayton to whom it was related by an eye witness.

determined to make a peace with you, and set out for that purpose, but was taken sick by the way, which hindered me. The same resolution remained in my heart, and the governor of Carolina, agreeing with me, consented to send a vessel to New York, that we might meet you here at this treaty, which greatly rejoiced me, and when I came away my towns all shook hands with me, and desired me, for them, to make a peace; and I give this belt, which has all my towns upon it, signifying that they all join in my desire.

We are all friends to the English and desire to be so with our brethren the Six Nations; and as some of your people are now out, that do not know of the peace, when they are all returned, and the path clear and safe, I will come to your towns and houses, and smoke with you, as I would in my own."[1]

The king of the Catawbas, and the sachems with him, then advanced and shook hands with the Six Nations, who thereupon replied:

"*Brethren:* We are glad to see you here, and return you thanks for your kind speech. But as it is a thing of moment, we must take time to consider of it, and shall answer you this evening or to-morrow morning."

It was not, however, until the tenth, that the Confederates were ready to give their answer; when their chief sachem, having lighted a pipe and handed it to the Catawbas, thus spoke:

Brethren the Catawbas: You came to our towns and fires to make peace with us, and we have heard your kind speech, and thank you for it, and as a token that you came to make peace, and were received as our friends, we give you this white belt of wampum, to wear about your necks, that all that see it, may know that you have been here and were received as our friends.

This belt serves to make you more powerful, and give you short horns; it has been a custom among all Indian nations, that when they come to sue for peace, they bring

---

[1] Council minutes.

some prisoners with them, and when you return with prisoners, the peace shall be completed, and your horns lengthened, and we give you a year to return with your prisoners, and if you do not come in that time, we shall look upon the peace as void.

We will take your pipe up to the Mohawk's castles, being the first town you came to, as it were, and there sit and smoke, and think of you, and not go out to war, if you return within the time appointed by us."

The treaty having been thus made, Governor Clinton distributed the presents, brought by the commissioners, among the Indians, and the council was formally dismissed; but not until "the hatchet was buried irrecoverably deep, and a tree of peace planted, which was to be green as the Alleganies, and to spread its branches till its shadow should reach from the great lakes to the gulf of Mexico."[1]

The general effect of this council, upon the Indians at least, was satisfactory. Although Governor Clinton was unsuccessful in persuading the several colonies to join in an alliance against the machinations of the French, yet the main object—that of prevailing upon the Six Nations to conclude a treaty with the Catawbas—was accomplished. Early in June of the following year, the Catawbas, desirous of performing their part of the agreement, sent to the Confederates a Cayuga prisoner in charge of four of their warriors; and thus the feeling of hatred entertained by the Six Nations toward that nation—which had been so bitter before the treaty, as to cause the confinement of the Catawba chiefs in a separate apartment—was now changed to that of cordial friendship.[2]

---

[1] Bancroft.

[2] Manuscript letter: John Ogilvie to Colonel Johnson. The Catawbas, at the time of the treaty, held in captivity three of the Six Nations; but during the year one had died, and the other refused to come by sea, preferring to remain in South Carolina until he could come by land.—*Governor Glen to Governor Clinton.*

Shortly after the arrival of the Catawba braves, Johnson wrote to Clinton, that the peace between that people and the Confederates was fully

Previous to his departure for Albany, Mr. Clinton had requested a farther appropriation for Indian presents in addition to the sum voted at a former session; and the legislature, in a better spirit than usual, had at that time promised to supply any deficiency in that regard, which might arise, in brightening the covenant-chain with the Six Nations. In the fall session of the assembly, however, the spirit of faction was again manifest, notwithstanding three of the chief leaders of the opposition had died since its last sitting—Mr. Clarkson, Mr. Philipse and Mr. Michaux. In his opening message, on the eighth of October, Mr. Clinton communicated to the house the result of the late treaty. The resignation of Colonel Johnson was attributed to its negligence in omitting to pass bills adequate for the support of the Indian department; and the designs of the French, and the consequent importance of sending agents to the distant western tribes, urged. The message closed by asking for the usual supplies for the maintenance of the government.

The house in its answer, the following day, said that it would cheerfully provide for the support of his majesty's government, and make provision for all the just debts that, on examination, should be found chargeable on the colony; that it was well aware that the security of the colonies depended, in a great degree, upon the fidelity of the Indians, but it had hoped that the sum of one thousand pounds, voted for that purpose, would have been amply sufficient to place the Indian affairs on such a basis, as to render a farther sum unnecessary. In the mean time, the several particulars of his excellency's speech should be attentively considered, and that which was judged best for his majesty's service, and for the welfare of the colony, should be done. Finally, it reminded his excellency, that many of the members had not been notified by the usual

---

ratified; and that the Catawbas had returned into their own country, escorted by several Iroquois warriors, who had volunteered to see them safely through those nations, who might not have heard of the recent peace.

circular letters of the present session of the assembly, a circumstance which it hoped would not again occur. Mr. Clinton, in his answer, stated that while it was true that the presents which he had given the Indians, at Albany, had produced a favorable effect, yet, unless the expense of daily providing for them was met, the good impression made at that time would soon be obliterated by the French priests. He also promised to lay before the assembly in a few days information lately received upon this point, which would render his remarks more clear. Alluding to the thousand pounds to which reference had been made, nothing, he said, would give him greater pleasure than to send down to the house a full account of the manner in which it had been expended; and as to the neglect, of which he had been accused, in not notifying the members, it was not true, as his deputy secretary had sent letters to all the members, with the exception of the speaker. He farther added, in conclusion, that he had made this explanation to show how entirely he was influenced by the desire of advancing the security and welfare of the colony.[1]

In accordance with his promise, Mr. Clinton, on the ninth, sent to the house the accounts relating to the disposition of the thousand pounds, accompanied with extracts from the minutes of the late council.[2]

On the thirteenth of September, Mr. Clinton had laid before his privy council letters from Colonel Johnson and Captain Stoddard, the contents of which were indeed startling. From a French deserter the Colonel learned that a convoy of twelve hundred French, accompanied by two hundred Adirondack Indians, had passed by Oswego about a fortnight before, with the object, so far as could be ascertained, of cutting off those western tribes friendly to the English, and driving off the Pennsylvania traders, who were erecting trading posts on the Ohio. Captain Stoddard's letter, also, confirmed this

[1] Journals of the assembly.
[2] Council minutes.

intelligence. Johnson farther wrote, that on the reception of this news, he had immediately dispatched a messenger, in the governor's name, with a belt of wampum, to all the castles of the Six Nations, informing them of the march of the French. Letters arrived, at nearly the same time, from Lieutenant Lindesay, in command at Oswego, to the effect that a Cayuga sachem had arrived from the Mississagas, bringing the intelligence that the French were building a large vessel at Cadaracqui, with the design of attacking his post.[1] Copies of these letters, Mr. Clinton now laid before the assembly, for its perusal and careful consideration.

The apparent good temper, however, with which the proceedings between the executive and the assembly had thus far been conducted, was destined to be of short duration. The house having on the sixteenth sent up to the council for its approval "an act for paying several demands made on the colony," the latter replied, on the eighteenth, by sending Colonel Johnson to request of that body the vouchers for the several demands provided for in the bill. This was applying the torch to the powder. The house flamed at once. It immediately resolved, that "the demand was of an extraordinary and unprecedented nature;" and that its consideration should be postponed until after the first of the ensuing May. No sooner had this action been communicated to the council, than they, in turn, becoming indignant, resolved that it was

---

[1] John Lindesay, founder of the Cherry Valley settlement, was a native of Scotland, and in December, 1730, received from his countryman, Governor Montgomerie, the commission of naval officer for the port of New York. He filled various other important offices, until, in 1744, Mr. Lindesay assumed the command of the fort at Oswego, Lieutenant Congreve resigning in his favor. In 1747, at the request of the Oswego traders and the Six Nations, Lieutenant Lindesay was continued in command of that post until 1749, when he was appointed Indian commissary and agent for Oswego, which latter situation he retained until his death, which occurred in the latter part of this year. At the time of his death, Mr. Lindsay was a lieutenant in Captain Clark's company of Independent Fusileers.—*Campbell's History of Tryon County.*

their unquestionable right to call for the vouchers; inasmuch as the sum, sufficient for the demand, was to come out of the royal revenue, and that their consent was therefore necessary. They also resolved, that they would not proceed on the bill until the vouchers appeared before them; and at the same sitting, in no very amiable state of mind, sent Colonel Johnson again to the house with a bill of their own, for "applying the sum of five hundred pounds, for the management of Indian affairs, and for repairing the garrison at Oswego." The passage of this bill by the council, as might have been foreseen, was not calculated to molify the temper of the house inflamed, as it was, by the demand of the council for the vouchers. The bill was therefore refused a second reading; and a motion was forthwith carried,—that inasmuch as the bill intrenched on the "great, essential and undoubted right of the representatives of the people of this colony to begin all bills for raising and disbursing of money, it should be rejected."[1] Directly upon the passage of this resolution, the house sent up to the governor an address, prepared in the same churlish manner as in times past. In it, the lack money for Indian affairs was greatly lamented—as if, indeed, it was not owing to themselves that a larger sum had not been voted. They even carried their spleen so far, as to hint that the governor had used the thousand pounds for purposes other than the public benefit; and that it was through his neglect that the Indian affairs were in such a condition. In conclusion, they threw upon the council the evil effects which would result from its refusal to pass the bill for the discharge of the colony debt; and prayed the governor to pass straightway those of the bills which he approved. Three or four more days were taken up in wrangling and puerile resolves, until Mr. Clinton, who had learned by experience the folly of any farther altercation, passed all the bills without farther discussion, and without any notice and to the astonishment of all,

---

[1] Minutes of the assembly.

dissolved the assembly. On the part of Mr. Clinton this was a master stroke of policy. The assembly were fairly caught. But having passed the support bill so early in the session, they were left without a remedy. "This gratified Mr. Clinton and the other officers of the government; while the neglect of the colony creditors, added to the governor's party, already strengthened by the appointment of Colonel Johnson to the council, and Mr. Chambers to the second place on the bench."[1]

Meanwhile the French were planning still farther encroachments upon the territory of New York. Already they possessed Crown Point, La Presentation and Niagara, and encouraged by the pusillanimity which had allowed them to take possession of those posts, they were now meditating the establishment of a military and missionary post on the banks of Onondaga Lake, which, while it would secure a foothold in the very heart of the province, would also, they thought, greatly strengthen their influence over the Six Nations. Preliminary to this audacious step, it was necessary that the Confederates, especially those residing in the immediate vicinity of the lake, should be courted into giving their consent. Accordingly the Jesuit emissaries insinuated themselves deeper than ever into the affections of that fickle people, and with such success, that at the close of the summer, several of the principal Onondagas had granted the desired permission.

Such a design, however, could not long escape the vigilance of Colonel Johnson, who no sooner heard through the Mohawks of the scheme afoot, than, braving the autumnal rains, he set off for the old fire-place of the Confederacy, hoping, if possible, to defeat the machinations of La Galissonière and his wily priests. Arrived at Onondaga, he lost no time in summoning the chief men of that castle to a conference, in which after laying before them the dangerous consequences resulting from a French

---
[1] Smith.

settlement in the very centre of their Confederacy, boldly desired them, as a proof of their esteem, to grant him Onondaga Lake with the land around it for two miles in width—promising them in return a handsome present. This sudden appearance of the colonel upset at once all the deep laid plans of the Jesuits. Mortified at being thus caught in the very act of lending an ear to their ancient enemies, the chiefs hung their heads and in confusion agreed to his proposition. A deed conveying the entire lake with its two miles of land, was accordingly made out on the spot, and signed by the entire castle, the latter receiving in return, the sum of three hundred and fifty pounds sterling. Immediately on his arrival home, the colonel who had in making this purchase no other object than that of securing the property to the crown, and the consequent defeat of the French, communicated an account of the transaction to Mr. Clinton,—at the same time offering the land to the government of New York at the same price which it had cost him. Refusing, however, to appreciate the important service which he had thus rendered, the assembly declined to reimburse him for the land; and the matter thus rested until the summer of 1753, when a minute was made in council, granting this tract to him and his heirs, by way of reimbursement for the sum advanced by him for the Indian department.[1] Otherwise than this, his debt from the colony was never paid.

---

[1] Manuscript council minutes.

CHAPTER XII.
1752—1753.

With the opening of the year, dawned a new era in American literature. Signs of a greater appreciation of learning and a desire for literary pursuits among the colonies, are in this year too apparent not to deserve a passing notice. The clang of steel and the midnight alarms had now ceased; and in the calm thought which followed, the literary seeds that had for so long a period lain dormant, found a rich soil in which to germinate and bring forth fruit. As in the age of the Reformation, and of Louis XIV, a company of stalwart literary giants sprung forth from the previous darkness, so in the period we are now upon, a score of men of power and vigorous intellect rose up in America, infusing new vigor into every department of letters with which they came in contact. The theological writings of Jonathan Edwards, with all their depth of philosophical eloquence, gave an impetus to that branch of scholarship hitherto unknown. It was in this year that Franklin electrified the savans of the Old World with his grand discovery. The universities of New England awoke to new life and activity. Schemes for the advancement of learning sprung up in the different provinces with wonderful rapidity. Libraries and philosophical societies were formed in every direction. Several men distinguished in the walks of scientific research visited America, and by their cordial sympathy encouraged greatly the enquirer after truth. The eye turns with pleasure to the names of John Winthrop, professor of mathematics at Cambridge, Thomas Godfrey, the inventor of Hadley's Quadrant, David Rittenhouse of Pennsylvania, and numerous others, whose names shine with lustre upon the page of history.[1] Confining ourselves to the province of

---
[1] Grahame.

CHAP. XII.
1752.

New York, Cadwallader Colden had just completed that remarkable book—the "History of the Five Nations;" and in this year the founding of Kings College began to be seriously urged.

It is not to be supposed that with this literary zeal pervading every mind, an intelligent man like Johnson could fail to be affected by it. Although in his spare moments, heretofore, he had always manifested a great fondness for literary pursuits and had repeatedly sent out to England for books, yet having a little leisure this year by his resignation of Indian affairs, he seems to have devoted much of his time to improving his own mind, and also the moral and social condition of those around him. The manner in which a portion of his time was spent at this period, may be inferred by the following letter to his agent in London.

"MOUNT JOHNSON, August the 20th, 1752.

" Sir:

Having the pleasure of an intimate acquaintance with your brother, Doctor Shuckburgh of New York, whom I have a singular regard for, induces me to apply to you for what I may want in your way, although but a trifle. Having lately had a pretty large collection of books from London, shall at present only desire you will please to send me what pamphlets are new and worth reading; also the Gentleman's Magazine from Nov'br. 1750 to the last, and the Monthly Review from the same time; also the Newspapers regularly and stitched up. You have only to deliver them to Mr. John George Liberwood, merch't. there, who will forward them to me, and will pay your am't. yearly.

Having nothing farther to add at present (but beg you will send me those things regularly and punctually) I conclude sir,

. Y'r very humble serv't.,   W. J.
To Mr. Shuckburgh, stationer, London.¹"

---

[1] Manuscript Letter. See also appendix No. II. of vol. I.

The intellectual culture of the Mohawks was a subject in which the colonel took special interest. The mission school at Stockbridge for Indian children, the plan of which was first projected by John Sergeant in 1741, and which after the death of the latter was carried on for a time by Jonathan Edwards, received at this time his particular attention. Sir Peter Warren in 1751 had donated for the support of this institution seven hundred pounds, and about the same time had expressed to his nephew a very favorable opinion of its purpose, requesting that he would use his influence in its favor.[1] Had Johnson previous to this request no other incentive for his interest in it, this would have been sufficient. His efforts were now unremitting to persuade the Mohawks to send their children thither; and a correspondence was kept up between himself and the committee of this school on the subject. His advice upon its management was freely asked and as freely given; and in a letter to him upon this topic, the writer says: "I can't but hope and pray for your further assistance in encouraging the Indians to send their children and continue them steadily here, and your thoughts with regard to any measures that may naturally tend to promote this affair, and be proper for us further to do or attempt, will be very acceptable.[2]

Nor were his efforts to benefit his savage neighbors confined solely to the school at Stockbridge. He was equally interested in other missions wherever located, and always used his influence for their support and encouragement. In the course of the following year (1753) Rev. Mr. Hawley was sent from Boston to establish an Indian mission school

---

[1] Manuscript Letter to Johnson from Joseph Dwight, one of the committee of the mission school.

[2] Extract from the same. Hon. Joseph Dwight, whose letter is here referred to, was a liberally educated man. He had been speaker of the house of Massachusetts Bay, and a counselor, and led a regiment in the successful attack on Cape Breton. He married the widow of the Rev. Mr. Sergeant, the same who is mentioned in the text as the founder of the mission school at Stockbridge.

west of Albany. On his way he stopped over night at Mount Johnson, hoping to obtain the colonel's countenance in his project. This was cheerfully granted, and the missionary sent on his way with a godspeed.[1] The colonel was also at this time in correspondence with Doctor Eleazer Wheelock, who had recently established a school in Lebanon, Connecticut, similar in its object to the one at Stockbridge, and which afterwards grew into Dartmouth college. Several years later, the celebrated Joseph Brant, sent by the colonel, received at this school his English education. It is pleasant to dwell upon this phase of Johnson's character, showing, as it does, that his mind was not wholly engrossed—as some would have us believe—in amassing a private fortune.

It will be recollected that when I last spoke of Sir Peter Warren, he had been obliged to retire through ill health to his country seat in Westbury, and had shortly afterward been elected to parliament from the city of Westminster. The capture of the French fleet of East Indiamen, of which an account has been given in a former chapter, was the last service he lived to perform; for peace being concluded in the following year, the fleet was of course dismantled. But even in his retirement honors followed him. In May, 1748, he received a distinguished mark of royal favor in being appointed vice admiral of the Red; and in the early

---

[1] Rev. Mr. Hawley was before this an instructor of the Iroquois children at the Stockbridge mission under Mr. Edwards. Mr. Hawley thus speaks of his visit at this time to Colonel Johnson in a letter to Rev. Dr. Thatcher, published in the Mass. His. Col. vol. iv. "On Friday we left Albany. Mr. Woodbridge and I set out for Mount Johnson, about thirty-six miles off, to pay our compliments to Colonel Johnson, and obtain his countenance in favor of our mission. * * * At sunset we were politely received at Colonel Johnson's gate by himself in person. Here we lodged. His mansion was stately, and situate a little distance from the river, on rising ground, and adjacent to a stream which turned his mill. This gentleman was well known in his civil, military and private character. He was the first civil character in the county of Albany at that day. * * * It was favorable to our mission to have his patronage, *which I never lost.*"

part of the present year, the citizens of London presented him with the freedom of the city and the Goldsmith's company. They also wished to make him an alderman for Billingsgate ward in the place of the lord mayor, deceased. This latter honor, however, Sir Peter courteously declined, " assigning as a reason, that his past profession must prevent him in a great measure, from discharging properly the duties of that office." The citizens nevertheless persisted in electing him for their alderman; upon which Sir Peter, on the twenty-third of June, wrote to the court of aldermen declining to serve, and enclosing at the same time the fine of five hundred pounds. Shortly afterward, Sir Peter hoping that the air of his native hills would improve his health, went to Ireland. The hope was fallacious, for scarcely had he landed when a severe inflammatory fever carried him off on the twenty-ninth of July. He died " universally lamented by all persons, who agreed that there could not exist a better and honester man, or a more gallant officer. Few men ever attained to a greater share of popularity. It was said of him that he had not only the singular happiness of being universally courted, esteemed, and beloved, but had the additional consolation of having passed through life without making a single enemy." [1]

By no one was the death of Admiral Warren felt with more acuteness than the Johnson family. Sir Peter had been to them all the kindest of benefactors; and was looked up to with feelings of gratitude and affection. This is evident from the following letter, written to Colonel Johnson by his brother, a few days after his uncle's decease.

"LONDON, Aug. 4th, 1752.

"*My Dear Brother:* It's with the utmost sorrow I give you the most dismal account of the death of our most dear, dear uncle, who died in Dublin last Wednesday night, 29th July, of a most violent fever, which carried him off

---

[1] *Biographia Navalis.*—Charnock.

in four days. I was up day and night with him, and would to God I'd have died in his stead. Oh my dear brother, such grief as our poor family are in, is inexpressible, for we have lost our all in all. And you, I am sure, will be as much shocked as mortal living, but let me beg of you to muster up all of your resolution to bear this most dismal account. I arrived here in two days from Dublin with the melancholy news to Lady Warren, whom from my very heart I pity, and hope God will preserve her life for her poor family's sake. He made his will two days before he died, and how he has settled his affairs no one as yet knows, nor I till I return with her directions to have it opened. I set out in two hours and expect to be in Dublin the 7th. He is to be interred at Pock Mark in a private manner. His executors are Lady Warren, Captain Tyrrell, and the Chief Justice De Lancey, and be assured of a faithful account of everything as soon as his will is opened.

"I hope in God, my dear brother will endeavor to bear this shock with patience. Our loss is very, very great, and what to do now with myself I know not. I shall let you hear from me by the first opportunity after my arrival in Ireland. I shall write this miserable account to my cousin Captain Tyrrell, who will be, I am sure, greatly shocked. I have not time to add more. My love to brother Ferrall,[1] and believe me, my dear brother, ever yours,

"Most affectionately and faithfully,
"WARREN JOHNSON."[2]

To Colonel Johnson the death of his uncle must indeed have been a terrible blow. Although I have not been able to find among his papers the answer to the above letter, yet undoubtedly it was full of corresponding sympathy and affection.

As by Sir Peter's death, the council lost one of its members, William Smith, at the recommendation of Mr. Clin-

---

[1] Johnson's brother-in-law. He was killed in the action of the 8th of September, 1775, at Lake George.
[2] Manuscript letter.

ton, was appointed by the crown to fill the vacant seat. This gentleman was at this time a flourishing lawyer in the city of New York, and had first gained Mr. Clinton's good will, by his prosecution of Mr. Oliver De Lancey—brother of the chief justice—for his abuse of the governor.[1] On the death of the attorney general in this year, Mr. Clinton appointed him to that office, which he filled with great credit and reputation, until the arrival from England of William Kempe, who had received the appointment from the crown, unknown to the governor.[2] The latter did not present the claims of Mr. Smith, without opposition;— Colonel Morris, formerly a member of the council under Governor Montgomery, sending in at the same time a memorial praying for the appointment. The influence, however, of Mr. Clinton at court, was too powerful to be overcome, and Mr. Smith took his seat at the council board, upon the thirtieth of April of the following spring.

To the new assembly, which met in October, many of its former members, friends of the chief justice, were returned. Its principal feature was the absence of the long messages both from the executive and the house, which had characterized its former sessions. Both parties seemed resolved to make them models of brevity. Mr. Clinton's opening message was comprised in fifteen lines; and the address of the house in reply, scarcely exceeded it in length. This is attributed by Mr. Smith to the fact of his own advice and that of Mr. Alexander having been taken by the governor, rather than that of Mr. Colden, "whose incautious and luxuriant compositions had so frequently kindled the party fires," which had increased the popularity of the chief justice "whom he was most anxious to pull down."[3] Be this as it may, it is certain that during the

---
[1] Manuscript letter.
[2] Governor Clinton to the Lords of Trade.
[3] Smith. Mr. Clinton had recently lost the support of Dr. Colden, by his having urged, in opposition to the latter's wishes, Robert Hunter Morris for lieutenant governor. Mr. Alexander was chosen by Clinton as his chief adviser in place of Colden.

present session, there was none of that bitterness which had characterized former sessions.

1752. The most noticeable action of the present assembly, was its voting to provide, at their next sitting, for the repairing of the different fortifications along the frontier; for the rebuilding of the trading-post at Oswego, now in a ruinous condition; and for the founding of a college for the education of the youth of the colony. A new board of commissioners was also appointed to take charge of the Indian department, which, by the resignation of Colonel Johnson, had been deprived of his services. It would appear, however, by the following extract from a letter written by Mr. Clinton to the colonel, under date of November fifth, that the former commissioners were still sore from their previous dismissal. The letter itself is addressed to the colonel, in the care of Captain Ross, New York, whither the former had come to attend the council:

"I find the assembly are determined to go upon commissioners for Indian affairs again, and as I cannot, without inconvenience, prevent it, I send for your perusal a list of persons proposed for my approbation for that commission. I cannot help observing that they are picked out of almost all your inveterate opposers; therefore should be glad of your opinion, for I can but think it justice, that I should have the nomination of one-half, at least, of them. I shall be at the fort Tuesday next, when I shall be glad if you would dine with me, and in the interim think what I can do in it."[1]

The result was a compromise—the governor rejecting six or one-half of the names sent in for his approval, and the house putting in their place, the members of the executive council, the commanding officer at Albany, the representatives of the general assembly, and the mayor and recorder of Albany *ex-officio*.[2] The affair of Indian

---

[1] Manuscript letter.

[2] Manuscript council minutes. The list for commissioners enclosed in Mr. Clinton's letter to the colonel, was Myndert Schuyler, Philip Schuyler, David Schuyler, Johannis Janse Lansingh, Hendrick Bleecker, Hans Han-

commissioners being thus settled, Mr. Clinton, on the eleventh of November, passed all the bills, including the one for providing for the payment of the salaries of government officers out of the duties, and prorogued the assembly to the first Tuesday of the following March.

It may at first appear singular that as Mr. Clinton had dissolved the last assembly on account of his trouble with the opposition, the tone of this new one should be so entirely different, especially since, as before observed, nearly all of the opposition had been returned. The solution of this is found in a glance at the political complexion of affairs, as they now stood. Mr. De Lancey began to fear that he had gone a little too far. He knew that Mr. Clinton held in his hands a commission for him as lieutenant governor; and his object thus far had been to render his position so uncomfortable that he would be obliged to resign and thus give him greater scope for his ambition.[1] Mr. Clinton's success, however, at court, as shown by his securing for his friends seats at the council board, caused alarm. He knew, also, from his friends in England, that the governor, who was thinking of soon leaving the province on account of ill health, had written several letters to the board of trade, requesting permission, without producing De Lancey's commission, to leave Colden, by virtue of being president of the council, in command of the colony.[2] The very idea of his most inveterate enemy, being thus placed in power, drove the chief justice well nigh distracted. Mr. Charles, moreover, had written to the speaker of the assembly, that measures were on foot to have the commission appointing De Lancey lieutenant governor revoked, and to have Robert Hunter Morris

---

son, Jacob H. Ten Eyck, Johannis Cuyler, Sybrant G. Van Schaick, Johannis Glen, Gerardus Groesbeck, and Johannis Van Rensselaer. The commissioners retained and substituted, were Myndert Schuyler, Cornelius Cuyler, Hendrick Bleecker, John Beekman, Johannis Lansingh, jr., and Jacob C. Ten Eyck.

[1] Review of military operations in America.
[2] Clinton o the board of trade.

appointed in his stead.[1] The chief justice, therefore, fearing the loss of the commission—than which nothing was farther from his thoughts—saw that he must play his cards differently if he would win. In addition to all this, the disputes between the provinces of New York and New Jersey in relation to the boundary line, were still unsettled; and it was evident that so long as the disputes between the assembly and the governor continued, they would be as far off from an adjustment as ever. Those families of the province who held large estates, had grown weary of these continual wranglings; and now gave the chief justice pretty plainly to understand, that if he would retain his popularity, he must cease his opposition. This was touching Mr. De Lancey in a vital spot; for he could not, for the present at least, afford to lose anything that might tend to further his ambition. He therefore became more cautious and less open in his opposition; and the remainder of Mr. Clinton's administration was passed in comparative freedom from those storms of faction, which had raged so fiercely between himself and the assembly.[2]

Serious difficulty was experienced this year in the collection of the Oswego duties. Considerable complaint had arisen of late in regard to the irregular manner in which the duties were collected; and hints of a dishonorable nature had been freely expressed against those who had them in charge. Now, however, direct charges of peculation were brought against John De Peyster and Peter Schuyler Jun., two of the commissioners; who, to say the least, had been guilty of great ill management and criminal neglect. The dissatisfaction at length grew so serious, as to lead Mr. Clinton to take the matter in hand; and he accordingly wrote to Colonel Johnson, requesting him to ferret out the true facts. The following extract from the colonel's reply, seems to show that the charges were not ill founded.

---

[1] Morris was appointed governor of Pennsylvania in 1754.
[2] Smith.

"As to that affair of the Oswego duties," he writes, "although a cursed piece of villainy, yet it is very difficult to find out. De Peyster has owned to me that he has not entered into recognizance these several years. The mayor tells me, also, that when he sent for Peter Schuyler to qualify, he then sent for De Peyster likewise, and he refused it, notwithstanding he has acted all the time. On talking to him some time ago about the yearly amount of duties, he acknowledged that they amounted to upwards of £1000, the year 1749, so that the other three years, which he mentions in his accounts delivered to the assembly, the duties are but about £145, as you'll see in the last notes, p. 32—a most damnable imposition on the public, yet I cannot sift it out, without he is to produce his books."[1]

Doubts as to the duties having been honestly collected, had arisen in the assembly the previous year, and they had at their sitting in the fall ordered "that the commissioners, for collecting the duties on goods carried to Oswego, do, with all convenient speed, lay before the house, a particular account on oath, of what the said duties have amounted to, from the delivery of the accounts, to the first of September last."[2] In accordance with this order John De Peyster sent in his accounts on oath, by which it appeared, that the duties, from June 1746 to September 1750, amounted to £1145, 17s. 8d. Thus, from the acknowledgment made to the mayor, it would appear, as Johnson observes, that only a trifle over £145 was left for the years '47, '48 and '50—a fact which fully justified the suspicion of unfair dealing. No farther action however, was taken; for although scarcely any one doubted their dishonesty, yet owing to the want of positive proof, it was difficult to fix the charges upon the parties to this transaction, and they therefore escaped. They were nevertheless more cautious in future, and De Peyster in his next accounts for the year 1751, showed the amount of

---

[1] Manuscript letter.
[2] Journals of the general assembly.

duties received to be something over £940! Johnson interfered grievously with their knavish plans, and hence, the bitter malignity with which he was pursued by a few individuals, during the remainder of his life.

Clouds still hung along the border of the northern frontier. In the summer of this year, a scalping party of St. Francis Indians surprised four young men, who were trapping beaver along the head waters of the Connecticut river. One of these was John Stark, a native of New Hampshire, and a bold and fearless hunter. When he found himself surprised, he shouted to his brother, who was in a canoe, to gain the opposite shore. This he did and escaped, though not before a young man with him in the boat had been shot at and killed. Stark, with his companion Eastman, was carried up the Connecticut river, and down Memphremagog to the chief village of the tribe. While there, he conducted himself with so much courage and good humor, as to win the affection of his captors, who dressed him in their finest robes, and cherished him with so much kindness, as to allow him, upon receiving a ransom, to return to his friends. The lessons of woodcraft which Stark learned in this early captivity, qualified him to render efficient service in the next war, from which by his courage and energy he rose to the rank of brigadier general in the armies of the United States.[1]

The general assembly met in March, but was by successive prorogations, prevented from sitting until May. In his opening message on the thirtieth, Mr. Clinton expressed his satisfaction at the resolves passed during the last session,—to take at this meeting, the state of the frontier fortifications, and the Indian affairs into consideration; having, as he said, the fullest confidence in their honor and justice. Nor did he fail to speak in the warmest terms of their determination to advance the cause of

---

[1] Belknap.

learning, by the founding of a college; and he hoped that the plan would receive their warmest encouragement, and be speedily carried into effect. He, also, informed them of the encroachments which had been made upon the province by the colonies of New Hampshire and Massachusetts Bay; advising, that committees from both houses should be appointed to concert the proper measures to be taken in this affair, in which, he assured them of his hearty assistance. He then alluded to the colony debts, among which was the long standing claim of Colonel Johnson; and closed with a promise to do everything in his power to promote the welfare of the colony.[1]

The assembly in its reply, two days afterward, thanked the governor in the warmest terms for his kind offer of assistance, promising to do everything in its power for the interest of the colony. Both the executive and the house seemed to be animated by the same spirit of harmony, which, indeed, continued throughout the entire session. Nor did the assembly confine itself to words. A committee, of the legislative council and the house, met on the New England encroachments, and passed a bill authorizing a committee to prepare a representation upon this grievance for the king's ministers.[2] A bill was also passed for raising a sum by lottery for the college; the colony debt, incurred during the late war, discharged; money voted for the fortifications; and the sum of eight hundred pounds appropriated for Indian presents.[3]

While the general assembly was sitting, a letter to Colonel Johnson from Captain Stoddard, and one also from Lieutenant Holland to Mr. Clinton, both dated at Oswego, informed the executive council that the French were again active and threatened serious trouble. On the fourteenth of May, thirty French canoes, with five hundred

---

[1] Journals of the assembly.
[2] The committee were all members of the house, and consisted of David Jones, John Thomas, Paul Richards, William Walton, Henry Cruger, and John Watts.
[3] Smith.

Indians under the command of Monsieur Marin, passed that post on their way to the Ohio River. By a Frenchman, lately arrived at Oswego, it appeared that this was only the advance guard of an army of six thousand men, which the French had been concentrating, preparatory to their taking possession of the Ohio Valley. Their object was to support—by building forts along the Ohio, and if necessary, by force of arms—their claim to the lands bordering upon that river; and to eject those English traders who had already settled along its banks.

Intimation of this movement was received by Johnson early in April. A party of the Six Nations hunting in the early part of that month near the rapids of the St. Lawrence, had descried a large company of French and Indians, on their way to Ontario. Two of their swiftest of foot were immediately dispatched with the intelligence to their council fire at Onondaga. Thence the news was borne to the colonel, who was awakened at midnight, on the nineteenth of April, by terrific whoops and yells, and presented with a belt of wampum which was to urge the English to protect the Ohio and the Miami Indians.[1]

The Six Nations, especially the Mohawks, straightway took alarm, considering the Ohio as their property, and any attempt therefore to erect forts upon that river, as a direct infringement on their rights. This conduct of the French was not calculated to assuage the temper of the Mohawks, already in an alarming state, caused by their having been overreached, as they alleged, in some sales of land to the whites. Added to this, while they witnessed the active movements of the French, they saw no corresponding activity on the part of the government of New York, either for resisting these encroachments, or for protecting them in their castles. In truth, there was cause for this feeling. The strange apathy of the parent government in thwarting the designs of the French, and the criminal neglect of the assembly to protect the fron-

---

[1] Colonel Johnson to Governor Clinton, 30th April 1753.

tiers, gave truth to the remark of King Hendrik, that
" the council and assembly dont take care of Albany, but
leave it naked and defenceless, and dont care what becomes
of our nation, but sit in peace and quietness, while we
are exposed to the enemy." The Indian commissioners
at Albany never had had either the confidence or the
affection of the Six Nations, and since the resignation of
Colonel Johnson, they had been sadly neglected. The
Mohaws at length became so uneasy, that, after appealing
in vain to the commissioners at Albany, they determined to
apply at head quarters for the redress of their grievances;
and accordingly Hendrik, accompanied by several of the
Mohawk chieftains, visited Governor Clinton at New York
during the session of the assembly.

The reproaches of the great Mohawk chieftain against
the council and assembly, for their indifference and cruel
neglect of his nation, were affecting, yet bitterly severe.
The grievances, to which they had been subjected in being
imposed upon in the sales of their lands, were especially
dwelt upon. Reminding them of the aid which they had
received from him in times past, he accused them of
having embroiled his nation with the French, and then
refusing to protect their castles from the revenge of their
enemy; the hatchet, also, which had been placed in their
hands by the government, was still there, never having
been taken back.[1] Hitherto, he continued, you have desired that the paths should be kept open by us, but now,
you make no effort to keep the French from closing them,
but throw the whole burden upon us. If, therefore, you
do not endeavor to redress our grievances, the rest of our
brethren of the Six Nations shall know of it, and all paths
shall be stopped. Dreading, also, the formalities of diplomatic etiquette, which always was a terror to the Indians,

---

[6] It was always customary, at the close of hostilities, to make their Indian
allies presents, when the hatchet was formally buried. Hendrick alludes
here to this ceremony having been neglected.

and recollecting the long delay in the exchange of prisoners, Hendrik, now grown desperate, could not brook any delay. He therefore closed his speech with this caustic remark: "We beg you will not be long considering it. You may, perhaps, tell us, you will write to our Father the King, but that will be too long. We therefore desire you will do something immediately, or tell us at once, you will do nothing at all for us."

Before Mr. Clinton replied to Hendrik, the committee, to whom had been entrusted the business of investigating the complaints of the Mohawks regarding their land sales, reported, through Mr. Holland, that all the lands, in the purchase of which the Indians alleged they had been defrauded, had been patented many years before his excellency had taken the reins of government; and that it was therefore impossible, by examining the grants registered in New York, to determine whether the persons who had purchased of the Indians had imposed upon them or not. This, Mr. Clinton explained to Hendrik in his answering speech, but stated, that a conference would be held with them at Albany during the summer; and as regarded the alleged land frauds, he would put their complaints into the hands of the Indian commissioners, who would see that justice was done them. The angry feelings, however, of Hendrik and his brother chiefs, were too deeply rooted, to be thus easily eradicated by the promise of a conference. Having but a poor idea of the justice to be obtained at Albany, they immediately retired in disgust, but not before Hendrik had delivered the following philippic:

"*Brother:* When we came here to relate our grievances about our lands, we expected to have something done for us, and we have told you that the covenant chain of our forefathers was like to be broken, and you tell us, that we shall be redressed at Albany; but we know them so well, that we will not trust to them, for they are no people, but devils, so we rather desire that you will say nothing shall be done for us. By and by, you will expect to see the nations down, which you shall not see, for as soon as we come home, we will send up a belt of wampum to our brethren the Five Nations, to acquaint them the covenant chain is broken between you and us. So you are not to expect to hear of me any more, and we desire to hear no more of you. And we shall no longer acquaint you with any news or affairs as we used to do."

The alleged grievances respecting the land frauds might be redressed; but these threats, in the present critical state of the country, and the ruinous condition of the fortifications, might not so easily be ignored or despised. Accordingly, Mr. Clinton sent down a message to the assembly, on the ninth of June, informing that body of the conference which he had just held with the Mohawk chief; urging that immediate measures should be taken to calm the temper of the Indians, and to secure their alliance. This intelligence at once aroused the assembly from its shameful apathy, and showed them the necessity of immediately providing for the interests and safety of the colony. It forthwith voted the sum of two hundred pounds, in addition to the eight hundred before voted, to be given to the Indians to assist in burying the hatchet; and, on the sixteenth, it resolved, that an humble address should be presented to his excellency, praying that he would be pleased, " in this *extraordinary conjunction* of Indian affairs, to meet the Six Nations of Indians at Albany this summer in person, to renew the ancient alliance with them, and to bury the hatchet."

A few days afterward, Mr. Clinton sent down to the house copies of Hendrik's speech, with the suggestion, that it would be expedient to send forthwith some man of influence to the several castles of the confederacy, who should lay before it the injustice done to the Mohawk chiefs, and prevent the mischievous consequences which would arise, should the threats of Hendrik be carried into effect. In answer to this message, and in accordance with its resolve of the sixteenth, the house, on the twentieth, prepared and sent in to the governor an elaborate address, in which it confessed that the Indian affairs were in such a critical state, that, "in their opinion, no commissioner that could be appointed would have so much weight among the Six Nations as himself." It hoped, therefore, that he would not hesitate a moment in determining to meet the Six Nations at Albany during the summer; and, at the same time, advised, that in accordance with his suggestion, two persons of weight among the Indians should be dispatched with all possible haste to the several Indian castles, to induce them to meet him at Albany, there to adjust all their difficulties and complaints.

The health of Mr. Clinton rendering it doubtful whether he should be able to meet the Indians during the summer, he proposed to authorize such persons to attend in his place, as both branches of his legislature should agree in appointing. This suggestion was immediately acted upon by the assembly; and the man that was selected to be the sole distributor of the presents, and the confidant of both houses, was Colonel Johnson![1] Perhaps no better proof can be adduced of the confessed ascendancy of the latter over the Indians, and of his known ability, than the joint address signed by James De Lancey and David Jones, to Mr. Clinton, requesting a treaty for "appeasing the ill temper of the Indians," and praying that Colonel Johnson might be sent to Onondaga to meet the Confederacy.[2] It is very certain, that with the known enmity with which at this time he was regarded by the chief justice, and with all the obstacles which had been continually thrown in the way of his collecting his accounts, if any other person had been capable, Johnson would have been the last one selected. But at this critical juncture, private enmity was forced to yield to the public good; and both branches of the legislature united in declaring, "that, in their opinion, Colonel Johnson was the most proper person to be appointed to do

---

[1] Manuscript council minutes.

[2] De Lancey and David Jones were at this time the speakers, respectively, of the council and the assembly.

this service; and they humbly hoped his excellency would commissionate him."

Agreeably to this request, Colonel Johnson at once set out on his mission. His journey was somewhat hastened by intelligence, received prior to his departure, that a party of the Six Nations, in violation of their treaty, had recently returned, from the country of the Catawbas, bringing with them scalps and prisoners; and as serious trouble was likely to result from this, unless such conduct was speedily stopped, no time was to be lost. On his arrival at Mount Johnson, both of the Mohawk castles were summoned to meet him at his house the twenty-sixth of July. The Indians came with alacrity, delighted, as they expressed it, that he was again " raised up," and was once more to be the organ of communication between their people and the English. Weary of the frauds practised upon them, since he had resigned the charge of their affairs, the Indians came to him as to a father anxious to unbosom all their griefs; for, in the language of Hendrik on this occasion, " where should they resort to when anything laid heavy on their hearts, but where they had always found satisfaction, whatever might trouble them." Contrary to the usage of the Indians, when called to a council, Hendrik opened the conference by speaking first. If any one, other than Johnson, he said, had sent for them, they would not have "moved a foot;" but now they would cheerfully listen to what he had to say.

The answer of Johnson was kind, yet full of stern reproof for their past behavior. The unreasonableness of their demands and threats which they had so freely expressed in New York, was dwelt upon at length. The governor, he said, was grieved to think that they whom he had always supposed were such sincere friends, should with such loud and foul words, soil that chain, which had been made by their wise forefathers, and which had remained until now bright and unsullied; the expectation of Governor Clinton, of soon leaving the province, together with his ill health, prevented him from meeting them at this time, but his successor would have time to hear their complaints and to quiet their minds; hence, he was empowered to go to Onondaga, and treat with the Six Nations in the governor's name, and he now invited them all to join with him in such steps as would insure a harmonious meeting. The Indians, in their reply on the following day, said they had heard his remarks with "willing ears," which would never be effaced from the minds of the youngest person present. Although sensibly affected by the neglect with which they had been treated, yet they would once more, on his solicitation, bury their animosities in a pool so deep as never to be thought of again." Thus, through the singular ascendancy of Johnson, the Mohawks, lately so fierce and implacable, once more became docile and good humored.

In September, the colonel set out for the great council fire of the Six Nations, which was ever kept burning, and arrived there on the eighth of the same month. About a mile from the town he was met by the sachems, and escorted, with all the forms of Indian ceremonial, to the shore of the lake, where he encamped. The chiefs having signified their readiness to receive him that same day he went directly to the council. As soon as he was seated, Red Head, the chief sachem of the Onondagas, rose and presented him with a belt of wampum, requesting him to "wipe away his tears, and speak freely."[1]

---

[1] "The original wampum of the Iroquois, in which the laws of the league were recorded, was made of spiral fresh-water shells, *ote-kó-á*, which were strung on deer skin strings, or sinew, and the strands braided into belts, or simply united into strings. Hubbard thus speaks of wampum in general: "It is of two sorts, white and purple. The white is worked out of the inside of the great conch into the form of a bead, and perforated to string on leather. The purple is worked out of the inside of the muscle shell. They are woven broad as one's hand, and about two feet long. These they call belts, and give and receive at their treaties as the seals of their friendship." It was first known in New England as wampumpeag, and the art of making it was obtained from the Dutch, according to Hutchinson, about 1627."—*Morgan's League of the Iroquois.*

Having by the distribution of a few presents disposed the Indians to a favorable hearing, the colonel announced the expected arrival of a new governor, who would meet them in a short time with presents, and hear all of their grievances. Until then, he charged them to live in harmony with their English brethren. In reference to the incursions upon the Southern Indians, he was exceedingly grieved to learn that some of their people had returned with scalps and prisoners from the Catawbas, with whom, in his presence, they had made such a solemn treaty; and that unless this affair was speedily settled, it would remain an indelible stain upon the character and faith of their nation. He therefore urged them to immediately return the prisoners, and commit no farther hostilities. In regard to the French—" are you willing," said he, "that they should dispossess you of the rich lands and fair fields along the Ohio, your ancestral inheritance! No, rather quench the fire already lighted by them, at Swegachey,[1] and call in your warriors that have wandered off, that united, you may crush them! The paths, likewise, to this place, are almost choked with weeds, and the fire that once burned so brightly, nearly extinguished." He was therefore charged by the governor, to rekindle the fire with such wood, as should never go out. "I now," he continued, "renew the fire, sweep and clean all your rooms with a new white wing, and leave it hanging near the fire place, that you may use it for cleaning all the dust and dirt, which may have been brought in by strangers, no friends to you or us." By such appeals, was there a direct road opened to the hearts of these metaphor-loving people.

Two days afterwards, Red Head thanked him for giving the Six Nations notice of the expected arrival of the new governor; adding that whenever he chose to convene them they would cheerfully attend. In the meantime, brother Warraghiyagey might rest assured that the ancient friendship for the English was undiminished. It was not

---

[1] La Presentation, now Ogdensburgh.

CHAP. with their consent, he continued, that the French had
XII. occupied the Ohio, but really they did not know what the
1753. English and French together intended; "for they were
already so hemmed in by both, that hardly a hunting place
was left; so that even if they should find a bear in a tree,
there would immediately appear an owner of the land, to
challenge the property." Regarding the Catawbas, their
answer was less satisfactory. They deplored, it is true, the
violation of the treaty, but declined giving a definite
answer upon this point, until the meeting with the new
governor.

This conference, considering the previously excited state
of the Indians, was considered by the colonel as quite
successful; a full account of which was enclosed by him
in a letter to Mr. Clinton upon his return home on the
twenty-fourth.[1]

Mr. Clinton was at his country seat at Flushing, Long
Island, when his successor, Sir Danvers Osborne, arrived.[2]
This was on Sunday, the seventh of October. The council, mayor, corporation, and the chief citizens, met the new
governor on his arrival, and escorted him to the council
chamber. The following day, Mr. Clinton called upon
him, and they both dined with the members of the council.
On Wednesday morning, Mr. Clinton administered to him

---

[1] For this letter, as well as for a full and detailed account of this meeting at Onondaga, the reader is referred to the *Documentary History of New York*, ii, 630.

It will be noticed that nothing was said to the Indians at this time in relation to "burying the hatchet." Shortly before the conference, Colonel Johnson wrote to Mr. Clinton that in the present state of hostilities with the French, he did not think it advisable to take the hatchet out of their hands; and by the advice of the council, to whom his letter was referred, Mr. Clinton countermanded his instruction to Johnson in this particular.—*Council minutes.*

[2] Mr. Clinton, whose health had been much impaired by the severity of the American winters, had often requested to be recalled, and at one time had disposed of all his furniture preparatory to that step. It was not, however, until this year that the crown saw fit to grant the required permission and appoint a successor.

the oath of office and delivered to him the seals; at the same time delivering to James De Lancey his commission as lieutenant governor. As soon as these forms were finished, Governor Osborne, attended by the council and Mr. Clinton, set out for the town hall, where the new commission was usually read to the people. Scarcely, however, had the procession advanced a few steps, when the rabble, incited, it is said, by the De Lancey faction, insulted Mr. Clinton so grossly, as to compel him to leave the party, and retire into the fort. In the evening cannon were fired, bon fires lighted, fireworks displayed, and the whole city was given up to a delirium of joy. Amid all these rejoicings, the new governor sat in his room gloomy and sad, and seemingly averse to conversation retired early. On Thursday morning he informed the council that his strict orders were to insist upon an indefinite support for the government, and desired to have the opinion of the board upon the probabilities of its success.[1] It was universally agreed by the members present, that the assembly never would submit to this demand, and that a permanent support could not be enforced. Turning to Mr. Smith, who had hitherto remained silent, he requested his opinion, which being to the same effect as that just expressed, Mr. Osborne sighed, and leaning against the window with his face partially concealed exclaimed, in great mental distress, "Then what am I sent here for!"[2] That same evening he was so unwell that a physician was summoned, with whom he conversed for a little time, and then retired to his chamber, where he spent most of the night in arranging his private affairs. In the morning he was found suspended from the top of the garden fence, dead.[3]

Sir Danvers Osborne had lost a wife to whom he was passionately attached, shortly before coming to New York.

---

[1] Council minutes.

[2] Smith.

[3] Manuscript affidavits of Philip Crosby and John Milligan before the council. Sworn to, Oct. 12, 1753, and now preserved in the secretary of state's office. Albany, N. Y.

This acting upon a mind morbidly sensitive, had thrown him into a melancholy bordering upon insanity. He came to the government, charged with instructions much more stringent in their tone than those given to his predecessor; and knowing the difficulty which Mr. Clinton experienced during his administration, he saw before him only a succession of storms and tempests. Almost the first words of the city corporation in their address to him in the town hall, —"that they would not brook any infringement of their liberties civil and religious,"—convinced Mr. Osborne of the utter impossibility of the task assigned him. All these causes working upon a morbid state of mind,—wishing to carry out his instructions on the one hand, yet seeing its utter hopelessness on the other,—produced a temporary insanity, in which state he committed the rash act. Party rage, it is true, threw out suspicions of unfair play; and the council even thought it worth while to appoint a committee to investigate more fully the circumstances of his death; but these suspicions, it was made clearly evident, were entirely without foundation.[1]

Immediately on the death of Governor Osborne, Mr. De Lancey, by virtue of his commission as lieutenant governor, assumed the reins of government. The role which he was now to play, though difficult, was acted with his usual shrewdness and address. He had now to convince the ministry that he was zealous in the promotion of the interests of the crown; while at the same time, if he would retain his own popularity, he must show the assembly that he was true to his former principles, and by no means required a compliance with the instructions, which, on the part of his majesty, he should present to them. Of the instructions given by the crown to Osborne, which were now to be submitted by his successor, the thirty-ninth article was the most obnoxious. The impression was prevalent that the increasing power of Mr. De Lancey, and the ferment raised against Mr. Clinton's administration,

---

[1] Council minutes.

was the occasion of the insertion of this article; providing as it did, for an indefinite support, and a competent salary to all the civil officers of the colony.[1]

The lieutenant governor in his opening message to the assembly, the last day of October, with consummate tact, said: "You will perceive by the thirty-ninth article of his majesty's instructions to Sir Danvers Osborne, (copies of which I shall herewith deliver you) how highly his majesty is displeased at the neglect of and contempt shown to his royal commissions and instructions, by your passing laws of so extraordinary a nature, and by such your unwarrantable proceedings, particularly set forth in this instruction; hence also his majesty's royal pleasure as to these matters will appear, and what he expects from you. On this head, I must observe to you, that by our excellent constitution the executive power is lodged in the crown; that all government is founded on a confidence that every person will discharge the duties of his station; and if there shall be any abuse of power that the legal and regular course is to make application to his majesty, who, having a fraternal tenderness to all his subjects, is always ready to hear and redress their grievances." To the assembly, in particular, he adds: "I must earnestly press it upon you, that in preparing your bill for the support of government and other public services, you pay a due regard to his majesty's pleasure signified in his instructions; and frame them in such a manner, as, when laid before me for my assent, I may give it consistent with my duty to his majesty." Could anything be more satisfactory to the ministry *in appearance* than this message? "As his majesty's representative, he was obliged to urge their compliance with seeming sincerity and warmth; but as James De Lancey, their old friend and best adviser, it was his real sentiment,

---

[1] Letter to a nobleman. Mass. Hist. Col., vol. 7, II series, p. 81.

The members comprising the executive council at this time, were Messrs. Colden, Alexander, Kennedy, De Lancey, Clarke, jun., Murray, Holland, Johnson, Chambers, and Smith

that never ought they to submit.[1] The answer of the assembly was equally studied;—"On reading the thirty-ninth article of his majesty's instructions to Sir Danvers Osborne, your honor's immediate predecessor, we are extremely surprised to find that the public transactions of this colony have been so maliciously represented to our most gracious sovereign. We can, sir, with truth and justice affirm, that his majesty has not in his dominions, a people more firmly, and that from principles of real affection, devoted to his person, family and government, than the inhabitants of this colony. And we are greatly at a loss to discover in what instances the peace and tranquility of the colony have been disturbed, or wherein order and government have been subverted. If the course of justice has been obstructed, or in any case perverted, it has been by the direction or through the means of Mr. Clinton, late governor of this province, who sent peremptory orders to the judges, clerk, and sheriff of Dutchess county, to stay process, and stop the proceedings in several cases of private property depending in that court, and also did in other counties commissionate judges and justices of known ill character and extreme ignorance; and others were so shamefully ignorant and illiterate, as to be unable to write their own names, from whence we greatly fear that justice has in many cases been partially, or very unduly administered."[2] By such false charges did the assembly attempt to injure Mr. Clinton, for the sake of gratifying its personal enmity. False they undoubtedly were. The suits commenced in Dutchess county, to which allusion is here made, were brought against their captains by those who had deserted the expedition to Canada in 1746; and Mr. Clinton had confessed at the time to the house, that his letters to the justices had been written ignorantly and in haste, and that if any one was injured he would pay out of his own purse his damages. As to the charge of

---

[1] Letter to a nobleman.
[2] Council minutes.

appointing ignorant men, he was not the only governor who had erred in a similar manner; and indeed Mr. De Lancey himself was not free from the same charge.[1]

The change in the administration, was, however, productive of one good result—that of infusing into the assembly a desire to take active measures for the defence of the province. All the wishes of the governor on this point—as indeed on every other—were promptly responded to. On his sending down to them a letter from the earl of Holdeness, urging that measures should be immediately taken to resist the incursion of the French, it was determined to assist the neighboring colonies, some of whom had written for aid, and to meet force by force. Eight hundred pounds were voted for Indian presents, and one hundred and fifty pounds for his voyage to Albany. Fifteen hundred and fifty pounds were voted for his salary,—a much larger sum than ever before given to any lieutenant governor; and also the arrearages of his pay as chief justice up to the twelfth of October.[2] Before the close of the session, an elaborate complaint to the crown, and a representation to the board of trade against Mr. Clinton were drawn up, and forwarded through Mr. De Lancey and Mr. Charles to the home government. The assembly was then prorogued to the first Tuesday of the following March,—the lieutenant governor "tenderly remarking before they parted, that they "must be sensible they had not acted with his majesty's royal instructions."[3]

Upon the death of Sir Danvers Osborne, Mr. Clinton retired to the west end of Long Island, whence he embarked shortly afterward for England. Before he sailed, Mr. De Lancey, anxious to secure his influence in England, endeavored to effect a reconciliation, and doubtless would have succeeded, had not Mrs. Clinton, by her influence,

---
[1] Letter to a nobleman.
[2] Council minutes.
[3] Smith.

thwarted his designs.[1] On his return home, Mr. Clinton received the governorship of Greenwich hospital, a sinecure,[2] and on the death of Admiral Stewart in the month of March, 1757, became admiral of the fleet. " Having thus obtained the highest rank in the service, with unsullied reputation, and the justly acquired character of meriting, on all occasions, the good will of his countrymen, he died on the tenth of July, 1761, in the seventy-fifth year of his age."[3]

The character of Mr. Clinton has not, I think, been fairly drawn. Those, upon whose opinions his character rests, were persons living at the same day, and who, influenced by party strife, were not in a position to judge impartially. He was an uncouth and unlettered admiral, who had been, through the Newcastle interest, appointed to the chair of governor. He was evidently unsuited to his position; and his former profession, in which he had always been accustomed to command, illy fitted him to brave the rebuffs and the opposition of party faction. His manner, too, was not such as to win friends. Having to depend entirely upon the advice of those around him, he was often the dupe of those better versed in the arts of diplomacy than himself. But I look in vain for that love of ease, to the neglect of his official duties, of which he is accused by Mr. Smith. On the contrary, although he relied too much on the advice of others for his own good, yet it was caused more by a consciousness of a lack of education, than by a desire to shirk action. In the care of the Indians he was indefatigable, as appears by his large correspondence with Colonel Johnson and the officers of the different frontier posts. He labored incessantly with his assembly to make them realize the condition of the colony, and had they met his views half way, or even manifested a tythe of his energy,

---

[1] Letter to a nobleman.

[2] The administration of Mr. Clinton, as governor of the colony, occupied ten years, he having arrived as governor in September 1743.

[3] *Biographia Navalis*, by John Charnock, London, 1790.

the province of New York would not have presented such an inviting field for the encroachments of the French. He is accused of amassing by unfair means a large fortune while governor, yet he freely advanced out of his private purse large sums for the exigencies of the Indian affairs, and many times saved the Six Nations from defection, and the province from the horrors of a predatory warfare, when it was impossible to rouse the assembly to a sense of danger. Indeed, I think it may safely be said, that had it not been for the untiring efforts of Mr. Clinton and Colonel Johnson, the Six Nations would have been completely won over by the French, and the fire-brand and tomahawk carried down to the very gates of New York.

CHAPTER XIII.

1753—1754.

CHAP. XIII.

1753.

The period is now reached, when the active public life of Colonel Johnson begins. In order to correctly appreciate his future career, it is necessary to understand fully the complications which had again arisen between the English and the French; and which led to a renewal of hostilities between those two nations, finally culminating in the war, which shook both hemispheres to their very centres.

The treaty of Aix La Chapelle, as remarked in the last chapter, was in its effect only a truce. The boundaries between the lands belonging to the crowns of England and France, were left as indefinite after, as before the treaty; and consequently, those lands, to the possession of which both claimed a right, were still in dispute. The valley of the Ohio, with its noble forests and alluvial meadows, presented to the eyes of both governments a tempting prize, which each was unwilling to relinquish. The grounds on which France founded her right to the ownership of this fair domain, were discovery and occupancy. She insisted that La Salle, Father Marquette and others had sailed down the Mississippi, and that settlements had been made in the vicinity of Lake Michigan and on the Wabash, long before it had been travelled by any Englishman. On this point, however, the statements of the early French writers are very confused, and the fact itself is difficult to substantiate. The claims of England were infinitely broader. She had from the very first claimed from the Atlantic to the Pacific, on the ground that the discovery and possession of the sea board, was a discovery of the whole country lying between the two oceans. So far, indeed, as actual discovery was an argument, she insisted upon it very little. It is true, that in 1742, John Howard, crossing the mountains, launched a canoe of Buffalo hide, and sailed down the Ohio, reaching the Mississippi, only to be captured by the French. Conrad Weiser, the Pennsylvania interpreter, had also in 1748 taken a trip to Logstown, an Indian canton on the Ohio, and distributed presents to the Indians. This, however, could give the English no claim, as neither of those persons made any settlements; and besides, the entire valley through which the former sailed, had been trapped and traversed long before by the French hunters and traders.

But the chief argument on which the English based their claim to the ownership of the lands west of the Alleghanies was, that the Ohio valley belonged to the Six Nations, and that when they in 1684, at Albany, placed all their lands under the protection of England, this valley was also included. Aside from this right to protect their lands, which—under the supposition that the Six Nations were correct in their claim to the lands in question—was undeniable, the English declared that many of the western lands were actually purchased by them from the Indians at the treaty held in Lancaster in 1744. A few deeds of land were at that time unquestionably given; and among them one in which was recognized the right of the king "to all lands that are or by his majesty's appointment shall be within the colony of Virginia." Under this deed —although it was repudiated by the Indians at Logstown, in 1752—the English relied in all their subsequent proceedings. After this, settlements were farther extended westward, as the desire of the whites to enlarge their trade with the Indians increased, until in 1748 several individuals, among whom were Augustine and Laurence, brothers of George Washington, formed an association under the name of the Ohio Company; and petitioned the crown for a grant of six hundred thousand acres of land west of the Alleghanies. The object of this enterprise was to own lands, upon which to establish trading houses, and import the furs obtained from the Indians, receiving in return European goods.[1] These lands were to be principally located upon the south side of the Ohio, and to include all the region that was embraced between the Monongahela and the Kanawha rivers; the company reserving to itself the privilege of settling a portion upon the north side, should it be deemed advisable. As no permament settlement, however, could be made by the company with any hope of success without some definite arrangement with the Indians, the government of Virginia was petitioned to invite them to a treaty, at which a better title to the lands to be settled, could be obtained. As a preliminary step to this measure, Christopher Gist was sent to explore the country, and report his observations to the board. Pursuing his instructions, Mr. Gist, in the winter of 1751, went down the south bank of the river as far as the Kanawha, in the vicinity of which, he spent several months, taking accurate observations of the quality of the land, and its suitableness for the object proposed.[2] Finding, however, that no farther progress could be made until the Indians—who influenced by the French traders now regarded with extreme suspicion the designs of the English—had been won over, commissioners were sent in May 1752, to Logstown to treat with the Mingoes, Shawnees and Ohio Indians. On the Lancaster treaty being produced, and the western lands under that treaty claimed, the chiefs indignantly replied that "they had not heard of any sale west of the warriors' road, which ran at the foot of the Alleghany ridge." While they acknowledged the treaty of Lancaster, and the authority of the Six Nations, they denied that it gave the English any claim to land west of the Alleghanies; but, added the half king, "as the French have already struck our friends, the Miamis, we

---

[1] Sparks's *Washington*, ii, 478.
[2] Idem.

therefore desire that our brothers of Virginia will build a strong house at the fork of the Monongahela." Not satisfied, however, with this, the commissioners prevailed upon Captain Montour to use his influence with the Indians, to effect a sale of the lands in question.[1] The influence of the half breed was successful; and upon the thirteenth of June a deed, signed by all the chiefs, was given, "confirming the Lancaster treaty in its full effect" and guarantying that the settlements south-east of the Ohio should not by them be molested.[2]

The French, meanwhile, were not indifferent to the designs of the English. It was evident to them, that if the latter were allowed to establish settlements and trading posts along the Ohio, it would interfere grievously with their own plans for its possession. The governors of Canada —generally military men—had watched their rivals with jealous eyes; and for several years had selected and fortified such positions as would best command an ascendency over the Indians, and secure a rendezvous from which to make incursions upon the northern frontiers.[3] The spiritual arm was also called to their aid, and missionary stations, "deep in the wilderness," quietly went on with the work of conversion. As soon therefore as La Jonquière, the Canadian governor, heard of the formation of the Ohio company, deeming it an intrusion into "the dominions of his most Christian majesty," he wrote to the governors of New York and Pennsylvania, informing them of the encroachments of the English traders upon French territory, and threaten-

---

[1] Probably Henry Montour, the Indian Interpreter—son of Catherine Montour—to whom allusion has been made in a former chapter.

[2] In this discussion of the French and English claims to the Ohio valley, I have freely consulted a very able paper in the *North American Review* for July 1839,—entitled, "A review of travels through the interior parts of North America, in the years 1766, 1767, and 1768." It has been stated that a few Iroquois chiefs were present at the Logstown treaty. This however, is denied by Colonel Johnson in a letter to Governor Clinton. *Doc. His. N. Y.*, ii, 624.

[3] Marshall.

ing that unless they immediately withdrew he should seize them "wherever found."[1] No notice being taken of this threat, La Jonquière proved its sincerity by seizing, in the summer of 1752, some English traders among the Twigtwees, and confining them for a time at Presque Isle on Lake Erie, where a strong fort at that time was erecting. Simultaneously, by a chain of posts along the French creek and Alleghany river, a communication was opened from Presque Isle to the Ohio, which was kept clear by detachments of troops stationed at convenient distances;—twelve hundred men being sent at one time, as was mentioned in the last chapter, for this purpose.

The Ohio company, justly considering these proceedings as a direct intrusion upon the lands which, as part of Virginia, had been granted it by the crown, complained bitterly of this grievance, and called upon Robert Dinwiddie, the lieutenant governor of that province, to demand that these aggressions should be stopped. This gentleman having laid the matter before his assembly, that body resolved that a messenger should be sent to Le Gardeur St. Pièrre, commander of the French troops then stationed in the west, to remonstrate with him against these encroachments.

The messenger to whom was entrusted this delicate mission, was George Washington. His coolness, knowledge of woodcraft, and familiarity with hardship, acquired in his profession of surveyor, eminently qualified him for the undertaking. Late in October, 1753, he set out from Williamsburgh, and arrived at Wells creek[2] in fourteen days. Here being joined by an Indian and a French interpreter, the young envoy, with Gist as a guide, hastened forward. Before he would reach his destination, four hundred miles of a trackless wilderness was to be traversed, full of savage men and savage beasts, and deep with the early snows of winter. Yet in the face of sleet, and rain, and

---

[1] Marshall. La Jonquière to Clinton, Col Hist. N. Y.
[2] Cumberland.

snow—through tangled underbrush and across icy precipices—he pushed on, and upon the eleventh of December reached fort La Boeuf,[1] at the head of the western branch of French creek, the headquarters of the French commandant. St. Pièrre received him with great courtesy; and after remaining three or four days, during which he employed himself in taking accurate observations of the strength and position of the fort, he set out on his return, bearing with him a sealed letter to Dinwiddie from the French commandant[2]

The answer of St. Pièrre,—which was to the effect that he had taken possession of the Ohio under the authority of his general, the governor of Canada, to whom he would refer the matter and abide by his decision,—convinced the assembly of Virginia that the Ohio would not be given up without a severe struggle. Acting with these views, Governor Dinwiddie wrote to the board of trade informing it that a descent of the Ohio was meditated early in the spring by some fifteen hundred French and Indians, having for its design the entire occupation of the valley of that river. At the same time he sent expresses to the governors of New York and Pennsylvania for aid, and proceeded, at the suggestion of his council, to raise two companies of troops—one of which was to be given to Washington, while a backwoodsman, by the name of Trent, was to raise the other and proceed at once to the frontier, to aid in completing a fort, already begun by the Ohio company at the confluence of the Alleghany and the Monongahela.

Having thus briefly sketched the progress of events in the Ohio valley up to the opening of this year—1754, I now return to affairs in the province of New York.

The general assembly met on the ninth of April. In his opening message, Mr. De Lancey informed the legislature of the recent encroachments of the French upon the terri-

---

[1] Waterford.

[2] For a full account of this journey, see Washington's journal on this occasion in Sparks's *Washington*, vol. ii, Appendix.

tory of his majesty, and of their preparations for its secure occupancy by the erection of a chain of forts from Lake Erie to the Ohio. In connection with this, the determination of Virginia to resist these aggressions, and her request for aid from the colony of New York was alluded to—as was also the defenceless condition of their own northern frontier, and the urgent necessity for the erection of more forts for its protection. The importance of the trading post at Oswego, moreover, was such as to need no argument to induce them to vote a sum sufficient for its thorough repair, for, situated on the direct route of the French to the Ohio, it was liable at any time to be attacked. It was his hope, therefore, in view of the expectations which his majesty had expressed in the earl of Holdernesse's letter, that ample means would be granted not only for transporting two of the independent companies to Virginia, treating with the Six Nations, and fortifying the northern frontier, but also for their share of any expense that might be incurred by the colonies for the public welfare. The assembly, in their answer on the twelfth, admitted that the several matters recommended by his excellency were certainly of the utmost importance "to all his majesty's colonies upon the continent, and ought to be esteemed a public concern." In view likewise of the active operations of the French, and their efforts to secure all the Indian nations in their interest, Virginia, they thought, was deserving of all praise for her vigorous action. So far all was well; but with a niggardly spirit, rendered the more glaring by their seeming appreciation of the critical state of affairs, they regretted, in the very same paragraph, that the paucity of the colony would prevent them affording all that assistance to their sister colony that they could wish. The reason of this inability, they said, was the large debts that the colony had already incurred for its own protection,—especially the great expense to which it had been subjected in building the forts at Albany, Schenectady, Fort Hunter and Oswego. Morover, all that the colony could raise would be hardly sufficient for the defence of its own frontiers, menaced as much by the French settlement at Crown Point, as were the southern colonies by the forts along the Ohio[1] They, however, voted one thousand pounds for the aid of Virginia, four hundred and fifty-six pounds for doubling the garrison at Oswego, and eleven hundred and fifty-six pounds for Indian presents, and the expense of the coming treaty. They also agreed to pay the charges incident to repairing Oswego, and bear their share in erecting forts along the frontier for mutual protection.[2]

The excuse of the assembly for not doing more in aid of its sister colony, had it come from a body of men that had uniformly proved its patriotism by being ever alive to the interests of the colony, would have been amply sufficient; but emanating, as it did, from an assembly which had always manifested the greatest indifference to the welfare of the province, and which had left the settlers upon the frontier exposed to all the horrors of a merciless predatory warfare, its excuse was little better than a miserable shift. The trading house at Oswego had been left for two years past with a miserable roof of bark, although its condition had been frequently called to their attention,[3] and the frontier fortifications were not in a much better condition. The fort at Saratoga had been burned and abandoned because they had refused to keep it in a proper state of defence; the friendship of the Six Nations had been spurned, and Colonel Johnson quarreled with, for bringing these matters to their attention,—so that this sudden anxiety for the security and welfare of the colony, was simply ridiculous. The argument, advanced by the assembly—that the king should afford the means for the protection of his own dependencies was true, so far as the *rights* of the crown were involved in the defence of the colonies; but the protection of the firesides of the colonists themselves, when

---

[1] Journals of the assembly.
[2] Idem. See also Smith.
[3] Manuscript council minutes.

only their individual interests were at stake, certainly should not have been a burden upon the home government.

Mr. De Lancey, deeming the answer of the assembly unsatisfactory, reminded it in a special message on the nineteenth, of the resolution passed at its fall session "to repel force by force." Quoting an extract from a letter lately received from the board of trade—to the effect that high expectations had been raised in the mind of his majesty by that resolution,—he begged that it would act promptly upon this occasion, and send to Virginia the assistance which she so earnestly requested. To this the house replied by referring him to the resolution in question—" that they would assist any of his majesty's colonies to repel force by force *in case they were invaded*," and evasively resolved that there had as yet been no invasion, as the fort which had been built by the French was at French creek, and " at a considerable distance from the river Ohio," the cause of the dispute. The executive at once answered this quibble by stating that the forts in question had been erected in the country of the Eries—a nation entirely annihilated by the Six Nations—and that as by the treaty of Utretcht, the Six Nations were the subjects of Great Britain, the building of the forts "was evidently an invasion of his majesty's territories, though perhaps, not so clearly within the limits of any colony." The assembly, however, was not to be moved, and besides the bill for raising the supplies had already been sent up to the council for the action of that body. This bill, which provided that the different sums should be issued by the treasurer on the receipts of the persons named therein, and not by the warrant from the governor, nor with the "consent of his majesty's council," was deemed by the council not to be in accordance with the "commission and instructions," and was therefore sent back to the house for revision. This the latter refused to do, alleging that the bill was according "to a method long pursued, settled with, and solemnly agreed to, by the late Governor Clinton;" but in answer to another message from the executive, counselling unanimity and dispatch, it agreed to frame a bill which should not be obnoxious to the above objections. Before, however, the bill was reconsidered, it proceeded to vote the supplies which it was to contain, but made no allusion to the one thousand pounds lately voted to Virginia. This omission was pointed out to their notice by Mr. De Lancey in a special message on the fourth of May; and the assembly were specially urged not to omit the sum allowed to Virginia, which, by its having been previously voted, would remain an indellible stain on its reputation. In its answer the same day the house bluntly charged the council with the delay, and the withdrawal of aid from Virginia. They farther said that when they promised to frame a bill which should obviate all objections, they referred only to those provisions which were absolutely necessary for the security of the colony—and that they did not consider themselves chargeable with any ill faith. In conclusion they uttered a growl at the large sums of money they were forced to expend by so long a sitting, especially when they could be of no service, and requested that they might all be dismissed to their homes. Mr. De Lancey in his reply stated that he should lay a candid statement of their conduct before the king; and having given his assent to those bills that were ready, prorogued the assembly.

Meanwhile, Virginia was not idle. The assembly, though not without great unwillingness, voted ten thousand pounds for the defence of the province, and increased the two companies already formed to six.[1] In answer also to the solicitations of Dinwiddie, a few troops arrived from South Carolina, and intelligence was received at nearly the same time that South Carolina had voted twelve thousand pounds for defence, and that four hundred volunteers would soon be on the way to Winchester. The prospect now looked more cheering; and a regiment of six hundred men was immediately raised and placed under the command of

---
[1] Governor Dinwiddie to Lieutenant Governor De Lancey.

CHAP. XIII.
1754.

Colonel Joshua Fry, Washington being made second in command, with the rank of lieutenant colonel. The governor, in order to stimulate the military ardor of the people and give energy to enlistments, issued a proclamation, offering a bounty of two hundred thousand acres of land on the Ohio river, to be divided among those troops who should enlist for the proposed expedition, free from all quit rents for fifteen years. [1]

All now was bustle and activity. Captain Trent, with forty-one men, pushed ahead to occupy the fort at the Monongahela. Young men, lured on by the tempting bounty, and seeing themselves in the future snugly esconced in comfortable farms, hastened to enlist. Cannon which had arrived from England for the fort at the fork, were hurried forward. All day long the farrier plied his forge, and at night the sparks from its huge chimney told of the work that was still going on within. Wagons were got in readiness, old firelocks mended, and swords which had been handed down as heir looms from father to son, were taken down from over the fireplace, polished, and made ready for service.

As soon as the genial rays of the sun had unlocked the icy chains which bound the western streams, Colonel Washington set out from Alexandria, with two companies —all that had been collected. The march was slow and painful. The melting snows and the warm days and cold nights of early spring rendered the roads nearly impassable. The baggage moved forward slowly from the scarcity of wagons in which to transport it, and the "self-willed and ungovernable" recruits under Washington rendered efficient concert of action almost impossible. Wills creek was at length reached upon the twentieth of April. Just before his entrance into this settlement, Colonel Washington was met by the ensign of Captain Trent's company. The intelligence brought by this messenger was mournful in the extreme. It was, that while his company were at work

---

[1] Sparks.

upon the fort, a body of one thousand French troops, commanded by Contrecœur, in three hundred and sixty bateaux, had dropped down the river from Venango, and planting their artillery before the fort, summoned them to surrender.[1] Although this estimate of the French forces was greatly exaggerated, yet resistance was of course hopeless, and the garrison surrendered, being allowed to retain their arms and tools. The fort was forthwith occupied by Contrecoeur, completed and fortified with the cannon he had brought with him, and named in honor of the Canadian governor, Fort Du Quesne.[2] This was the beginning of the war.[3]

On the reception of this news Washington halted, and sent back expresses to the governors of Virginia and Pennsylvania, informing them of his critical situation, and urging them to hasten forward reinforcements. At the same time he called a council of war, in which, after considering the evils that would result from the raw and undisciplined troops being left in idleness, it was determined to push forward at once to the confluence of the Red Stone creek and Monogahela, and employ the men in erecting a fortification at that place. While Washington, with his men, was preparing to cross the Youghiogeny by constructing a bridge over that river, a belt of wampum on the twenty-fifth of May reached him from the Half King. "Be on your guard," said the belt, "the French army intend to strike the first English whom they shall see." Another report, the same day, confirmed this warning, with the additional intelligence that the French were only eighteen miles distant. Being ignorant of their strength or of their movements, Washington fell back to the Great Meadows, threw up entrenchments, and cutting away the underbrush, prepared, to use his own language, "a charming field for an encounter." Scouts, mounted upon wagon horses, were at the same time sent out to reconnoitre, but they returned without discovering any signs of the enemy.

---
[1] Manuscript letter: Washington to Governor Hamilton of Pennsylvania.
[2] Now Pittsburg.
[3] Sparks.

CHAP. On the twenty-seventh Gist arrived from Wills creek, and
XIII.
reported that a party of fifty French had visited that settle-
1754. ment the day previous, and that he had himself seen their
trail within five miles of the Great Meadows. In the evening of the same day, another express arrived from the Half King, who, with a party of his warriors was about six miles distant, to the effect that an armed body of the French were skulking in the vicinity of his camp. Washington at once took forty men, and pushing out into the night, black with wind and tempest, and stumbling through windfalls and over sharp rocks, reached the camp of the Half King a little while before day. A council was immediately held, and two Indians having discovered the position of the enemy in a rocky ravine, it was determined at once to attack. Marching in single file with the troops on the right and the Indians on the left, they came suddenly upon the French, though not so quickly, but that they had time to seize their arms. Both parties fired simultaneously, and a brisk action ensued, which, lasting for a quarter of an hour, resulted in the complete discomfiture of the enemy, whose commander, M. De Jumonville, and ten of his men were killed, and twenty-two taken prisoners.

Colonel Fry dying suddenly two days afterward at Patterson's creek, as he was hastening forward to unite his forces with the advance, the entire command devolved upon Colonel Washington. Fearing that so soon as the news of De Jumonville's defeat reached the main body of the French, a large force would be sent out to meet him, he set his men to building a stockaded fort at the Great Meadows, which was appropriately called Fort Necessity. Several companies from South Carolina arriving at this time, serious difficulty arose between the commander of the South Carolina troops and Washington, in relation to rank, and the latter to avoid altercation, ordered his own men to advance with the intention of investing Fort Du Quesne. Scarcely, however, had he advanced thirteen miles, when intelligence was received through Indian runners, that Fort Du Quesne had been largely reinforced by troops from Canada, and that a large force of French and Indians were on their way to avenge the death of Jumonville. On the receipt of this intelligence, Washington immediately fell back to Fort Necessity, and began a moat around the stockade. Hardly had the hastily constructed works been made at all tenantable, when De Villiers, at the head of six hundred French and one hundred Indians, appeared in sight, and took possession of one of the eminences by which the fort was encompassed. A brisk fire of small arms was kept up by the French from behind trees, which was feebly returned by the men in the fort, owing to the rain which fell heavily having filled the trenches with water, and disabled many of their muskets, already sadly out of repair. The firing began at eleven o'clock in the morning, and lasted until eight in the evening, when De Villiers, fearing his ammunition would give out, sounded a parley, and sent into the garrison terms of capitulation. These terms, being interpreted to Washington, were accepted; and the next morning, on the fourth of July, the garrison, taking with them everything but their artillery, marched out of the fort, with colors flying and drums beating.

Thus were the French left in undisputed possession of the basin of the Ohio; and the evening guns, from the waters of Lake Erie to the Delta of the Mississippi, saluted the lillies of France, which now waved proudly in the evening breeze.

CHAPTER XIV.
1754.

While Washington was engaged in erecting his rude little fortress at the Great Meadows, an event of far greater moment was occurring at Albany. This was no less than a congress of commissioners from seven of the colonies, for the purpose of treating with the Six Nations, and uniting upon a plan of union for resisting the common enemy.

The letter from the earl of Holdernesse, advising that the colonies should "repel force by force," had first directed attention to the importance of concerted action in resisting French aggressions; and the reception, in the spring of this year, of letters from the lords of trade to the different colonial governors, directing that commissioners should be appointed to assemble at Albany—there to devise concerted action against the French—hastened the carrying out of this project. The object of this congress had been at first, nothing more than to conciliate the Six Nations, and prevent them from going over to the interest of the French.[1] Governor Shirley, however, had conceived, early in this year, a general union of all the colonies for mutual protection, and had taken the opportunity presented by this meeting, to suggest to the different governors that the delegates to the convention should be instructed by their constituents to mature a plan for a general union.[2]

The day appointed for the meeting of the commissioners was the fourteenth day of June, but they did not all arrive until the nineteenth.[3] The colonies of New Hampshire,

---

[1] Sparks. Governor De Lancey to the lords of trade.
[2] Holmes. Grahame. Shirley to Holdernesse January 7, 1754.
[3] The commissioners from the several colonies were James De Lancey, Joseph Murray, William Johnson, John Chambers and William Smith—

Rhode Island, Connecticut, Massachusetts, New York, Maryland and Pennsylvania, were all represented, making the whole number of delegates present twenty-five. Early in March, the governor of Virginia had written Mr. De Lancey that he was too much engaged in the military preparations necessary to repel encroachments along his own frontier,[1] to be present at this time; and the Carolinas were also too much occupied in treating with their own southern tribes, to give the treaty at Albany their attention. The sachems of the Six Nations, were still more backward, not making their appearance till the latter part of the month. The Mohawks were the last to arrive, and, indeed, the entire number of Indians present during the whole of the treaty did not exceed one hundred and fifty. There were those who did not scruple to attribute their delay to the influence of Johnson, who, they said, wishing to magnify his influence over the Indians, purposely held them back; and writers, who should have been better informed, have not failed to give countenance to this report.[2] The truth is, that the Indian commissioners felt piqued at the contrast presented between the reluctance shown by the Indians in coming to this council, and the alacrity with which they had attended the one held in 1748, when Johnson had the charge of their affairs, and prompted by jealousy, threw out these insinuations, as false as they were malicious. Hendrik explained the delay, so far as the Mohawks were concerned, by stating that the speech of Colonel Johnson at the Onondaga castle the preceding summer, had been attributed by the Six

---

New York. Samuel Welles, John Chandler, Thomas Hutchinson, Oliver Patridge, John Worthington—Massachusetts. Theodore Atkinson, Richard Wibird, Meshech Weare, Henry Sherburne—New Hampshire. William Pitkin, Roger Wolcott, Elisha Williams—Connecticut. Stephen Hopkins, Martin Howard—Rhode Island. John Penn, Benjamin Franklin, Richard Peters, Isaac Norris—Pennsylvania. Benjamin Tasker, Benjamin Barnes—Maryland.

[1] Manuscript council minutes.
[2] Messrs Livingston and Smith.

Nations to the Mohawks; and therefore lest they should be accused of the same in relation to the governor's speech, they tarried until the other castles should have arrived before them. The true cause, however, of the reluctance displayed by the Indians in coming to this treaty, and the fewness of their number was, that the continual rebuffs which they had met with in their endeavours to obtain assistance from the colony for the defence of their castles, discouraged them from any farther effort to obtain redress. The council, held at Onondaga the previous year by Colonel Johnson, although it had quieted, had not satisfied them. They still felt sore from the imposition to which they had been subjected in the sales of their land. Many of them,—especially the Senecas—were absolutely in a starving condition, caused by their having abstained, at the request of the English, from their annual hunts;[1] and numbers of the Onondagas and Cayugas had already gone to Oswegatchie and taken up their abode at that mission, finding there plenty to eat and ample protection under the guns of the fort for themselves and families. Indeed, the wonder is, considering these untoward circumstances, that so many of the Confederates were present; and had it not been for the influence of Hendrik —still, through his affection for Colonel Johnson, the fast friend of the English,—scarcely any castle of the Six Nations would have been represented.

The first few days were occupied by the commissioners in consulting upon the principal topics to be presented to the Indians, and in listening to several chiefs of the lesser castles in relation to the fraudulent surveys of their land. On the twenty-ninth, Mr. De Lancey,—who being the only governor present had been called to the chair— opened the treaty with a general speech which was interpreted to the Indians by Myndert Schuyler. In his speech, the lieutenant governor stated to the Confederates, that they had been invited hither to receive the presents sent by

---
[1] Manuscript council minutes.

the king, their father, and renew the ancient treaty made between all the colonies and their own nation; and that all the colonies had united in sending commissioners for this purpose except Virginia and the Carolinas, who though detained by the importance of their own affairs at home, nevertheless wished to be considered by them as present. " We come," he said "to strengthen and brighten the chain of friendship," and, continued he, at the same time handing Hendrik the chain belt, "this chain hath remained firm and unbroken from the beginning. This belt will represent to you our disposition to preserve it strong and bright, so long as the sun and moon shall endure; and in the name of the great king our father, and in behalf of all his majesty's colonies, we now solemnly renew, brighten, and strengthen the ancient covenant chain, and promise to keep the same inviolable and free from rust; and we expect the like confirmation and assurance on your part." The scattered manner, in which, departing from their ancient custom, the Confederates for the last few years had lived, was then adverted to; and they were specially urged to live together in their castles, and to call back those of their Onondaga and Cayuga brethren who had removed to Oswegatchie in defiance of the ancient covenant. "The French profess to be in perfect friendship with us as well as you. Notwithstanding this they are making continual encroachments upon us both. They have lately done so in the most insulting manner, both to the northward and westward. Your fathers, by their valor above one hundred years ago, gained a considerable country which they afterwards, of their own accord, put under the protection of the kings of Great Britain. The French are endeavoring to possess themselves of the whole country, although they have made the most express treaties with the English to the contrary. It appears to us that these measures of the French must necessarily soon interrupt and destroy all trade and intercourse between the English and the several Indian nations on the continent, and will block up and obstruct the great roads, which have hitherto been open, between you and your allies and friends who live at a distance. We want, therefore, to know whether these things appear to you in the same light as they do to us, or whether the French, taking possession of the lands in your country, and building forts between the lake Erie and the river Ohio, be done with your consent or approbation." "Therefore," he concluded, " open your hearts to us, and deal with us as brethren."

Three days afterward, the lieutenant governor attended by all the commissioners, in behalf of his majesty and the several colonies, met the Indians in the court house to hear their reply. As soon as they were seated, the sachems of the Six Nations, glittering with ornaments and clothed in their richest robes and feathers, came in and seated themselves with all the pomp of Indian ceremonial. Then amid a deep silence, Abraham, a sachem of the upper castle of the Mohawks and a brother of King Hendrik, rose and said:—" Brethren, you the governor of New York, and the commissioners of the other governments, are you ready to hear us?" The governor having replied in the affirmative, King Hendrik, venerable in years, rose and with all the dignity which his white hairs and majestic mien gave him, holding up the chain belt to the gaze of all, advanced a few steps, and thus spoke:

"*Brethren :* We return you all our grateful acknowledgements for renewing and brightening the covenant chain. This chain belt is of very great importance to our united nations, and all our allies. We will therefore take it to Onondaga, where our council fire always burns, and keep it—so securely, that neither thunder nor lightning shall break it. There will we consult over it; and as we have already added two links to it, so we will use our endeavors to add as many more links to it as lies in our power;[1] * * In the meantime we desire that you will

---

[1] The allusion is to two small Indian tribes which the Six Nations had lately taken into the Confederation

strengthen yourselves, and bring as many into this covenant chain as you possibly can.

"*Brethren:* As to the accounts you have heard of our living dispersed from each other, 'tis very true. We have several times endeavored to draw off these our brethren who were settled at Oswegatchie; but in vain, for the governor of Canada is like a wicked deluding spirit. However, as you desire, we shall persist in our endeavors." Then burning with indignation, as he recalled the long neglect with which his services had been rewarded by the English—his eyes flashing, and his whole frame quivering with the honest anger, which had so long been pent up within him—he exclaimed "You have asked us the reason of our living in this dispersed manner. The reason is *your neglecting us for three years past.*" Then taking a stick and throwing it behind him—"you have thus thrown us behind your backs and disregarded us; whereas the French are a subtile and vigilant people, ever using their utmost endeavors to reduce and bring our people over to them. * * *

"This is the ancient place of treaty, where the fire of friendship always used to burn; and 'tis now three years since we have been called to any public treaty here. 'Tis true there are commissioners here, but they have never invited us to smoke with them.[1] But the Indians of Canada come frequently and smoke here, which is for the sake of their beaver. But we hate them. We have not as yet confirmed the peace with them. 'Tis your fault, brethren, that we are not strengthened by conquest; for we would have gone and taken Crown Point, but you hindered us. We had concluded to go and take it, but we were told that it was too late and that the ice would not bear us. Instead of this, you burnt your own fort at Saratoga, and ran away from it, which was a shame and a scandal to you!" Then again kindling as he thought of the shameful remissness, which had left their own castles

---

[1] That is—have never invited us to any conference.

defenceless, he concluded in the same scathing language. "Look about your country, and see, you have no fortifications about you; no, not even to this city! Look at the French; *they are men;* they are fortifying every where! But, we are ashamed to say it, you are all like *women,* bare and open, without any fortifications!"

Thus closed one of the most eloquent Indian speeches ever uttered. A speech, which for its truth, vigor, and biting sarcasm, has never been equaled by any Indian orator—scarcely excelled by one of any other race—and which, " containing strains of eloquence which might have done honor to Tully or Demosthenes,"[1] will ever stand among the finest passages of rhetoric in either ancient or modern history.[2]

As soon as Hendrik had ended, his brother Abraham, rising up, spoke:

"*Brethren:* We would let you know what was our desire three years ago, when Colonel Johnson laid down the management of Indian affairs, which gave us great uneasiness. The governor then told us, it was not in his power to continue, him but that he would consult the council at New York; that he was going over to England, and promised to reccommend our desire, that Colonel Johnson should have the management of Indian affairs, to the king, that the governor might have power to reinstate him. We long waited in the expectation of this being done; but hearing no more of it, we embrace this opportunity of laying this belt before all our brethren here present, and desire them, that Colonel Johnson may be reinstated and have the management of Indian affairs; for we all

---

[1] *Gentleman's Magazine;* referring to this speech.

[2] This is not empty panegyric. In a manuscript letter before me written by Governor Shirley to Hendrik, through Colonel Johnson, Governor S. expresses himself in terms of the warmest admiration for Hendrik both as an orator and as a man; thanks him for his speech at Albany; and promises to recommend him to his majesty as the warm friend and fast ally of the English. Governor Livingston alluding to this speech also speaks of Hendrik as a "consummate orator."—*Vide Life of Livingston by Sedgwick,* 98.

lived happy whilst they were under his management, for we love him, and he us, and he has always been our good and trusty friend." Then before he sat down, he added with significant irony:—"*Brethren:*—I forgot something. We think our request about Colonel Johnson, which Governor Clinton promised to convey to the king our father, is drowned in the sea." Then turning himself around and facing the New York commissioners for Indian affairs, he closed by telling them that the fire at Albany was burned out, and requesting that they would take notice of what he said.

These speeches, as exponents of the state of feeling existing among the Confederates, were considered so important, as to cause them to be debated, by the commissioners, paragraph by paragraph; and the same committee—which had drafted the opening speech of the lieutenant governor upon the nineteenth, was requested to prepare a suitable answer to these also.[1] On the third of July the draft of the answer was submitted to the board of commissioners by Colonel Johnson, as chairman, and being approved, it was delivered to the Indians, by Mr. De Lancey on the fourth. Its tone was eminently kind and conciliatory. In it, the lieutenant governor expressed the gratification which it afforded all present, to learn of their good intentions, and know that it was not with their countenance that the French had entered upon the Ohio, and their lands. Some of the information, moreover, which they had communicated in their speech, was to himself and the commissioners not a little surprising. Although, he said, he had known for the past five years, of the encroachments of the French, yet it was only lately, that he was aware that they had been building forts for the protection of themselves and the Indians. "It is fortu-

---

[1] This committee consisted of William Johnson, Samuel Welles, Theodore Atkinson, Elisha Williams, Martin Howard Jr., Isaac Norris, and Benjamin Tasker Jr.

nate" he added, "that Mr. Weiser, who transacts the public business of Virginia and Pennsylvania with your nations, and is one of your council, and knows these matters well, is now present. Hear the account he gives, and this will set the matter in a true light." Conrad Weiser was here introduced, and a brief sketch of the French encroachments on the Ohio, was given by him to the Indians. Mr. De Lancey then continued—As to their dissatisfaction at the resignation of Colonel Johnson, he was sensible that while he had the management of their affairs they all lived happily and contentedly, but as Albany was the place where the ancient council fire was kindled, which was now almost extinguished, and as Colonel Johnson still declined acting, he had thought proper to rekindle the fire by appointing commissioners. "These" said he, "I shall direct to receive and consult with you upon all business that may concern our mutual interests; and I expect that you will for the future, according to the custom of your forefathers, apply to them. I shall give them directions that they treat you with the affection due to you as brethren. I shall therefore make trial of them another year; and if you do not meet with the kind treatment you have a right to expect, complain to this government, and effectual measures shall be taken for your satisfaction." Mr. Kellogg, the interpreter from Massachusetts Bay, then closed the conference for the day, by telling the Indians of several forts which the French were erecting on the Kenebec and Connecticut rivers, and also of some depredations lately committed in the colony of New Hampshire, by a party of the St. Francis Indians.

While the congress was sitting, Colonel Johnson, at the request of the commissioners, submitted a paper, containing his views on the management of the Six Nations, and the best method of defeating the designs of the French upon the Confederates. The suggestions were considered so judicious, as to lead the congress to vote that Mr. Franklin should be desired to give the thanks of the board to

Colonel Johnson, and request him to allow a copy to be taken by the commissioners of each colony for the consideration of their respective governments.

The chief measures urged by the colonel were, that garrisons should be established immediately in the most commodious situations among the Six Nations, from which the Indians should be supplied with food, until their own lands could be so protected as to furnish them with the means of subsistence. The French, moreover, obtained much of their influence over the Indians by having large stores of clothing and other necessaries for them at their different forts; and such kind of encouragement should likewise be extended by the English at Oswego, and at any other posts or trading houses that might hereafter be built in the Indian country. A strict look out at Oswego and at other points was recommended, to hinder the French from tampering with the Confederates; and military officers, he thought, should reside at each castle, and keep the government well advised of every occurrence. The building of a fort, also, at the Onondaga castle, properly garrisoned, was strongly urged, where should be stationed a missionary and a smith to repair their arms and utensils. The colonel, moreover, respectfully suggested, that young men well versed in grammar should reside among the Onondagas, Senecas and Mohawks, in order that they might become good interpreters in every dialect—a thing much needed. Finally the Six Nations should be reminded of their promise to extend the covenant chain to Detroit unless hindered by the French; consequently, if the latter were removed, there would be nothing in the way of the fulfilment of their agreement. This, the colonel thought, might " serve to show them the early and contrived encroachments of the French." These suggestions were considered so valuable, that Mr. De Lancey forwarded a copy of them to the board of trade, recommending their adoption.

Several more days were occupied in hearing and answering speeches from the Six Nations, the Schaticook and

River Indians; and on the eleventh, the Confederates, having renewed all their covenants, and sworn uncompromising hostility against the French, were dismissed seemingly pleased with the result.[1]

The Indians were not allowed to depart however, until the famous purchase from them of the Wyoming lands was effected;—an account of the origin of which, from the important bearing of the transaction on future events, must not be omitted.

"The first grants of land in America by the crown of Great Britain, were made with a lavishness which can exist only where acquisitions are without cost, and their value unknown; and with a want of provision in regard to boundaries, which could result only from entire ignorance of the country. The charters of the great western and southern Virginia companies, and of the colonies of Massachusetts Bay and Connecticut, were of this liberal and uncertain character. The charter of the Plymouth company covered the expanse from the fortieth to the forty-sixth degree of northern latitude, extending from the Atlantic to the Pacific ocean."[2] This charter was granted by King James I., under the great seal of England, in the most ample manner, on the third of November, 1620, to the duke of Lenox, the marquise of Buckingham, the earls of Arundel and Warwick and their associates, "for the planting, ruling, ordering and governing of New England in America." The charter of Connecticut was derived from the Plymouth company, of which the earl of Warwick was president. The grant was made in March, 1621, to Viscount Say and Seal, Lord Brook, and their associates.

---

[1] At this congress, a present from the king was distributed to the Indians, "of much greater value than ever before." The commissioners from New Hampshire made them a separate present. It is a custom among the Six Nations to give a name to their benefactors upon such occasions. The name which they gave to the province of New Hampshire was *So-Sâguax-owâne.* I have inquired of the Rev. Mr. Kirkland, the meaning of this name. He informed me that *So* signifies again; *Sâguâx*, a dish: and *owâne* large." Again a large dish.—*Belknap.*

[2] Gordon's *History of Pennsylvania.*

it was made in the most ample form, and also covered the country west of Connecticut to the extent of its breadth, being about one degree of latitude from sea to sea.[1] This grant was confirmed by the king in the course of the same year, and again in 1662. New York, or to speak more correctly in reference to that period, the New Netherlands, being then a Dutch possession, could not be claimed as a portion of these munificent grants, if for no other reason, for the very good and substantial one, that in the grant to the Plymouth company, an exception was made of all such portions of the territory as were "then actually possessed or inhabited by any other Christian province or state." But the round phraseology of the charters opened the door sufficiently wide for any subsequent claims, within the specified parallels of latitude, which the company, or its accessors, might find it either convenient or politic to interpose. And it appears that even at the early date of 1651, some of the people of Connecticut were already casting longing eyes upon a section of the valley of the Delaware. It was represented by these enterprising men that they had purchased the lands in question from the Indians, but that the Dutch had interposed obstacles to their settlement thereon. In reply to their petition, the commissioners of the united colonies asserted their right to the jurisdiction of the territory claimed upon the Delaware, and the validity of the purchases that had been made by individuals. "They protested against the conduct of the Dutch, and assured the petitioners that though the season was not meet for hostilities, yet if within twelve months, at their own charge, they should transport to the Delaware one hundred armed men, with vessels and ammunition approved by the magistrates of New Haven, and should be opposed

---

[1] Trumbull's *History of Connecticut*. Colonel Timothy Pickering, in his letter to his son, giving the particulars of the highhanded outrage committed upon him in Wyoming in 1788, in speaking of these grants, remarks:—" It seems natural to suppose by the terms of these grants, extending to the western ocean, that in early times the continent was conceived to be of comparatively little breadth."

by the Dutch, they should be assisted by as many soldiers as the commissioners might judge meet; the lands and trade of the settlement being charged with the expense, and continuing under the government of New Haven."[1] The project, however, was not pressed during the designated period, nor indeed does it seem to have been revived for more than a century afterward. Many changes of political and other relations had occurred during this long lapse of time. Disputes had arisen between the people of Connecticut and the New Netherlands, in regard to boundaries, which had been adjusted by negotiation and compromise. The colony of the New Netherlands had moreover fallen, by the fortunes of war, under the sway of the British crown. The colonies of New Jersey and Pennsylvania had also been planted. Various additional grants had been given by the crown, and other questions of territorial limits had been raised and adjusted. But in none of these transactions had Connecticut relinquished her claims of jurisdiction, and the preëmption right to the lands of the Indians lying beyond New York, and north of the fortieth degree of latitude, as defined in the original grant to the Plymouth company. The grant of the Plymouth company to Lord Say and Seal and Lord Brook, had been made fifty years before the grant to William Penn, and the conformation of that grant to Connecticut by royal charter, nineteen years prior to that conveyance.[2]

Unfortunately, moreover, from the laxity that prevailed among the advisers of the crown, in the granting of patents, as to boundaries, the patent to William Penn covered a portion of the grant to Connecticut, equal to one degree of latitude and five of longitude; and within this territory, thus covered by double grants, was situated the section

---

[1] This quotation is from Gordon. Colonel Pickering, in the letter already cited in a preceding note, addressed to his son, and privately printed for the use of his own family only, supposed that Connecticut did not set up any formal claim to lands west of New York and New Jersey, until just prior to the revolution. He was in error.

[2] Trumbull.

of the Delaware county heretofore spoken of; as also the yet richer and more inviting valley of Wyoming, toward which some of the more restless, if not enterprising sons of the Pilgrims were already turning their eyes with impatience.

The project of establishing a colony in Wyoming was started by sundry individuals in Connecticut in 1753, during which year an association was formed for that purpose called the Susquehanna company, and a number of agents were commissioned to proceed thither, explore the country, and conciliate the good will of the Indians. This commission was executed; and as the valley, though at that time in the occupancy of the Delawares, was claimed by the Six Nations, a purchase from that Confederacy was determined upon. To this end, a deputation of the company, the associates of which already numberd about six hundred persons, embracing many gentlemen of wealth and character, was directed to repair to this present congress at Albany, and if possible effect the purchase. Their movements were not invested with secresy, and James Hamilton, the governor of Pennsylvania, becoming acquainted with them, was not slow in interposing objections to the procedure—claiming the lands as falling within the charter of Penn, and of course belonging, the preëmptive right at least, to the proprietaries for whom he was administering the government. Hamilton wrote to Governor Wolcott upon the subject, protesting strongly against the designs of the company. To this letter Wolcott replied, that the projectors of the enterprise supposed the lands in question were not comprised within the grants of William Penn; but should it appear that they were, the governor thought there would be no disposition to quarrel upon the subject. Governor Hamilton also addressed Colonel Johnson in relation to the matter, praying his interposition to prevent the Six Nations from making any sales to the agents of the Connecticut company, should they appear at Albany for that purpose.

But these precautionary measures on the part of Governor Hamilton did not defeat the object of the Connecticut company, although the Pennsylvania delegates were especially instructed to that end before leaving home for Albany. A purchase was made by the Connecticut agents or delegates, through Lydius, of a tract of land extending about seventy miles north and south, and from a parallel line ten miles east of the Susquehanna, westward two degrees of longitude.[1] This purchase included the whole valley of Wyoming, and the country westward to the sources of the Allegany.[2] The Pennsylvania delegates did all in their power to circumvent the agents of the Susquehanna company, holding several private councils with the chiefs of the Six Nations, and endeavoring to purchase the same lands themselves. In the course of their consultations, Hendrik, thinking that some reflections had been cast upon his character, became excited and declared that neither of the parties should have the land. But the Connecticut agents succeeded, as already stated, and the Pennsylvanians also effected the purchase of "a tract of land between the Blue mountain and the forks of the Susquehanna river;— purchases which were to involve Pennsylvania in a long and savage war, in which the blood of her best settlers flowed like water. Strong efforts were subsequently made by the Pennsylvanians, aided by the influence of Colonel Johnson, to induce the Indians to revoke the sale to the Susquehanna company, and Hendrik was induced by the colonel to make a visit to Philadelphia upon that business And in justice to the Pennsylvanians it must be allowed that they always protested against the legality of this purchase by their rivals—alleging truly that the bargain was

---

[1] Trumbull.

[2] Chapman. Another association was subsequently formed in Connecticut called the *Delaware company*, which purchased the land of the Indians east of the Wyoming tract, to the Delaware river. This company began a settlement on the Delaware at a place called Coshutunk in 1757, which was the first settlement founded by the people of Connecticut within the territory claimed by them west of New York.

not made in open council; that it was the work of a few of the chiefs only; and that several of them were in a state of intoxication when they signed the deed of conveyance.[1]

During the session of the congress, at the suggestion of the Massachusetts commissioners, the plan for a general federal union was taken into consideration. A committee, consisting of a delegate from each of the colonies represented, was appointed to draft plans for this object;[2] and the subject was debated "hand in hand with the Indian business daily, for twelve consecutive days."[3] Finally, after several different plans had been submitted to the board and debated, the one drawn by Franklin—the chief heads of which had been prepared by him before he left home, was adopted. Every member of the council approved of the plan except Mr. De Lancey, "and he made no great opposition."[4] The plan, in many of its features, was similar to the federal constitution, which its author assisted in framing many years afterward. It proposed first, that application should be made to parliament for an act to establish a general government in America, which was to consist of a president general, to be supported by the crown, and a grand council of forty-eight members,

---

[1] Gordon. In this opinion Gordon is supported by Colonel Pickering, who remarks:—These purchases were not made, I am well satisfied, at any public council, or open treaties of the Indians to whom they belonged, but of little knots of inferior and unauthorized chiefs, indifferent about the consequences, provided they received some present gratification, if comparatively of little value.

[2] This committee was composed of Franklin of Pennsylvania, Tasker of Maryland, Smith of New York, Hutchinson of Massachusetts, Atchinson of New Hampshire, Pitkin of Connecticut, and Hopkins of Rhode Island— all distinguished men.

[3] Franklin.

[4] Smith. See also Governor Livingston *Mass. His. Col.* viii, 77. Authorities, I am aware, differ on this point of unanimity. Franklin and Hutchinson say the plan was *unanimously* agreed upon, and Trumbull directly affirms the contrary. The balance of authority however, serves to sustain the view taken in the text.

who were to be chosen by the different colonial assemblies.[1] The number of members from each colony was to be never more than seven, nor less than two; and was to be "in proportion to the sums paid by each colony into the general treasury." To the grand council was to be committed the entire management of all civil and military affairs. The president general was to have a veto power on every act of the council, and in him was to be lodged the whole executive authority. To him also was given "the appointment, with the advice of the council, of all military officers, and the entire management of Indian affairs." The president and council together might declare war against the Indians, or make peace with them; conclude treaties; buy lands either in the name of the crown or the union; raise troops; build forts; and in short do everything for the general defence and welfare of the colonies. The seat of this government was to be located in Philadelphia, which, it was supposed, might possibly be reached from either South Carolina or New Hampshire in fifteen or twenty days!

This plan was not adopted. The several assemblies deeming it too much of an encroachment upon the liberties of the people, refused their assent. The parent government, equally jealous of the prerogative, rejected it on the ground that it favored the democratic at the expense of the aristocratic element; and the colonial governors, "too inconsiderable to hope for so illustrious a seat as the president's, could not brook the exaltation of private citizens to stations in the grand council, inflating their vanity, and enabling them not only to traverse their interests at court,

---

[1] The assemblies were to choose the members for the grand council in the following proportion:

Massachusetts	7	Pennsylvania	6
New Hampshire	2	Maryland	4
Connecticut	5	Virginia	7
Rhode Island	2	North Carolina	4
New York	4	South Carolina	4
New Jersey	3		

Total. 48

but lessen their authority."[1] The plan, therefore, meeting with coldness from both the crown and the colonists, fell through; yet not until it had proved the leaven, which, working for many years, prepared the minds of the people to receive with alacrity a similar federal constitution, thirty-three years afterwards.

Thus closed the labors of the most august assemblage that had ever yet been convened upon the American continent. Composed of men distinguished in the walks of science, statesmanship and philanthropy, it commanded attention alike from the humblest of the people to the highest dignitary of the crown. Though in some respects it was a political failure, yet it stands another link in the chain of events which were rapidly hastening the colonies into the maintenance of an independent existence.[2]

Scarcely had the last commissioner departed from Albany, when the whole frontier from the meadows of the Ohio to the forests of Maine, became alive with savage hordes let loose upon the settlements by the French. Intimations of this however, had been received through the mouths of Indian runners in the spring. As soon as hostilities had fairly begun on the frontiers of Pennsylvania, reports came that a fort had been erected on the head waters of the Kennebec by the French. Immediately on the receipt of this news, Governor Shirley, at the suggestion of Dinwiddie,[3] proceeded up that river with five hundred men to Tacconet falls where he built Fort Halifax. Having explored the country above Nimdynock without discovering any signs of the enemy, Governor Shirley built Fort Western at Cushenoc, and leaving a sufficient number of men to garrison the forts, returned to Boston to find the enemy almost at the very gates of that city.

The storm which had been so long gathering had indeed burst with all its fury upon the colonies. On the twenty-

---

[1] Smith.
[2] For a full account of this congress, see *Mass. His. Col.* v, 3d series.
[3] Governor Dinwiddie to Lieutenant Governor De Lancey.

eighth of May a body of one hundred Schaghticoke Indians fell upon Dutch Hoosick, about ten miles west of Fort Massachusetts, and attacking some men at a mill on the borders of the town, killed one and wounded another. Seemingly infuriated by the sight of blood, they next rushed into the settlement—firing houses, barns and stacks of grain, and killing large numbers of cattle. On the following day they burned the little village of Coick, but as most of the inhabitants had fortunately taken the alarm and fled the day previous, the loss of life was not great.[1] The villagers presented a lamentable spectacle as they came the next day into Albany, some half naked, others with one or two articles of household goods—all that they had been able to secure in their sudden flight—and all foot-sore and weary. The sight, says an eye-witness, was pitiable in the extreme.[2] The garrison of Fort Massachusetts being too weak to furnish efficient aid, a party of militia immediately left Albany for the scene of devastation; but the Indians escaped into the woods, whither the militia dared not follow.[3] Hardly had the yells of the savages died away, when, as if to add intensity to these horrors, intelligence came that the tomahawk was doing its bloody work upon the borders of New Hampshire. On the fifteenth of August, the Indians made their first appearance at Bakerstown, killing a woman, and capturing several others. A few days afterwards they surprised the house of James Johnson at Number Four, in the night, and rousing his family from their slumbers, conveyed him, his wife and six others to Crown Point, and thence into Canada.[3]

Finding the enemy intent upon slaughter, Governor Shirley at once took active measures for the defence of the Massachusetts frontier. Colonel Israel Williams, who had

---

[1] Hoyt's *Indian Wars*.

[2] Letter from the Indian commissioners at Albany to Lieut. Gov. De Lancey.

[3] In this raid 14 houses, 28 barns, and 28 barracks of wheat were destroyed.—*Statement of Captain Chapin, then in command of Fort Massachusetts.*

proved himself such an efficient officer in the last war, was again called to the defence of the western border. That officer, having in his previous service become thoroughly conversant with the topography of the country, submitted to Shirley a sketch of the land,—together with a plan for a vigorous prosecution of the war. He proposed that those forts which had afforded little or no protection heretofore to the borderers should be given up, and in their place, a line of small fortifications should be erected through the valley of Charlemont; Forts Dummer and Massachusetts were to be strengthened and supplied with light cannon, and with two additional forts to the westward, were to form a chain of forts connecting with the line of fortifications in New York[1] Having seen, also, the advantage which the Indians, by their system of warfare, had always possessed over the whites, Colonel Williams now proposed to meet them with their own weapons and upon their own ground. For this purpose, bodies of rangers well skilled in woodcraft and in bush fighting, were to be selected and kept constantly traversing the wilderness,[2] keeping at the same time a sharp look out upon the routes to and from Crown Point.[3] The plan of Colonel Williams was laid by Governor Shirley before the general court, and its main features were adopted. A body of rangers, such as the colonel had recommended, was also raised and stationed on the western frontier under his command. At the same time troops were raised for the defence of the north-western quarter of the province, in the counties of Worcester and Hampshire, and Captain Ephraim Williams appointed to the command, with the rank of major.[4]

While these vigorous measures for the defence of Massachusetts were being pushed forward by Governor Shirley, the lieutenant governor of New York was not idle. As

---

[1] Hoyt's *Indian Wars.*

[2] The present state of Vermont.

[3] Hoyt's *Indian Wars.*

[4] Idem.

soon as the latter received intelligence of the destruction of Hoosick, he sent orders to the authorities of Albany to repair the stockades around that city, and put the block houses in a suitable condition for defence. Simultaneously, by his orders, the only company remaining in New York —the two independent companies having sailed for Virginia—marched to Albany—a sergeant and a few invalids only being left in the city to garrison the fort.

While these measures were in progress to guard Albany against surprise, rumors reached Colonel Johnson from the north, that the French were meditating a descent upon the lower settlements of the colony, and that a large force in advance of the main body had already begun their march.[1] Although these reports were not credited by the colonel, yet he did not think it prudent to relax the preparations which he had already begun, shortly after the burning of Hoosick, for putting the frontier towns in a posture of defence. Measures were therefore immediately taken by him for placing the militia of the province in a condition to render efficient service. Acting with this object, he wrote at once to the captains of the several companies within his district, ordering them to have their men in readiness to march at a moment's warning.[2] At the same time, he directed the commanding officer at Schenectady to see that all the companies stationed there were instantly equipped and provided with proper arms and ammunition. The officer was further ordered to keep a strict watch by night and by day, and to report to him the state of the block houses.[3] Considerable difficulty having arisen between the militia and the regulars stationed at Schenectady, the colonel in these same orders thought proper to add :—" the guard must be regular, and not allowed to com-

---

[1] Manuscript orders of Colonel Johnson to the captains of the different companies within his district.

[2] Idem.

[3] Manuscript letter; Johnson to Captain Jacobus Van Slyck, the commanding officer at Schenectady, Aug. 30th, 1754.

mit any indecency, or give any insults to the king's garrison."

Meanwhile the general assembly was convened by the lieutenant governor on the twentieth of August. His reason for convening it at such an unusual season of the year was given in the opening message. It was, he said, to inform them of Colonel Washington's defeat upon the east side of the Ohio, within the undoubted limits of his majesty's dominions; and as it was plain that the king's lands had *now been invaded,* there was therefore no excuse for not voting their promised aid to Virginia, which they had refused at the last session. The defenceless condition of Albany was then pointed out, and the consequent necessity for erecting a fort upon Hudson river for its protection; equally necessary, he continued, in view of the importance of the Six Nations as allies, was the erection of a fort in the Seneca's country, where a smith could permanently reside. As the Confederates, moreover, at the last congress, had complained of the pernicious effect of the sale of rum amongst them, he urged a more stringent act to prevent its sale to the Indians, as the one formerly passed for that purpose had proved totally ineffectual. A stronger militia act, for the formation into companies of those able to bear arms, yet exempt from military duty by law, was advised; and also that a quantity of arms and accoutrements should be provided at New York and at Albany, to be on hand in case of any emergency. Directing his remarks more particularly to the house, he informed it of the plan of union which had been unanimously agreed to by the commissioners at Albany, which he, concluded, "I shall now order to be laid before you."

The answer of the house was of the same general tenor as its reply to the lieutenant governor's message at the preceding session—full of quibbles in justification of its refusal to grant the desired aid. While it deemed it the reciprocal duty of the colonies to assist each other, yet "these principles," said the house, "your honor will not extend to an unlimited sense;" there may be instances where the particular colonies which are invaded, ought to exert their own strength and "not call too loudly upon others more exposed than themselves;"—yet such, it said, was the condition of the colony of New York, burdened with taxes, and threatened by the enemy at their very doors. "The other colonies," it continued, "make themselves strong and defensible by settling in townships, or some other close order, while our frontier lands are granted away in patents, almost without bounds or number, regardless of settlements or the public welfare."

"Would any man," says Mr. Smith, alluding to this answer of the assembly, "would any man without doors, and not in the secret, believe what is a fact, that they had already, that very morning, voted a gift of five thousand pounds to their fellow subjects in Pennsylvania and Virginia?" Yet such was the fact. By granting the aid to Virginia and Pennsylvania, the ministry were humored; while by doing it with seeming reluctance, the parsimonious spirit of the people was gratified and suspicions of a sacrifice of the colony's interests to the De Lancey faction, prevented.[1] Nothing worthy of special note occurred during the remainder of this sitting; and the members of the assembly, after thanking Mr. De Lancey for the *faithful* manner in which he had distributed the presents to the Indians at the late congress—intending by this a direct hit at Mr. Clinton—were dismissed to their homes.

In the general assembly which met on the fifteenth of October, was first manifested the want of that harmony, which had hitherto been so flattering to Mr. De Lancey's administration. The reluctance of the lieutenant governor at the congress to accede to the plan of union, first awakened suspicion in the public mind that his sympathies were on the side of the crown; and that the affection which he professed for the people, was only a cover to his

---

[1] Smith.

own ambition. There were also a few of Mr. Clinton's friends left, around whom were gathered a small opposition; and the partiality which Mr. De Lancey had shown to his partizans since coming into power, disgusted others and added to the discontent which was now quite general. To this was added another source of dissatisfaction, viz.: the course he had taken in the founding of the college. To understand this latter point more clearly, it is necessary to glance at the origin of the controversy which was now raging fiercely, and which had already divided the assembly into two parties.

The province of New York at this period was divided, in its religious views, into two sects—the Episcopalian and the Presbyterian—the former being led by James De Lancey, and the latter by Wm. Livingston. The Presbyterians, though outnumbering ten to one the Episcopalians,[1] had not fairly recovered from the oppressions of the early governors, Fletcher and Cornbury; and they would probably have remained quiet, had not the Episcopalians, with great lack of judgment, stirred up anew the embers of controversy.[2]

The people of New York, awakened to the importance of stimulating education, raised by successive lotteries, the sum of three thousand four hundred and forty-three pounds for the purpose of founding a college; and in the fall of 1751, passed an act for placing the money thus raised in the hands of ten trustees. Of these, seven were Episcopalians, two belonged to the Dutch church, and the tenth was Wm. Livingston, an English Presbyterian.[3] This manifest inequality in favor of the church of England, at once raised a well founded alarm in the minds of the other sects, who very justly perceived in this, an attempt to make the college entirely sectarian, by which only those in the Episcopal church could participate in

---

[1] Smith.
[2] *Life of Livingston*, by Sedgwick Jun.
[3] Wm. Livingtson, afterward governor of New Jersey.

CHAP. XIV.
1754.

its benefits. Nor were they left long in suspense, for it soon became well understood that the majority of the trustees were to have the college under their control, and were intending shortly to petition the lieutenant governor for a charter, in which it was to be expressly stipulated that no person out of the communion of the English Church should be eligible to the office of president.[1] Far seeing men uttered gloomy forebodings; and a belief soon diffused itself through the minds of intelligent dissenters, that this was only the foreshadowing of an attempt to introduce into the colony an established church.

This idea was to a majority of the colonists repugnant in the extreme. The union of church and state, with its tythes and taxes, was, like the "skeleton in armor," ever present to their imaginations, stimulating them to the utmost resistance. Mr. Livingston, therefore, partially with a view to expose the evils of a college founded upon such sectarian principles, established a paper called the *Independent Reflector*.[2] The articles which successively appeared from his pen on this subject were able and pungent. Under his lash the leaders of the church party winced;[3] and in their agony, charged him with the design of breaking up the plan of any college whatever, and dreaded lest he should obtain a charter "for constituting a college on a basis the most catholic, generous and free."[4] These attacks of the church party were returned with

---

[1] *Life of Livingston.*

[2] Idem.

[3] In a letter from the Rev. Samuel Johnson of Connecticut to Bishop Secker (published in the *London Documents* xxx, 6), the writer says: "The church at New York is about founding a college with free liberty to dissenting pupils to go to what meeting they please; nay not excluding dissenters from being even tutors. * * * Nay they contend that no religion at all should be taught in the college rather than the church should have any precedence. So bitterly are they set against us! and however so much they are otherwise at variance among themselves, yet they unite *with their utmost force* against us, and do all they can to disaffect the Dutch towards us, who otherwise were peaceably disposed."

[4] *Independent Reflector*, No. 18.

redoubled violence, and the controversy had now risen to fever heat.[1]

The efforts of Mr. Livingston and other able writers to prevent the incorporation of the college under these principles, were fruitless; and Mr. De Lancey accordingly granted the charter. Rev. Samuel Johnson from Stratford, a worthy man, was called to the president's chair, and Mr. Livingston was appointed one of the governors, in the hope of silencing his opposition.[2]

The granting of this charter was so displeasing to the majority of the people, that the lieutenant governor thought it advisable, in order to win back their former confidence, to urge at the present session the passage of several popular acts. Among them was one for supplying the garrison at Albany and the fortifications along the frontiers, and another for the discharge of the claims of the public creditors, especially the one of Colonel Johnson.

It may at first appear singular that Mr. De Lancey should be found using his influence in favor of Colonel Johnson. His opposition to the latter, however, had arisen more from a desire to harass Governor Clinton, than from any personal animosity; and the cause being now removed, he not only ceased his enmity, but continued his warm friend until his decease.

In a message which the lieutenant governor sent down on the twenty-fifth, the house was informed that the Mohawks of the lower castle were dissatisfied on account of a piece of ground which they had formerly sold to the

---

[1] The following are a few of the titles of the articles written and published by Mr. Livingston at this time.

"No XXXI. Primitive Christianity, short and intelligible—Modern Christianity, voluminous and incomprehensible.

"XXXIV. Of the veneration and contempt of the clergy.

"XXXVI. The absurdity of the civil magistrate's interfering in matters of religion.

"XXXVIII Of passive obedience and non-resistance."

[2] Sedgwick.

Rev. Mr. Barclay. The land, they said, they never intended should pass in fee, but remain forever for the use of any missionary who might be stationed among them. Rev. Mr. Barclay, having given up his situation as missionary to the Mohawks, for the rectorate of Trinity Church, would gladly deed the land back to the Indians, provided he was reimbursed for the improvements which he had put upon it. The message therefore recommended that a sufficient sum of money should be appropriated for this object, as well as for the erecting of a church among the Canajoharies, which the latter very much desired.

The assembly had already proceeded to vote the arrears of salaries, and a farther sum of one hundred and fifty pounds for the extraordinary expenses of the lieutenant governor at the late treaty, when on the twenty-first of November, a letter was communicated to them by Mr. De Lancey, from the lords of trade. The latter, he said, were of opinion, that the council had done right in refusing its assent to the late application bill, as such annual grants might be employed "to the purpose of wresting from the crown the nomination of all officers whose salaries depended upon the appointment of the assembly, and of defeating all the necessary services of government;" and that they were, therefore, at a loss to understand what end the plan of granting a yearly revenue could serve. If, however, the assembly persisted in these attempts to weaken the power of the crown by such measures, it must not flatter itself that it could give them either stability or permanency. "I hope, therefore," continued Mr. De Lancey, "you will take these weighty reasons into your most serious consideration, and provide a permanent revenue for the support of government, in such a manner as may put an end to any dispute on that head." "There is another point in their lordship's letter," he farther added, "on which it is proper you should know their sentiments. Their lordships are inclined to believe, from the nature of paper currency in general, that the making such paper money a legal tender in all payments, is unnecessary, improper, and inconsistent with the sense of parliament," and therefore "I cannot give my consent to any act of this sort, without a clause being inserted therein, suspending its execution, until his majesty's pleasure be known."

The result of this communication was an address in which, while the assembly denied any intention to encroach on the executive, it refused to recede from the new mode of a yearly support. It was impossible, it said, on account of the colony debt, to erect forts without a farther issue of paper; and it boldly declared, that unless the bills were made a legal tender without any restriction, it would not even accede to that; when however he had it in his power, to give his assent to an act that should not be impeded by any *restraining clause*, it would cheerfully provide for the defence of the colony. The assembly nevertheless was so alive to the importance of erecting a fort forthwith upon the Hudson river above Albany, that it directed him to have one built, promising to defray the cost when the amount should be known.[1]

The granting of a charter to the new college had not utterly crushed out opposition to its obnoxious principles. The house still had the disposal of the money which had been raised; and the sectaries having a majority, the trustees were ordered to report their transactions by virtue of the act under which they had been appointed. The latter accordingly on the first of November handed in two separate reports, Wm. Livingston reading one, and James Livingston and Mr. Nicoll the other. After the two reports had been considered, the house unanimously resolved " that it would not consent to any disposition of the moneys raised by lottery for erecting a college within this colony, in any other manner, than by an act of the legislature hereafter passed for that purpose." Permission at the same time was given Mr. Robert Livingston to

---

[1] Journal of assembly.

bring in a bill for incorporating a college, which he introduced that same afternoon.[1]

The introduction of this bill astonished both houses. It was vain to suppose that the council would give its assent to an act so distasteful to its religious prejudices; nor was the lieutenant governor likely to directly contradict the letters patent which, on behalf of the crown, he himself had granted—while the assembly, composed chiefly of dissenters, dared not reject it.[2] In this predicament, a motion was made by Mr. Walton—prefaced with the remark "that the subject was of the utmost consequence to the people they represented, with respect both to their civil and religious liberties"—that the consideration of the bill be deferred until the next session, by which time the sentiments of their constituents could be obtained. This motion was gladly seized upon as the only mode which presented an honorable retreat from the position they had so hastily assumed, and was therefore immediately carried.

Thus, with the close of the year, practically terminated the college controversy. A controversy, which considered in itself, was not perhaps of much importance; but which should not be omitted by the historian, who would show the progress which the colonists were making toward that civil and religious freedom which they afterward attained.

---

[1] Smith.
[2] Idem.

CHAPTER XV.
1755.

Blood had been spilled, Washington defeated, and the scalping knife unsheathed from the Ohio to the Kennebec, yet England and France were still at peace. Notwithstanding the bold assumptions of France, the vascillating course of the Newcastle ministry rendered a definite policy toward that government impossible; and although the defeat at the Great Meadows roused the ministry sufficiently to ask the advice of Horatio Gates, a youthful officer just arrived from Nova Scotia, yet they soon relapsed into their former imbecility, leaving the charge of American affairs to the duke of Cumberland, at that time the captain general of the armies of Great Britain.[1]

The duke of Cumberland, who has been described as "cruel and sanguinary," regarded the opportunity thus afforded for indulging in his favorite pastime, war, with delight; and rightly judging that the French were bent on hostilities, he dispatched in January, while the ministry were still hesitating, two regiments to America under the command of Edward Braddock. The French, thoroughly cognizant of the intentions of the English, notwithstanding the flimsy diplomatic subtleties with which "England's foolish prime minister" was amusing the French court, immediately made preparations for sending large reinforcements into Canada. With this design, a fleet of transports carrying troops under the command of Baron Dieskau, a veteran soldier, and having also on board De Vaudreuil, who was to supersede Duquesne in the government of Canada, sailed from Brest early in May. Scarcely

---

[1] Bancroft. Walpole's *George II.*

had its sails caught the ocean breezes, when the English, who had watched this movement with a jealous eye, sent Admiral Boscawen in pursuit. Both fleets arrived nearly at the same time off Cape Race, but were prevented by a dense fog, from seeing each other. The larger part of the French fleet, taking advantage of this circumstance, escaped up the St. Lawrence, and safely landed the troops, with Dieskau and Vaudreuil, at Quebec. Two vessels, however,—the Alcide and the Lys—were not so fortunate, for on the sixth of June they fell in with the Dunkirk and the Defiance of the British fleet. The Alcide was commanded by Hocquart, and the Dunkirk by Howe,[1] both brave men—and a sharp action ensued, which, lasting several hours, resulted in the discomfiture and surrender of the French men-of-war.[2] Meanwhile, as the prospect of a war became more certain, and the defenceless condition of the frontiers more apparent, the alarm of the colonists grew so great as to induce the lieutenant governor, with the advice of his council, to convene the assembly on the fourth of Feburary. The opening message informed that body of the active measures which his majesty was taking for the security of his subjects in America, and of the armament which had already sailed under General Braddock. It farther reminded them of the weak state of the frontier fortifications, should the French make—which was quite possible—a descent upon the province. In order effectually to prevent this, the defences around the city of New York should at once be strengthened, and other works constructed, which the commander in chief, with the advice of his council and the best engineers, might think advisable. The northern frontier next demanded their serious attention. The defences of the city of Albany were in such a deplorable state, as to excite the derision even of the Indians; and yet should that city be taken, there was nothing to prevent the French from sweeping

---

[1] Afterward Lord Howe.
[2] Smollet.

down into New Jersey and Pennsylvania. Albany should therefore be fortified without delay, and a strong fort built at some advanced place on the Hudson, whence scouts could be sent out to gain intelligence and give timely notice of the enemy's approach. All these preparations, added the message, would require a large amount of money; but as security could not be purchased at too high a price, it hoped that, throwing aside any ill-timed parsimony, they would provide such funds as would be sufficient to defray all expenses necessary for their own preservation. The assembly needed no urging to prompt action. Its alarm was too great, and the enemy too near for it to be indifferent to the exigency of the occasion. It immediately, in defiance of the royal instructions, authorized an issue of forty-five thousand pounds in bills of credit, to be sunk at stated intervals by a tax; prohibited any supplies of provisions from being sent to the French colonies; and made the militia subject to such penalties as should be imposed by the executive.

Meanwhile, the Mohawks of the upper and lower castles became alarmed at the prospect of hostilities, which would let loose the hordes of French Indians upon their castles, now entirely defenceless. Hearing of Colonel Johnson's intended departure for New York to take his seat at the council board, they hastened to transmit by him a message to the executive, representing their unprotected condition and beseeching aid. Their appeal was delivered by the colonel, shortly after his arrival in the city, to Mr. De Lancey in person, who communicated it to his council on the twenty-eighth. The letter was addressed to the lieutenant governor, and was as follows:

"*Brother Goragh:* When we had the pleasure of seeing you last summer at Albany, the air seemed to be pleasant and the sky serene and clear, but to our great concern we now observe thick and heavy clouds arising on all sides and driving this way, which seems to portend a storm. Should it blow, we are very apprehensive of danger, having no shelter. To you, therefore, Brother, (in whose power it is to draw or disperse those dark clouds) we make known our fears, not doubting but you, out of a brotherly affection, will either remove them or ease the minds of our old and young people, or cover us from the impending storm." The council, after considering this letter, wisely resolved that to comply with their wishes would be a better argument in dissuading them from yielding to the intrigues of the French, than all the words that could be used, and determined forthwith to have both their castles stockaded and such other works erected as would best protect their uncovered old men. They also authorized the executive to draw upon the contingent fund for this purpose; and directed the colonel to estimate the expense of such works as the Indians desired, and construct, on his arrival home, such defences as in his judgment might be deemed advisable.

While the assembly was sitting, Governor Shirley, who had for a long time been in correspondence with the ministry upon the importance and feasibility of conquering Canada, sent commissioners to the several colonies, urging them to assist him in his long cherished project of driving the French from the continent of America. Thomas Pownal,[1] the commissioner sent for this purpose to the colony of New York, met with so lukewarm a reception from De Lancey, as to lead him to seek sympathy from the party opposed to the latter. This party had now acquired considerable influence, and as Mr. Pownal received from it cordial support, the lieutenant governor thought it not advisable to create any more ill feeling against himself, by provoking it farther. He accordingly sent down to the assembly, upon the twenty-sixth, a special message, in which he requested supplies for the quartering of the troops, and informed it that the garrison at Oswego was in danger of succumbing through want, as Colonel Johnson had

---

[1] Brother of John Pownal, at that time one of the secretaries to the board of trade.

refused any longer to provision that post, while the debt which he had already incurred in supplying it was unpaid. Accompanying the message, were copies of Mr. Shirley's letters, and he urged it to take the suggestions therein contained into consideration. On the same day, Mr. John Chambers was sent by the council to request the house to unite in a joint committee to confer with Mr. Pownal upon the suggestions made by Governor Shirley. This was acceded to, and after the committee had met the Massachusetts commissioner, it was unanimously resolved "that the scheme was well concerted, and that if Massachusetts would raise fourteen hundred men, they ought to find eight hundred, and that they would agree to contribute to a general fund for the common charge of the war." Before however this resolution should be acted upon, it was proposed to submit it to General Braddock for his approval; and the house adjourned on the twenty-ninth until his opinion could be obtained by Mr. De Lancey, who had been called to confer with that general and five of the colonial governors at Alexandria.[1]

This conference had been called by Braddock shortly after his arrival in Virginia, to meet upon the fourteenth day of April.[2] Its object was to devise measures for a vigorous prosecution of the war against the French. Yet at the same time it was distinctly understood that Canada was not to be invaded, but only French encroachments along the frontier repelled.

Four separate expeditions were planned by Braddock and the royal governors—the first for the complete reduction of Nova Scotia, was to be commanded by Lawrence, the lieutenant governor of that province; a second was to recover the Ohio valley, under Braddock himself; the

---

[1] The colonial governors present upon this occasion, were, De Lancey of New York, Shirley of Massachusetts, Morris of Pennsylvania, Sharpe of Maryland, and Dinwiddie of Virginia. Commodore Keppel was also present.

[2] Braddock sailed from Cork with one thousand men upon the fourteenth day of January, and arrived in the Chesapeake the latter part of February.

third, under command of Shirley, was to expel the French from Fort Niagara, and form a junction with Braddock's forces; and the fourth was to be given to Colonel Johnson, having for its object the capture of Crown Point. This last appointment was made through the influence of Governor Shirley. The energy which Colonel Johnson had displayed in his command of the militia of New York, and the vigor which he had infused into that branch of the public service, first led Shirley to desire that he should have the command of the expedition.[1] Early in this year, he had announced to the general assembly of Massachusetts, under a pledge of secrecy, his intention to appoint Johnson to the command of the expedition against Crown Point;[2] and at this conference, General Braddock, at his suggestion, gave the colonel the command, with the rank of major general. The latter was to have under him the provincial militia and the warriors of the Six Nations; and his acknowledged influence over the latter especially, gave promise of success. General Johnson held his commission from the governors of those colonies that were to furnish the provincials—the respective quotas of each being fixed at Alexandria.[3]

At this conference, Johnson, who was also present at the solicitation of General Braddock, received from the latter the appointment of superintendent of Indian affairs, with full power to treat with the Confederate Nations, and to secure them and their allies to the British interest. For the furtherance of this latter object, Braddock advanced Johnson two thousand pounds, which, it was understood, should be reimbursed to him by the colonies, according to the proportions which had been settled upon by the commissioners, the previous summer at Albany.

Immediately upon Johnson's return, he sent belts of wampum to all the castles of the Confederate Nations, now

---

[1] Manuscript letter: Shirley to Johnson.

[2] Letter to a Nobleman. *Mass. His. Col.*

[3] Johnson's commission from Governor Shirley as major general, is dated the 16th April of the present year.

increased to nine,[1] informing them of a grand council which he proposed to hold, and desiring that they would meet him at Mount Johnson with all possible dispatch. The Indians did not require urging to attend. The news that their brother Warraghiyagey had again been raised up among them, spread like wild-fire;[2] and in a very short time, in response to his call, over eleven hundred Indians of every age and sex, assembled at the place designated. So unprecedented and unexpected was the number present —by far the largest assemblage of Indians ever before convened—that Johnson, as well as his larder, was completely taken by surprise.

On the twenty-first of June he opened the council by a speech, which was interpreted to the Indians by Red Head, the chief sachem of the Onondagas.[3] In this address the Indians were informed of the arrival of General Braddock, who had come with "a large number of armed men, great guns, and other implements of war," to protect those Indians against the French, who remained firm in their attachment to the English. In the course of his remarks, the speaker also took occasion to inform them in their own poetical language, of his late appointment from General Braddock. "The tree," said he, "which in your public speeches and private applications to me, you have so often and so earnestly desired might be again set up, is now raised and fixed in the earth by so powerful a hand, that its roots will take a firm and deep footing, and its branches be a comfortable and extensive shade for you and all your allies to take shelter under it. And by this belt, I now invite you and all

---

[1] By taking into the covenant chain the Tiederigoenes, Schanadarighroenes and Delawares.

[2] The Indians appear in extreme good humor, and mightily pleased at your having solely the superintendency of their affairs." Manuscript letter: Colonel Stoddard to General Johnson, June 13th, 1755.

[3] Although Johnson was perfectly acquainted with the Indian tongue, and could have spoken to them directly in their own language, yet it was always considered by the Indians as etiquette to be addressed at a formal conference through a third person.—*Manuscripts of Sir William Johnson.*

your allies to come and sit under this tree, where you may freely open your hearts and get all your wounds healed. I do, Brethren, at the same time, remove the embers which remain at Albany, and rekindle the fire of council and friendship at this place; and this fire I shall make of such wood as will give the clearest light and greatest warmth, and I hope it will prove comfortable and useful to all such as will come and light their pipes at it, and dazzle and scorch all those who are or may be enemies to it." In conclusion, they were informed that he had a message to give them from General Braddock, and also presents which the king had sent them by that warrior. These he would deliver to them in a day or two, together with a speech of his own.

On the twenty-third, however, the Indians having informed Johnson that they were desirous to answer his late speech, he consented to put off the delivery of the one he had promised for that day, and listen to theirs. Accordingly Hendrik rose, and addressing his brother warriors, announced that in accordance with their ancient custom, the speaker at a council was always chosen from either the Mohawks, Onondagas, or Cayugas, in deference to their being the elder brothers of the Confederacy; and he therefore gave them notice that Brother Kaghsuaghtioni (Red Head) would be the speaker on this occasion.[1]

The answer of this sachem was, in its principal features, an expression of satisfaction for the restoration of Johnson. The Six Nations, he said, had long been in darkness, and now were extremely obliged to the king their father, for restoring to them that clear and comfortable light which in old times cheered their forefathers, by appointing him to the sole management of their affairs—who had always treated them *kindly* and *honestly*, and whom they looked upon as their own flesh and blood. As to the fire at Albany, it was so low and bad that they could not even

---

[1] In the private council of the sachems held in reference to the reply to be given to Johnson's speech, Hendrik had been nominated as their speaker, but he declined in favor of Red Head.

find a spark with which to light a pipe. "We look on you, Brother," concluded the orator, "as the king, our father's representative. We are under your direction and disposition, and the fire you have kindled here, as well as that at Onondaga, we will cherish, and all other fires we thus kick away, as unnatural and hateful to us." Here, suiting the action to the word, Red Head gave a violent kick. Then presenting to General Johnson a belt of wampum, he bowed three times very low, and sat down amid an universal shout of approval.

As soon as the Onondaga orator had finished, the chief sachem of the Oneidas came forward, and presenting a boy to Johnson and to the Indians, announced the death of one of their sachems, and asked permission to raise up this lad in his place, and confer on him the name of the deceased. The general thereupon, taking the boy from his hand as a token that he was pleased with the selection, told him that if the sachems of his nation would introduce the boy on the morrow, he would clothe him as became a chief. The Indians were then thanked for the cordial manner in which they had responded to his speech, and notified that the firing of two cannon would be the signal of his being prepared to answer their speech, when he hoped that all of them "great and small, would be in attendance to hear what he had to say."

On the twenty-fourth, the sachems and warriors of the nine cantons having assembled, Johnson opened his speech by pointing impressively to four large volumes of Indian records which lay on a table before him—"These are," said he, "the records of the many solemn treaties which have passed between your forefathers and your brothers, the English. They testify that upon our first acquaintance we shook hands, and finding we should be useful to one another, entered into a covenant of brotherly love and mutual friendship. * * * And now my brethren, I ask you, and I desire every man present to put his hand on his heart and ask himself seriously this question; *who have* been, who are the friends and brethren of the Five Confederate Nations and their allies? the English or the French? Does it require any time to consider? does it require any argument to determine? If you can be one moment in doubt, I must tell you, you will not act like the children of those brave and honest men, whom you call your forefathers, but like Frenchmen in the shape of the Five Nations. Are you indeed our Brethren? Are you the children of our ancient friends and brothers? Are you those sachems and warriors of the Five Confederate Nations, whom the great king of England, the best and most upright prince in the world, loves and honors as his wise, his warlike and dutiful children? * * * *Stand by your Brethren the English*—don't break your covenant chain with them; let not the French boastings or lies deceive you. The English have indeed been long asleep, but now they are thoroughly awake: they are slow to spill blood, but when they begin, they are like an angry wolf, and the French will fly before them like deer." [1]

After the Indian warriors had been wrought up by these stirring appeals to the highest pitch of frenzy, Johnson informed them that he had received a message from the Half King, stating that their brethren southward had already offered their services to General Braddock. This being the case, continued he, will you allow your southern brethren to outstrip you in zeal and bravery? No, rather set them an example. If you desire to treat me as a brother, go with me. "My war-kettle is on the fire, my canoe is ready to put in the water, my gun is loaded, my sword by my side, and my axe is sharpened. By this large

---

[1] In the first rough manuscript draught of this speech, in Johnson's own hand-writing, now before me, the reading is "*angry bear*," instead of "*angry wolf*," as it is written in the speech published in the *N. Y. Col. Doc.* The expression in the text, however, is the most forcible. The wolf frequently preys on the deer; the bear, rarely, if ever—the food of the bear, especially in the northern wilderness of New York, being chiefly berries and young twigs. Johnson probably altered the first expression in the last draught.

belt, therefore,"—at the same time handing the Sachem Abraham a war-belt—" I call on you to raise up like honest and brave men, and join your brethren and me against our common enemy, and by it, I confirm the assurances I have given you."

The following day, the speech of General Braddock was delivered to the Indians by Johnson. The latter threw into its delivery all the fire and energy of which he was master, and at its conclusion flung down, in the general's name, the war-belt. It was immediately picked up by an Oneida sachem, and, at the same time, Arent Stevens, the interpreter, began the war dance, in the chorus of which he was joined by all the sachems present. A large tub of punch was thereupon brought forward for the Indians to drink the king's health, and the council broke up for the day.[1]

The result of this council was flattering. Although of late, the activity of the French had won over several chief warriors of the upper castles, among whom was Red Head, yet their minds were so mollified by the exertions of Johnson, that he was able to write to the lords of trade shortly after, "that there were very few amongst the whole Confederacy, who, in the present disputes between the French and our crown, do not sincerely wish us success, and are disposed to assist our arms."

As soon as the plans of the four campaigns had been definitely arranged at Alexandria, Shirley hastened to Boston to prepare for the expedition under his command; to expedite the departure of the provincials who were to join General Johnson's command; and to urge forward the troops destined for Nova Scotia. He was detained, how-

---

[1] The efforts of Johnson with the Indians upon this occasion were not confined merely to his public interviews. He labored incessantly with them in private; and finally prevailed upon the Six Nations to send a message to those of the Onondagas who had settled at La Presentation, and also to the Caughnawagas, urging them to remain at least neutral in the coming struggle.—*N. Y. Col. Doc.*, vi.

ever, a few days in New York, while engaged in removing some objections which De Lancey had raised to the form of Johnson's commission; and also in Connecticut, where he tarried to hurry forward the provincial troops from that province. Having at length arrived in Boston, he worked with so much diligence that the troops for Nova Scotia, under the command of Colonel Winslow, were soon on their way; and having seen them fairly started, he returned to New York, and sailed for Albany on the fourth of July,—his own regiment having preceded him by a few days.[1]

Lieutenant Governor De Lancey likewise hastened from Alexandria to New York, and having convened his legislature, informed it in a short message, on the twenty-third of April, that General Braddock had given his assent to Governor Shirley's plan, and urged it to act on the resolution of the joint committee. The assembly, now thoroughly aroused, entered with alacrity into the proposed expedition. Bills were immediately passed for levying and supplying eight hundred men to act under General Johnson in erecting forts near Crown Point, and for impressing ship carpenters and laborers to construct boats and other articles that might be necessary for the expedition.

On the twenty-seventh, in another message, the assembly were informed that Connecticut had consented to furnish three of the eight companies at the expense of New York, and that a loan of a sufficient number of arms to equip the entire eight companies had been requested of Governor Dinwiddie. In case, however, the executive should be disappointed in obtaining a sufficient quantity, it was suggested that provision should be made for supplying the deficiency. Inasmuch, also, as it had been agreed at Alexandria that presents should be given to the Indians, it was thought that money should be appropriated for that purpose, and likewise for the expenses of Major General Johnson, suitable to his rank. The assembly responding

---

[1] *Mass His. Col.*, vii

promptly to these suggestions, agreed to give fifty pounds as their share toward the pay of the workmen employed in erecting forts; four hundred and fifty pounds for Indian presents; and fifty pounds to Major General Johnson for his table—at the same time granting as much to the colonel of their own regiment.[1]

While the lieutenant governor and the assembly of New York were thus actively engaged in preparing to meet their share of the expenses of the coming hostilities, the expedition under Colonel Winslow, for the capture of the two French forts in Acadia, had already sailed. At the head of the bay of Fundy the New England troops were joined by Colonel Monckton with three hundred regulars, and a small train of artillery, and the forces now increased to about eighteen hundred men, appeared on the second of June, before Beausejour. De Verger, the officer in command of that fort, although having a plentiful supply of ammunition and artillery, yet, with a strange lack of energy, took no pains to prevent the English from disembarking. A day was spent by the provincial troops in repose, and upon the fourth of June, they invested the fort. No sally or even a respectable defense was attempted, and upon the twelfth the garrison, "weakened by fear, discord and confusion," surrendered.[2] The garrison, by the terms of the surrender, were to depart forthwith for Louisburg; and three hundred of the Acadians who were found aiding in the defense of the fort, were pardoned, it appearing that they had been forced into the service much against their will. The fort was garrisoned with English soldiers, and its name changed to Cumberland in honor of the warlike brother of George Second.

Beausejour having been reduced, the provincials next directed their efforts against the small palisaded fort on the

---

[1] Journal of the assembly. Smith.
[2] Bancroft.

CHAP. Gaspereau, garrisoned by only twenty men, and forced its surrender on the same terms. At the same time Captain Row was dispatched with four vessels, to attack the French fort on the river St. John. Before he arrived, however, the French taking alarm, burned the fort and the surrounding dwellings and fled, leaving a barren victory to the conquerors.[1]

Had the British and the New England commanders stopped at this point, the conquest thus achieved would have presented an unsullied record. But not content with a success which left them in safe and in undisputed possession of the whole of Nova Scotia, they next turned their attention to the dislodgement of the inhabitants of Acadia.

The Acadians were a simple, harmless, and pious people, leading a pastoral life among their flocks and herds; and tilling the soil, which, for more than a century and a half, had descended from father to son. Their morals were pure, their temper cheerful, and their religion sincere. The parish priest was the sole arbiter of their disputes, and beyond him there was no appeal. Happy in the consciousness of harboring no ill-will towards their fellow men, they lived contentedly in their little cottages; and while the husbands and brothers went forth with the early morn to the severer labors of the field, the wives and sisters nimbly plied the shuttle, or trained the woodbine and the honey-suckle over the doors of their peaceful homes. Their happiness was soon to be rudely shattered.

The fertile fields and rich meadows of the Acadians, brought into the highest state of cultivation by their own industry, had long been coveted for the crown by the governor of Nova Scotia; and regarding this as a favorable opportunity for securing their possession, he lost no time in thus representing it to the ministry.[2] His representations were but too successful, and under the flimsy pretext, that to allow so large a body of French to reside

---

[1] Bancroft.
[2] Lieutenant Governor Lawrence to the lords of trade, Aug. 1, 1754.

in Acadia, would render insecure the possession of Nova Scotia, it was determined to send adrift the entire colony. Accordingly a proclamation was issued commanding the males of all ages to assemble at their several villages on the fifth of September. Utterly unsuspicious, in the simplicity of their hearts, of any hostile intent, four hundred and eighteen unarmed men assembled at Grand Pré, one of the places designated. As soon as they had been like a flock of sheep huddled together in the church, the doors were closed and secured, and it was told them by Colonel Winslow, that all their lands, houses and live stock were confiscated to the crown, and that they were to be removed immediately from the province. They were, however, "through the goodness of his majesty,"—to be permitted to take with them their money and as much of their household goods as would not encumber the vessels in which they were to sail.

It was a sad day, when for the last time the Acadians looked upon their homes which for so long had contained all that life holds dear. As the embarkation was in progress, the men, as they marched to the boats, were greeted with the blessings of the women and children, who kneeling, joined with them in "praying, and singing hymns." Although Colonel Winslow was a humane man, and exercised as much kindness as was consistent with his orders, yet it is to be feared that the New England troops, actuated by that same intolerance which caused their ancestors to burn out the tongues of Quakers, entered into this horrid work with alacrity. As there was not a sufficient number of transports to carry them all at one time, the women and children were left behind until they could be taken off in other vessels. "The embarkation of the inhabitants goes on but slowly," wrote the brutal Monckton; "the most part of the wives of the men we have prisoners are gone off with their children, in hopes I would not send off their husbands without them." They were indeed bitterly deceived; and as the last anchor was weighed, and the white sails, filling with the breeze, bore their loved ones from the sight of those that were left behind, one universal wail of anguish rose up to heaven.

Cruel was the fate of these unfortunates. Full seven thousand of them were distributed throughout the colonies. Some were sent to Georgia and South Carolina, and others to New England, where scorning to receive assistance from those who had so cruelly wronged them, they died in obscurity and indigence.[1] For many months afterward the provincial newspapers contained advertisements of husbands seeking their wives, lovers their betrothed, and brothers their sisters. A few, after weary months of wandering, found again their lost ones; but the majority never again beheld the faces of those whom they loved.

Thus was consummated a deed, the most needless, wanton and fiendish, that it has ever been the lot of an historian to record,—a deed which has left upon the reign of George Second, and upon all those who were engaged in this expedition, a stain so dark and damning, as needed not the pen of one of our most loved poets, to render its memory lasting, so long as the sanctity of the family tie shall remain in the hearts of men.[2]

General Braddock had intended to have advanced against Fort Duquesne in the early part of spring. Difficulties, however, in procuring a suitable number of wagons and a proper supply of provisions, retarded his movements so greatly, that he was not ready to start until June. On the tenth of that month, with Washington as one of his aids, he left Wills creek at the head of twenty-two hundred men. The roughness of the roads and the impossibility of hastening forward the wagons,—loaded not only with the neces-

---

[1] Grahame.

[2] English writers have indeed attempted to justify this cruelty on the ground of "military necessity;" but the duty, which each one seems to consider himself under to explain it away by elaborate reasoning, is only a **confession of the utter needlessness and inhumanity of the act.**

sary supplies, but with much unnecessary baggage, which the regular officers would not consent to leave behind,—rendered the progress of the troops slow and tiresome. Under these circumstances, Braddock, at the suggestion of Washington, pushed ahead with twelve hundred picked men lightly equipped, while Colonel Dunbar, with the remainder of the troops and the heavy artillery, followed in slow marches. At length upon the eighth of July, the fork of the Monongahela and Youghiogheny was reached.

The next day's sun was just appearing above the eastern hills, when the army, having forded the Monongahela, pursued their journey along the southern bank of that river. Their polished helmets and rich trappings, glittering in the dewy foliage like so many diamonds, were in keeping with the cheerfulness visible upon each countenance, while a fresh breeze, which had just sprung up infused new life into the jaded steeds, who champed their bits, and seemed scarcely less impatient to hasten forward than their riders. At noon the river was again forded, and the troops were upon a level plain which, extending for half a mile, terminated in a gradual rise of ground to the hills beyond. The road from the fording place to Fort Duquesne, was across this plain and up this ascent.

"By the order of march, a body of three hundred men, under Colonel Gage, made the advance party, which was immediately followed by another of two hundred. Next came the general with the columns of artillery, the main body of the army and the baggage. At one o'clock the whole had crossed the river, and almost at this moment a sharp firing was heard upon the advanced parties, who were now ascending the hill, and had proceeded about a hundred yards from the termination of the plain. A heavy discharge of musketry was poured in upon their front, which was the first intelligence they had of the proximity of an enemy, and this was suddenly followed by another on their right flank. They were filled with the greatest consternation, as no enemy was in sight, and the firing seemed to proceed from an invisible foe. They fired in their turn, however, but quite at random and obviously without effect.

"The general hastened forward to the relief of the advanced parties; but, before he could reach the spot which they occupied, they gave way and fell back upon the artillery and the other columns of the army, causing extreme confusion, and striking the whole mass with such a panic, that no order could afterwards be restored. The general and the officers behaved with the utmost courage, and used every effort to rally the men, and bring them to order, but all in vain. In this state they continued nearly three hours, huddling together in confused bodies, firing irregularly, shooting down their own officers and men, and doing no particular harm to the enemy. The Virginia provincials were the only troops who seemed to retain their senses, and they behaved with a bravery and a resolution worthy of a better fate. They adopted the Indian mode, and fought each man for himself behind a tree. This was prohibited by the general, who endeavored to form his men into platoons and columns, as if they had been manœuvring on the plains of Flanders. Meantime the French and Indians, concealed in the ravines and behind trees, kept up a deadly and unceasing discharge of musketry, singling out their objects, taking deliberate aim, and producing a carnage almost unparalleled in the annals of modern warfare. More than half of the whole army which had crossed the river in so proud an array only three hours before, were killed or wounded. The general himself received a mortal wound, and many of his best officers fell by his side."[1]

Upon the fall of General Braddock, Colonel Washington assumed the command, and having succeeded in rallying the troops, fell back with them in tolerable order upon Gist's settlement, where Colonel Dunbar was encamped. Here a panic again seized the troops, and hastily burning

---

[1] Washington's journal, ii, 469.

their stores and destroying their artillery, they retreated in the wildest confusion to Will's creek, which a second time received an army broken and routed by the French. The English left on the field dead seven hundred and fourteen privates, while, with the exception of Washington, not an officer escaped unhurt. The French remained in possession of the field and vast quantities of ammunition, together with six brass field pieces, four howitz-carriages, and eleven small grenade mortars.[1] Their loss in killed was only three officers and thirty men.

Thus terminated this expedition, from which so much had been expected, and upon the result of which the eyes of both continents had been turned in anxious solicitude. It was an expedition moreover lost through sheer folly. During the march, Washington had repeatedly urged his commander to accept of a body of Indians under the Half King, who, at the solicitation of Johnson, had offered themselves to serve as scouts,[2] but Braddock, who, though a brave man, was imperious and self-willed, at first refused; and though he finally accepted them, yet they were treated with such neglect, that they left in disgust. Had Washington's advice been followed, so far even as to have sent in advance of the main body half a dozen Indians, the calamity would not have occurred.

Well would it have been for the colonists of Pennsylvania and Virginia had the effects of the rout ended here. But the French, when they unexpectedly saw that this defeat was followed by the retreat of the remainder of the army, found themselves at liberty to resume the offensive. The prestige of British troops among the Indians was gone, and taking advantage of this, the French prevailed on several of the Indian nations to take up the hatchet against the English—a result which was accomplished the more readily from the fact that the Indians still considered

---

[1] An account of the battle of the Monongahela.—*Paris Doc.*, x, 308.
[2] Manuscript letter: Johnson to George Croghan, April 23d, 1755.

themselves aggrieved by the sale of their lands by the Six Nations two years before at Albany. Although a part of the Shawnees were always perfidious and had declared for the French in the previous war, yet the majority of that nation, together with the Delawares, had always been depended on by the government of Pennsylvania, to preserve the western tribes in its interest, or at least to prevail on them to remain neutral. Now, however, those two nations, having declared war against the English with great solemnity, took up the hatchet with alacrity, and fell with great fury upon the settlements, carrying on a most sanguinary and cruel war, and burning and laying waste all before them from beyond the Apalachian hills in Virginia to the river Delaware.[1] From the fact that the Indian towns were scattered along both banks of the Ohio and Delaware, and on both branches of the Susquehanna, the Indians were capable of doing much mischief; and the terror of the inhabitants became so great, that it was feared, that following the Blue Ridge in their desolating course, they would fall upon the provinces of New Jersey and New York[2]

The Susquehanna and the Catawba tribes remained faithful. Rumors, however, becoming prevalent that the French were tampering with the Southern Indians, and a message being received to that effect from the chief warrior of the Cherokees, Governor Glen held a council among the hills of western Carolina, with five hundred warriors of that nation, with whom he renewed the covenant chain, and obtained from them a grant of lands, and also permission to erect a fort on the banks of the Savannah river.[3]

An evil star hung over the expedition against Niagara from its very inception. It was to have started early in

---

[1] Manuscript letter: Governor Morris of Pennsylvania to Governor Shirley, 3d December, 1755.

[2] Manuscript letter: Governor Morris to Governor Shirley.

[3] Fort Prince George.

the spring, but the troops, who were to take part in it, composed of Shirley's, Pepperell's and Colonel Schuyler's regiments, did not arrive in Albany till early in July. Just as Shirley and Pepperell, with their regiments, were embarking at Schenectady for Oswego—Colonel Schuyler's regiment having preceded them by a few days—the news of Braddock's defeat reached Albany. The effect of this intelligence was disastrous in the extreme. Such was the terror excited by it, that many of the troops deserted, and so great a number of the bateau men went home, that a large portion of the necessary stores had to be left behind, while over the spirits of all was cast a deep gloom. This caused more delay, and it was not until the latter part of July that General Shirley was fairly on the way to Oswego, where he arrived on the twenty-first of August.

At the council held at Alexandria in the spring, it had been determined that Oswego should be reinforced, and that vessels should also be built to intercept more readily the bateaux of the French. Accordingly, upon the seventh of June, three hundred and twenty ship carpenters arrived at that post; and at the same time Captain Bradstreet marched thither with two companies to reinforce the garrison. Meanwhile the carpenters worked so expeditiously, that when General Shirley arrived, he found several good vessels already built and ready for the transportation of his troops to Niagara. More boats, however, had to be built, and weeks passed before a sufficient number for transporting six hundred men—all that Shirley proposed to take with him—could be completed. Scarcely were they finished, when a storm set in so severe as to render it unsafe for the troops to venture on the lake in open boats. The storm abated upon the twenty-sixth of September, but hardly had the orders been given for their embarkation, when a succession of head winds and tempests arose, which continued for thirteen days. Sickness now prevailed; the Indians dreading a voyage on the water, deserted; and the season was far advanced. Under these circumstances

CHAP. a council of war was held, at which it was the opinion of
XV. all, that it would be more prudent to defer the expedition
1755. until another year. Accordingly on the twenty-fourth of
October, General Shirley, leaving Colonel Mercer in command of a garrison of seven hundred men, with instructions to erect two new forts for the farther security of the place, returned to Albany with the residue of his army.

Two of the expeditions so confidently planned at Alexandria, had thus signally failed. The hopes of all the colonists were now centered, in fearful suspense, upon the result of the expedition under Major General Johnson. Crown Point had been strongly reinforced. Dieskau, with the flower of the French army, was watching with eagle eye his movements. Should Johnson fail all hope is lost.

CHAPTER XVI.
1755.

By the end of June, all the forces destined for the reduction of Crown Point had assembled at Albany. They were composed chiefly of provincial militia from the colonies of Massachusetts and Connecticut. New York had contributed one regiment to the expedition, and New Hampshire had raised for the same object, five hundred sturdy mountaineers, and had placed them under the command of Colonel Joshua Blanchard.[1] The latter was first sent by Governor Wentworth to the Connecticut river to erect a fort at Cohoes, under the impression that it was on his route to Crown Point. While on the way, however, advices being received from Governor Shirley, urging him to hasten to Albany, he marched forthwith for that city, where he arrived with his men, after a tiresome march through the woods by way of Number Four, in time to join the rest of the troops.[2]

In the beginning of August, General Lyman was sent forward with the greater part of the troops, to erect a fort on the east bank of the Hudson river, at the great carrying-place between that river and Lake George, and which afterward received from General Johnson the name of Fort Edward.[3] It was the intention of Johnson to have gone on at the same time, and he would have done so, had he not been detained by the leaky condition of the bateaux, and also by difficulties which arose at this time between himself and Governor Shirley. The author of *A Letter*

---

[1] John Stark, the hero of Bennington, was, at this time, one of Blanchard's lieutenants.

[2] Manuscript letter: Governor Wentworth to Johnson. See also, Belknap.

[3] The fort was first named Fort Lyman after the builder.

to a Nobleman has seen fit to misrepresent so greatly the origin of this difficulty, and the conduct of General Johnson in this affair, that it is but just that the reader should have the benefit of an extract from a letter written by the general upon this subject to the board of trade. The letter is written from the camp at Lake George shortly after his arrival:

"Governor Shirley, soon after his arrival at Albany, on his way to Oswego, grew dissatisfied with my proceedings, and employed one Lydius, of that place—a man whom he knew, and I told him was extremely obnoxious to me, and the very man whom the Indians had in their public meetings so warmly complained of, to oppose my interest and management with them. Under this man several others were employed. These persons went to the Indian castles, and by bribes, keeping them constantly feasting and drunk; calumniating my character; depreciating my commission, authority and management; in short, by the most licentious and abandoned proceedings, raised such a confusion amongst the Indians, particularly the two Mohawk castles, that their sachems were under the utmost consternation; sent deputies down to me to know what was the occasion of all these surprising proceedings; that I had told them I was appointed sole superintendent of their affairs, which had given an universal satisfaction through all their nations, but that now every fellow pretended to be vested with commissions and authority. I sent several messages and the interpreters up to quiet their minds, for my military department would not suffer me to leave Albany, as I was about marching with the troops under my command, or I would have gone up and should have soon arrested all these violent measures.

*   *   *   *   *   *

"I shall only say, in general, that a complication of more scurrilous falsehoods; more base and insolent behavior; more base and destructive measures to overset that plan of general harmony, which I had with infinite pains, and at a great expense to the public, so lately established, could not have taken place, than did in the conduct of these agents of Governor Shirley. I spoke of it to Governor Shirley; I wrote to him of it, but without success. They pleaded his authority for all they did, and said they had his commission; and I can't but presume that it must have been done with his knowledge and consent, in which I am confirmed in his letter to me.   *   · *   *

"The reasons, or the pretended reasons which Governor Shirley gives for opposing my Indian management and employing these persons is, that I would not get him some Indians to escort him from Schenectady to Oswego. I had indeed mentioned it to some of the sachems, who told me that as his way to Oswego lay through their several countries,—and Oswego itself is in the Senecas country—they could not conceive there was any occasion for their escorting him, and that when he came to Oswego there was no fear but that many of the Six Nations would, according to my desire, meet him there and assist him. Numbers of the troops had gone up without any molestation; not the least interruption had been given to any one, the traders to Oswego daily going and returning with single bateaux. Those who are acquainted with Indian affairs well know that it would have been the worst of policy for the French at that time to violate the tranquillity of the country of the Six Nations. It is true, some small parties of enemy Indians had been discovered between Schenectady and my house, but they are looked upon as a set of freebooters, and Governor Shirley's body guard would have been a full security to him against any such. Even his premier Lydius, when I talked to him on this head, told me he *saw no want of Indians to escort him*, and that he would endeavor to dissuade him from it.

"It is with reluctance that I trouble your lordships with these matters, but as I have been honored with a station of great importance, and entrusted with money belonging to the crown, it behooves me on my account, not to be wholly silent; and I have said as little as I possibly could to give your lordships some idea of affairs, for which I apprehend myself accountable to your board.

"Governor Shirley's conduct not only shook the system of Indian affairs, and gave me fresh anxieties and perplexities, but occasioned considerable and additional expenses, which would otherwise have been saved; the profuse offers which his agents made to the Indians in order to debauch them from joining me, though it did not succeed with but a very few, yet gave to all such self-importance, that when I urged to any of them who made demands upon me, the unreasonableness of them, they reproached me that they had refused Governor Shirley's great offers, from whom they would have had anything they wanted. Under these circumstances and the account coming out at that time of our unhappy defeat on the Ohio, I was forced to make compliance, which otherwise they would not have expected nor I submitted to."

The truth is that Governor Shirley, who was an exceedingly consequential man, was piqued at the seeming neglect shown to his position. He had expected to find Johnson, like Lydius, a ready tool in his hands, and to be escorted through the Indian country, with all the ceremony of an Eastern prince. In this, Johnson, who had no time to give to anything that was not absolutely essential to the success of the expedition, could not further him, and hence Shirley's dissatisfaction. But even if Mr. Shirley did think that Johnson was not acting with judgment, his proper course would have been to lodge his complaints—if any he had—before the lords of trade, and not, for the sake of gratifying his animosity, to descend to these means. They could do no good; and to say the least, it was very ill-judged at this time,—when the utmost unanimity was necessary to further the expedition, then on the very eve of embarking,—to do anything which would create jealousies and dissensions among the Indians.

The character of Governor Shirley, which Mr. Bancroft

very justly describes as artful, favors the representation of this transaction as given by Johnson. The Six Nations, moreover, required peculiar management, which Johnson, after years of study and observation, alone was qualified to undertake. If he, likewise, was to have the entire control of the Indians and was alone responsible to the crown, it was natural, as well as perfectly right and just, that he should resent any interference, especially by one who, residing in New England, could not properly appreciate the exigencies which were continually arising among the Indians in the province of New York. The remarks of the author of a *Letter to a Nobleman* are as unjust to General Johnson, as his eulogy of Governor Shirley is gross and fulsome. General Johnson very properly, therefore, tells the ministry, in the letter which we have quoted, that the management of Indian affairs had not been sought by him; and that if he continued in it, he must be allowed to have it under his own control, untrammeled by the interference of the Massachusetts governor.

Before the general could join his army the dissensions sown among the Indians by Lydius must be healed. This caused a delay of several days; and even then, just as he had arranged everything, as he supposed, to the satisfaction of the Indians, a deputation came to him on the eve of his departure, refusing to proceed with him farther, until matters had been explained to them more clearly.[1]

These difficulties having been finally adjusted, the general upon the eighth of August, set out from Albany with the stores and artillery, and—with the exception of the New York and Rhode Island militia, which were still behind— with the rest of the troops. He was also accompanied by King Hendrik with fifty Mohawk warriors, and also by Joseph Brant, then a mere lad of thirteen years.[2] Upon his arrival at the great carrying place, on the fourteenth, he was joined by two hundred more braves, thus increasing

---

[1] Manuscript letter: Johnson to De Lancey, 8th August, 1755.
[2] *Christian Register.*

the number of his Indian allies to about two hundred and fifty.

The general found the New England troops burning with ardor and impatient of delay. The news of Braddock's defeat far from disheartening, only made them more desirous to be led against Crown Point. To them this expedition was for the defense of their firesides. "I endeavor to keep myself calm and quiet under our slow progress, and to wait God's time," wrote one of the provincials at this time, to his wife in Massachusetts.[1] But to them the advance was slow. General Lyman felt equally restive under the delay. So much so, indeed, that before Johnson's arrival, he had set three hundred of his men to work cutting a road to Fort Ann, supposing that the army would proceed against Crown Point by way of Wood creek and Lake Champlain. Johnson, however, in view of a council of war, which he proposed to call for the purpose of deciding upon the best route, countermanded the order, and sent out a scouting party of forty soldiers and three Indians to reconnoitre the whole country in that vicinity.[2] The scouts having returned, a council was called on the twenty-second, in which the officers, upon hearing their report, unanimously gave it as their opinion, "that the road to Lake St. Sacrament appeared to them the most eligible, and that it ought to be immediately set about." It was also determined to send forward two thousand men to cut a road through the woods to the head of the lake, and erect suitable buildings in which to store arms and other munitions of war when they should arrive.

Leaving General Lyman to await the arrival of the rest of the troops, and the New Hampshire men to complete and garrison the fort, Johnson set out on the twenty-sixth,

---

[1] Manuscript letter: Thomas Williams to his wife. Thomas Williams, who accompanied this expedition as a surgeon, was a brother to Colonel Ephraim Williams, and the same one who was dispatched from Fort Massachusetts to Albany for supplies, when that post was attacked by De Vaudreuil.

[2] Manuscript letter: Thomas Williams to his wife.

with thirty-four hundred men, for the lake—a distance of fourteen and a half miles—reaching it at dusk of the twenty-eighth. The position which he selected for his camp was a strong one, being protected on the rear by the lake, and on both flanks by a thickly wooded swamp. His first act on his arrival was to change the name of the lake from St. Sacrament to Lake George, "not only," as he loyally writes, "in honor of his majesty, but to ascertain his undoubted dominion here."[1] Although for many years previously this lake had been used as a means of communication both for warlike and commercial purposes between Canada and Albany, yet Johnson found a primeval forest, where "no house was ever before built, nor a spot of land cleared." The soldiers were immediately set to work clearing a place for a camp of five thousand men, and providing shelter for the military stores. Meanwhile General Lyman, having left at the carrying place two hundred and fifty New England troops, and five companies from New York which had finally arrived, joined the camp at Lake George on the third of September, bringing with him all the heavy artillery.

All now was activity in the provincial camp. Wagons laden with munitions of war, came and went across the

---

[1] Manuscript letter: Johnson to De Lancey. Also Johnson to the lords of trade.

The ancient Iroquois name of this lake is *Andiatarocte*—" there the lake shuts itself." The French missionary, Father Jogues, named it *St. Sacrament*; not, as some suppose—Mr. Cooper among them—on account of the purity of its waters, but because he arrived at the lake upon the eve of the festival day of that name.[1] The early Roman Catholic discoverers, says the Rev. Mr. Van Rensselaer, "frequently connect the discovery of places with the festival name, on the calendar." Mr. Cooper, in his *Last of the Mohicans* suggests the name of Horicon, for this lake. This, though quite poetical, is merely fanciful, as indeed he claims, and has not the merit of historical truth.

[1] "Ils arriverant, la veille du S. Sacrament, au bout du lac qui est joint au grand lac de Champlain. Les Iroquois le nomment Andiatarocte, comme qui diçoit *la ou le lac se ferme*. Le Pere le nomma le lac du S. Sacrament "—*Relations*. 1645-46.

portage. The wild flowers of the forest bent beneath the rude tread of armed men. The noise of a hundred hammers echoed through the mountain fastnesses; and keel after keel cut the crystal waters of the lake. By day, the French mountain frowned defiantly at those by whom its repose had first been broken; and at night, the panther, from the neighboring thicket, looked forth upon the stalwart forms reclining by the watch fires. "Prayers," wrote Johnson, "have a good effect, especially among the New England men;" and on the sabbath, while the Indians were reclining at a distance under the forest shade, or skimming the waters in their birchen canoes, the New England troops had gathered around the man of God,[1] to listen to his words of comfort, and to unite with him in supplication at the throne of the most High.

Johnson had expected to be joined at the lake by many more warriors of the Six Nations. In this he was disappointed. A few braves, it is true, dropped in at the camp, but by no means in the numbers which the Indians had assured him would come. The old Sachem Hendrik was mortified at the paucity of the number, and availed himself of a council, held on the fourth, to explain to Johnson and his officers why so few warriors had joined their standard:

"Some time ago," said he, "we of the two Mohawk castles, were greatly alarmed and much concerned, and we take this opportunity of speaking our minds in the presence of many gentlemen concerning our brother, Governor Shirley, who is gone to Oswego;—he told us that, though we thought you, our brother Warraghiyaghey, had the sole management of Indian affairs, yet that he was over all; that he could pull down and set up. He farther told us that he had always been this great man, and that you, our brother, was but an upstart of yesterday. These kind of discourses from him caused a great uneasiness and con-

---

[1] Rev. Stephen Williams, of Longmeadow, Mass., chaplain of Williams's regiment.

fusion amongst us, and he confirmed these things by a large belt of wampum.

"I just now said, these matters made our hearts ache and caused a great deal of confusion in our castles. Governor Shirley further told us: 'you think your brother Warraghiyaghey has his commission for managing your affairs from the king our father—but you are mistaken—he has his commission and all the moneys for carrying on your affairs from me, and when I please I can take all his powers from him; it was I gave him all the presents and goods to fit out the Indians with.'

"He further told us when he came to our fort: 'This is my fort; it was built by my order and directions; I am ruler and master here, and now brethren, I desire twenty of your young warriors from this castle to join me as your brother Warraghiyaghey promised me you would do, and be ready at a whistle. Brethren, you may see I have the chief command; here is money for you, my pockets are full; you shan't want; besides I have goods and arms ready for all that will go with me.' He said a great deal more of the like kind, which time will not permit us to repeat at present.

"He was two days pressing and working upon my brother Abraham to go with him as a minister for the Indians—he said to him: 'Warraghiyaghey gives you no wages, why should you go to Crown Point, you can do nothing there; but with me there will be something to do worth while.' These speeches made us quite ashamed, and the Six Nations hung down their heads and would make no answer.

"But brother, notwithstanding all these temptations and speeches, we that are come and now here, were determined to remain steadfast to you, and had it not been for Governor Shirley's money and speeches, you would have seen all the Six Nations here.

"Brother, we have taken this opportunity to give you this relation, that the gentlemen here present may know

CHAP. and testify what we have said, and hear the reasons why
XVI. no more Indians have joined this army."[1]

1755.   Thus closed the last formal speech that the great Mohawk chieftain lived to make. True as tempered steel to the interests of the English, his last moments were in harmony with those of his life—spent in keeping the Six Nations steadfast to their ancient alliance. Although he was a rude brave of the forest, yet his noble appreciation of the exigencies of the public welfare, the more polished governor of Massachusetts might well have imitated.

General Johnson's plan of operations was to build a fort at the head of the lake, and to remain there until a sufficient number of bateaux could be constructed in which to transport his stores and artillery. As soon as these were in readiness, he designed to proceed down the lake, with all his available forces, to Ticonderoga, and there remain until, strengthened by sufficient reinforcements, he could successfully attack Crown Point. Ticonderoga had long been considered by military men as a "very dangerous and important pass;" and it was his design to construct on that promontory a fort which would command the only two water passes to the lower settlements. This movement was therefore well planned; for if it should not be deemed advisable to attack Crown Point, the French could at least be prevented from passing down either of the lakes. The general was also the more anxious to proceed, from intelligence received through scouts, that a small party of French had already occupied this import-

---

[1] All these statements of Shirley, it is perhaps unnecessary to remind the reader, were false. 1st, Johnson acted at this time as superintendent of Indian affairs under a commission from General Braddock, and not from Shirley; 2d, The money which he held for the Indians, was given to him by Braddock, and he was responsible for it to him alone; and 3d, The fort was built—as stated in the last chapter—by the direction of Mr. De Lancey and his council, on the application of Johnson, with a portion of the "fund for contingencies," in the hands of the lieutenant-governor. Hendrik's well known character for strict integrity forbids us to doubt the correctness of the facts mentioned in his speech.

ant pass. Before, however, his arrangements could be completed, the rapid movements of the enemy foiled his design.

Early in July, De Vaudreuil, who was informed, through papers taken from Braddock, of Shirley's proposed expedition against Niagara, arranged a well concerted attack upon Oswego. Learning, however, that the English were advancing by way of Saint Sacrament against Crown Point, he changed his purpose; and calling back the troops already on their march to Oswego, sent them, under Baron Dieskau, to meet the forces of General Johnson.[1] Leaving a large force at Crown Point, the baron took six hundred Indians, seven hundred Canadians, and two hundred regulars,[2] and proceeding up Lake Champlain, landed at the head of that lake. The intention of the French general was first to attack Fort Edward, and then cut off the retreat of Johnson and annihilate his army. This accomplished, Albany and the lower settlements were to be destroyed. This plan was in harmony with the motto upon the baron's arms, "BOLDNESS WINS;" and though it was brilliant, it was also rash.[3]

On the evening of the fourth day after disembarking, the French army found itself, through the treachery of the Iroquois guides, on the road to Lake George, four miles distant from the fort.[4] Here the baron halted, and sent forward a party of Indians, under the direction of M. de St. Pièrre, to reconnoitre. They soon returned, having killed a courier, whom General Johnson had sent to warn the garrison at the carrying-place of their danger. As it was evident from this, that the commander of the fort was now on the alert, Dieskau gave the Indians the choice

---

[1] M. de Lottiniere to Count d' Argenson, 24 Oct., 1755.
[2] Chevalier de Montreuil to the same, 14 Oct., 1755.
[3] " I avow that I had a recent presentiment that misfortune would overtake him, (Dieskau) because I knew him to be too great a stickler for the dangerous principle that intrepidity alone can accomplish the most difficult things."—*Doreil to the Minister*, 28 Oct., 1755.
[4] Dieskau to Count d'Argenson, 14 Sept., 1755.

of either attacking the fort or marching against the camp at the lake.[1] The Indians, who had a peculiar horror of artillery, having learned through a prisoner, that the camp at the lake was destitute of cannon, positively refused to attack the fort, but expressed their willingness to be led against the latter. Having thus ascertained the disposition of the Indians, Dieskau gave up for the present his former design, and marching through the forest in the northerly part of the present towns of Kingsbury and Queensbury, encamped on the margin of a small pond, on the east of the Lake George road, and near the southern spur of the French Mountain.

On the evening of the seventh of September, Johnson was apprised, through his scouts, that a road had been cut from South bay, and that a large body of men were marching to the Hudson. The general immediately sent expresses to New York and New England for reinforcements, and at the same time dispatched two messengers to Fort Edward to warn Colonel Blanchard of the advance of the French army. One of these couriers was, as has been stated, intercepted and killed, but the other returned at midnight, bringing the startling intelligence that the enemy were only four miles from the fort. A council of war was called early the next morning, in which it was the general opinion of both officers and Indians that a detachment of one thousand troops, and two hundred Indians should be sent out in aid of Fort Edward "to catch the enemy in their retreat, either as victors or as defeated in their design." Hendrik alone disapproved of the number. "If," said that sage counsellor, "they are to fight they are too few; if they are to be killed they are too many;" and again, when it was proposed to send out the detachment in three parties, the Mohawk, picking up three sticks from the ground, said, "Put these together and you cannot break them; take them one by one, and you will do

---

[1] "An account of what has occurred this year in Canada."—*Department de la Guerre, Paris.*

it easily." His advice, however, on both these points was disregarded, and the Provincials, under the gallant Colonel Ephraim Williams, and the Confederate warriors, led by the venerable Mohawk brave, set out without delay in three divisions, and marched toward the fort, where it was supposed the enemy would be found. As soon as they left the camp, Johnson had some trees felled to form, with the wagons and bateaux, a rude breastwork; and at the same time, some heavy cannon, destined for the attack on Crown Point, were drawn up from the shore of the lake, and posted in advantageous positions.

Meanwhile, Dieskau, advised through his Indian scouts of the advance of Colonel Williams, arranged in a defile near at hand, an ambuscade in the shape of a crescent; the regulars being stationed in the center, and the Canadians and Indians on either side, where they were concealed on the right by thickets, and on the left by rocks and trees.

Colonel Williams advanced with his division to Rocky brook, about two miles from the camp, and halted until he should be overtaken by Lieutenant Whiting and Hendrik with the rest of the party. As soon as they came up, the colonel, singularly unsuspicious of danger, and neglecting his usual precaution of throwing ahead skirmishers, gave the order to advance; and the entire column, preceded by Hendrik and his warriors, marched briskly forward and entered the fatal defile. It had been the express orders of Dieskau, that his men should reserve their fire until the English were entirely within the half circle. Fortunately, however, before the detachment were entirely within the ambush, one of the enemy's muskets went off accidentally. Instantly, terrific yells and rattling of musketry filled the air, as volley after volley was poured with murderous effect upon the left of Williams's column, and upon the Indians in front. Hendrik, who was in advance of his braves, and who being corpulent and mounted on horseback, formed a conspicuous mark for the enemy's bullets, fell dead at the first fire. Colonel

CHAP. XVI.
1755.

Williams was also killed in the early part of the action, being shot through the head as he was standing upon a rock which he had mounted, the better to direct the movements of his men.[1] A hurried retreat of the Provincials now followed, with the enemy close on their heels, alternately yelling and firing. Reaching a small pond near the road,[2] a portion of the Provincials rallied, and stationing themselves behind it, each man for himself, checked the pursuit, until the arrival of Lieutenant Colonel Cole, whom Johnson, as soon as he heard the firing, had sent out with three hundred men to cover the retreat. Under the guidance of Whiting and Cole, this was successfully effected; and the party which a little before had gone forth confident in their strength, clambered over the barricades weary and dejected.

Had the French commander been able, as he intended, to have taken advantage of the confusion produced in Johnson's camp by the arrival of the panic stricken fugitives, and while his men were flushed with success, rushed forward and carrred the breast-works by storm, he would doubtless have been successful. But the Indians and Canadians, coming in sight of Johnson's cannon, halted, and finally skulked off to the edge of the woods, leaving the regulars to begin the attack. This delay lost the baron the victory, and gave the Provincials full fifteen minutes, in which to improve their defences, and recover from their previous trepidation.

The attack was begun by the regulars, who advanced in perfect order against the center, firing by platoons. As their polished arms were first descried advancing from the woods, a slight tremor seized the Provincials, but after the first few volleys they lost all fear and fought with

---

[1] For a sketch of Williams and Hendrik see Appendix No. III and IV of this volume.

[2] Since called Bloody pond, from the tradition that many of those slain in this skirmish were thrown into it.

coolness and desperation.[1] Finding that no impression could be made upon the center, Dieskau changed his attack to the left with no better effect. He next attempted, by a desperate charge, to turn Johnson's right, where were stationed the regiments of Ruggles, Titcomb, and the late Colonel Williams. A terrific fight followed; both parties feeling that the issue of the struggle had now arrived. In the words of an officer present, "there seemed nothing but thunder and lightning and perpetual pillars of smoke, and the bullets flew like hail-stones." The Provincials, said Dieskau "fought like devils," and in some instances leaping the breast-works and clubbing their arms they fought hand to hand and face to face. Finally, the old fashioned musket, in the muscular arms of the New England farmers, proving superior to the glittering bayonet, the regulars were again driven back, leaving the ground covered with their dead and wounded. During this attack upon the right, a party of Abenakis and Canadians, posting themselves in a morass, for a time made considerable havoc, but a few shells thrown among them scattered them in the greatest confusion. Thus driven back at all points, the enemy began to waver, which was no sooner perceived by the Provincials, than leaping their defences with a loud shout, they fought them until the lake became red as the crimson flowers that blossom upon its margin.[2] This fierce onset decided the day; and

---

[1] Joseph Brant, in relating the particulars of this bloody engagement to Dr. Stewart, acknowledged that this being the first action at which he was present, he was seized with such a tremor when the firing began, that he was obliged to take hold of a small sapling to steady himself; but that after the discharge of a few volleys he recovered the use of his limbs and the composure of his mind so as to support the character of a brave man, of which he was exceedingly ambitious.

[2] The *Lobelia Cardinalis*, commonly called the *Indian Eye-Bright*. The author has frequently seen large clusters of this beautiful blossom growing on the banks of the lake and upon the margin of Bloody pond. Alfred B. Street has embalmed this flower in a touching Indian legend, in his entertaining *Woods and Waters*.

the French, breaking their ranks, sought in wild disorder the cover of the woods.[1]

In this battle almost all the French regulars were killed. Dieskau, although he had received three balls in his legs and one across his knee while fighting close to the barricades, refused to leave the field; and supported by the stump of a tree, continued amid the whistling of bullets calmly to give his orders. Finally, as his troops were in full retreat, a renegade Frenchman maliciously discharged his musket through both of the general's hips, inflicting a very severe wound. Lieutenant Colonel Pomeroy coming up at this moment, the baron was conveyed to the tent of the American commander, where he received every attention due to a brave though unfortunate man—General Johnson refusing to have his own wounds dressed until those of the baron had been properly attended to.[2] Le Gardeur de St. Pièrre, the same who had defeated Washington the previous year on the Ohio, received his death wound in the skirmish of the morning. His last words were, "fight on boys, *this is Johnson not Braddock.*"

---

[1] The French suffered little in this action from the artillery, which, aimed generally too high, did but small execution—except, by the crashing of the balls in the tree-tops, to scare the Indians. All the credit is due to the personal valor of the soldiers and officers themselves.

[2] Account of the battle of Lake George; (1755) written by Baron Dieskau, in a dialogue entitled, *Dialogue between Marshal Saxe and Baron de Dieskau in the Elysian Fields;* also Dieskau's official account of the action—Department de la Guerre, Paris, published also in *N. Y. Col. Doc.* From these documents, it appears that the generally received impression that Dieskau was shot while feeling for his watch, &c., is a pure fiction.

"I know not what at present will be my fate; from M. de Johnson, the general of the English army, I am receiving all the attention possible to be expected from a brave man, full of honor and feeling." Baron de Dieskau to Count d' Argenson, Sept. 14, 1755.

Before the baron left America, a warm friendship sprung up between himself and his conqueror; and previously to his returning to France, he presented Johnson with a magnificent sword as a token of his regard. General Johnson acknowledged this gift in a feeling letter to the baron, which manuscript letter is in my possession. Dieskau died in 1767, of his wounds received in this action.

In the beginning of the action, General Johnson "displayed a firm and steady mind," and conducted himself with great bravery; but soon receiving a painful wound in the hips, he was forced to retire, leaving the command to Major General Lyman. During all of the fight, which lasted from half past ten in the morning until four in the afternoon, Lyman behaved with distinguished bravery; repeatedly showing himself in front of the defences, in order to encourage his men.[1]

The misfortunes of the enemy were not, however, at an end. Toward evening of the same day, as the shattered remnants of the French army were seated near Rocky brook, refreshing themselves after the late exhausting battle, they were suddenly attacked by a party of two hundred New Hampshire men under Captain Maginnis, who were on their way to Lake George, and completely routed, leaving, in the words of an eye-witness, "their garments and weapons of war for miles together, like the Assyrians in their flight." The brave Maginnis, however, received a contusion on the head from a spent bullet, and died soon after reaching the camp.

The bodies of those slain in this skirmish, were buried in the bottom of the glen, beneath the shade of everlasting rocks. It is a sweet, wild haunt,—the sunbeam falls there with a softened radiance,—and the brook near by murmurs plaintively, as if mourning for the dead.

In the three actions of this day, about two hundred and twenty of the Provincials were killed, and ninety-one wounded. Their loss was greater than it might otherwise have been, from the fact that several were hit by poisoned bullets; thus mere flesh wounds soon mortified, some of the soldiers dying in convulsions.[2] Of the Six Nations

---

[1] For a map of this action see appendix No. v.

[2] "Mical Harrington died of the wound he received through the fleshy part of the thigh, the ball undoubtedly poisoned; as also one Jonathan Burt, of Brimfield, by a poisoned ball through the arm; and one Brisbee, by a slight shot in the leg which threw him into convulsions. The art of man could not stop the mortification which seized the wounded part, and

nearly forty of their braves perished. The loss of the French was probably between three and four hundred.[1]

General Johnson, under the direction of a council of war held immediately after the action, sent circular letters, containing an official account of the action of the eighth, to Boston, whence they were to be sent to the several colonial governors. His thus acting according to direction, is a sufficient answer to those who have censured him, for not advising Governor Shirley at Oswego of the result. It is true that he might have written him unofficially by a private express; but this was a mere matter of preference. That he did not prefer so to do, after the efforts of Shirley to weaken his influence, is not surprising.

Three days after the battle, the Indians in council announced to Johnson and his officers, through Aguiotta, an Oneida sachem, their intention of returning forthwith to their homes. It was in vain that the general remonstrated, and told them that the object of the campaign was not yet accomplished,—that in fact he had "not yet got half way,"—they were determined in their purpose. While, however, they were not to be moved from their design, they assured their brother, "that their going home arose not from any coldness of heart, but was in accordance with their invariable custom of returning after an engagement, in which they had sustained loss, to cheer their people;" and they promised soon to return and use the hatchet with fresh vigor against the French. The Indians were also fearful that the Abenakis, in revenge for the loss of their braves, would fall upon their own castles left by their

---

presently a few hours shut up the scene. Oh cursed malice, that the fatal lead should not be thought sufficient without being rolled up with a solution of copper and yellow arsenic, as I am thoughtful was the case, by many of the poisoned balls which were brought in out of their bullet pouches, taken among the plunder."—Manuscript letter, Surgeon Thomas Williams to his wife. This is the only instance, that I recollect, of the use of poisoned bullets in battle.

[1] Dieskau estimated it at six hundred, and Johnson placed it in his first report of the action also at six hundred, but afterward at four hundred.

absence in a measure unprotected. It being useless to detain them against their inclination, the general, after consulting his officers, dismissed them to their castles, giving them some strouds, with which to cover the graves of their dead.[1]

The months of October and November were chiefly occupied in building a strong fort at the head of the lake.[2] A fortification at this point, was justly considered by Johnson extremely important, as it would thus command the pass into Canada by way of Lake George, in the same way as Fort Ann commanded the one by way of Wood creek. Its importance had also been seen by the lieutenant-governor of New York, who, in the previous year, had written the lords of trade, urging the erection of a fort at the "southern extremity of Lake St. Sacrament," on the ground that it would be a "defense against the French, and a protection for the Mohawks."[3] A council of war, held at the camp, on the seventh of September, had recommended the expediency of building a small picketed fort without delay. This was opposed by the general, who thought that a strong fortification should be constructed capable of holding, in an emergency, five hundred men. He, however, yielded to the will of the majority, and a small fort was begun, which went on so slowly, that by the last of September it was not nearly completed; only a dozen men at one time being found by Johnson engaged on the work.

On the twenty-ninth, advices were received from Sir Charles Hardy, the new governor of New York, stating that it was the wish of himself and his majesty's council, that a

---

[1] Minutes of council held at Lake George. *N. Y. Col. His.*

[2] Mr. Bancroft, I think, is mistaken in calling this "a *useless* fort of wood." It was successfully defended in the spring of 1757, against a force of two thousand troops, supplied with three hundred scaling-ladders; and it was only surrendered the ensuing summer by the cowardice of General Webb. While it was not of course a fortification of the first class, nor its site well chosen, it was far from *useless*.

[3] De Lancey to the lords of trade, December, 1754,

durable and commodious fort should be constructed as soon as possible. Upon this wish of the governor being communicated to a council of war, it was immediately decided to erect a fort, which should meet his views. The general accordingly sent to Fort Edward for all the shovels and spades which the officer at that post could spare, and the fort was forthwith begun. The work, however, did not progress so rapidly as Johnson desired. "The fort," he writes on the seventh of October, "goes on, all things considered, *pretty well.*" The New England men, impatient to proceed, and not seeing the necessity of a fort, did not enter into it with alacrity.[1] It was using their services, they selfishly thought, solely for the benefit of New York,—not perceiving that a fort at this place which would hold the French in check, was as much needed for the protection of their own frontiers as for those of their sister province. The work therefore lingered along; and it was not until the middle of November that the fort was completed, receiving from Johnson the name of William Henry, in honor of two princes of the royal blood.[2]

The want of unanimity shown in the erection of the fort, was not the only symptom of the jealousy which, for so many years, had existed between the provinces of New England and New York. The troops from the latter colony were as much elated at the defeat of Dieskau, as those from New England were depressed at the abortive attempt of Shirley; and other signs of ill feeling were soon manifest, which threatened to impede seriously the operations of the campaign. General Johnson was indefatigable in his endeavors to allay all jealousies and promote harmony among his troops. How well he succeeded may be inferred from the following extract from a

---

[1] "It [the fort] has met with many obstructions, and the men have been very backward in working there, which has been partly owing to several of their officers." Letter from Johnson, Nov. 4th, 1755.

[2] For a plan of this fort originally carved on the powder horn of a provincial while doing garrison duty in 1756, see Appendix vi.

letter written by a *New England* officer, from the camp at Lake George, to his wife, in Deerfield, Massachusetts:

"I must say, he (Johnson) is a complete gentleman, and willing to please and oblige all men; familiar and free of access to the lowest sentinel; a gentleman of uncommon smart sense and even temper; never saw him in a ruffle, or use any bad language—in short, I never was so disappointed in a person in the idea I had of him before I came from home, in my life; to sum up, he is almost universally beloved and esteemed by officers and soldiers as a *second Marlborough for coolness of head and warmness of heart.*[1]

This encomium, coming from a New England officer who, according to his own admission, joined Johnson's army prejudiced against him, is testimony which is deserving of the careful consideration of the candid reader.

But little more was accomplished during the remainder of the campaign. Scouting parties, it is true, under Captain Rogers, the famous ranger, amused themselves with surprises upon the enemy; executing them so adroitly, that many of the French, in the vicinity of Fort Frederick, bit the dust,—one Frenchman being killed and scalped by Rogers under the very walls of that fort. It was now, however, late in the autumn, and a council of war having decided on the twenty-eighth of November, that it was too late in the season to proceed farther with the expedition, General Johnson disbanded his army; and leaving six hundred men to garrison the fort, resigned his commission, and returned in the middle of December to his home at Mount Johnson.

In the conduct of this campaign, General Johnson has been severely censured in two particulars; first, in not following up the routed army of Dieskau, and thus pre-

---

[1] This manuscript letter is dated Oct. 8th, 1755. I have in my possession many manuscript letters testifying to the same thing. The one in the text is selected, that, coming from a *New England man*, it may have more weight. It is from Surgeon Williams to his wife.

venting its escape down Lake Champlain: and secondly, that instead of boldly advancing against Crown Point, he allowed the autumn to pass away in comparative inactivity, contenting himself with constructing a useless fort.[1]

Regarding the first of these charges, there can be no question, that in not following up the French army, the general allowed his caution to prevail over the better judgment of his officers. General Lyman begged that with his men flushed with their recent victory and anxious for the pursuit, he might be sent after the enemy. The reply given to him by the general—"that he had reason to expect a renewal of the attack, and that it would be dangerous to weaken the main body of the army by sending out detachments to scour the country," is not sufficient to justify his refusal of Lyman's request. Exhausted and dispirited as the enemy were, they were, in no condition to have made a successful defense, much less to have resumed the aggressive; and the probability is, that if General Lyman's suggestion had been followed, the gates of Fort Frederick never would have opened to receive the broken ranks of Dieskau's army.

Respecting the second and more serious of these criticisms, however, General Johnson is not so culpable as may at first appear. It was well known to the general, both through the baron's papers, and through scouts which he had dispatched for that purpose, that Crown Point was heavily garrisoned, and that at Ticonderoga, strong breast works had been thrown up.[2] The experience of the last engagement had shown him how difficult it was for even thoroughly trained troops to capture rude and hastily constructed defences; and he therefore very wisely hesitated before attacking, with raw and undisciplined militia, breast works which had been carefully put up, and which were

---

[1] Vide: Review of military operations, in a *Letter to a Nobleman*. See also Bancroft, and Dr. Dwight's *Travels*, vol. iii.

[2] Major General Johnson to Lieutenant Charles Hardy, Sept. 16th, 1755. See also Capt. Roger's *Journal*.

defended by regulars, trained under the best generals of Europe.[1] In addition to this, the artillery of the enemy which on his first movement down the lake, could be easily transported from Crown Point to Ticonderoga, was such as to make an attack hazardous in the extreme, unless with a very strong army of disciplined troops, and with a sufficient supply of heavy ordnance, neither of which Johnson possessed. That he was sadly deficient in the requisite artillery, is sufficiently evident from the following official correspondence between himself and Captain William Eyre, who was chief of the ordnance department, and considered a very accomplished and skillful officer:

General Johnson to Captain Eyre.

"CAMP AT LAKE GEORGE, Sept. 29th, 1755.

" Sir: I desire you will give me your opinion in writing whether the artillery and stores thereunto belonging at this camp, at Fort Edward, and left on the road between said fort and Albany, are, according to the late intelligence we have received relating to the enemy, sufficient for proceeding on the present expedition.

"I am, Sir, &c.,
" WM. JOHNSON.

Captain Eyre to General Johnson.

"LAKE GEORGE, Sept. 29th, 1755.

"Sir: Pursuant to your order of this day, to know my opinion whether the artillery and stores here, at Fort Edward, and on the road from Albany to the last mentioned place, are sufficient to proceed against Crown Point, I answer NO, upon the supposition that our accounts from the French are to be depended on; as this information acquaints us that they have, (meaning the enemy,) thirty-three pieces of cannon, many of them 16 and 24 pdrs., equal or nearly

---

[1] The experience of Abercrombie, in 1758, in attacking the breastworks erected by Montcalm at Ticonderoga, shows that Johnson did well to hesitate.

to our 24 and 32 pdrs., and also thirty-five mortars. Now our strength consists of four battering pieces, viz: two 32 pdrs., and two 18 pdrs., two 12 pdrs., and eight 6 pdrs., besides one 13 inch mortar, with four smaller ones from five inch and a half diameter to seven inches: and add to this a scarcity of 6 pd. ball. These are my reasons for determining me to think our present state of artillery not sufficient.

"I am, Sir, &c.,

"WILL. EYRE, Engineer.

"N. B. Our howitzers split during the late engagement."[1]

It was the duty of General Johnson to be guided by this advice; and had he, with the knowledge of this state of facts, attempted an attack on Crown Point and failed, the caustic, but prejudiced and unreasonable pen of the author of *A Letter to a Nobleman*, would have been equally wielded in demonstrating its folly. It is reasonable, also, to presume that a general on the spot, with a knowledge of the means at his command, and whose bravery and skill never has been questioned, should have been better able to judge of the expediency of an attack, than a civilian, comfortably seated in his easy chair, far removed from the scene of operations.

Want of energy was not one of Johnson's faults. He was anxious to proceed, and felt annoyed at the delay. Even if everything otherwise had been favorable, the lack of suitable means for transporting his supplies was sufficient to retard the expedition until too late in the season to advance. "Our Expedition," he writes, "is like to be extremely distressed and I fear fatally retarded for the want of wagons. The people of the county of Albany and the adjacent counties, hide their wagons and drive away their horses; most of the wagoners taken into this service have deserted; some horses are quite jaded, and some few killed

---

[1] This official manuscript correspondence, which I have found among the Johnson manuscripts, has never before seen the light.

by the enemy, and several run away. Most of our provisions are at Albany; a great part of our ammunition at the lower camp, and all our bateaux except a hundred and twenty. To bring a sufficient quantity of provisions here, and all other necessaries for an embarkation upon the lake in due time, will require four or five hundred wagons at least. I have written to the mayor and magistrates of Albany, and sent them an impress warrant and called upon a special commission to an active officer to superintend and dispatch the wagons. I sent, *some time ago*, a positive order to all the commissaries at Albany to forward all the provisions and stores in their hands; since which we have only sixty wagons, none of which, as I can find, were dispatched by the New York commissaries, who being livers in Albany, and men in power there, might, I apprehend, if they had properly exerted themselves, have forwarded the common cause very much with regard to wagons. We had not above *two days allowance* of bread in camp, when these sixty wagons arrived, and I hear they are short at the other fort."[1]

Thus hampered by the remissness of contractors, whom no exertions on his part could stimulate into activity, all the general could do was to employ his men in erecting a fort, hoping by this course to prevent any insubordination that might arise through idleness. He was moreover, unwilling to have his retreat cut off by way of Wood creek, in case he was unsuccessful, by not having an open communication with Fort Edward and Albany. Boldness alone does not constitute a good soldier, and he who neglects to provide for every *foreseen* contingency, is deficient in the first requisite for a good general.

Although General Johnson, owing to causes over which he had no control, was unsuccessful in the original object of the expedition, yet his services were appreciated both by the crown and by the people of his own province; the former creating him in November a baronet of Great

---

[1] Gen. Johnson to Sir Charles Hardy, Sept. 16th, 1755.

Britain,[1] and the latter greeting him with an illumination and a triumphal procession on his arrival at New York the last of December. Parliament, also, voted him its thanks for his victory, together with the handsome sum of five thousand pounds.[2]

The action of the eighth of September, so far as concerns the number of men engaged, was not a great battle; but when viewed in its immediate strategical results, it well deserves a prominent place among the battles of American history. The Rev. Cortlandt Van Rensselaer, in his admirable discourse upon the battle of Lake George, thus sums up its results:

"I. The battle of Lake George is memorable in defeating a well laid, dangerous scheme of the enemy, and in saving the province from scenes of bloodshed and desolation. If Dieskau had succeeded in overthrowing Johnson in his entrenchments, his advance upon Fort Edward would have been easily successful, and thence his march to Albany would have been triumphant. Old Hendrik, at the convention of the preceding year, had warned the province of its danger. "You are without any fortifications," said he; "It is but a step from Canada hither, and the French may easily come and turn you out of doors." The conflagration of our northern settlements would have been followed by the desolation of Albany and Schenectady; and although Dieskau must have soon been compelled to retreat, it is impossible to estimate the bloodshed, plunder, and general losses which might have taken place, had not God ordered it otherwise. His providence was on our side. The victory of Lake George undoubtedly rescued the province from injury and woe beyond computation; considered, therefore, in its immediate strategical results, the battle was one of the important engagements in American history.

---

[1] Johnson's baronetcy dates from Nov. 27th, 1755.

[2] For the manner in which Johnson invested the £500, the curious reader is referred to manuscript letter in Appendix vii

"II. The battle of Lake George is remarkable for *its influence in rallying the spirit of the American colonies.* Much had been expected from the three expeditions sent against the French; but disappointment and sorrow had already followed Braddock's terrible defeat. It was more than the moaning of the forest pine in the ears of the solitary traveler; it was the blaze of lightning falling upon the mountain oak in his very path, followed by the crash of thunder. All the provinces were amazed, awe-struck, paralyzed for a time; but recovering from the first shock of the calamity, they were aroused to avenge their loss. Their hopes were turned to Lake George and Niagara, and not in vain. Johnson's victory was received as the precursor of a recovered military position and fame, and was hailed as the means of deliverance from a bold and cruel foe. Few battles ever produced more immediate results in rekindling military and martial enthusiasm. Congratulations poured in upon General Johnson from every quarter. Not only were the colonies filled with rejoicing, but the influence of the triumph went over to England, and the deeds of our fathers at the camp of Lake George became familiar to the ears of royalty, and were applauded by the eloquence of parliament. The moral effects of a battle in which the forces arrayed against each other were comparatively small have rarely been greater and more decided in the whole range of military annals.

"III. Viewed simply in a military aspect, the battle of Lake George was the *only successful achievement within the thirteen colonies, during the campaign of* 1755; which is another item of its various renown. Braddock's defeat on the Monongahela, and Shirley's retreat from Oswego, brought ruin upon the expeditions framed for the reduction of Forts Duquesne and Niagara. Although the northern expedition failed in its object of reducing Fort Frederick, it had a show of glory in the brilliant success of a hard fought battle. Success in one direction often overbalances disappointment in another. The victory of General Johnson was the great event of the campaign of 1755, solitary in the honors of its military triumph, and shining out, bright as Mars, from the clouds of night.

"IV. The victory of Lake George occurred in a series of campaigns that *ended in the conquest of Canada and of the valley of the great west.* Here, in the forest, was the base of a line of operations on which were wrought out great problems of war. The mountains of the lake were landmarks to conduct our armies from summit to summit of achievement, until, passing over all barriers, they found their resting place in the valleys of St. Lawrence and Mississippi. Unknown results of territorial acquisition, and of political and religious destiny, lay concealed in the expedition which started for the capture of a single fort on Lake Champlain and for the defence of the limited boundary line of a province. God disposes of man's proposals. The lucid purposes of an all-comprehensive providence, undiscernible by mortal eyes, are brought to pass by the majestic developments of events apparently remote in their relations as trivial in magnitude. The American victory of Lake George was not an isolated item of one campaign. It was more than a simple triumph in an unbroken wilderness,—a military achievement of the New England and New York yeomanry which saved themselves from destruction. Far higher its moral, political and warlike connections. It headed a series of successes that were followed by the gain of kingdoms. It animated the determination of the country to take decisive measures for deliverance from French aggressions and agitations. "Canada, my lord," wrote a distinguished New Yorker, in reviewing the operations of the campaign, "Canada must be demolished,—*Delenda est Carthago,*—or we are undone."[1] The result was not anticipated at the beginning, but the natural tendency of the contest was the overthrow of French dominion on the continent. Johnson's victory had a true influence of relation to this end. As the south-

---

[1] Review of military operations.

ern inlet near Fort George joins itself to the lake, whose waters flow to the north, and, tossed over cascades and waterfalls, pass into the St. Lawrence, so the expedition of 1755, identifying itself with a vast expanse of agencies, pressed forward the natural current of its direction, over the rocks and reverses of campaigns, into Canada. But Canada was only a part of the great acquisitions of the war. The whole northwest was wrested from France, together with the valley of the Mississippi lying easterly of that river, with the exception of the island of Orleans.

"V. The battle of Lake George was furthermore memorable *in its suggestions of provincial prowess, and its lessons of warfare to the colonies preparatory to their* INDEPENDENCE. The battle was fought by provincial troops, and chiefly by the hardy sons of glorious New England. The veteran regulars of Old England had been beaten in the forests of western Pennsylvania, or remained inactive in the Niagara expedition. Through some unaccountable cause, the expedition, which was on the direct line of Canada, and nearest to the French reinforcements, known to be at hand, was consigned to the exclusive care of native colonial soldiers; and bravely did they do their duty. On these shores provincial prowess signalized its self-relying and unaided capabilities; and in this battle and in this war the colonies practically learned the value of union and the unconquerable energies of a free people. Putnam and Stark, and Pomeroy, came here, as to a military academy, to acquire the art of warfare; and they all exercised their experience at Bunker Hill. George Washington himself, as a military man, was nurtured for America and the world amid the forests of the Alleghanies and the rifles and tomahawks of these French and Indian struggles. Lake George and Saratoga are contiguous not merely in territory, but in heroic association. Correlative ideas, evolved under varying circumstances, they are proofs of the same spirit of liberty, the same strong energy of purpose."

CHAPTER XVII.
1755—1756.

CHAP. XVII.
1755.

The news that Sir Charles Hardy was to take the reins of government arrived, much to the chagrin of the De Lancey party, early in March, but it was not until the third of September that the new governor landed in New York. The ship of war in which he came anchored in the harbor upon the second, but the lieutenant governor detained him on board until the next day, under the pretence that the military were not quite ready to receive him; but in reality that he might have an evening with him alone to secure him to the interests of his faction.

Sir Charles Hardy, the one whom the ministry had selected to succeed Sir Danvers Osborne, was, like Clinton, an unlettered British admiral; and he had not landed long, before it became apparent that like him also, he had not sufficient executive talent to govern without a leader. He therefore soon resigned himself into the hands of Mr. De Lancey, who thus for the third time became governor.[1] His first message to the assembly on the fourth—three days after that body had been convened and opened by Mr. De Lancey,—fully endorsed the message of the latter; expressed his pleasure at the energy which they had shown in granting supplies; and closed with complimenting the lieutenant governor, who, said he, "from his attachment to his majesty's service, and great knowledge of the country, has laid this matter before you in a way that leaves me nothing to require, but that you would proceed with the utmost dispatch on the matters recommended in his message."

The house, however, resolved on the fifth, that the season

---
[1] Smith.

was too far advanced to raise men in time for the expedition against Crown Point; but as it understood that Connecticut was actually raising for General Johnson's army two thousand men, who from the forwardness of the levies could reasonably be expected to reach that general in time for action, it would contribute eight thousand pounds toward their equipment.[1] In order that this resolve might not seem to be dictated by a refractory spirit, the house on the eleventh sent up to the new governor an address couched in the most courteous language, in which, after congratulating him upon his safe arrival, it assured him that the great regard his most sacred majesty had shown his loyal colony by appointing a gentleman of his excellency's upright character to preside over it, was a happy presage of its future prosperity; "and your excellency may be confident of meeting with all the assistance for attaining that most desired end, that it is in the power of a dutiful people to give." He was also informed in this same message, of the custom, usual upon the arrival of a new governor, of dissolving the assembly and issuing writs for a new election; and that if he thought that such a measure, in the present state of affairs, would be consistent with his majesty's service, it would be agreeable to them, and to the people whom they had the honor to represent. The governor, in his answer on the ninth, thanked them for these expressions of good feeling, assuring him as they did, that a governor who made the welfare of the colony the rule of his conduct, would always meet with their confidence and assistance. "Whatever may appear," he added, "advisable at this juncture, for the peace and good of the province, I cannot but take notice of the honor that must redound to you, gentlemen, who from a consciousness of the rectitude of your conduct, thus refer yourselves to the voice of the people." He did not, however, think it advisable to dissolve the assembly; and after passing, on

---

[1] Journals of the assembly.

the eleventh, the bill of eight thousand pounds for Connecticut, he prorogued the assembly.

1755.   The day after the prorogation, a letter from Colonel Blanchard was received by Sir Charles, informing him in general terms of the action of the eighth of September;[1] but it was not until the fourteenth, that his excellency communicated to his council a letter of the tenth instant from Peter Wraxall,[2] aid-de-camp to General Johnson, containing a full account of the defeat of the French army and the capture of its general. At the same time he laid before the board letters from Governor Wentworth and Lieutenant Governor Phipps. The former wrote that New Hampshire had passed an act for raising three hundred men for the Crown Point expedition; and the latter informed him that Massachusetts had already in the field two thousand men in addition to their former quota of eight hundred, raised for the same object. These letters were accompanied by a suggestion from the executive that as these additional reinforcements might occasion a scarcity of provisions among the troops, it would be well to send at once to Albany an ample supply of stores. Acting upon this hint, the council directed Mr. Oliver De Lancey to forward the requisite supplies, and to purchase and send to Albany three hundred muskets, in addition to those belonging to the province which were already in his hands. After some farther suggestions respecting the health of the city in his absence, the governor, having appointed Thursday, the second of October, as a day of public thanksgiving for the defeat of the enemy, sailed for Albany the afternoon of the same day.[3]

The governor's object in going to Albany at this time, was, that being nearer the seat of operations, he might be better able to hasten the supplies delayed by the remissness

---

[1] Manuscript letter: Goldsbrow Banyar to Johnson, Sept. 13, 1755.
[2] Afterward private secretary to Johnson. He died July 11th, 1759.
[3] Manuscript letter: Banyar to Johnson. Sir Charles was accompanied on this voyage by De Lancey, Horsmanden, Rutherford and Pownal, the first three being members of his council.

of the Albany authorities, and personally superintend the forwarding of the Connecticut troops. His visit, however, accomplished little; and having concerted measures with the Massachusetts and Connecticut commissioners respecting the garrisoning of Forts Edward and William Henry, and giving a few general orders to the militia officers to hold themselves ready to march at a moment's warning, he returned to the city on the twenty-sixth of November.

The governor met his assembly on the second of December, and in his message the day following, announced the victory of General Johnson over Baron Dieskau. Although the expedition had not been attended with those important results which he had hoped for, yet it had been productive of much benefit. The two forts which had been constructed at the great carrying place and the head of Lake George, would not only facilitate any future attempt upon the French in that direction, but, if properly garrisoned, add greatly to the security of the frontier. In the same message, Sir Charles made public, for the first time, the disagreeable instructions with which he had been charged by the ministry; and therefore now demanded, in the name of the king, the passage of a law for settling a permanent revenue on a solid foundation—said law to be *indefinite and without limitation of time*—for salaries of governors, judges, and all the necessary charges of the government. As, moreover, the two forts, erected by the provincial army, were to be garrisoned with troops raised by each province, he recommended an immediate provision for their quota of the expenses incident to this service.

In their answer, on the ninth, the assembly applauded the governor in the warmest terms for his zeal in promoting the expedition against Crown Point. While they confessed that the success of that expedition had not equalled their expectations, yet the advantage gained by General Johnson was deserving of special notice,—as to it might be ascribed the comparative safety of the frontier. The measures, also, which had been taken in erecting and properly garrisoning the forts, were, in their estimation, well judged; and the executive might rest assured that they would not fail to defray their portion of the expense. To that part of the message demanding an unlimited support, their answer was in singular contrast to the manner in which Mr. Clinton's similar request had been met. "We wish," they courteously replied, "we could with equal satisfaction, reconcile to ourselves your excellency's recommendation of an indefinite support; but humbly beg leave to inform your excellency that we have no permanent funds on which to establish such a revenue ; *nor do any occur to us, without very apparent inconveniences to our constituents.* We therefore most humbly trust that we shall stand acquitted in the eyes of our most gracious sovereign, *if we decline a measure so directly opposite to the sentiments of almost every individual of the colony.*"

The quiet indifference with which the demand for an indefinite support was thus met, is ascribed by Mr. Livingston to the influence of the lieutenant governor, who, having a large sum due him for past services, for the passage of which the governor's consent would be necessary, thought it best to treat Sir Charles in a different manner and with more leniency than his predecessor. While, however, considerable allowance should be made for the rancor of that writer toward his political opponents, yet it is certain that there was a marked change in the course pursued by Mr. De Lancey ;—a course, moreover, in which he was aided by the conduct of Sir Charles himself, who, preferring the ease and emoluments of office to the bitterness of party strife, soothed the assembly " with hints of his disapprobation of the orders he had delivered from his master, and with intimations of his unwillingness to take umbrage at their non-compliance."[1]

The history of this year would be incomplete without some reference to the Indian ravages on the north-eastern

---

[1] Smith.

frontier. The provincial army under General Johnson, while it checked incursions along the chain of posts in the north-western portion of Massachusetts, did not stop the forays of the enemy on the Connecticut river, and along the New Hampshire border. From the St. Lawrence to the Connecticut river, an easy communication by Lake Memphremagog was open to the St. Francis Indians, of which they were not slow to avail themselves. In Keene, the fort was attacked, and though the enemy were repulsed, yet in their retreat they burned several houses, slaughtered many cattle, and killed two men.[1] Near Fort Dummer, a fortified house was entered in the evening, through strategy, by a party of Indians, and all of its inmates captured and conveyed to Crown Point. Many of the St. Francis Indians were in the army of Dieskau, and their defeat stimulated them the more to deeds of increased ferocity.[2] Their incursions at length grew so frequent, that the government of New Hampshire was appealed to for a body of troops to protect the frontier. This appeal being received with indifference, application was next made to Massachusetts with more success; and a body of troops was sent to the aid of the settlers, and the posts on the Connecticut supplied with small garrisons.[3] Notwithstanding this, however, armed bands of Indians continued to infest the woods, lying close by day, only to wield the hatchet with more fatal effect by night. Numerous were the midnight alarms, the individual murders, the burning dwellings. Farmers gathered their harvests in terror, or more frequently left them to rot untouched upon the field; so that in several instances the inhabitants were threatened with starvation.[4]

While the soil of New Hampshire was watered with the blood of her settlers, Governor Shirley, who, by the death

---

[1] Hoyt.
[2] Belknap.
[3] Hoyt.
[4] Idem.

of General Braddock, had become commander-in-chief of all his majesty's forces in America, arrived in New York the second of December. He came from Albany, where he had been engaged, since his arrival from Oswego, in forwarding stores and munitions to the garrison of that post. Always in a bustle, he never made progress; and although his plans were feasible and often brilliant on paper, yet in their practical workings they were sadly deficient. His magnificent scheme for the capture of Niagara having failed, the winter could not pass without his "revolving in his busy mind" another expedition against the enemy. Accordingly, on his arrival in New York, he immediately summoned a grand congress of provincial governors to meet on the twelfth, to discuss a plan of operations for the next year's campaign.[1]

The congress was opened by Mr. Shirley with an elaborate and strongly written statement of the importance of Oswego, both as a military harbor, and as being situated in the country of the Onondagas, the center canton of the Confederacy. Should that post be lost, the inevitable consequence would be, "the defection of the Six Nations, the loss of the whole country, for nearly three hundred miles from Oswego to Schenectady, and perhaps the reduction of Albany itself." Nor should he be surprised to hear any day of its capture, so long as the French held Fort Frontenac,—the possession of which, enabling them to build and maintain "vessels of force" upon the lake. Indeed, he already had reliable intelligence that the enemy were now constructing three large vessels in the harbor of Frontenac. "Hence," concluded Mr. Shirley, "could the French be dislodged from that post and the little fort at Toronto; and their entrance into Lake Ontario obstructed, all their other forts and settlements on the Ohio and the

---

[1] This council was composed of Governor Shirley, Sir Charles Hardy, Mr. Fitch of Connecticut, Mr. Sharp of Maryland, Mr. Morris of Pennsylvania, Colonel Peter Schuyler, Colonel Dunbar, Major Craven, Major Rutherford and Sir John St. Clair.

western lakes, would be deprived of their support from Canada, and must ere long be evacuated."

Having thus prepared the members of the congress to regard his projects with favor, Mr. Shirley laid before them his plan of operations. Five thousand men were to rendezvous early in the spring at Oswego, whence the forts at Niagara, and Frontenac were to be attacked, and *of course* taken; three thousand provincials were to march at the same time, by way of Will's creek, upon Fort Duquesne; and simultaneously with both these expeditions, ten thousand troops were to proceed against Crown Point, and having reduced that fort, erect a regular fortification in its place, and build and launch seven war vessels upon the lake. In addition to this large force, two thousand men were to march up the Kennebec, lay waste with fire and sword the French settlements on the Chaudière, and penetrate to within three miles of Quebec. Thus menaced at all points, disturbed and distracted, Canada must succumb, and the governor's long cherished project of expelling the French from Canada, would be accomplished! Preparatory, however, to the successful prosecution of the spring campaign, he proposed to take advantage of the freezing of the lake and attack Ticonderoga, which, from the weakness of its garrison, he was sanguine could be captured. This plan appeared so feasible, and was withal so confidently stated, that in its chief features it met with the almost unanimous approval of the congress. Sharpe, the lieutenant-governor of Maryland, alone augured ill for the success of the scheme. "We shall have good reason to sing Te Deum, at the conclusion of this campaign," he wrote, "if matters are not then in a worse situation than they are at present." He, however, yielded to the opinion of the majority; and Major Rutherford and Captain Staats Morris were dispatched to England, to lay the plan before the ministry. The business which had brought the governors together being finished, they returned to their several provinces, leaving Shirley in New York, busily

CHAP. XVII.
1755.

engaged in endeavoring to win the assembly's countenance to his winter expedition.

Success, in the estimation of the public, is always the criterion of an able chieftain; and however fair and plausible the plan appeared upon paper, yet its author had invariably been so unsuccessful in all his military undertakings, that the assembly looked coldly upon the design against Ticonderoga, and refused to appropriate anything for that object. Finding his measures feebly supported, Governor Shirley in disgust returned soon after the holidays to his own province, to induce it to assist him in his winter expedition, and receive from the people of Boston a balm for his wounded feelings in the form of an ovation, gotten up as an offset to the one lately given to Sir William Johnson in New York.

Sir William Johnson spent most of January in New York, during which month, a tart correspondence was held between himself and Governor Shirley respecting his commission as agent of Indian affairs. It has been seen that the Baronet, holding his commission from General Braddock, had long chafed under the interference of Shirley; and the reception by him at this time of a new commission and instructions from the latter, determined him to bring the matter to a definite understanding at once. If he held any commission in future it was his wish to hold it directly from the crown, and until this point was settled, he preferred to act, if he acted at all, under the one which he then held from General Braddock. "With relation to the new commission," he writes, "which your excellency has thought proper to send me, I must beg leave to observe to your excellency that I apprehend the late General Braddock's commission to me for the sole management of the affairs of the Indians of the Six Nations and their allies, was granted in consequence of the royal instructions, and with the concurrence of the council of Alexandria, of which your excellency was a member, and that it remains still in force. Under this opinion, I do not conceive the necessity of your issuing another commission to me, or that I can consistently accept of it."¹

To this rejection of the commission, Shirley objected, on the ground that if Braddock had given him such a commission it must have been by sinking the commission from the king, which his majesty had sent to be delivered to him. He however said that he should not insist on his acting under a commission from him, and thus gave up the point, much to the satisfaction of the Baronet, who replied, that he was happy his excellency had thought it advisable that he should not act under his commission, as otherwise he could not possibly have executed the trust reposed in him, nor do that service which the public cause required. "Your excellency," added the Baronet, "as commander in chief has an undoubted right to direct the measures of this his majesty's service, and to send me your instructions accordingly, which I shall think it my duty to obey, but how far at each particular juncture, and upon each particular occasion, and in what peculiar manner, I may be able to manage, and persuade the six Confederate nations (who tho' allies to the British crown are very jealous of being thought dependent upon us) to engage in this or that measure, must, I conceive, while I have the management of their affairs, be left to my conduct and discretion, without which, unless your excellency conceives them as vassals, you must know that no one can manage their affairs properly; and here I must beg leave to represent to your excellency, that there are now agents acting among the Confederate Indians, without any knowledge or advice, and what they are about and what may be the consequence of their measures, I cannot answer for. I must therefore beg that your excellency give orders that they be withdrawn, and that none hereafter be sent there, but by my direction or recommendation."²

---

[1] Sir William Johnson to Governor Shirley, Jan. 3d, 1756.
[2] Sir Wm Johnson to Governor Shirley 5th, January 1756.

In order, however, that this matter might be settled for the future on a permanent basis, the Baronet laid the whole case before the lords of trade; the result of which was, that in July he received through Mr. Secretary Fox, a commission as "COLONEL, AGENT, AND SOLE SUPERINTENDENT OF ALL THE AFFAIRS OF THE SIX NATIONS AND OTHER NORTHERN INDIANS," accompanied with a salary of six hundred pounds per annum. At the same time instructions came from the ministry forbidding each northern province to transact any business with the Indians. The Baronet was thus placed on the independent footing which he had so long desired; and the entire management of Indian relations was given into his hands, "with no subordination but to Loudoun."

APPENDIX.

No. I.

The adoption of the pale-faces as a compliment for distinguished services, or as a token of esteem, has always been usual among the Indian tribes. Dr. Cadwallader Colden was adopted by the Mohawks. The late duke of Northumberland, who served as Lord Percy in the American Revolution, was created a chief of the Six Nations through the influence of Joseph Brant, with whom he was on terms of warm friendship. Washington Irving was adopted into the Huron clan, a few years before his death; and the late General Peter B. Porter was long a chief of the Senecas by adoption. Edmund Kean, the tragedian, was also adopted by the Hurons of Loretto near Quebec.

In January, 1844, the late Colonel Wm. L. Stone was adopted by the Senecas, at a formal council, as a chief of that nation. The letter which Mr. Stone returned in reply to the compliment, shows so much good feeling as well as appreciation of the honor, that his son may be pardoned for introducing it in this place in full.

" *To the Senecas, Chiefs and Warriors of the Seneca Indians.*

Brothers : I have been told that at your general council, held at Cattaraugus, in the Moon of Juthoo, that is, in January last, you did me the honor to make me a chief of the Seneca nation; and I have read the talk made by your chief sachem, Sahdegeoyes, at that time. I know by the histories which the white men have written, and by the traditions preserved by the belts hung up in your council house, that the Senecas have always been a brave nation. When, many hundred moons ago, the Five Nations united to be one people, the Senecas were placed at the western door of their long house, to guard it from all the foes that might come from toward the setting sun. This was done because the Senecas never sleep, and because their hatchets were always sharp. To be known as a Seneca, therefore, is an honor which I accept with pleasure.

Brothers: When the first great canoe of the white man arrived at Man-na-hatch-ta-ninck, (which is now called New York,) although it created great surprise, the strangers were kindly received. You gave them of your venison to eat, and spread beaver skins for them to lie down upon. When the big canoe arrived at Albany, you all resolved to take the best care of it. For this purpose it was agreed to tie it fast with a great rope to one of the largest trees on the bank of the river. Afterward, fearing that the wind would blow down that tree, it was agreed to make the rope very long, and tie it fast at the great council fire at Onondaga, and the end put under your feet, that you might know by its shaking if anything touched the canoe; in which case you all agreed, as one man, to rise up and see what was the matter. After this a bond of friendship was formed between you and Corlaer, the governor of New York, with which he was so well pleased that he told you that he would find you a long silver chain, which would neither break nor rust, to bind you and the English together in brothership, that your people and they should be as of one head, and one heart, and one blood forever. After this firm agreement was made, our forefathers, finding that it was good, and foresecing many advantages that both parties would reap from it, ordered that if ever that silver chain should become rusty in the least, or if it should slip or break, it should be immediately brightened up again, and fastened stronger at the ends.

Brothers: These were the doings of our wise forefathers. But it was not so with the French, who also came across the great water, and paddled their canoes up the St. Lawrence to Cadaracqui. They joined your enemies the Ottawas, and the other Indians living about Montreal, and were always on the war-path against you, doing all in their power to drive you from the face of the earth. But the Five Nations were brave. Their brothers, the English, gave them guns and powder, instead of the bow and the arrow; and the warriors, your forefathers, after making the country of the Onondagas and Senecas fat with their blood when they came against you there, followed them like the swift winds into Canada, and made red their own war-paths even down to Montreal and the gates of Quebec.

Brothers: Many seasons afterward, when the old thirteen families of English colonies had become men, and wished to kindle fires and hunt venison for themselves, the king, who then called him-

self your father, would not let them. But he had been kind to
you, and it was natural that you should take the hatchet which he
put into your hands to strike us on the head. Yet, although the
blood of your warriors had run like water on the ground in the
cause of your pretended father, when he found that he was not
able to put out the thirteen fires, and agreed to smoke the pipe of
peace with us, he forgot his red children, and would have left them
without wiping away their tears and blood, or condoling with them
for their dead, or leaving them so much as a place whereon to
spread their blankets, or to kindle fires to warm their old men,
their women, or their little ones. Then it was that your Great
Father General Washington, made a new chain of friendship with
his red children, at Fort Stanwix, one end of which was fastened
at the great council house of the thirteen fires, and the other in
the Seneca country, because the great fire at Onondaga had gone
out. Your new father, though a great war chief, was nevertheless
a lover of peace. He saw your distress, and that you too wanted
peace. Nor did he wish to crowd you from your seats, but left you
broad hunting grounds with game, and fields to plant your corn.
He took the chiefs, your forefathers, by the hand, and told them to
use the tomahawk no more, but to bury it, and plant a tree over it,
that it might never be dug up again. Brothers, that new covenant
chain has been kept strong and bright ever since, though about
thirty years ago the king of England tried to break it. But you
kept fast hold of it, and when his troops attempted to stop up all
the roads, the Senecas sent their brave warriors with ours across
the Niagara, and soon made them open them again.

Brothers: The honor you have conferred upon me, by making
me one of your chiefs, has reminded me of these facts in your
ancient history, and the old covenants which have so long subsisted
between your ancestors and mine. Holding fast that covenant
chain which was made last, I hope we may speak with a free mind
to each other. Will you open your ears, then, brothers, and listen
to a few words more which I have to say?

Brothers: Listen! The Great Spirit has told us in the Good
Book which he has given his children, that he has made of one
blood all nations of men. The red men and the white are all the
same flesh. And he loves his red children as well as he does the
white. When we are in sorrow, if we ask him, he is always ready
to make our hearts glad. When we are called to weep, he will dry

up our tears. The red men and the white ought therefore to love one another, and do all the good they can to each other. The fire of amity and friendship should always blaze upon the hearths of their council houses, their ears should ever be open to the cries of distress, and the doors of their lodges to the feet of the stranger.

Brothers: The Great Spirit gave the red man a broad and beautiful country, with deep forests to cover you from the heat of the sun, filled with game for you to eat when you were hungry, and to clothe you in furs when you were cold. He gave you clear springs of water to drink; rivers filled with fishes, bright lakes for you to paddle your canoes upon, and flowers to make the air sweet and your paths beautiful. But the Great Spirit did not mean that you should always be hunters. The first man he made was a red man, and the first command he gave him, after he had sinned by disobedience, was to cultivate the ground, and to make his condition better than it would be in a state of nature. The birds build their nests, and the beavers make their dams, by instinct. But they never do anything better than they do at first. They are always the same. To man, the Great Spirit has given reason. He looks to him for improvement. And he sent the white man into your country to teach you how to live in a better way than by hunting and catching fish. He sent them to instruct you how to build fine houses in the place of your wigwams, and to plant fields, and cultivate beautiful gardens, and lay out orchards of delicious fruits;—to teach your women to spin and weave and sew, so that you might live comfortably and happily by your own bright fires, with everything delightful around you. Above all, the white man came to give you a better knowledge of the Great Spirit, to teach you to read, that you may know what he says to us, and to write, so that you can breathe your thoughts to each other when separated.

Brothers: You have seen from what I have told you about the arrival of the first big canoe, and the covenant chain that was made, that the red men were not displeased when the white men first came among them. I know that the white men were then few and feeble, and that you were many. Now they have become like the leaves on the trees, that cannot be counted, and they have pressed hard upon your seats. What is the reason of this great change? Brothers, the white men have grown rich and strong and many, because they obey the Great Spirit in tilling the ground. The earth is the mother of the red man and the white, and if we draw our sustenance from her breast, she will bountifully supply us all we can desire. Let us therefore labor, that we may live upon her bounty, and when weary "recline upon her bosom."

Brothers: There are bad white men as well as bad Indians. They often come to you with forked tongues to deceive you, and they put the fire-waters to your lips to stupify, that they may cheat you. But the Great Spirit is angry with such. He did not make the fire-waters, but gave you cool sweet springs to slake your thirst; and if you will drink nothing else, and be industrious, and open schools for your children, although your seats are not so broad as they were once, you may still become happy and numerous like the white men.

Brothers: I have told you that when the Great Spirit made man, he placed him in a beautiful garden, to till and dress it; and he bound him to himself by a golden chain. But the Spirit of Evil crept into that garden in the shape of a serpent, and contrived to break that chain. The Great Spirit then sent his own Son to make it over, and wash away the rust that had got on it. But the canker of that rust was so deep that it took his own blood to make it bright again. Now we must believe in that Son, and do as he has told us in the Good Book; and then, when the Master of Breath shall call for us, he will take us up to the fair hunting grounds through clouds bright as fleeces of gold, upon a ladder as beautiful as the rainbow, where we shall live with the Mannitoes—the happy spirits—forever!

Brothers: My talk is done. I am proud to be called a Seneca, to be numbered among a people who have raised such warriors and orators as Old Smoke and Young King, the Farmer's Brother, the Corn-Planter, Sa-go-ye-wat-ha and Captain Pollard, and a long list of other brave chiefs whose names I cannot remember, but who have long ago been called away by the Great Master of Breath. Brothers adieu! May you always possess your minds in peace.

I am, very truly, &c., &c.

WILLIAM L. STONE, or
Sa-go-sen-o-ta.[1]

To the Sachem, SAHDEGEOYES,
and the Chiefs, GAUGOO, and
HA-DYA-NO-DO, and others.
New York, April 15, 1844.

---

[1] That is, He renders their name conspicuous,—in other words an historian or biographer.

No. II.

A Memorandum for Trifles, sent to London for, through Captain Knox—by Sir William Johnson.

February 19th, 1749-50.

Two volumes quarto of Mathematical Elements of Natural Philosophy, confirmed by experiments—or an introduction to Sir Isaac Newton's Philosophy; translated into English by the late J T. Desaguliers.

Also the second edition of Doctor Desaguliers Course of Experimental Philosophy, adorned with 78 copper plates, in two volumes quarto.

Chambers Dictionary, 2 volumes.

Bakers Microscope made easy.

Rhodderick Randum.

The Gentleman's Magazine, from December 1748 to the present time.

The Family Magazine, in two parts.

An Historical Review of the Transactions of Europe from the Commencement of the War with Spain.

The whole proceedings in the house of peers against the three condemned lords.

Amarylis, a new musical design, well bound.

A good French horn, with the notes.

A good common hunting horn.

A good loud trumpet.

A dozen of good black lead pencils.

1 lb. of best red sealing wax.

1 lb. of black sealing wax.

2 Reams of good common writing paper.

200 lbs. of ground white lead.

100 lbs. of good red lead.

20 gallons of good linseed oil.

A good globe to hang in the hall with light.

A prism————Some prints as—

Titians Loves of the Gods,

Le Bruns Battles of Alexander.

Some numbers of Pousin's Landscapes by **Knapton**.

4 Seasons by Lancred.

4 Prints of a camp by Watteau.

Some numbers of Houbraken's heads.

The pictures of some of the best running horses at New Market

No. III.

Ephraim Williams.

The following sketch of this gallant officer, is taken from the Rev Cortlandt Van Renselaer's Historical Discourse of the BATTLE OF LAKE GEORGE.

Ephraim Williams was descended from the best Puritan ancestry. He was always enterprising. Having lost his parents early in life, he was brought up by his grandfather, Abraham Jackson. In his youth, he made several voyages to Europe, visiting England, Spain, and Holland, probably for commercial purposes. In 1744, he was made captain and put in command of Fort Massachusetts, in the western part of the province, in the valley of the Hoosic. After the war, he had an important agency in settleing that section of country. At the beginning of the campaign of 1755, he was made colonel, and commanded the third Massachusetts regiment. His aide was William Williams, a signer of the Declaration of Independence.

Colonel Williams, being well versed in warfare, especially with the Indians, was placed at the head of the detachment sent out against Dieskau's column. His great error on that day was in not sending out scouts. Colonel Williams was early struck with a ball through the head, and fell dead on the spot. Two of his companions immediately concealed the body from the scalping-knife of the advancing Indians. His body was found after the battle, unmutilated, and it was buried some fifteen or twenty rods rods southeast of where he fell, at the foot of " a huge pine beside the military road." About twenty years ago, his nephew, Dr. William H. Williams, of Raleigh, North Carolina, " disenterred and carried off the skull." The ancient pine has fallen, but the stump remains. Two smaller trees have sprung from the parent stock, and still shade the place of burial. E. W. B. Canning, Esq., who superintended the erection of the monument on the part of the alumni of Williams college, and who explored the ground carefully, says : " Directed by an aged man, who dug up the skull, I found the grave, and had it refilled, and a large pyramidal boulder set over it, with the inscription E. W. 1755."

The rock on which Colonel Williams fell is now surmounted by a marble monument, twelve feet high. The earth has been excavated a little around the rock, so that the top of the rock is now seven feet from the ground The monument was erected by the alumni of Williams College, in 1854, and is an appropriate, tasteful and worthy memorial. It is surrounded by a good iron fence, which visitors find the means of climbing. The writer, without recommending others to follow his example, went up to the monument for the purpose of *copying the inscription;* and as he now gives the inscriptions *verbatim et literatim,* this historical motive cannot be so well plead hereafter. The inscriptions were copied exactly according to the words in the lines, and the division of syllables, as cut upon the marble, but they are here given continuously, partly to save space, and partly to avoid the exhibition of an unskillful performance, for the words and syllables are arranged (at least on two sides of the monument) in not the most tasteful style. This is a matter of regret. I notice it simply to put the Lake George Committee of Monuments upon their guard, and to induce them to see that the stonecutter had a fac-simile of the work to be done. The beauty of a monumental inscription depends very much on the arrangement of the lines and of the words.

The following inscription is on the *east* side of the monument, towards the plank road:

To the memory of Colonel EPHRAIM WILLIAMS. A native of Newton, Mass., who after gallantly defending the frontiers of his native state, served under General Johnson against the French and Indians, and nobly fell near this spot in the bloody conflict of Sept. 8th, 1755, in the 42 year of his age.

On the *north* side, towards the lake:

A lover of peace and learning, as courteous and generous as he was brave and patriotic. Col. Williams sympathized deeply with the privations of the frontier settlers, and by his will, made at Albany on his way to the field of battle, provided for the founding among them of an institution of learning, which has since been chartered as Williams college.

On the *west* side, towards the old road:

Forti ac magnanimo Eph. Williams, Collegii Gulielmi Conditori; Qui in hostibus patriæ repellendis, prope hoc saxum cecidit; grati alumni posuerunt, A. D. 1854.

On the *south* side, towards the toll-gate:

This monument is erected by the alumni of Williams College: the ground donated by E. H. Rosekrans, M. W. Perrine, J. Haviland.

APPENDIX. 549

The monument makes a beautiful appearance from the road, and is looked for and admired by all travelers. The monument is more accessible from the old road than from the new; but the old road is not in a very good condition, although it can be used.

Joseph White Esq.,[1] thus sums up the traits of Colonel Williams character:—" For whatever is known of his opinions, as well as of his personal appearance, habits and manners, we are indebted to the impressions he made upon his contemporaries, as revealed in the scanty notices of the times and in the few traditions that yet linger amongst us." From these we learn that his "person was large and fleshy," his countenance benignant, and his appearance commanding; that he loved and excelled in the rough games of agility and strength so common in his day, and often engaged in them with his soldiers during the intervals of duty; that his " address was easy, his manners simple and conciliatory;" that he loved books, and the society of literary men, " and often lamented the want of a liberal education;" that to these endowments were added the higher qualities of mind—quick and clear perceptions, a solid judgment, a lofty courage, and an unwavering constancy in scenes of danger, and that military genius which needed only a fitting opportunity to place him in the highest walks of his profession. He knew both how to command and to conciliate the affections of his men. " He was greatly beloved by them while living, and lamented when dead." And, finally, in the language of Colonel Worthington, who knew him well, " Humanity made a most striking trait in his character, and universal benevolence was his ruling passion." He truly adds, " His memory will always be dear."

No. IV.
King Hendrik.

Although this great sachem has been called a *Mohawk*, yet his family was *Mohegan*, and he himself only a *Mohawk by adoption.* According to his own statement his father lived in the first years of his (Hendrik's) life, at Westfield in Connecticut. The exact

---

[1] "Joseph White's address before the alumni of Williams College, 1855, commemorative of Ephraim Williams abounds in historical incident and eloquent discription. I am indebted to this address for the biographical hints of Colonel Williams in the beginning of this sketch, and also for other items of information."

time of his birth is not known, though it is believed to have been between the years 1680 and 1690. Equally difficult is it, to ascertain at what time he moved into the Mohawk valley. His usual residence however, during the latter portion of his life was in the present town of Minden, in Herkimer county, N. Y., and near the Upper or Canajoharie castle. The site of his house is described by Dr. Dwight, as being a "handsome elevation, commanding a considerable prospect of the neighboring country." Mr. Schoolcraft, in his *Notes of the Iroquois* thus speaks of him:

"There was a time in our settlements when there was a moral force in the name of King Hendrik and his Mohawks, which had an electric effect; and at the time he died, his loss was widely and deeply felt and lamented even in Great Britain. It is said that he on two occasions visited his British sovereign. On one of these occasions, doubtless the last, which is conjectured to have been about the year 1740, his majesty presented him a rich suit of clothes,—a green coat, set off with brussels and gold lace, and a cocked hat, such as worn by the court gentry of that period. In these he sat for his portrait, which was executed by a London artist. From this portrait, which has no date, engravings were made, of a large cabinet-size, and colored in conformity with the original. I saw one of these engravings in the family of a relative in Schenectady, which has, however, been long since destroyed by fire; and recently I have seen another, which had been, for nearly a century, the property of Jeremiah Lansing Esq. of Albany, N. Y. The prosolopogical indicia of his countenance denote a kind disposition, honesty of purpose, and an order of intellect much above mediocrity. Although his complexion was the "shadowed livery of the burning sun," his figure and countenance were singularly prepossessing and commanding. The concurrent testimony of every traditionist awards to him great natural talents, judgment, and sagacity. As a diplomatist and orator he was greatly distinguished, and divided the palm only with his brother Abraham, of pious memory, who was exclusively devoted to civil pursuits."

Hendrik's most famous speech was the one delivered at the congress in Albany, 1754. It excited at the time universal attention, both in America and in England. In reference to it, a journalist of that day says: "For capacity, bravery, vigor of mind and immovable integrity combined, he excelled all the aboriginal inhab itants of which we have any knowledge." Hendrik was quite a lion in his day, and his spirit and martial powers were upon every tongue. He was also esteemed the bravest of the brave among the Iroquois." He led many war parties against the Canadian frontier in the old French and Indian war; and his staunch friendship for Sir William Johnson, caused him to use his great influence to keep the Six Nations, especially the Mohawks. faithful to their covenants. Indeed, many times, had it not been for his efforts, the entire Confederacy would have probably broken through all restraint and gone over to the French. He died lamented by many, and by no one more than by Sir Wm. Johnson. Judge Campbell in his *Annals of Tryon County* has preserved the following anecdote illustrative of the friendship that the Great Mohawk was capable of inspiring in the hearts of the whites towards himself:—" During some of the negotiations with the Indians of Pennsylvania and the inhabitants of that state, Hendrik was present at Philadelphia. His likeness was taken, and a wax figure afterward made which was a very good imitation. After the death of Hendrik an old friend, a white man, visited Philadelphia, and among other things was shown this wax figure. It occupied a niche, and was not observed by him until he had approached within a few feet. The friendship of former days came fresh over his memory, and forgetting for the moment Hendrik's death, he rushed forward and clasped in his arms the frail icy image of the chieftain."

The famous story of Sir William Johnson's dreaming with King Hendrik for the royal grant, or indeed for any other piece of land, is a pure fiction. See chapter xvi, vol. ii.

No. V.
Map of Battle of Lake George

References to map on opposite page.

First Engagement.—1. The road. 2. The French and Indians 3. Hendrik on horseback. 4. Our men. 5. Our Indians far within the ambuscade.

Second Engagement.—6. Canadians and French Indians. 7. Dieskau's regulars making the attack on the centre. 8. The road. 9. Our men in the action posted in front. 10. The trees felled for the breastworks. 11. Three of the large cannon. 12. One of the cannon posted "advantageously" on the eminence. 13, 14, 15, 16. Illustrating the attack on the right; particulars not known. 17. The guards on the flanks and rear. 18. Woods and swamp. 19. Low ground near the lake. 20. Cannon defending flanks and rear. 21. Baggage-wagons. 22, 23, 24. Military stores and ammunition. 25. Mortars. 26. Road to the lake. 27. Bateaux on Lake George. 28. Four Storehouses. 29. Storehouse. 30. Iroquois Indians. 31. General Johnson's tent. 32. Major-General Lyman's regiment. 33. Colonel Harris's regiment. 34. Colonel Cockcroft's regiment. 35. Colonel Williams's, now Colonel Pomroy's regiment. 36. Colonel Ruggles's regiment. 37. Colonel Titcomb's regiment. 38. Colonel Guttridge's regiment. 39. Officers.

The heading of the map is not quite accurate in the number of troops stated to be engaged on both sides, and is quite inaccurate in the number stated to be killed on the side of the French.

No. VI.
Powder Horn.

Through the kindness of the Rev. Henry Ballard of Brunswick, Me., Secretary of the Maine Historical Society, I am enabled to give on the opposite page a fac-simile of perhaps the only sketch of Fort Wm. Henry in existence. The Sketch was carved on a powder-horn by a Provincial doing garrison duty at the fort in October, 1756. The horn was presented to the Maine Historical Society in January, 1864, by the Hon. Wm P. Haines, of Biddeford, Me., who at the time of its presentation, accompanied it with an exceedingly interesting paper, relating to its history. Mr. Haines, who deserves great credit for his instrumentality in rescuing this interesting relic from oblivion, courteously sent me a copy of this paper, from which I take a few extracts.

"Recently I learned that Tristram Goldthwait Esq., an esteemed citizen of Biddeford and once its representative, had in his possession a powder horn which had a history. At my request he brought it to me, and now permits me to deliver it to the Maine Historical Society for safe-keeping and inspection of the curious, and, to use his precise words, probably never to be reclaimed by him. He informs me that it was delivered to him as the male representative of the original owner, and came down in the family.

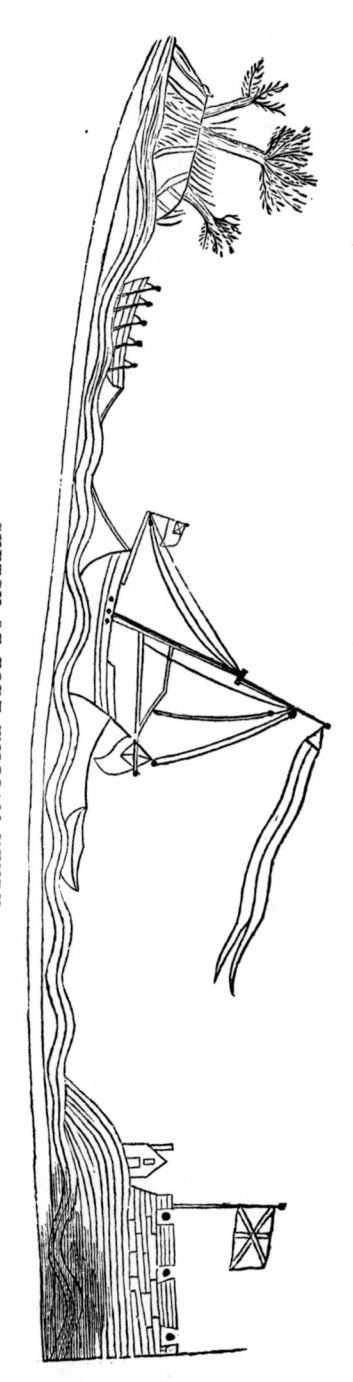

SKETCH OF FORT WILLIAM HENRY.

Upon inspection it will be noticed that this powder horn bears upon its face on the right, a well-carved and spirited sketch of Fort William Henry at the head of Lake George. Showing the outlines of the fort and its guns mounted, its barracks, lofty flag-staff, and at the top the English ensign unfolded to the breeze, and over against it, on the left, an island in the lake [Tea Island], and between these, a sloop being towed by a boat well-maned to the island, over the rough waters of the lake.

Beneath is the following inscription carved in beautiful letters, which are in perfect preservation.

" Michael B. Goldthwait's horn, 1756, at Fort Wm. Henry, October 2, A.D."

* * * * * * *

It was precisely at this period, October second 1756, the date of this inscription, midway between the building of the fort in the autumn of 1755, and its destruction in 1757, that the interesting relic before us was fashioned by its owner into the form in which it is now presented to us! A humble soldier, on duty at the fort, in his moments of leisure, turns artist, and with his rustic knife, gives us an animated and truthful outline of the scene then in his eye, the winding shore, the waters of the beautiful lake, the island, the headland surmounted by the fort, and floating over all the glorious flag of England, and thus daguerrotypes for posterity, the only picture in existence of objects of so much historical interest!

No. VII.

Manuscript Letter No. I.

This letter bears this endorsement in the Baronet's hand.

" Alderman Baker's letter about my money in the funds," and is as follows :

" *Sir William Johnson Baronet.*

" LONDON 31st March, 1757.

Sir.

" I have no letter from you since I wrote the original of the foregoing. I have received from Mr. John Pownall the money which he received from the exchequer being clear of fees, &c., £4945, 18s., 6d. You have the particulars annext which I have extracted from Mr. Pownall's letter to me. I have invested this money as near as I well could in three per cent bank annuities

APPENDIX. 555

which now stand in my name and cost you £4943, 2s., 6d., being the purchase of £5500, capital in said fund of which the particulars are annext. I have been extremely hurried of late, otherwise you should have had the advices sooner. Now I have only to add that I am:

"Sir
"Your most humble Serv't
"WM. BAKER."

An account of money received by John Pownall Esq. for
  Sir William Johnson granted by parliament,......... £5000:00:0
Fees at the treasury for the warrant order
  and letter,.. £8:04:6
Fees at the exchequer, viz. bills,   4:07
Tellers and poundage,................. 143:10
Auditor,................................. 9:07   157:04   165:08:6
                                                                                                              £4834:11:6

Received at the Exchequer poundage remitted, £125:0
Deduct fees at the treasury for that order,..... 1:1   123:19:0
                                                                                                       £4958:10:6
Paid for Sir Wm. Johnson's appointment to be Agent
  for Indian affairs 12:12:0
                                                                                               £4945:18:6

Received for Sir Wm. Johnson and transferred for his account into the name of Wm. Baker £5500 bank three per cent annusties, viz:

£4000 transferred by Theodore Crowley at 89¼ p.c. £3570.
  1500   Wm. Colsford   89¼ p.c.   1338:15
Paid I. Shipston broker a ⅛ p.c. on £5500....................6:17:6.
My commission   ½ p.c. on   do........................27:10.
                                                                                                  £4943:2:6"